Amplifications of Black Sound from Colonial Mexico

# CRITICAL MEXICAN STUDIES

Critical Mexican Studies
Series editor: Ignacio M. Sánchez Prado

Critical Mexican Studies is the first English-language, humanities-based, theoretically focused academic series devoted to the study of Mexico. The series is a space for innovative works in the humanities that focus on theoretical analysis, transdisciplinary interventions, and original conceptual framing.

Other titles in the series:

*The Restless Dead: Necrowriting and Disappropriation*, by Cristina Rivera Garza

*History and Modern Media: A Personal Journey*, by John Mraz

*Toxic Loves, Impossible Futures: Feminist Living as Resistance*, by Irmgard Emmelhainz

*Drug Cartels Do Not Exist: Narcotrafficking in US and Mexican Culture*, by Oswaldo Zavala

*Unlawful Violence: Mexican Law and Cultural Production*, by Rebecca Janzen

*The Mexican Transpacific: Nikkei Writing, Visual Arts, and Performance*, by Ignacio López-Calvo

*Monstrous Politics: Geography, Rights, and the Urban Revolution in Mexico City*, by Ben Gerlofs

*Robo Sacer: Necroliberalism and Cyborg Resistance in Mexican and Chicanx Dystopias* by David Dalton

*Mexico, Interrupted: Labor, Idleness, and the Economic Imaginary of Independence* by Sergio Gutiérrez Negrón

*Serial Mexico: Storytelling across Media, from Nationhood to Now* by Amy E. Wright

*Sonic Strategies: Performing Mexico's War on Drugs, Mourning, and Feminicide* by Christina Baker

*Subjunctive Aesthetics: Mexican Cultural Production in the Era of Climate Change* by Carolyn Fornoff

*Fatefully, Faithfully Feminist: A Critical History of Women, Patriarchy and Mexican National Discourse by Carlos Monsiváis*, translated and edited by Norma Klahn and Ilana Luna

*Biocosmism: Vitality and the Utopian Imagination in Postrevolutionary Mexico* by Jorge Quintana Navarrete

*"We, the Barbarians": Three Mexican Writers in the Twenty-First Century* by Mabel Moraña

# Amplifications of Black Sound from Colonial Mexico

Vocality and Beyond

Sarah Finley

Vanderbilt University Press
*Nashville, Tennessee*

Copyright 2024 Vanderbilt University Press
All rights reserved
First printing 2024
Library of Congress Cataloging-in-Publication Data

Names: Finley, Sarah, author.
Title: Amplifications of Black sound from colonial Mexico : vocality and beyond / Sarah Finley.
Description: Nashville, Tennessee : Vanderbilt University Press, [2024] | Series: Critical Mexican studies ; book 16 | Includes bibliographical references and index.
Identifiers: LCCN 2024013180 (print) | LCCN 2024013181 (ebook) | ISBN 9780826506849 (paperback) | ISBN 9780826506856 (hardcover) | ISBN 9780826506863 (epub) | ISBN 9780826506870 (pdf)
Subjects: LCSH: Music--Social aspects--Mexico--History--17th century. | Musicians, Black--Mexico--History--17th century. | Sopranos (Singers)--Mexico--History--17th century. | Castrati--Mexico--History--17th century. | Villancicos (Music)--17th century--History and criticism. | Music and race--Mexico--History--17th century. | Sound--Social aspects--Mexico--History--17th century. | African diaspora--History. | Mexico--History--Spanish colony, 1540-1810. | Mexico--Social life and customs--17th century.
Classification: LCC ML3917.M4 F56 2024 (print) | LCC ML3917.M4 (ebook) | DDC 780.89/00972--dc23/eng/20240403
LC record available at https://lccn.loc.gov/2024013180
LC ebook record available at https://lccn.loc.gov/2024013181

Front cover image: Detail from Gaspar Fernández, "Negrinho tiray vos." Cancionero de Gaspar Fernandes, vol. 1 (Instituto Nacional de Bellas Artes / Centro Nacional de Investigación, Documentación e Información Musical Carlos Chávez: Mexico City, 2001).

To academic friendship

# Contents

Acknowledgments ix
A Note on Translation, Nomenclature, and Transcriptions xi

|   | INTRODUCTION. Percussions | 1 |
|---|---|---|
| 1 | Black Male Sopranos in New Spanish Cathedrals | 19 |
| 2 | Musical and Lyrical Rememberings of Black Male Sopranos | 53 |
| 3 | Harmonizing Blackness in Urban Political Ceremonies | 85 |
| 4 | Harmonizing Blackness in Popular Religious Settings | 119 |
| 5 | Harmonizing Blackness in *Villancicos* | 153 |
| 6 | Black Women's Performance in Sor Juana's *Villancicos* | 183 |
|   | CONCLUSION. Black Sounds Echo in New Spanish Waters | 213 |

Notes 228
Bibliography 250
Index 268

# Acknowledgments

Writing a book is no small undertaking. At the outset, it is a rich, intellectual journey without a sure destination. As the process nears completion, it becomes clear to the author how the stories she tells interweave with her own. I wrote *Amplifications of Black Sound* during an introspective period. While solitary bouts of research and writing offered space for reflection, scholarly camaraderie was the project's most meaningful gift. I developed this book in concert with smart, generous colleagues whose friendship is a treasured keepsake of *Amplifications of Black Sound*'s voyage. Thus, it only seems fitting to dedicate the final product to the bonds that make us better scholars and human beings. From ideation to publication, the many voices involved in *Amplifications of Black Sound* are too numerous to list. Some provided thoughtful feedback, and others dialogued with my ideas in less formal settings. All offered warm companionship and gave me a sense of community that stretches from Mexico to the United States and beyond. I am especially grateful to the following individuals: Olivia Bloechl, Rafael Castañeda García, Ireri Chávez Bárcenas, Carlos Cuestas, Kate de Luna, Mónica Díaz, Patrick Erben, Sarah Eyerly, Cesar Favila, Barbara Fuchs, Glenda Goodman, Bonnie Gordon, Sara Guengerich, Paul Michael Johnson, Elisabeth Le Guin, Mary Caton Lingold, Omar Morales Abril, Jesús Ramos-Kittrell, Maria Ryan, Nuria Salazar Simarro, Miguel Valerio, Sherry Velasco, Lisa Voigt, and Emily Wilbourne.

A number of peoples' time and energy made this publication possible. Ignacio Sánchez Prado recognized *Amplifications of Black Sound*'s vision long before I did, and I am grateful for his support and encouragement. Likewise, the editorial team at Vanderbilt University Press made production a seamless process. Thank you in particular to Gianna Mosser, Patrick Samuel, and Zack Gresham for the care that you have taken with my monograph. Anonymous readers engaged with an initial draft, and their comments invaluably shaped the final project. Moreover, members of the Early Caribbean Music Working Group helpfully critiqued a draft of Chapter 2.

Financial resources are equally important for a project like *Amplifications of Black Sound*. Christopher Newport University provided necessary leave time to complete the book, and a Faculty Development Grant funded publication costs. Additionally, a generous grant from the Huntington Library enabled me to travel to Mexico to consult primary resources there. *Amplifications of Black Sound* particularly benefitted from two funded symposiums, where I was able to workshop chapter drafts and exchange ideas with colleagues. Intersections: Black and Indigenous Sound in the Early Atlantic World took place at Virginia Commonwealth University, with support from the Omohundro Institute for Early American History and Culture, Washington University in St. Louis, the Virginia Commission for the Arts, and Christopher Newport University. Mary Caton Lingold, Miguel Valerio, and Sarah Eyerly were tireless co-conspirators in the organization of this event. The UCLA Center for 17th- and 18th-Century Studies and the Clark Library hosted Approaches to Sound in the Early Modern Atlantic World. I owe particular gratitude to Barbara Fuchs for her guidance and vision in co-organizing the Clark symposium.

Finally, close friends and family have been invaluable for bringing this endeavor to fruition. I am grateful to have all of you in my life. Michael Davis, for the dance that led me here. Annie Shelby and Katy and Charlie Finley, for inspiring me to be curious about the world and grounding me in reality. Bob and Carol Smith, for teaching me that local stories matter and for letting me share in your histories. Mark Dalton, for gamely taking part in *Amplifications of Black Sound*'s geographic and intellectual path. Heather Weddington, for your wisdom and championship of writing and creativity. And last but certainly not least, Valentina Sorbera, for fierce support and sisterhood, every step of the way.

# A Note on Translation, Nomenclature, and Transcriptions

Unless otherwise indicated, all translations of primary and secondary sources in this book are mine. The seventeenth- and eighteenth-century *villancicos* in Chapters 3, 6, and 7 presented a particular set of challenges when I considered how to render them in English. In the lyrics of *villancicos de negros*, or Black villancicos, European and Creole authors signal characters' Blackness through *habla de negros*, or blackspeak, to use the English translation that Noémie Ndiaye coined.[1] The style appears in villancicos as well in plays, poems, and other literary forms from early modern Spain and Portugal. It uses phonetic and grammatical anomalies to mark African and Afro-descendant voices and also incorporates racial slurs and stereotypes. The result is a poetic imagining of Blackness that was not necessarily grounded in Afro-diasporic speech patterns. Instead, blackspeak reinforced racial essentialism and furthered the marginalization of people of color.

Such characteristics are problematic, especially in contemporary publications and performances. Consequently, there are few published translations to guide authors who seek to make Black villancicos available for study outside of Hispanic and Luso-Brazilian traditions. One model is Edith Grossman's English rendering of selections from Sor Juana Inés de la Cruz's villancico set for St. Peter Nolasco. This translation articulates Blackness by voicing some characters' lyrics as African American speech.

In the notes, Grossman affirms that she draws inspiration from writers like Mark Twain and Zora Neale Hurston.² Grossman's version is unquestionably faithful to Sor Juana's original. Nonetheless, it raises important questions about how a translator might approach racist texts, particularly when faced with questions of historical difference. Should one translate derogatory language, or is it acceptable to alter or even silence racial slurs and disparaging representations?

With these questions in mind, other scholars who have translated black-speak purposefully avoid reproducing the ways that it frames non-European voices. For instance, Ndiaye translates the grammatical and phonetic variations that mark speakers as Black into standard English and indicates any anomalies with an asterisk.³ Likewise, Nick Jones affirms that "the translation of habla de negros language into AAVE is not necessary. As a translator of habla de negros, my task, to echo Benjamin's 'The Task of the Translator' (1923), ultimately consists of finding that intended effect upon the language into which I am translating that produces in it an echo of the original."⁴ To the degree possible, both authors suppress the atypical Castilian that characterizes blackspeak and translate Black characters' utterances into standard English.

I follow a similar approach in *Amplifications of Black Sound*. Inasmuch as Black villancicos contribute to the racialization of sub-Saharan Africans, rendering them in another language requires careful reflection upon both the intended audience and the translator's positionality. Indeed, in a volume that explores multifaceted intersections of race and translation, Corine Tachtiris notes that "translation and translation studies are affected by the material conditions of racialization and racism at work in society, but they also produce their own racial meanings and structures."⁵ Such considerations are especially pertinent to my task in making *Amplifications of Black Sound* broadly accessible. Precisely, translating Black villancicos risks perpetuating their underlying racism and contributing to its legacies. With this in mind, *Amplifications of Black Sound* only includes textual excerpts that are central to my arguments. When translating these works, I opt not to reproduce the grammatical and phonetic inconsistencies that mark certain characters as dark-skinned. Instead, a general description of blackspeak's characteristics in the book's introduction is sufficient for orienting the Anglophone reader to the original texts.

Racial terms are another challenge that arises in *Amplifications of Black Sound*. With this difficulty in mind, it is important to underscore the distance between contemporary English uses of *Black* and more nuanced identifiers from seventeenth-century New Spain. Indeed, *bozal, ladino, moreno, pardo, mulato,* or even references to someone's country of origin are just a few examples of colonial Mexico's careful categorization of Black bodies. The system accounted for ethnicity, described whether someone was free or enslaved, and even indicated one's degree of assimilation to Hispanic culture. There are no contemporary English equivalents to these linguistic descriptors of New Spain's social and racial hierarchies, and identifying approximate terms can be challenging. When writing in my own voice, I use language like *Afro-descendant, Afro-diasporic, sub-Saharan,* and *Black* to refer to people of African descent. When translating, I avoid imposing additional layers of racialization by leaving words that describe Afro-descent in Spanish. I treat references to Indigenous people similarly, using words like *Amerindian* or *autochthonous* except when translating. In instances where the term *indio* appears, I maintain the original Spanish.

Finally, *Amplifications of Black Sound* incorporates evidence from manuscript sources. My transcriptions preserve the original orthography. They do not modernize punctuation, capitalization, or spelling, including accents and other diacritical marks. When I refer to people that these sources reference by name, I likewise maintain the irregularities of the primary text.

Que aunque samo neglo
savemo cantá

Although we are Black
we know how to sing

—**II Nocturno,** *Villancicos que se cantaron en la catedral de la Puebla de los Angeles, en los Maytines de la Natividad de Christo Nuestro Señor, este año de 1673*

# Introduction
## Percussions

The only written thing on slave ships was the account book listing the exchange value of slaves. Within the ship's space the cry of those deported was stifled, as it would be in the realm of the Plantations. This confrontation still reverberates to this day.

—Édouard Glissant, *Poetics of Relation*

In Juan Gómez de Trasmonte's 1628 map of Mexico City, an orderly collection of churches, streets, plazas, and dwellings peacefully rests in the middle of Lake Texcoco. In the background, twin volcanoes—Itzaccíhuatl and Popocatépetl—rise above the New Spanish capital, and the sun peeks out from behind mountainous surroundings.[1] The innermost parts of the city are densely packed with buildings organized into neat squares. At its outskirts, the tidy, geometric pattern gives way to a scattering of smaller abodes and floating agricultural plots known as *chinampas*. A network of canals winds its way through the urban space. In some places, the waterways yield to the imposed order of city planners from Spain, who associate the grid-like structure with civic harmony and peace. In other areas of the metropolis, however, the canals disrupt the plot with their diagonal paths and graceful curves. These spaces resist the imposition of colonial order, no matter how much architects and engineers try to bend the remnants of Mesoamerican dikes to their will.

For all of its detail, Gómez de Trasmonte's representation of Mexico City does not include a single inhabitant. It is curiously silent, but not soundless, for the urban layout itself resonates with harmony. Geoffrey Baker argues

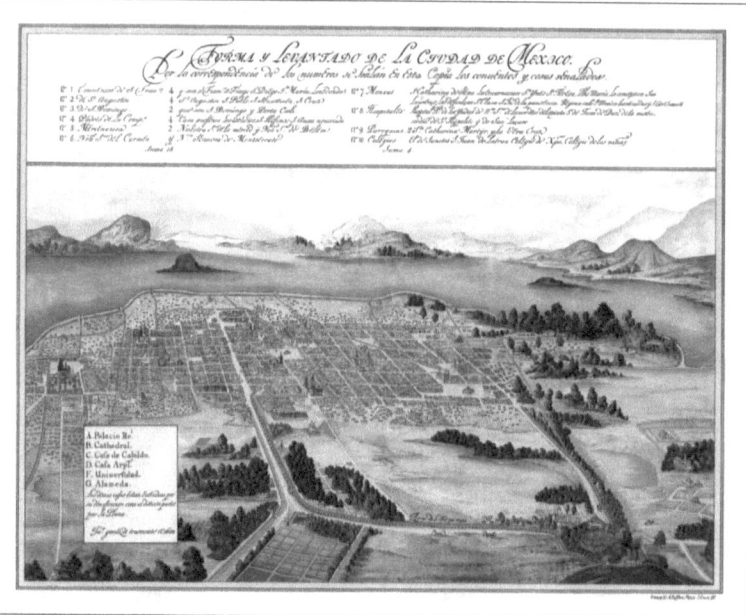

**INTRO.1.** Juan Goméz de Trasmonte, *Forma y Levantado de la Ciudad de México*, 1920 lithographic reproduction of 1628 original. David Rumsey Map Collection, David Rumsey Map Center, Stanford Libraries.

that in the colonial Latin American context "a correspondence can be drawn between urbanism and music, specifically between the urban ideal and the concept and practice of harmony that were transplanted from Europe to Latin America by the Spanish colonists. The city was conceived in terms of the *urbs*, or built environment, and the *civitas*, or human community that populated the city."[2] With the links that Baker draws out among spatial, social, and sonorous order in mind, *Amplifications of Black Sound* probes the boundaries of the unheard in Gómez de Trasmonte's map. The goal is to fill it with sounds—specifically, Black and African ones.[3] To do so, I turn to cathedral records, Inquisition cases, travel narratives, scores and lyrics from the so-called Black villancicos, and visual art as sources for recovering Afro-descendant sonorities from large, urban areas—predominantly Mexico City—in seventeenth-century New Spain. My readings position these auditory interventions within the viceroyalty's cityscapes, especially with respect to the social concord that the harmonic grids imagine. An interpretative framework of harmony amplifies the audio-racial politics that stand out in representations of Afro-descendant sound. Above all, my analyses consider how the participation of New Spain's Black and African people in dominant sound traditions afforded audibility, opportunity, and a sense of community. Where relevant, I call attention to the auditory as a site of cultural memory and draw out the possible persistence or "repercussion" of early Afro-Mexican sound culture.

## AFRO-DESCENDANT VOICES IN THE ARCHIVE: A PHONOGRAPHIC APPROACH

When one considers the number of Afro-descendants in the New Spanish capital and elsewhere in the viceroyalty, the survival of sonic customs from these inhabitants' countries of origin and the emergence of syncretic traditions seem unquestionable. Joan Bristol observers that "in the 17th century, Mexico City had 70,000 inhabitants, with the mixed population (which included Blacks and Mulattos as well as Mestizos) making up 35–40 per cent of the overall population."[4] More specifically, Herman Bennett uses data from 1646 to break down the demographics for each region, including racially mixed inhabitants designated as "Euro-Mestizo," "Afro-Mestizo," and "Indo-Mestizo." Indigenous people and Indo-Mestizos were by far the largest category, followed by about 182,000 people of European origin or ancestry. Bennett estimates that some 150,000 Africans and Afro-descendants lived in New Spain, making the population just slightly smaller than Spaniards, Creoles, and Euro-Mestizos.[5]

Given the prominence of Black and African people in New Spain, there is an ample corpus on the subject.[6] Some of these works shed new light on the socioracial hierarchy known as the "caste system" by contrasting its rigid depiction in visual art with fluctuating quotidian practices and experiences. Others consider the consolidation of Afro-Mexican identities through social institutions like confraternities, militias, or even networks among enslaved laborers. Still others offer detailed readings of agency and resistance in Black festive and devotional practices. Despite this wealth of analytical perspectives, however, there is no full-length study devoted to early African and Afro-Mexican music or sound culture in New Spain or indeed, elsewhere in Latin America. *Amplifications of Black Sound* addresses this lacuna with auditory re-readings of indispensable materials for the study of Afro-descent and also examines sonorous themes in understudied primary sources. To be clear, my aim is not to offer a comprehensive overview of Black and African soundways from New Spain. Rather, I tease marginalized sonorities out of materials long thought to mute them in order to showcase Afro-descendant prevalence in the region's auditory imagination.

Within this context, voice is a key concept for bridging the distance between writing and sound and also for considering the material, agential, and affective contours of the archive's embedded Afro-diasporic sonorities. In the introduction to the influential anthology *Afro-Latino Voices*, Kathryn McKnight and Leo Garofalo reflect upon how written records and official documents construct Afro-Latin subjects. They remind us that such histories are partial and frequently mediated by (colonial) hegemonies of writing: "in almost all the narratives in this book, European scribes have recorded the Afro-Latino voices, not with the word-for-word transcription enabled by modern recording devices, but as colonial officials intent on interpreting the speaker's words from within their own European ideological an discursive worldview."[7] In response, McKnight and Garofalo advocate for a critical practice that distances voice from inscription's illusion of stability and instead attends to its fluidity and multivalence. They approach voice from the symbolic realm and draw upon linguistic concepts like performance and diglossia in order to understand its fragmented relationship to identity.[8]

For all this, voice's centrality in McKnight and Garofalo's observation highlights an overlooked but intriguing line of inquiry. In addition to underscoring the limits of the written archive, it also opposes it to the sonorous histories that recording technologies can provide. Gary Tomlinson, Ana María Ochoa Gautier, and Kathryn de Luna have built upon these ideas with sound-based approaches to lettered records. They argue that Western writing is a limited mode for capturing non-European sonorities in the early Americas. For instance, in a study of pre-Contact musical practices, Tomlinson grapples with the limits of logocentric thought when faced with non-European auditory interventions, which he argues exceed Western definitions of voice and resist lettered reproductions. He seeks to access early Amerindian song, whose practices and philosophies are obscured unsatisfyingly in Eurocentric accounts. In response, Tomlinson interrogates the letter itself, arguing that European writing systems are inadequate for capturing the sound-based ideologies that informed autochthonous practices in the Americas.[9]

For her part, de Luna considers how the colonial archive writes African Atlantic voices into official discourses, but it also suppresses their extra-logic (*logos*) possibilities. Taking an African Atlantic view, she locates this "epistemological violence" in its inability to conserve the linguistic flexibility of African oral traditions. She argues that scholars might overcome written lacunae by attending to the plurality of African words themselves.

> In oral societies, it was *words naming ideas*—not testimonies, letters, and treatises—that were exchanged, debated and revised in political projects. Words reveal durable ontologies in their etymologies, and their various forms and

meanings carry evidence of the historical processes by which such durability was sustained or rejected in changing circumstances. In this way, words illuminate the content of contests between men and women of different backgrounds who fought to create alternative meanings in the world through arguments literally cast in the same terms. Words are as much historical sources as political treatises or court testimony because language is a product of the history of its speakers and words bear the content of that contested history.[10]

From de Luna's perspective, European chroniclers' accounts of language in the African Atlantic are like a game of "telephone," filled with erred hearing and misunderstanding. This process of misquotation illustrates the epistemological limits of Contact, both between Western and sub-Saharan worldviews as well as among diverse African ethnicities. Rather than take an occidental perspective that casts the resistance to linguistic singularity as a loss, however, de Luna suggests an approach that understands these discrepancies as syncretic products of Atlantic Encounter and privileges African thought as crucial for understanding their significance beyond archival bounds.

For all this, it is clear that while written accounts of Contact in the Americas contain echoes of non-European sounds, they require a more nuanced approach than textual methods of literary and historical inquiry can offer. Ochoa Gautier responds with a "an acoustically tuned exploration of the written archive."[11] She observes that "many of the acoustic dimensions of the colonial and early postcolonial archive are not presented to us as discrete, transcribed works or as forms neatly packaged into identifiable genres. They are instead dispersed into different types of written inscriptions that transduce different audile techniques into specific legible sound objects of expressive culture."[12] Here, Ochoa Gautier argues that while linguistic and notated representations of sound render it legible, they are not always audible. This is especially true in multicultural contexts like New Spain, where European writing systems were ill-equipped to capture Indigenous or African soundways. As a result, written records tend to mute voices and auditory forms of meaning-making that resist inscription. These absences give the impression of a homogenous sound culture where non-Western interventions are either silent or ring out as dissonances to be harmonized within socio-political hierarchies. However, as I will argue in this book, Afro-descendant interventions in New Spanish sound culture were rich and varied. While one can easily pinpoint examples of extreme discord within archival records, cases of hyper-consonance with European musical traditions are also noteworthy, for these instances illustrate how Black and African people adapted to dominant soundways in order to gain agency and audibility. Such harmony is striking, but alas, it is rarely audible when scholars listen through the critical dichotomies that condition understanding of race, including (Western) self and (African) other, writing and orality, center and periphery, dominance and subjugation, or sound and silence. In order to attend more fully to muted voices in the archive, it becomes necessary to appreciate the plural manifestations of Afro-descendant sound in New Spain.

In light of these complexities, *Amplifications of Black Sound* takes a phonographic approach Black and African voices in the colonial archive. In a nutshell, this line of inquiry relates writing to recording technologies. My aim is to draw out embedded sonic materiality and also attend to the ways script interrupts vocal signification by distancing voice from speaker or singer and also from the spatiotemporal context of its utterance. By recognizing these distances, *Amplifications of Black Sound* frees Black voices in the archive from their scripted intersections with discourses of self and other. Instead, it allows them to resonate freely and attends to consonances and dissonances that, while conflictive at times, form an integral part of Afro-diasporic identity.

A reading in this vein should begin with the most basic of questions: what is phonography? For most readers, the first resonance that comes to mind is likely the phonograph, which Thomas Edison patented in 1877. One of the inventor's first recordings was his own recitation of "Mary Had a Little Lamb." It was etched into tinfoil, which turned out to be a poor way of preserving one's voice for all posterity. Just a few years later, however, scientists like Alexander Graham Bell and Emile Berliner began to experiment with materials that would produce a more permanent recording, including wax, rubber, and glass. The National Museum of American History holds of number of artifacts from early sound-capturing technologies. In collaboration with the Smithsonian and the Library of Congress, researchers at the Lawrence Berkeley National Laboratory have made some of these recordings available online.

Beyond mere objects of interest, these early recordings are useful for thinking about the process of preserving or archiving sound, in written accounts as well as through recording technology. Indeed, complementary to the primary sounds that are recorded, we are also faced with what Michel de Certeau describes as a "scattered and secondary vocalization [that] traverses discursive expression, splicing or dubbing it."[13] De Certeau argues that this "minor voice," with its extra-semantic sonorities, unsettles the grand linguistic narratives that the "major voice" establishes. He uses an extended sonorous metaphor to describe such disturbances, situating them firmly within the auditory realm. "From the clamor of voices overrunning and breaking up the field of statements comes a mumble that escapes the control of speakers and that violates the supposed division between speaking individuals. It fills the space between speakers with the plural and prolix act of communication and creates, mezza voce, an opera of enunciation on the stage of verbal exchange."[14] In the context of speech, the philosopher struggles to reconcile linguistic meaning with voice, a singular, sonorous fiction and symbol of identity whose slippery essence is indeed difficult to grasp. Furthermore, he underscores the unknown auditory fabric of coughs, "umms," and even fingers tapping on the table as interpretable signs of discourse—and presence— that do not always make their way into histories or epistemologies, perhaps due to their disruptive nature. By drawing out these "secondary voices," de Certeau also implies that one might interpret them, perhaps using an approach that privileges language's extra-semantic content.

The interdisciplinary field of sound studies offers ample fodder and methods for interrogating the secondary (auditory) discourse that troubles de Certeau and also eludes inscription in the colonial archive. In the introduction to *Digital Sound Studies*, Mary Caton Lingold, Darren Mueller, and Whitney Trettien reflect upon these same themes. The trio's opening remarks describe their first encounter with the Jazz Loft Project, a large collection of photojournalist W. Eugene Smith's recordings that dates from 1957–65, some of which feature puzzling "thumps" in the background. In conversation with archivist Dan Partridge, they learn that the noises are Smith's cats, passing by the recording device as he works. Lingold, Mueller, and Trettien reflect upon the deep listening in which Partridge was able to engage once he had identified the sounds properly:

> Dan spent his days in a quiet basement, his ears locked under headphones, listening to the recordings on a computer. As he listened, scrubbing the audio back and forth to hone in on particular noises, his ears became attuned to what he was hearing, and he began to develop a mental map of the acoustic space in Smith's loft. Eventually he could interpret sounds that would be unintelligible to a casual listener—understanding indistinct commotion, for instance, a cat jumping onto a table. . . . Dan's descriptions are now part of the collection's finding aid and thus render an impenetrably large amount of audio data accessible to researchers.[15]

Partridge's experience illustrates the richness of attending to secondary or unexpected discourses in the sonic archive, for his observations lend important insight into aspects of the recording that exceed its primary message.

All of this clarifies phonography's capacity for documenting sounds that exceed writing's major voice and thus resist script. While the devices that this overview explores are emblems of sound writing, the tradition's history predates its nineteenth-century mechanization. Indeed, Shane Butler's history of phonography does not begin with Edison, tinkering in his Menlo Park laboratory. Rather, it opens with the anonymous inventors of inscription and considers the problematic but pervasive desire for vocal legibility in Antiquity poetry, rhetoric, and other literary forms. From Butler's perspective, Western philosophy's difficulty in relating speech, voice, and text is rooted, in part, in continued phonographic slippage among the three concepts. He traces the challenge back to "a root ambiguity in the Greek word *phōnē*, the principal meanings of which not only include 'voice' but also the human faculty of 'speech.'"[16] In Western thought, the vagaries of translation amplified this hazy distinction between speech and voice. Broadly, epistemological and ontological discourses associate the former concept with language and reason and struggle to hear the latter. On one hand, voice designates the unscriptable auditory contours of vocalization. On the other, it is a metaphor for presence. Together, these constructions constitute a sonic metaphysics that eludes systems of writing, even those that purport to privilege auditory legibility.

In its material form, phonography is a means of capturing sound's impressed vibrations. In a reading of sonic technologies' signifying role within modern African American culture, Alexander Weheliye argues that

> inscription seems to be at the root of any kind of recording: more than recording itself, it seems that sound necessitates transposition into writing to even register as technology. The place of script as a preferred, if not dominant, cultural technology in the West makes for the authority that it relays in relation to speech and sound, which, in contrast to writing, have to be reiterated and imagined as writing in order to operate as recordings.[17]

For Weheliye, sound's materiality enables its scripted representation, which, in turn, imbues *phōnē* with writing's ontological authority. He maintains that "the murky domains of reproduction and reception" are loci of meaning in sonic recordings and suggests that the mechanical distancing of sound and source in modern devices like Edison's invention disturbed the relationship between voice and presence.[18] In this way, Weheliye aligns phonography with writing and beckons interpretations that attend to its acousmatic instability. Just as text conceals the authorial hand that transcribes pure thought, so sonic recordings muffle the larynx, tongue, and lips that produce their content. In phonography, engraved frequencies and imprinted vibrations reproduce voice and distance the vocalizer. In order to interrupt the process and unscript the speaker or singer's inaudible presence, then, it becomes necessary to attend to phonography's underlying pulsations.

Viet Erlmann's observations about the Latin root -*cutere* (to shake or strike) and its sonic derivatives as a threat to reason's separation of subject and object are useful for understanding how writing and vibration intersect. Erlmann attends to the concept's resonances in René Descartes's *Meditations on First Philosophy* (1641), where he draws out tension between the thinker's definitive use of *inconcussum* (unshakeable)—a term that Descartes relates to truth—and its trembling foundation. Erlmann notes that

> while the philosopher's desire for certainty thus clearly appears to be premised on the absence of sound, the rich etymology of *cutere* and its various ancient derivatives such as *percussion, concussion*, and *discussion* ... suggest that Descartes was actually grappling with a more complex set of issues. These issues not only cast doubt on the philosopher's hidden claim that the sought-after certainty can only occur in a soundproof space free of the noise of the crackling fire and even that of the philosopher's own breathing, they entangle the philosopher's strategy of securing the ego by means of reasoning in a web of uncanny affinities with the very phenomenon of -*cutere* the strategy is meant to negate.[19]

Beneath the Cartesian certitude that banishes the senses from the epistemological realm, something pulsates just below the textual surface, a barely audible disturbance that throbs against unvoiced thought and threatens to puncture it. The contemplative silence that Descartes imagines is like the noise-canceling headphones of philosophy. It is an artificial dampening of sound that seeks to amplify the thinker's voice as a single, dominant narrative. However, as Erlmann's history of early modern otology illustrates, concepts like frequency or resonance are noisy interferences in fictions of the thinking self and its written manifestations. Given -*cutere*'s inherent linkage of sound and vibration, percussion stands out as useful motif for puncturing lettered alterity.

Continuing, Jacques Derrida's auditory critique of Western thought's reliance on the self/other binary in *Margins of Philosophy* (1972) resonates with the vibrations that disturb Cartesian silence. Here, the philosopher's opening meditation on the tympanum—the membrane that transmits auditory stimuli from the outer to inner ear—represents the eardrum as a porous threshold of subjectivity. Derrida's remarks are ideal for thinking about how listening can disrupt self-presence, especially with respect to speech's resistance to writing. He observes:

> If Being is in effect a process of reappropriation, the "question of Being" of a new type can never be percussed without being measured against the absolutely coextensive question of the proper. Now this latter question does not permit itself to be separated from the idealizing value of the *very-near*, which itself receives it disconcerting powers only from the structure of hearing-oneself-speak. The *proprius* presupposed in all directions on economy, sexuality, language, semantics, rhetoric, etc., repercusses its absolute limit only in sonorous representation.[20]

Precisely, the ear's anatomy transduces vibrations into sound, passing them through the filter of the self along the way. It would seem that the process depends upon the distinction between a sounding object and a listening subject. And yet, the absolute proximity of sound perception shakes being's foundational alterity. The uncanny act of hearing the other speak as oneself lies at the core of this disruption and offers a position from which to interrogate the colonial archive's inscription of non-European voices. If we were to return to that initial vibration and separate it from audition's inescapable self-hearing, then it might be possible to access the sounding voice's subjective registers.

Like Gayatri Chakravorty Spivak has pointed out, the infinite openness of Derridean deconstruction make it possible to interrogate Western philosophy's general deafness before polyphonies of gender and race.[21] With this in mind, I turn next to audio and rhythmic themes in the works of scholars like W. E. B. Du Bois or Paul Gilroy. My argument is that these refrains offer useful counterpoint to attempts to distance vocalized subjectivities from a liminal sensory context in which the embodiment of alterity interrupts self-presence. By attending to the quivering haptics of voice in inscriptions of Black and African sound, *Amplifications of Black Sound* amplifies affective contours that exceed the archive's lettered bounds.

Black and Africana studies have long considered sound and music as indices of Afro-diasporic experience. Indeed, the trope stands out in Du Bois's 1903 classic *The Souls of Black Folk*. The activist and scholar saw music as a cultural archive that captured the unscriptable realities of the enslaved and their descendants. He maintained that oral materials from the American South encoded dissonant voices and emotions.

> I know that these songs are the articulate message of the slave to the world. They tell us in these eager days that life was joyous to the black slave, careless and happy. I can easily believe this of some, of many. But not all the past South, though it rose from the dead, can gainsay the heart-touching witness of these songs. They are the music of an unhappy people, of the children of

disappointment; they tell of death and suffering and unvoiced longing toward a truer world, of misty wanderings and hidden ways.[22]

In this passage, Du Bois privileges music's affective properties as a site for remembering Afro-diasporic histories. For the pivotal thinker, song is an essential legacy of Black and African people in bondage. While time and repetition have diluted the original connotations, Du Bois argues that an extra-linguistic filter can enable contemporary listeners to appreciate the experience of the enslaved.

In a gesture that further underscores music's centrality for Black epistemologies, Du Bois opens each chapter with a poetic epigraph and several bars of music. He explains that "before each thought that I have written in this book I have set a phrase, a haunting echo of these weird old songs in which the soul of the black slave spoke to men."[23] Both the structure of Du Bois's book and his clarification reinforce the idea that music encodes Afro-descendant knowledge and histories in a way that exceeds the archive's written limits. In addition to links with memory and affect, the connection also relates to music's resistance before script.

All of these qualities stand out in a fragmented, familial tune that Du Bois includes in the final chapter of *The Souls of Black Folk*. His great-great-grandmother remembered her homeland by singing the piece, and the writer affirms that family members handed it down through the oral tradition. "My grandfather's grandmother was seized by an evil Dutch trader two centuries ago; and coming to the valleys of the Hudson and Housatonic, black, little, and lithe, she shivered and shrank in the harsh north winds, looked longingly at the hills, and often crooned a heathen melody to the child between her knees."[24] In Du Bois's description, the tune becomes a trans-historic echo that recalls his familial place of origin and mourns its loss. While the book's other musical examples are without lyrics, this piece, the "Do bana" song, features words whose linguistic meaning remains buried. Abigail Manzella remarks that "the lyrics of the song, however, are untranslatable, not just to the reader not versed in African languages, but even to those people. It appears that the words over time have been corrupted because they were not understood by their singers."[25] From this perspective, it is possible to hear the Duboisian tune as an archive, though not in the sense of writing or printed images. Instead, it is a record of voice whose sonic ephemerality and unstable transmission are spectral reminders (remainders) of an unwritable past.

The challenging excavation of the legible past that Manzella underscores in "Do bana" is central to its particular meaning-making, especially in the context of Black and African studies. According to Manzella, "we see a tie across generations represented through the transmission of the song, a much more immediate passage of memory than that of the sorrow songs that had to be indirectly relearned."[26] Indeed, just as the intimacy of performance binds families across time and space, so the melody's sonic contours represent the fractured memory of enslaved people and their descendants. Du Bois describes the transmission process: "the child sang it to his children and they to their children's children, and so two hundred years it has travelled down to us and we sing it to our children, knowing as little as our father what its words may mean, but knowing well the meaning of its music."[27] Two centuries after the author's great-great-grandmother arrived on American shores, her progeny continues to voice the experience of bondage. The lyrics' impenetrable semantics recalls the unspeakable histories of people taken forcibly from their homelands. As a corporeal sonic practice, singing remembers bodies long separated from their mother tongues, even as the words' meaning eludes performers and repetition transforms phonic contours.

The oral legacy that Du Bois describes recalls Diana Taylor's concept of "repertoire." In a landmark study of performance and memory in the Americas, Taylor explains how embodied histories or "repertoire" can complement the lettered archive. She notes that

> the repertoire, on the other hand, enacts embodied memory: performances, gestures, orality, movement, dance, singing—in short, all those acts usually thought of as ephemeral, nonreproducible knowledge. Repertoire, etymologically "a treasury, an inventory," also allows for individual agency, referring also to "the finder, discoverer," and meaning "to find out." The repertoire requires presence: people participate in the production and reproduction of knowledge by "being there," being a part of the transmission. As opposed to the supposedly stable objects in the archive, the actions that are the repertoire do not remain the same. The repertoire both keeps and transforms choreographies of meaning.[28]

For Taylor, repertoire amplifies the performer's role as co-creator of meaning and challenges writing's iterability. Along the same lines, as a ghostly shell of its performance, "Do bana" quietly resists textual representation. Although Du Bois attempts to transcribe the piece, the lettered sounds of English are undoubtedly a poor substitute for once-Africanized syllables, and the melody's septuple meter is at odds with the 4/4 time signature that the stave indicates. Tensions like these illustrate the difficulty of reducing an embodied practice like singing to written forms and also signify distance between the piece's African origins and the Western codes through which the author presents it.

For all this, Du Bois's observations in *The Souls of Black Folk* codified music as a locus of Black thought. Some ninety years after its publication, Paul Gilroy's foundational study of the Black Atlantic echoed these ideas and inserted them into debates about writing and racial identity. For Gilroy, music is a means of hearing beyond the writing's essentialist narrative of Black cultural experience—in particular, its future-oriented, utopic yearnings. He notes that "the politics exists on a lower frequency where it is played, danced, and acted, as well as sung and sung about, because words, even stretched by melisma and supplemented or mutated by the screams which still index the conspicuous power of the slave sublime, will never be enough to communicate its unsayable claims to truth."[29] Once again, resistance before script stands out as key to Black experience and epistemology in Gilroy's observations.

In *Listening to Images*, Tina Campt develops Gilroy's "lower frequencies" as a framework for examining photographic representations of the Black and African Atlantic. She proposes a methodology of listening to the visual archive in order to attend more fully to Black subjectivity. Campt maintains that

> it is through sound that I seek a deeper engagement with the forgotten histories and suppressed forms of diasporic memory that these images transmit. I theorize sound as an inherently embodied process that registers at multiple levels of the human sensorium. To invoke another counterintuition that serves as a second point of theoretical departure, while it may seem an inherent contradiction in terms, sound need not be heard to be perceived. Sound can be listened to, and, in equally powerful ways, sound can be felt; it both touches and moves people. In this way, sound must therefore be theorized and understood as a profoundly haptic sensory contact.[30]

Here, Campt opposes the auditory and haptic models that Gilroy invokes with visual epistemologies that dominate Western thought. She deepens notions of perception that link external stimuli to a single sense organ and instead argues for sensory epistemologies that account for the fullness of bodily experience. In archival records throughout the Atlantic, Campt reads sound as a physical and affective index of Black presence and experience. While Du Bois and Gilroy highlight auditory ephemerality as resistance to Eurocentric forms of recordkeeping and representation, Campt argues that in visual histories, inaudible sound paradoxically voices the refusal that is central to Afro-descendant experience.

Much like Sor Juana Inés de la Cruz reminds us in her musings on silence in the *Response to Sor Philotea de la Cruz* (1691), for Campt, inaudibility is a ghostly remnant of the limits of writing and other forms of inscription before subaltern subjectivities.[31] As a result, the voices the trope encodes remain inaccessible through traditional methods of literary analysis or visual art. In response, Campt draws upon Gilroy's ideas about frequency and proposes an auditory filter for hearing Black subjectivity in the archive.

> What is the frequency of these images? Quiet. A quiet hum full of reverb and vibrato. Not always perceptible to the human ear, we feel it more in the throat. To look at these images is to see genre and form. To look at them is to look through their sitters and see function and format, to "oversee" them in ways in which black people have been erased and overseen for centuries. To listen to them is to be attuned to their unsayable truths, to perceive their quiet frequencies of possibility—the possibility to inhabit a future as unbounded black subjects.[32]

For Du Bois and Gilroy, sound resists the illusion of stable meaning that writing and other visual forms provide. From their perspective, music remembers unscripted histories and voices longing for better days ahead. Meanwhile, for Campt, it is an affective mode that resists the visual hegemonies that dominate Western philosophy. To this end, Campt's reading distances audition from listening. Instead, she employs a theoretical motif of "frequency" to emphasize sound's haptic qualities and thus highlights its capacity to move the auditor, both physically and emotionally. Her analysis highlights the physical process of aural transmission, in which vibrations from the sounding body generate resonance with the tympanic membrane, or eardrum, as well as other organs to facilitate perception. Moreover, it underscores Western sound's persistent relationship with physical, spiritual, and emotional health.[33] By showing how embodied, sonic themes resist the structures of discipline and marginalization that frame photographs of Black subjects, Campt develops a praxis of echolocation that uses sound to draw out Afro-diasporic presence in the visual archive. I will return to the concept in the final chapter.

In sum, this audio-philosophic medley undergirds *Amplifications of Black Sound*'s interpretative approach. Instead of focusing on language as a foundation of meaning-making—what de Certeau calls the "major voice"— I listen to the uneasy shaking that haunts inscriptions of Black sounds, audible only as pops or cracks in the lettered recording.[34] By attending to the intimate haptics of pulses, frequencies, and rhythms that pepper the archive, I strive to re-embody Afro-descendant voices and shake them free from the shackles of written records. In some cases, my readings are firmly anchored in the colonial archive, where they probe unexplored nooks and crannies to draw attention to Black and African presence in New Spanish sound practices. In others, I employ a more experimental praxis of remixing to highlight diasporic and transhistorical resonances. Here, the work of contemporary Mexican hip-hop group Rak Ric Rack! or folkloric dances from Veracruz and the Costa Chica region echo Afro-descendant voices from New Spain, providing a contrapuntal response that opens new interpretative possibilities.

**CHAPTER OUTLINES**

*Amplifications of Black Sound* is divided into three interrelated sections. First, voice is the theoretical nucleus that guides Chapters 1 and 2. This portion of the book delves into the histories of Afro-descendant singers—possibly eunuchs, or *capones*—who sang in prominent New Spanish cathedrals during the early seventeenth century. Chapter 1 explores the tensions among these singers' prominent position in church ceremonies, where they were often the headliners of the chapel choir, the privileging of (castrate) sopranos within the early modern musical imaginary and the marginal status of enslaved Black and African people in New Spanish society. I maintain that discordant vocal identities enabled performers like Puebla's Juan de Vera and Mexico City's Luis Barreto to amplify their presence in contexts that might have otherwise muted them.

Complementarily, Chapter 2 draws out the persistence of Black and African sopranos within New Spain's audio-racial imaginary. Here, I approach early to mid-seventeenth-century Black villancicos as recordings that can lend insight into male high voices. From this perspective, musical and poetic renderings of Afro-descent stand out as valuable phonographic sources whose auditory tropes prescribe and describe the celebrated Black voices that rang out in the region's cathedrals.

Harmony and urban space are unifying themes in the next two chapters, which turn a listening ear to audio-racial themes in political (Chapter 3) and religious (Chapter 4) performances of Afro-descendant harmony in New Spanish cities. Baker's reading of inherent harmonies of urban space in Latin America informs my argument that these ideological filters imagine Black sounds as either consonant or dissonant with dominant socio-political and spiritual ideals.

Chapter 3 examines Afro-descendant performers in civic ceremonies, including viceregal entries, the private parties of Spanish officials and equestrian ballets. I argue that in these events, the participation of dancers and musicians from marginalized castes can be read from two perspectives. From one angle, they perform loyalty and obedience to colonial authorities through actual harmonies that accompany the acts and also through concordance with social hierarchies. From another, however, staging Black bodies at political events centers them and offers opportunities to perform Afro-diasporic memory before a diverse audience.

Chapter 4 explores some of the same themes in the context of paraliturgical and popular devotion. I draw out evidence of Afro-descendant sonorities from confraternity accounts, descriptions of private oratorios, villancico representations of Black festive practices, funerals, and Inquisition cases against enslaved *bozal* women (recent arrivals from Africa) who practiced divination. Although these sources do not often give detailed or accurate explanations of the performances they record, they strengthen understanding of the strategies that New Spanish Afro-descendants employed to amplify their voices in a culture that otherwise muffled them.

Chapters 5 and 6 turn to Black villancicos as phonographic archives of Afro-descent. These are musico-poetic pieces that lend a popular tone to liturgical readings. During the seventeenth and eighteenth centuries, churches throughout the Spanish world commissioned poets and composers to pen villancicos for feast day performances. While villancicos touch on a variety of things and draw in diverse elements of popular culture, the representation of Afro-descendants, gypsies, and autochthonous and other marginalized people in the *villancicos de remedo* or "ethnic" villancicos has drawn the most critical attention. As regards Afro-descent, these pieces' reproduction of stylized imaginings of Blackness from all over the Hispanic world is indisputably problematic. Nonetheless, I affirm that sonic renderings of Black villancico characters can lend insight into actual Afro-descendant sonorities as well as their perception among New Spanish elites.

Chapter 5 shows how the language, song, and dance of Black figures in villancicos typically disorder the concordant urban space in which they perform. Despite these dissonances, however, the characters' music-making is almost always an affective response to church festivities and the figures they honor. I contend that this tension is a necessary element of villancicos, whose role on city stages is to perform the evangelization of Afro-descendants, Indigenous people, and other new or recent Christians.

The sixth chapter applies a feminine lens to intersections of text, voice, and urban sounds in the New Spanish archive, specifically with respect to poet Sor Juana Inés de la Cruz's villancicos. Although the nun authored numerous lyrics for the genre, there are no complete extant scores for original performances of her work. Nevertheless, Sor Juana's villancicos include frequent references to musical instruments, dances, and vocal qualities, to say nothing of their sumptuous poetic rhythms. These lyrical sonorities are ripe for further interpretation. My readings concentrate on sonic performance of Afro-descent in two of Sor Juana's villancicos. In *Villancico* 258 (Assumption, 1679), a pair of Black female "princesses" (street vendors) abandons their daily activities in order to sing and dance in the Assumption festivities. Similarly, the attributable *Villancico* lviii (Assumption, 1686) imagines the voices and frenetic motions of two Afro-descendant women's musical tribute to the Virgin Mary. More than mere literary convention, I contend that Sor Juana's lyrics give body and voice to Black and African sonorities that rang out just beyond the convent walls. Through writing, *Villancicos* 258 and lviii re-sound acousmatic echoes of urban spaces to which the nun had little visual access. In this way, they function as both historical record and Afro-Atlantic performance.

The conclusion of the book reflects upon how sound's ability to move across space and time might enable scholars to hear the archive differently. The closing analysis of *Amplifications of Black Sound* centers on early Mexico City's aquatic infrastructure as well as other watery spaces as emblems of the region's multiethnic past. Along these lines, Barbara Mundy's award-winning study *The Death of Aztec Tenochtitlan, the Life of Mexico City* draws out the colonial persistence of an aqueous politics of civic authority and Indigenous cultural identity. Complementarily, I maintain that the city's lakes and aqueducts are metonymic reminders of the transatlantic exchange that was essential to Mexico City's cosmopolitan identity. As regards Afro-descent, I follow Ayesha Hameed's *Black Atlantis* and frame the aquatic as an embodied, sensory archive of the Black Atlantic and its enduring legacies.

With this pluricultural symbolism in mind, the conclusion attends to Afro-descendant echoes in seventeenth-century Mexico City's vast waterways. Its readings of seventeenth-century chronicles, travel narratives, and visual art highlight harmony and related terms as recurring descriptors for the city's dikes and canals. For instance, although Bernardo de Balbuena's *La grandeza mexicana* (1604) elides non-European sounds as "deafening noise," sonic descriptions from other seventeenth-century materials can amplify the quiet legacy of empty descriptors like Balbuena's. Baker's observation that consonant sounds and geometries were important for ordering New World urban space elucidates the auditory language that peppers these materials. Here, as elsewhere in the book, I maintain that concordant reverberations in representations of the canals harmonize these spaces' dissonance in accord with the city's sounds. Nevertheless, the murky depths dampen the auditory sense. Just as the canals resist the geometric grids that stand out in Gómez de Trasmonte's map, so they also muddy the harmonic order that governs urban land. I affirm that Black bodies and voices move more freely in these watery spaces. By adapting one's listening positionality to the aqueous environment, it is possible to hear them quite clearly.

Finally, having partially reconstructed Afro-descendant soundways in seventeenth-century New Spain, *Amplifications of Black Sound* closes with a brief reflection upon the work that is needed to connect historical details to present-day practices. While the book highlights some examples of the persistence or repercussion of Afro-Mexican sound culture, additional research can develop these tentative connections and draw out additional ones. This "retuning" of the collective ear can be frustratingly painstaking and slow. Nonetheless, it is essential if we are to one day hear Black sound as integral to Mexico's local and national sound cultures.

CHAPTER 1

# Black Male Sopranos in New Spanish Cathedrals

He said he was not a man, not a mortal, but part of the angel race, the dark spirit / angel race (an archangel, of course), a different order of being. . . . Angels of music are God's instrument: they glow with the color of their song, and every light and sound is an echo of God's voice and eyes. All men are the instruments they play on.

—**John F. Szwed**, *Space is the Place: The Lives and Times of Sun Ra*

June 19, 1611: Just days after the Corpus Christi festivities, on a warm Sunday afternoon, Mexico City prepared to welcome its new viceroy, Fray Francisco García Guerra. The Spanish clergyman and politician had already made one ceremonial entry into the celebrated city, when he arrived as archbishop of New Spain in 1608. Now, three years later, García Guerra traveled in a carriage through Mexico City's Indigenous outskirts. Inhabitants greeted him with music and exhibitions, including a display of flying dancers, or *voladores*. When the new viceroy reached the street of Santo Domingo, he mounted a steed adorned with wreaths and black velvet and continued onward. At this juncture, the viceregal court and military regiment came forward to accompany their leader. Black hats with white plumes, bright red tunics, and golden swords glittered in the sunlight as the procession journeyed toward the city center. Peninsular, Creole, Indigenous, and Afrodescendant faces in equal proportion looked on, and they raised their voices in support of the ruler as he passed. At the Plaza de Santo Domingo, García Guerra rode through one of New Spain's first triumphal arches, a festive construction that celebrated the leader's heroism with architecture, painting, and poetry. The chief magistrate handed the viceroy a golden key, and he opened the arch's gates, a metaphorical doorway to the city. In celebration, municipal officials and soldiers raised a silken canopy embroidered with golden flowers to protect García Guerra from the sun as he made his way through the crowded streets.

Soon, García Guerra and his entourage arrived at the Metropolitan cathedral, whose extensive remodel was underway. During those years, artisans and stonemasons were erecting the church's outer walls. The work was backbreaking, and Indigenous and Afro-descendant laborers toiled daily in service to the church and crown. On the day of his entry as viceroy, García Guerra stood before a massive skeleton of the volcanic rock called *tezontle* that loomed over the city's bustling *zócalo* (main square). At the heart of the construction site, religious services continued in the humble temple that architect Martín de Sepúlveda had designed some eighty years earlier. The procession prepared to enter the sacred space, but first, the church canons and clergy ordered them to remove the splendid shade "por q aqella majestad i gloria, solo a Dios pertenecia i no a criaturas umanas" (for such majesty and glory only belonged to God and not to mankind).[1] Indeed, even an archbishop-cum-viceroy needed to comply with standards of humility.

García Guerra led the crowd to the cathedral's main door, the *puerta del perdón*, or pilgrim's entry. There, priests, deacons, and the cathedral's music ensemble (the chapel) all awaited his arrival, sweltering under their heavy copes. García Guerra knelt on a ceremonial seat that had been brought outside for the occasion. The rest of the party followed suit. One of the priests raised a crucifix, and everyone genuflected. Then, the clergy and chapel greeted the leader with the *Te Deum laudamus*, a hymn of thanksgiving sung at Matins and on solemn celebrations. In all likelihood, singers intoned the Ambrosian lyrics while shawms, cornets, dulcians, sackbuts, and perhaps guitars accompanied them, much like in the *Te Deum laudamus* performance that Thomas Gage described when he disembarked at the Veracruz port alongside viceroy and Marquess of Cerralvo Rodrigo Pacheco y Osorio de Toledo in 1625.[2] When the hymn ended, García Guerra and his court made their way to the main altar, and an attendant placed the ceremonial seat nearby, in the area where the viceroy normally sat when attending mass. The party enjoyed the cathedral ensemble's performance of two *chanzonetas*, a paraliturgical genre with all of the hallmarks of the villancico, and then they left through the opposite door, raised the canopy once more, and made their way to the viceregal palace.[3]

The church council spared no expense in putting on a lavish celebration to commemorate García Guerra's entry, and music was central to the festivities. Given the viceroy's penchant for the art form and his subsequent role in shaping New Spanish music culture, the council most certainly recruited the city's best singers (*cantores*) and instrumentalists (*ministriles*) to perform in his honor.⁴ Among them, the cathedral musicians were the cream of the crop. Under chapelmaster Juan Hernández's direction, these expert performers took part in mass and also made music at paraliturgical and civic ceremonies, including the Corpus Christi octave; the Feast of San Hipólito, patron saint of New Spain; funeral ceremonies; and processions to honor ecclesiastical and political dignitaries.⁵ Their repertoire was vast, incorporating mass settings from France, Italy, and Spain; the *chanzonetas* of New Spanish and Peninsular composers; and even theater pieces like devotional *coloquios*.⁶ The choir consisted of a dozen or so men who sang *tiple* (soprano), *contralto*, *tenor*, or *contrabajo* (bass).

During this time, fulfilling the high voice parts was a particularly difficult task. Church mandates prevented women from performing in ecclesiastical spaces, and young boys could only sing in the choir for a few years before puberty lowered their pitch. Consequently, the church council was always on the lookout for adult *tiples* who sang falsetto or whose voices had been preserved through castration. There were several sopranos in the chapel when García Guerra became viceroy, but financial records from the Archivo del Cabildo Catedral Metropolitano de México suggest that he particularly favored one voice: that of enslaved *mulato* Luis Barreto.

Alfredo Nava Sánchez has detailed the career of the famed New Spanish singer extensively and drawn him into the cathedral music canon. Nava Sánchez's account of Barreto's wages and the privileges he enjoyed are of particular interest for understanding how the church valued the Black, high-voiced singer. A year after archbishop García Guerra's arrived, the council awarded Barreto a salary of 12 gold pesos a month, in recognition of his service to the church and "por ser de tan singular voz y destreza para el canto de órgano" (for having such a singular voice and talent for organum).⁷ One month later, officials voted not to discount the costs of the singer's upkeep from his salary.⁸ The singer's 144-peso annual wages were just slightly less than his peers' earnings. By comparison, the council awarded soprano Matheo Marín a salary of 150 gold pesos in November of the same year.⁹ Following the establishment of his regular wages, Luis Barreto received several luxurious outfits and a one-time bonus of 100 pesos for his stellar performance during the 1611 Corpus Christi festivities.¹⁰ In 1615, the singer petitioned the cathedral council for his freedom, offering a purchase price of 1,500 pesos and five years of salaried service.¹¹ After some deliberation, ecclesiastical authorities granted Barreto his liberty in exchange for the proposed fee and six additional years of service as a paid singer in the cathedral chapel.¹²

Barreto is just one prominent Black voice in early seventeenth-century New Spain's sacred music industry. Around the same time, another enslaved, Afro-descendant soprano rose to distinction in the ranks of the Puebla cathedral chapel. As Omar Morales Abril's research has shown, Juan de Vera had a storied career both in and beyond the Puebla cathedral. He regularly sang with the cathedral chapel, a prestigious group of some of the city's best-trained musicians that performed at mass and on feast days. In addition, he sang at events like the city's Corpus Christi festivities, worked as a musical scribe, and carried out a number of other musical tasks in cathedral and municipal settings. In fact, Juan de Vera even composed *chanzonetas* for the 1604 Corpus Christi celebration, when Puebla found itself in dire straits following the sudden departure of chapelmaster Pedro Bermúdez, to whom it would have fallen to write the pieces. During that year, a desperate council paid Vera "ochenta y dos pesos cinco tomines y nueve granos que se le libraron de los coloquios y chanzonetas que hizo en la fiesta de Corpus y su octava de este año de seiscientos y cuatro" (eighty-two pesos, five *tomines*, and nine *granos* were ordered in payment for the *coloquios* and *chanzonetas* that he prepared for the Corpus celebration and its octave from this year of 1604).[13] Within the musical economy of the day, 82 pesos seemed like a mere pittance in exchange for the enormous musical task that Vera undertook. As a point of comparison, Morales Abril has remarked upon the lavish 830-peso salary that lured Bermúdez to Puebla in 1603.[14]

A year later, the council awarded 100 pesos in additional compensation to both Vera and subcantor Francisco Alfonso, who had prepared the choir for Corpus Christi in Bermúdez's absence. In 1606, the council raised Juan de Vera's annual salary to 300 pesos and offered additional pay for his continued work as interim composer. Morales Abril transcribes the terms of payment, which indicate that Juan de Vera was to compose *chanzonetas* for the cathedral until such time that the council appointed a new chapelmaster.[15] These details are of interest for several reasons. First, as Morales Abril remarks, it demonstrates the high esteem in which the Puebla cathedral held Juan de Vera's musical talents, although, it is equally noteworthy that the enslaved man did not assume the chapelmaster's responsibility of directing the choir. Additionally, the record is valuable evidence that composition was among the church musicianship duties assigned to enslaved Black and African people in New Spain. Indeed, Juan de Vera's extensive training as a singer also prepared him to write music for the villancico cycles that would accompany some of the most important feast days of the year. All together, these activities paint a portrait of a talented and well-trained musician whose community greatly valued him.

Barreto and Vera's careers raise a number of questions about race, voice, and performance in seventeenth-century New Spain's sacred music industry. Although case studies like those Morales Abril and Nava Sánchez have undertaken offer tantalizing details about individual vocalists, additional research is necessary to gain broader insight into the ways that Afro-descendants participated in New Spanish sound culture and how musical activities intersected with these individuals' social statuses. Indeed, there is a strong need to diversify our understanding of cathedral music culture, where scholars have long read Black, Indigenous, and other non-European voices through a lens of exceptionalism that dampens these ethnic groups' contributions to New Spain's sacred sound culture.

Despite assumptions, non-white musicians are far from absent in seventeenth-century cathedral records from New Spain. Beyond the singers whose careers this chapter examines, there is evidence of musicians of African and Indigenous descent in urban cathedrals throughout New Spain. The viceroyalty's first bishop, Juan de Zumárraga, took a keen interest in the Indigenous choirboys who received training in plainchant and polyphony, Spanish, and theology at Pedro de Gante's convent school of San Jose de los Naturales.[16] As ecclesiastical music became more professionalized in the viceroyalty, the church council began to contract native musicians. Church ledgers document the presence of autochthonous performers in the Mexico City cathedral relatively soon after Contact. In fact, Stevenson observes that the practice dates back to 1543.[17] Likewise, Celina G. Becerra Jiménez remarks upon Indigenous choirboys who sang in the Guadalajara cathedral during the mid- to late sixteenth century.[18] Complementary to these references, the Musicat database, which offers digitized access and a search function for acts of the cathedral chapter relevant to the study of music, includes references to free and enslaved instrumentalists of African descent. Pedro de Rivera, a *pardo* man in bondage, and Francisco Rivera, a *moreno* man in bondage, respectively played the bassoon and the bugle in the Oaxaca cathedral during the 1650s.[19]

In light of this evidence, recent research on New Spanish cathedrals moves toward scholarly frameworks that account for a greater diversity of race and cultural experiences. Some scholars extend Stevenson's pioneer work by de-centering the cathedral as a primary locus of musical activity. Along these lines, Baker's study of how race, urban space, and music-making intersect in sixteenth- through eighteenth-century Cuzco is especially valuable.[20] Others interrogate notions about race and class that inform analyses of cathedral sound culture. For instance, David Irving examines musical Encounter in the Philippines through a contrapuntal lens that draws out the interplay of European, autochthonous, and African musical practices, forms, and performers in the region's festivals and religious institutions.[21] With a focus on eighteenth-century New Spain, Jesús Ramos-Kittrell has shown how participation in musical activities influenced mutable categories that determined social standing, including race and "decency," a concept that reflected bloodline, reputation, and education, among others. Ramos-Kittrell's study valuably shifts paradigmatic readings of cathedral music-making as an upper-class, Iberian, or Creole activity.[22] In light of these advances, scholarship that continues to listen to New Spain's sacred music industry through a multiethnic filter can further diversify the canon.

The presence of sopranos like Juan de Vera and Luis Barreto beckons additional research on Black performers' audibility within New Spain's sacred music culture. While Barreto and Vera are perhaps the best-known Afro-descendant cathedral singers of their day, they are not the only ones. For example, Stevenson referenced the popularity of a choir with an Afro-descendant director in mid-seventeenth-century Mexico City. Apparently, the group competed with chapelmaster Fabián Ximeno and the cathedral musicians on special occasions. In 1651, Ximeno brought a complaint about the rival choir before the cathedral chapter and asked that they cease to allow performances by "las capillas de musicos, Y en particular, Vna de vn negro, por la indecenssia, con que cantan, y disparates que dicen en el officiar las missas" (musical ensembles, And in particular, One led by a *negro*, because of the indecency, with which they sing and the mistakes they make when officiating mass).[23] In order to justify the chapel's superiority, Ximeno references the mistakes that the unsanctioned ensemble makes, calling their music "indecent." According to the word's historical and contemporary usage, the chapelmaster's description might portray the Afro-descendant or mixed-race group as disreputable or even provocative.[24] A reading from this angle resonates with the lewd characterization of Black and African dances that Nicholas Jones has drawn out in early modern Iberian texts and neatly aligns with assumptions about how viceregal society devalued Black cultural interventions.[25]

Nonetheless, there are other ways to read Ximeno's description. For instance, Ramos-Kittrell has shown that in the context of eighteenth-century cathedral music-making, *decencia*, or decency, referred to one's position in the community, including lineage, moral disposition, and public and professional profiles.[26] Likewise, the *Diccionario de Autoridades* defines the term as "compostúra, aseo, adorno que excíta el culto y veneración de las cosas santas y sagradas" (ornamentation, cleanliness, embellishment that inspires the devotion and veneration of holy and sacred things). From this perspective, decency describes art's potential to move an audience through masterful beauty, particularly in religious contexts.

In the passage that Stevenson quotes, Ximeno uses "indecency" with specific reference to a Black or mixed-race choir's singing. He relates "indecency" to the group's musical and textual errors and thus underscores its resonances with performance training in the Western tradition. The classification purposefully portrays the offending choir as a group of unskilled outsiders whose musicianship is inferior to cathedral chapel singers. While it is impossible to ignore the racial undertones of "indecency," Ximeno's complaint appears to focus more emphatically on the group's musical proficiency or their ability to affect parishioners. The chapelmaster makes a case for excluding Afro-descendant singers from paid positions in religious ceremonies because of their technically inferior performance, which may or may not relate to race.

In light of contemporary sensibilities about the topic, it would be easy to fall prey to facile essentialism and read Ximeno's indication as evidence that Afro-descendant musicians are less skilled than their Creole or Spanish counterparts. In fact, one might even hypothesize that Black singers and instrumentalists in New Spain received lower-quality music instruction, or none at all. After all, Black villancicos regularly depict Afro-descendant musicians as amateurish. In addition to the broken Castilian of *habla de negros*, these pieces abound with lyrical references to the discordant, unmusical sound of Black singers, and some musical settings lend sonorous context to dissonant imagery. In addition, accounts of Afro-descendant music in New Spanish streets describe it as disruptive or cacophonous.[27] While the humble social status of Black and African people in New Spain may have limited access to formal musical training, interpretations that read Afro-descendant participation in professional spheres as exceptional risk furthering long-held notions about marginalized castes' limited access to the cathedral chapel and the musical formation that it entailed. This chapter challenges such notions with a discussion of the pedagogical and performance practices that shaped the careers of singers like Vera and Barreto.

## COMMODIFYING SOPRANO VOICES

As adult, male sopranos, Juan de Vera and Luis Barreto were valuable members of the chapel. While their wages were comparable to their white peers' salaries, these figures' enslaved status lends a new dimension to our understanding of the worth of church musicians, particularly as it relates to voice. Precisely, the elevated prices that both Barreto and Vera fetched in bills of sale beckon explorations of vocal commodification and its relationship to bodies in bondage. The theme can be uncomfortable in the face of Western philosophy's longstanding association of voice with agency and identity.[28]

Fred Moten has explored these connections from a Black and African studies perspective that opposes voice to commodification. Moten's reading focuses on an otherwise-voiceless commodity's imagined response to capitalist valuing in Karl Marx's *Capital*. Inasmuch as Western philosophy imagines speech as a property of the subject, Marx's envoicement of the object draws it into the field of subjectivity and therefore destabilizes the subject/object dichotomy that makes capitalist exchange possible. Moten reasons that "we can think how the commodity who speaks, in speaking, in the sound—the inspirited materiality—of that speech, constitutes a kind of temporal warp that disrupts and augments not only Marx but the mode of subjectivity that the ultimate object of his critique, capital, both allows and disallows."[29] For Moten, Aunt Hester's scream in Frederick Douglass's *Narrative of the Life of Frederick Douglass, An American Slave* precedes the spoken resistance to commodification that he draws out in Marx. He asserts that "every approach to Mark's example must move through the ongoing event that anticipates it, the real event of the commodity's speech, itself broken by the irreducible materiality—the broken and irreducible maternity—of the commodity's scream."[30] Moten relates the thick aurality of Aunt Hester's shriek to sonic expression in Black performance. Along these lines, he draws out resistance in Black sound: an auditory refusal of objectification, enslavement, and the written and musical forms that guide Western thought. Furthermore, he sees Black aurality as a non-scripted history that gives voice to people who are otherwise reduced to commodities in record books.

Barreto and Vera's cases do not fit neatly into Moten's reflections on sound, resistance to objectification, and Black performance. Indeed, what of the commodity of who sings? And in particular, what of the commodity whose voice is a product of intensive training, a regimen of vocal care, and perhaps, surgical alteration? In a study of early modern *castrati* from Italy, Bonnie Gordon observes that the commodification of these voices distanced them from Western ideas about subjectivity and self-determination.

> Because the castrato voice was so explicitly made by surgeons, teachers, and the singers themselves, it foregrounds the technical practices and materials that animate song. This particular voice highlights the ability of technology of all kinds, including vocal training, to separate the voice from the presence of an essential speaker, and it debunks the Western premise of the human voice as necessarily invested with unmediated presence and agency. The castrato's now totally absent sounds remind would-be listeners that voices are material—produced through bodily actions and bodily training—and that they are always produced in ways that disengage them from an essential body or subjectivity.[31]

Whether or not Barreto and Vera were castrati, they were valuable instruments of the church. Like I will argue here, the enslaved men's technical education, diet, and costuming all served to hone their much-needed soprano voices for cathedral performances. From a Black studies perspective, it can be difficult to attend to the vocalic resistance in the figures of Vera and Barreto, for their voices are a site of commodification. Nevertheless, these singers ameliorated their enslaved condition in other ways.

As financial records show, a musician in bondage was an attractive asset for both church and slaveholder. First, it is important to bear in mind that in New Spain's urban centers, many enslaved men labored as craftsmen or artists. Owners permitted and even encouraged their workers to acquire marketable skills like carpentry or stonemasonry, for these abilities were a source of income. Indeed, Pablo Sierra Silva observes that New Spain's Afro-descendants in bondage took on domestic duties, ran errands, sold food in marketplaces, drove carriages, and looked out for their masters' physical safety. Such details draw out enslaved laborers' significance for their masters' personal finances as well as for the viceroyalty's economic development. Sierra Silva observes that "these blurred boundaries between the domestic, artisanal and political were integral to urban slave-ownership. Most masters trusted their slaves and depended on their mobility to profit from their subjection."[32] Complementary to financial gains for slaveowners, the freedoms that New Spain's urban workers enjoyed also benefitted laborers themselves. Movement throughout the city enabled enslaved men and women to build networks among their peers, and artisanal skills offered opportunities for increased visibility and better living conditions.

Like details that Morales Abril recovered from Juan de Vera's performances suggest, owning an Afro-descendant soprano was a particularly lucrative business. Indeed, Juan de Vera's owners, Francisco de Céspedes and later, Antonio de Vera, made a handsome profit from the enslaved man's wages, for he earned a steady income as a member of the Puebla cathedral chapel. From 1590 onward, account records document Juan de Vera's participation in the city's lavish Corpus Christi festivities, for which he received supplementary pay as recompense. Morales Abril observes that Vera's responsibilities for these celebrations extended well beyond singing or even acting.[33] Surviving records of cathedral expenses can shed some light on Juan de Vera's other duties and thus afford a clearer understanding of the enslaved man's day-to-day life. Morales Abril details expenditures like paper for writing compositions, materials to re-string the cathedral's harp—an instrument that Vera purportedly stole—and even clothing for special celebrations.[34]

Above all, Juan de Vera's history is especially interesting for its rich insights into the economy of Black voices as well as other duties that such singers might undertake in New Spain. Indeed, Morales Abril's careful documentation of Vera's earnings illustrates his voice's financial worth. As a cathedral musician in the late 1570s, he earned about 100 *pesos de minas* "por cantor y por puntador de la música" (for being a singer and for being a musical scribe).[35] The enslaved man's salary fluctuated, depending upon his responsibilities, and at the height of his career, he earned around 300 *pesos de minas* per year, plus one-time bonuses for festival performances or compositions. In addition to the enslaved man's regular salary, both Céspedes and Antonio de Vera, Juan de Vera's subsequent owner, earned additional stipends for his contributions. According to documents that Morales Abril recovered, Céspedes received an additional 100 *pesos de oro común* each year in recognition of Vera's services to the cathedral.[36] A few years later, in 1578, the cathedral paid Antonio de Vera an annual supplement of 150 *pesos de oro común* in exchange for the enslaved man's services.[37]

Although Juan de Vera's wages may have supported his upkeep, they formed part of his owners' estate, as Antonio de Vera's will indicates: "Mando que [Juan de Vera] viva en los aposentos en que hoy vive y acuda como tal músico a cantar a la dicha iglesia. Y los dichos trescientos pesos que se le da y gana por año, dé y acuda con ellos al dicho Juan Velásquez, primero patrón, para que los ponga y junte con la demás renta del patronazgo que dejo fundado" (I direct that [Juan de Vera] should live in the quarters where he lives today and attend the aforementioned [cathedral] church as a singer. And as for the aforementioned 300 pesos that he is given and earns each year, he should give them to the aforementioned master, Juan Velásquez, so that Velásquez can add them to the other tributes from the patronage that I established).[38] Antonio de Vera's will makes the singer's financial worth clear, for he views Juan de Vera as a legacy whose continued service and earnings will benefit the cathedral and also add wealth to the canon's estate.

Ample returns like these came at a high price for slaveowners, though. When Céspedes first brought the young Black man to Puebla, Bishop Antonio Ruiz de Morales y Molina offered him a handsome raise so that the Puebla Cathedral might make use of his servant's astonishing vocal talents. As it turns out, Céspedes was a shrewd businessman. When the chaplain contemplated leaving Puebla, the bishop responded with a recommendation to purchase the singer so that he could continue to participate in the cathedral's musical activities. Morales Abril notes that the proposed price was an exorbitant 1,400 pesos, more than three times as much as the cathedral would pay for other enslaved Afro-descendants some twenty years later.[39]

Although the cathedral was not successful in their bid to acquire the singer, documentation for the potential sale clarifies that Vera's vocal talent determined his value: "es muy necesario a la dicha iglesia el dicho negrillo, por ser, como es, muy buen cantor y de muy buena voz para la capilla de la música" (the *negrillo* boy is very necessary to the church, being, as he is, a very good singer with a very good voice for the cathedral choir).[40] In light of the handsome price that the performer fetched because of his extraordinary voice, Morales Abril puts forth a convincing hypothesis: "era caponcillo o la iglesia tenía la intención de emascularlo" (he was castrated or the church intended to emasculate him).[41]

The Mexico City cathedral paid a comparably hefty sum of 1,500 pesos for Barreto in 1595, when they purchased him in Veracruz and placed him in the care of subcantor Bartolomé Franco. Nava Sánchez details the muddled story of Barreto's acquisition and custody. Apparently, Franco quickly tired of his headstrong charge and requested that the council house the enslaved man elsewhere. The church obliged and removed Barreto from Franco's care. When the council considered selling the servant, however, the subcantor himself offered to buy the twenty-something singer.[42] Perhaps, Franco hoped to profit from the enslaved performer's salary. Just as in the case of Juan de Vera, Luis Barreto's purchase price was exorbitant. Nava Sánchez observes: "No cabe duda que era realmente la voz del mulato esclavo la que valía tal cantidad de dinero, por lo que interesó al cabildo conservarla en buen estado y hacer todo lo posible para que aquél no sufriera ninguna desgracia que dañara su valioso tesoro" (There is no doubt that it was actually the *mulato* slave's voice that was worth such a large sum. For this reason, the council became interested in maintaining it in a good state and doing everything possible so that the enslaved man did not suffer any misfortune that might damage his valuable treasure).[43] Precisely, Luis Barreto was a luxury item, and his worth related to the unique voice that the church so esteemed. Like Morales Abril, Nava Sánchez concludes that the enslaved man's elevated value reflects his status as a castrate singer.[44]

### MAKING THE PERFECT SOPRANO

The presence of eunuch singers in New Spanish cathedrals may come as a surprise, for the popular imagination tends to relate castrati to superstar leads of Italian opera during the eighteenth and nineteenth centuries, including Carlo Broschi ("Farinelli," subject of the eponymous 1995 film) or Alessandro Moreschi, whose 1902 and 1904 wax cylinder recordings offer a glimpse of the celebrated vocal type. Nonetheless, the tradition's musical roots stretch much farther back. In sixteenth-century Europe, a growing preference for eunuch singers responded to two shifts in church music culture. The post-Tridentine rise of four-part, liturgical polyphony required a broader range of voices than the plainchant that preceded it, spanning from bass to soprano or tiple, to use the nomenclature of Spanish-language scores. At the same time, however, the Catholic church discouraged and even banned women from singing during worship. As justification, ecclesiastical leaders cited the Pauline command to "let women keep silent in the churches" (I Corinthians 14:34). While young boys could sing the soprano part in church services, laryngeal growth and thickening vocal cords at puberty wrought havoc on their upper registers. Instead of investing years of training in singers who could only serve in their positions for a few years, the church turned to male falsettists and castrati to fill high-voiced roles. Throughout the sixteenth century, debates raged on about the authenticity of the two types of male sopranos.[45] In 1589, Pope Sixtus V's *Cum pro nostro pastorali munere* codified a preference for castrate sopranos in religious settings by advocating for their presence in the Sistine Chapel Choir, his private ensemble.

While Sixtus V's 1589 bull is a landmark for understanding vocal preference in early modern churches, the presence of castrati in Italian churches and elsewhere in Europe predates his decree. Indeed, Feldman observes that Spanish singer Hernando Bustamante was the first documented eunuch—of any nationality—in the papal choir.[46] However, Ángel Medina traces the presence of castrate singers in Spanish churches to 1506, when the Burgos Cathedral hired a *capón* or castrated male.[47] While castrati performers seem to have been rare in most European countries during the first half of the sixteenth century, there are proliferate records of this vocal type's presence in Spanish religious ensembles. For this reason, Medina argues that the practice of creating and training eunuch singers originated in Spain during the early sixteenth century and quickly spread to the Spanish Americas. During the latter half of the epoch, the phenomenon made its way to Italy via court connections.[48]

Like other Spanish cultural practices, the use of castrate singers in the church made the Atlantic passage and took roots in the Americas, especially during the late sixteenth and early seventeenth centuries. For example, Jorge Hidalgo Lehuedé, Nelson Castro Flores, Alberto Díaz Araya, and Priscilla Cisternas hypothesize that early seventeenth-century Aragonese cleric and capón singer Francisco Otal took advantage of the demand for soprano voices to overcome his humble origins and gain positions in the Lima and

La Plata cathedrals.[49] Eunuch performers also forged musical and ecclesiastical careers in New Spanish churches. Contracts from the Archivo del Cabildo Catedral Metropolitano de México indicate that the practice flourished in the viceroyalty's largest churches. For instance, in 1590, the Metropolitan cathedral paid for the passage of two young Spanish capones, Tomás Lopez and Pedro de Salzedo. Each musician received an annual salary of 120 gold pesos in exchange for four years of exclusive service.[50] While archival records from New Spain sometimes distinguish castrated sopranos from their falsettist peers, scribes were not always copious in their notetaking.

Although direct references like these are somewhat limited, details from a 1594 order to bring another castrate singer, Joan de Villarubia, provocatively suggests that the number of capones in the cathedral at the turn of the century far exceeds scant entries in treasury accounts. While the order to bring Villarubia to New Spain ultimately passed, several members of the chapter were against it. They argued "que esta Santa Iglesia tenía al presente la voz de tiple muy copiosamente proveída con la del maestro de capilla, tres capones y cuatro muchachos, no les parecía enviar por más tiples a costa y riesgo de la Fábrica, y para voz que no se conocía ser buena o mala, más que de relación" (that this Holy Church had at the time the soprano voice very well supplied, with that of the chapel master, three capones, and four boys, it did not seem necessary to send for more sopranos at cost and risk to the Treasury, and all for a voice that was not known to be good or bad, except for by word of mouth).[51] Indeed, the reference here to three capones is intriguing, for it supports a hypothesis that the employment of eunuch singers in the cathedral was common, perhaps as much as that of young boys.

Finally, there is evidence for the presence of Afro-descendant eunuch singers as well. In 1599, Pedro de Pisa, precentor of the Tlaxcala cathedral, sent his enslaved *mulato* Juan Marín to the Mexico City cathedral for vocal training. Apparently, the young musician displayed such promise that the church sought to purchase him as a chapel singer. The bid was unsuccessful, however, for Morales Abril discovered a record for Marín's 150-peso annual salary in the Archivo del Venerable Cabildo de la Catedral de Puebla.[52]

While scholars can only speculate about Barreto and Vera's castration, Morales Abril cites a record of the Mexico City cathedral's proposal to purchase Marín that directly mentions his emasculation:

> Tratando de cosas tocantes al servicio de Nuestro Señor y de su iglesia, se advirtió que sería bien tratar de que entre en la capilla el mulato capón que el doctor Pisa ha enviado a esta ciudad para que le enseñen a cantar, *por ser*

*su voz acomodada y buena para el facistol.* Y por serlo tal, se acordó que el señor doctor Ribera escribe al dicho doctor Pisa lo venda a esta santa iglesia, el cual se encargó de hacerlo.⁵³

With respect to things pertaining to the service of Our Lord and of His church, it would be advisable to try to accept the castrated mulato that Dr. Pisa has sent to this city in the choir so that he might be taught to sing, *because his voice is well-proportioned and suited to the choir lectern*. And as it is so, it was agreed that the gentleman Dr. Ribera would write to the aforementioned Dr. Pisa so that he might sell the enslaved man to this sacred church, and he agreed to take charge of it.

Given the entry's specific classification of Juan Marín as a capón, the reference to the singer's "voz acomodada" is curiously vague in detail. According to the *Diccionario de Autoridades*, "acomodar" means "ordenar, componer, y ajustar las cosas, distribuyéndolas, y disponiéndolas con orden y méthodo, segun el fin à que son destinadas" (to order, arrange, or adjust things, distributing them and arranging them with order and method, according to the use for which they are destined). The term underscores the harmonic proportions of the enslaved man's voice and furthers the argument for his acceptance in the choir. In addition, however, the definition implies outside interventions and thus underscores the ways Juan Marín's physical alteration and training intentionally maximized his vocal potential.

If, indeed, slaveholders like Antonio de Vera or Dr. Pisa profited from the voices of castrate laborers, Juan de Vera and Juan Marín's cases extend Medina's observations about the "rentabilidad" or profitability of the eunuch's voice in early modern Spain. The scholar observes that the church's ongoing need for male sopranos generated an entire industry, where a talented castrate singer often earned significantly more than his falsettist peers or other voice types. To this end, Medina remarks upon castration among lower-class Peninsular boys as a means of securing a better place in society.⁵⁴ In an intriguing complement to Medina's observations, John Rosselli also reads the practice as a financial strategy whose potential benefit for the family paralleled preparing a child for the clergy or convent. He argues that "[a] castrato could be thought of as an enforced celibate with an unusual chance of securing his family an income, perhaps a fortune."⁵⁵ For these scholars, castration is part of an economic transaction to preserve young boys' voices for church, court, and other performance venues. Although such interpretations rightly attend to the financial circumstances of testicular ablation, they marginalize the spiritual and affective repercussions of the voices that the process created.

Rosselli's comparison to religious celibacy is not without merit, and it opens the door for new approaches by allowing scholars to compare eunuch singers in the church with religious counterparts whose vow of chastity also hampered the possibility of bearing legitimate offspring, albeit to a lesser degree. For instance, Colleen Baade has observed that postulant nuns from families of lesser means were sometimes granted admission to early modern Castilian convents based on their musical abilities. Instead of paying the traditional dowry, some of these novices contributed to their communities as performers. Baade underscores the situation's advantages and drawbacks, which are similar to those of New Spain's enslaved castrati. Sometimes, nun musicians who served their community to satisfy a debt had limited freedom and lower standing within the convent. Nevertheless, however, their musical professionalization offered new avenues of agency and authority, and some communities greatly valued the "hired" nun musicians, to use Baade's term.[56]

Resonances among these groups—particularly enslaved castrati—can lend insight into music as a vocation in early modern religious institutions. Precisely, talented performers with few or no means could serve the church as literal instruments. Although these musicians had little autonomy over their training or scope of labor, heightened audibility offered opportunities to envoice their otherwise marginal presence from prominent positions. Indeed, Medina highlights the castrato's audibility in cathedral choirs and other ensembles.

> Entre los músicos de una capilla esa condición sobresaliente tiene que ver, en una primera aproximación, con su propia ubicación sonora en el reparto de las tareas musicales. El del capón tiple es un lugar privilegiado desde el punto de vista musical, en el ámbito más llamativo, más sonoro, de la composición. Un lugar en lo más alto que atrae inmediatamente los oídos, que centra su figura en el imaginario aéreo como rey de las regiones agudas, diáfano objeto de admiración y no menos nítido blanco de la infamia y de la envidia.[57]

> At first glance, this distinctive condition among the chapel musicians has to do with their sonorous position in the distribution of musical tasks. The tiple capón's place is privileged from a musical standpoint, as the showiest and most sonorous of a composition. [It is] an elevated place that immediately attracts the ears, that centers his figure in the aerial imaginary as king of the highest musical pitches, diaphanous object of admiration and no less clear target of infamy and envy.

Rhetorical embellishment aside, Medina's description draws out the capón's particular audibility, especially in religious contexts. The physical anomalies of castrate singers inevitably made their voices louder and more resonant than those of their falsettist counterparts.

Moreover, musical thinkers privileged the soprano range for a variety of reasons. French polymath Marin Mersenne imagines it in close proximity to the heavens and observes that "our experience is that both vocal and instrumental high parts attract our attention more readily, and that they are more pleasant because they are closer to Heaven and life than low voices are."[58] In the music theory treatise *Escuela Música según la práctica moderna*, Pablo Nassarre explains that the higher sounds move air more quickly and thus heighten perception. He argues

> la razon de que son mas sensibles los sonidos agudos, que los graves, es porque el movimiento del ayre es mas veloz en los agudos, y esta mayor velocidad llegando a los oídos mas pronta, mueve la membrana, con el ayre connatural, que está encerrado dentro de los Organos, como dice Titelman [sic], y tanto, quanto mas fuere la velocidad del ayre, será la del movimiento de la membrana, y tanto mas lo armonico del sonido. Y tanto quanto mas agudo, ó alto fuere el sonido, tanto mas claro se percibe, porque a proporción de la agudeza se aumenta la velocidad del ayre.[59]

> the reason that high-pitched sounds are more sensible than low-pitched ones is because the air's movement is quicker in high-pitched sounds, and this greater velocity arrives at the ears more quickly, moves the membrane, with its implanted air, which is contained in the Organs, as Titleman says, and thus, the faster the air's velocity, the faster the movement of the membrane, and the more harmonic the sound. And thus, the more piercing or higher the sound, the clearer it is perceived, because air's speed increases in proportion to pitch.

Here, Nassarre favors the soprano voice for its acoustical principles. According to the day's scientific discourse, air was the medium of sound. Theorists like Helkiah Crooke, Francis Bacon, and Mersenne all agreed that vapor, motion, and physical contact were the stuff of hearing. Indeed, the auditory process began when sounding a body set the surrounding air in motion. Upon reaching the ear, that moving air would strike, shake, or percuss the tympanic membrane and move the ear's internal air. Higher pitches vibrated more vigorously and thus had a greater physical impact upon the auditory organs.

Because of its connections to voice, song amplifies the affective principles of musical sound. Early modern approaches to this notion hearken back to Aristotle's *De anima*, which imagines voice as an airy vestige of the soul, pushed out by the throat, tongue, and lips. From this perspective, vocalized sound is an audible echo of ontological and epistemological essences. Katherine Larson argues that "the voice's close connection to the soul, manifested in terms of both the meaningful air produced by a speaker or singer and its effect on a hearer, differentiates its communicative impact from other respiratory noises."[60] Gina Bloom underscores the voice's connection with sacred wisdom in Biblical sources and, in particular, the Holy Spirit. She notes that "Christian tradition ... had long associated breath with spiritual authority."[61] Indeed, some of Christianity's greatest revelations are the result of divine audition. These include Gabriel's Annunciation to Mary (Luke 1: 26–28) and the acousmatic, heavenly voice that commands the disciples: "This is my Son, my Chosen; listen to him" (Luke 9:35). Likewise, auditory hallucinations abound in hagiographic accounts of religious men and women and become symbols of exemplarity.

### LISTENING TO BLACK SOPRANO VOICES

For all this, it is clear that the high-pitched voices of New Spain's eunuch singers sounded vocal skill and spiritual devotion. In the case of Afro-descendant sopranos like Juan de Vera or Luis Barreto, their celebrated voices emanated from some of society's lowliest subjects. Indeed, these singers' skilled performances demanded attention for their dissonance with scripted representations of Black vocalization, which frequently reduced Afro-descendant song and speech to discordant squawks and nonsensical babble. While accounts like Sor Juana's *Villancico* 258, which I will discuss in Chapter 6, or Fabián Ximeno's complaint, cited earlier in this chapter, depict Afro-descendant musicians as boisterous outsiders who disrupt Christian ceremony with rowdy, untrained music and muddled understandings of the liturgy, the cathedrals' Black castrati possessed some of the finest manufactured voices of their day. Given the strident expectations for chapel singers, there can be little doubt that these performers were also well-versed in religious doctrine, so as to better communicate the liturgical subjects about which they sang. Along with their prominent positions as cathedral musicians, such dissonances with scripted representations of Afro-descendant sound made the Black sopranos that I examine here challenge the racialized, essentialist sound that written descriptions sought to impose. This position enabled Afro-descendant singers to ameliorate their living conditions and assume positions of musical authority far beyond material reaches of their voices.

The tension that arose between the sounds of skilled singers like Vera and Barreto and inscriptions of Black vocality raises questions about voice, body, and race. Pooja Rangan has examined these themes in a scene from Julie Dash's 1982 film *Illusions*, where a Black, female assistant sings Ella Fitzgerald's "Starlit Hour" on a film set while a white actress lip syncs for the camera. Rangan reads the scene through an acousmatic lens, and she extends Mladen Dolar's logocentric analysis of the heightened authority of disembodied voices. Dolar's discussion focuses on how the Pythagorean tradition of teaching from behind a curtain or veil distances vocalic authority from the enunciating subject's body. Along these lines, Ranga argues that "the idea of the vocalic body as invisibility cloak in this originary scene of acousmatic listening vividly illustrates the often imperceptible but thoroughly ideological practices of perceptual disciplining that cloak the subjective, embodied origins of *certain* idealized voices, framing their traits as divine or disembodied."[62] Rangan's observations are useful for considering how voice and race intersect (or fail to intersect) in New Spanish listeners' perceptions of African and Afro-diasporic cathedral singers. According to Rangan, Dash's film simultaneously underscores the striking distance between voice and racialized body and also highlights the arbitrary, imagined links between the two. From the same Pythagorean perspective, the idealization of Barreto and Vera's vocal authority shrouds their Black bodies, even as those bodies labor at the cathedral's service. Such corporeal invisibility contrasts with the racialized sonic tropes that stand out in *habla de negros*, and it illustrates complex dissonances in how colonial Mexicans perceived and imagined Black vocality.

If, indeed, Barreto and Vera were castrati, then questions about how listeners imagined links among race, voice, and body become even more complex. While these singers were of sub-Saharan descent, early modern Europeans may have associated capón performers with North African Muslims. Such connections would have complicated the racial perception of Vera and Barreto's voices, for European vocal training, dark-skinned bodies, and Moorish resonances all converged in their song.

Despite castrati's prominence in Italian music history, Medina's reasoning about the Spanish origins of castrate musicians in the Catholic church is astute. Spain's Moorish roots combined with the longstanding tradition of enslaved performers in Islamic courts make Medina's hypotheses especially convincing, particularly given the apparent taste for women and eunuchs as captive laborers.[63] In fact, George Junne details longstanding trade in eunuchs in West and North Africa. As far back as the fifteenth century, Sudanese rulers castrated prisoners of war and profited from their sale. Likewise, Sunni Muslims in present-day Burkina Faso and Nigeria sold enslaved eunuchs to the Maghreb and the Ottoman Empire. Thriving Mediterranean trade routes brought many castrated servants to European soil, and the French town of Verdun even specialized in fabricating eunuchs for Spanish Muslims.[64] As it turns out, the French were not the only suppliers of castrates for their southwestern neighbors. Ronald Segal has documented the persistence of slave emasculation in al-Andalus, where, among other duties, captive performers likely made music in the courts.[65]

With these cultural antecedents in mind, the persistence of the Moorish castrate trope in early modern European imaginaries sheds some light on its continuity. For instance, Virginia Mason Vaughn discusses gendered and racial themes in William Hemings's *The Fatal Contract* (penned between 1638 and 1639), where the female role Chrotilda assumes the disguise of a castrate Moor named Castrato and seeks revenge for her rape.[66] For popular examples from the seventeenth-century Hispanic world, one need look no further than Cervantes' exemplary novel *El celoso extremeño*, where a Black eunuch guards the doors of Leonora's house (and consequently, her honor). While the Cervantine castrate's Moorish identity is somewhat veiled, here it important to attend to the religious overtones of imaginings of Blackness in early modern Spain. Indeed, as K. Meira Goldberg observes, in fifteenth-century ideology and beyond, the non-Christian Moor's spiritual darkness justifies the forced servitude of sub-Saharan Africans.[67] Given this context, the Spanish capón's Moorish origins and intersections with racial and religious difference beckons attention.

Questions of gender have long fascinated scholars of castrati; however, most analyses overlook the underlying racial discourses that inform the figure's construction and reception. In part, scholarly muting of castrate singers' racial overtones is a result of the whiteness of the early modern musicological canon.[68] Within this context, there is a particular reticence before non-white constructions of the castrato voice, especially given its deep entrenchment with Italian opera. Nevertheless, as I will argue in the next chapter, New Spain's Afro-descendant male sopranos loomed so large in sacred and popular sound culture that their voices shaped imaginings of Black vocality in repertoire like villancicos, as well as in other liturgical and festive compositions.

Amid silences surrounding Muslim and Black African eunuch singers, Emily Wilbourne's research on sub-Saharan African musicians and writers in early modern Italy notably stands out. Wilbourne reflects on the challenges that she faced in making a case for the enslaved entertainer Giovanni Buonaccorsi's authorship of "Sogno di Giovannino Moro," an unattributed poem whose colorful characters reflect the flamboyant atmosphere of the Medici court where Buonaccorsi served. She observes that "the purportedly neutral skepticism of academic practice requires a higher burden of proof for exceptions to the straight, white, male model, insisting on the foreignness of the enslaved Black man and presuming his incapacity."[69] Continuing, Wilbourne calls out a scholarly tendency to assume that Black artists, writers, and performers were less skilled at their professions. All too often, the erroneous alignment of deficiency and authenticity in scholarship on early modern cultural production mutes or even excludes non-masculine and non-European voices.

While scholars like Wilbourne, Goldberg, Jones, Miguel Valerio, and others offer increasing evidence for the impact of free and enslaved Afro-descendants on cultural canons in early modern Europe and beyond, scholars continue to view the cases of Black sopranos in New Spain through a lens of cautious exceptionalism. To this end, Morales Abril highlights the value of singers like Juan de Vera but also cautions against readings that overvalue the performer's importance for understanding colonial Mexican music culture. He draws out tension between the racialized discourses surrounding the scorned bodies of Black, high-voiced singers—members of society's lowest ranks—and their song, through which churchgoers experienced echoes of celestial harmony.[70] To some degree, these highly regarded vocal abilities allowed Afro-descendant eunuch singers to access education and intensive musical training that may not have been available to them in other contexts.

Morales Abril is not the only scholar to attend to apparent dissonance between Black bodies and male soprano voices in New Spain. Similarly, Nava Sánchez underscores the presence of enslaved, Afro-descendant capones in American cathedrals as different from Peninsular practices, where scholars have not uncovered any evidence for professional church musicians of color. He argues that

> podría decirse que en el caso de estos capones novohispanos existía una separación todavía más grande entre el cuerpo y la voz, pues parecería que el hecho de que algunos cantores fueran castrados, esclavos y mulatos—características que por sí mismas remitían a una calidad negativa de lo corporal—no significó ningún problema para la Iglesia con tal de que sirvieran en el oficio divino.[71]
>
> it could be said that in the case of these New Spanish capones there was a much greater separation between body and voice, since it would seem that the fact that some of them were castrates, slaves, and mulattos—characteristics that in themselves had negative corporeal connotations—did not present a problem for the church as long as they served in the divine office.

There is little doubt that with continued archival work and attention to Spain's Black African roots, scholars working in the field will soon challenge Nava Sánchez's hypothesis that there were no Black capones in Spanish cathedrals or courts. Nevertheless, the tension he underscores between the enslaved bodies with their negative cultural connotations and the celebrated voices of eunuch singers in the cathedral will be a key area of inquiry as the field advances. As the next chapter will illustrate, my perspective on the topic is that the dissonance between these musicians' powerful vocal identities and liminal corporeality makes Afro-descent audible in sacred contexts that scholars long imagined as the domain of Creole and Peninsular musicians.

### TRAINING THE PERFECT SOPRANO

Beyond possible castration, what, exactly, did it take to become a prized soprano in New Spain's cathedrals? Like Nava Sánchez has shown, aspiring singers in the Spanish-speaking world undertook an intensive training regimen designed to produce some of the most skilled singers in the region. Their preparation covered subjects like music performance and theory as well as related topics in rhetoric or theology.[72] While the latter subjects may seem irrelevant from a contemporary standpoint, early modern theories of acoustics and musical expressivity closely related them. Cathedral singers were charged with reproducing celestial harmony through skilled lyrical and musical performance. Their affective capacity depended upon vocal prowess, which was a combination of technical skill and divine resonance. Singers developed the former in codified training programs, under the instruction of cathedral chapelmasters or other church musicians. In addition to practical considerations like the ability to read or copy music, students also refined vocal qualities, including agility, aptitude for ornamentation, breath control, and tone.

The reason for such strident training has to do with music's function within Catholic ritual at the time. Precisely, music and the skill with which singers and other performers executed it were intended to heighten liturgical messages with a near reproduction of celestial accord. In agreement with the neo-Platonic music of the spheres, the art form's harmonic structure echoed heavenly concord, a sacred consonance that was otherwise inaudible (*musica mundana*, in Boethian terms). This cosmic structure organized earthly elements as well, including the human soul (*musica humana*). During the Catholic mass, attentive and devout worshippers sought animistic resonance with the divine. Because of its structural resemblance to *musica mundana* and *musica humana*, *musica instrumentalis*, their audible counterpart, effectively acted upon the soul's order and harmonized it with the cosmos. Andrés Lorente explains the relationship in his 1672 treatise *El porque de la mvsica*.

> En quanto a la Musica humana, dize Augustino: vn espíritu, que es muy cercano a Dios, y vn cuerpo, que es *quasi nihil*, ponerlos en proporcion, solo el saber, y poder diuino fue para ello suficiente; de forma, que de cosas distintas, que son el Anima, y el cuerpo en el hombre, nace esta Musica humana; y como Dios aya puesto en el hombre esta natural Musica, assi el hombre tiene esta natural inclinacion, y amistad con ella: todo semejante aparece a su semejante, y con él le goza, y con su desemejante se turba: de aquí es, que oyendo las disonancias nos dan pena, y tristeza; las consonancias de alegría.[73]

> As regards musica humana, Augustine says: a spirit, which is very close to God, and a body, which is *almost nothing*, only wisdom and divine power are sufficient to put them in proportion; therefore, from different things, which are the Soul and the human body, this musica humana is born; and since God has put this natural Music in man, thus man has this natural inclination, and friendship with it: all similar things appear alike, and rejoice in their likeness, and are disordered by differences: for this reason, hearing dissonance gives us pain and suffering; and consonance, happiness.

Like other theorists of his day, Lorente treats music as a form of divine knowledge and imagines the human relationship with God in harmonic terms. This privileging of musico-spiritual epistemologies elevates the musician's status, particularly in sacred settings. Indeed, just as Lorente points out in subsequent remarks, an expert performer echoes celestial concord and makes heavenly mysteries audible.[74]

For all this, skilled musicianship was a key element of Catholic ritual. Nava Sánchez notes that New Spanish cathedrals selected candidates for their chapel based upon aptitude and then trained them in vocal pedagogy as well as related subjects in order to create ideal religious singers in terms of both musical ability and character. His observations merit quotation in full.

> Estas voces [formadas para honra de Dios] . . . debían encarnar en el cantor una excepcionalidad respecto del resto de la gente. Servir como tal en cualquier catedral de mundo hispánico requería una dedicación completa a aprender música y, sobre todo, a ejercitar adecuadamente las capacidades vocales. Mediante este adiestramiento y disciplina se buscaba alcanzar ciertas habilidades, según la teoría y la práctica musical de la época. En este

punto en donde se cruzaban el sentido religioso del canto—como alabanza y devoción—y la técnica vocal dependiente del conocimiento musical, pues ésta debía expresar y subrayar la profunda unión espiritual de los feligreses con Dios durante el ritual litúrgico. El canto se perfeccionaba mirando siempre este objetivo, pero se hacía echando mano de herramientas musicales que no necesariamente eran producto directo del conocimiento proveniente de la Iglesia. De esta manera, en el cantor eclesiástico debían buscarse dos cualidades, ser buen cristiano, conocer a la perfección lo que se canta, y ser habilidoso en la música, destacar por su pericia y destreza vocal. Ninguno de la [sic] dos, en teoría, podía descuidarse. Sin embargo, para el cantor, evidentemente, la voz lo era todo, pues dependía de ésta para subsistir. En los templos, y más en las catedrales, se procuraba contratar siempre a los mejores, lo cual significaba un grado de exigencia mayor para aquellos que deseaban conseguir algún lugar en la capilla de música de esos sitios. En este sentido, era la música, como disciplina con presupuestos teóricos y prácticos, la que determinaba cuáles debían ser las características del buen cantor. Por lo tanto, había que practicar y formar la voz según los dictados de este arte, el cual, a su vez, imponía una serie de normas que establecían cuál era el mejor momento para iniciarse en la práctica vocal.[75]

These voices [created to honor God] . . . should have embodied in the singer a sense of exceptionalism compared to other people. Serving in this way in any cathedral in the Hispanic world required complete dedication to learning music and, above all, to adequately training one's vocal capacities. This preparation and discipline were intended to achieve certain abilities, according to the music theory and practice of the time. In this point in which the religious sense of song—as prayer and devotion—and vocal technique depending on musical knowledge converge, given that the letter should express and underscore the faithful's profound spiritual union with God during liturgical ritual. Song was always perfected with this objective in sight, but it was carried out with the help of musical tools that were not necessarily a direct product of the Church's knowledge. In this way, two qualities were sought in the ecclesiastical singer, being a good Christian, that is, knowing the perfection of what is sung, and being musically skilled, defined by skill and vocal ability. None of the two, in theory, could be neglected. Nevertheless, for a singer, evidently, his voice was everything, since he depended on it for subsistence. In temples, and even more in cathedrals, they made sure to contract the best singers, which meant a higher degree of rigor for those who wished to obtain a place in the musical chapel of those places. In this sense, it was music, as a discipline with practical and theoretical premises, that determined which were the characteristics of a good singer. Therefore, one needed to practice and develop the voice according to the dictates of this art that, at the same time, imposed a series of norms that established which was the best moment to begin vocal studies.

All of this amounts to a music industry designed to manufacture exemplary singers for spiritual ceremonies, with the most extreme case being the surgical alteration of castrate vocalists. Nava Sánchez highlights voice's material qualities as the industry's nucleus and details specific characteristics intensive training sought to develop.

Just as pedagogical practices developed singers' dexterity and sonic contours, so they also shaped the voice's symbolic qualities. Indeed, Medina remarks that aspiring singers underwent rigorous examination of their musical talents and also their character. He notes that vocal talent, musical skills, reputation, bloodline, temperament, and spiritual inclination all informed the evaluation of candidates for the cathedral choir.[76] Institutional needs influenced and sometimes justified such decisions as well, like Drew Edward Davies indicates in his description of how the Durango cathedral hired chapelmaster Alonso Ascencio because of a shortage of skilled candidates. Ascencio, a *pardo* (of mixed Spanish, African, and Indigenous descent), was a talented curtal player in the Mexico City cathedral and rose through the musical ranks to become the Durango cathedral's first chapelmaster 1657. Davies notes that records of Ascencio's position underscore his skill and strong character but rhetorically frame his appointment as less than ideal, given his heritage. He argues that "the cathedral chapter exempted Ascencio from the requirement of blood purity on account of his merit and ability to serve the needs of the Church and for being a virtuous person, as well as noting the lack of musical capability otherwise available at the time."[77] Here, Ascencio's musical talent, integrity, and ability to serve a fundamental liturgical role exceed the limitations prescribed for his race and social class.

### FASHIONING THE PERFECT SOPRANO

Of the three Black sopranos for whom scholars have recovered details, Luis Barreto is perhaps the best known. Pioneer Robert Stevenson first referenced Barreto in a 1964 article that details musical activities in the Mexico City Cathedral.[78] Nava Sánchez has since expanded Stevenson's reference to shed additional light on the singer's role in the Mexico City Cathedral. By all appearances, Barreto was one of the most famed singers of New Spain. During a tenure of more than twenty years in the cathedral choir, he made frequent appearances in the lavish festivals for which the region's capital was known. The performer's progression from a headstrong young man to a well-respected musician is a product of his ability to negotiate an audible position for himself despite the limits that society imposed upon an enslaved *mulato* like Barreto. In this case, the musician's success resulted in the purchase of his own freedom.

According to Nava Sánchez's account, Luis Barreto's experience as an enslaved performer was similar to Juan de Vera's. Indeed, Nava Sánchez tells the story of a prized Black singer whose voice was worth its weight in gold. Among other details, Barreto's case is notable because there are extensive records of privileges that the enslaved man enjoyed and also of his numerous transgressions, including an attempt to flee to Spain. Detailed descriptions of his unruly behavior can shed some light on the figure's personality, particularly as early modern thinkers might have perceived it in relation to his emasculated body (or, as it were, the manner in which high-voiced singing might suggest an emasculated body). Roger Freitas has situated the castrato within seventeenth-century ideas about the physical origins of gender dispositions. He notes that "the man whose appearance belied his more feminine humors—that is, the prepubescent boy and castrato—was regarded as a highly sensual creature, wanting in the 'masculine' virtues of restraint and abstinence."[79] Church records do not offer any details about Barreto's sexual appetite, but accounts of his unruliness resonate with general perceptions of women as having less stable dispositions than men.

From this perspective, archival reports of Barreto's constant insubordination align with Freitas' description. Nava Sánchez notes that the singer caused such disruption in Franco's home that the prebendary imprisoned him.[80] The acts of the cathedral chapter describe the singer's defiance. "El racionero Franco dio cuenta de los latrocinios, embustes e insolencias del mulato Luis Barreto, cantor, esclavo de la Fábrica de esta Santa Iglesia, y el castigo que iba haciendo en él, teniéndole preso. Pareció esto bien, respecto de tenerle a su cargo el dicho racionero y por serlos excesos de este esclavo tan continuos y tan graves" (The prebendary Franco gave an account of the thefts, lies and insolence of the young *mulato* Luis Barreto, singer, slave of the Treasury of this Holy Church, and the punishment that he imposed upon him, imprisoning him. This seemed fine, given that he was in the aforementioned prebendary's care and because the excesses of this slave were so continuous and serious).[81] This and other descriptions characterize Barreto as hotheaded and uncontrollable. While the performer may well have possessed a volatile nature, stereotypes of the rebellious slave as well as ideas about the unrestrained temperaments of castrati could have informed accounts of Barreto's behavior. Within these contexts, references to sexual excess are curiously absent. The omission is noteworthy, since such irrepressible bodily appetites were associated with capones. One possible explanation for the archive's silence before such behavior is that as an enslaved member of the cathedral chapel, Barreto was subject to the same high standards of decorum as his peers. Sexual licentiousness would have been out of the question.

Above all, the church's treatment of Barreto's enslaved body is of significant interest for delving into the relationship between the vocal instrument and mechanized body of Afro-descendants in bondage. For example, Nava Sánchez describes the exorbitant expense of feeding and clothing Luis Barreto. Indeed, in 1600–01, the cathedral spent 475 gold pesos to maintain the singer, more than organist Alonso Rodríguez de Mesa's salary.[82]

Beyond recompense for the singer's talent, there is little doubt that this investment responds to the strident dietary guidelines that some of the epoch's vocal pedagogy outlined. Nava Sánchez underscores numerous links between digestion and vocal production that Pietro Cerone details in *El melopeo y maestro*. In a chapter on methods for conserving the voice, the theorist recommends light, easily digestible meals and wine in moderation, preferably diluted with water. He counsels singers to avoid fatty meals and nuts and even suggests that they abstain from all food except pulses before performances.[83] In his reading of Cerone's instructions, Nava Sánchez draws out resonances with Catholic asceticism: "la moderación a la que, según el tratadista italiano, debía someterse el cantor recuerda la abstinencia del cristiano de los placeres en general y de los de la comida en particular" (the moderation to which the singer should submit himself, according to the Italian theorist, recalls Christian abstinence from pleasures in general, especially those related to food).[84] From this perspective, the singer's diet is a sign of his professional and spiritual dedication. In fact, Barreto's abstinence from particular foods recalls devotional practices among religious men and women. Asunción Lavrín describes fasting among New Spanish nuns as a performative act of piety: "In its 'heroic' mode, as described in the biographies of exceptional nuns, it took a spiritual meaning that affected the body in a very direct manner. The best proof of spiritual achievement was a body that suffered the affliction of hunger and deprivation with love and humility."[85] Along these lines, while Barreto's "voice-healthy" diet further illustrates his instrumentalization as a voice of the church, it also aligns him with exemplary Christians and thus elevates his social standing.

Similar to his strict diet, Luis Barreto's clothing distinguished him in performance and served as a visual symbol of the church's wealth. According to the cathedral chapter acts, the singer dressed richly, in a wardrobe that flaunted imported fabrics, rich in ornaments.[86] These included: "manteo y sotana de paño de Castilla, jubón, camisas, calzones, medias, zapatos, sobrero, sábanas y lo demás que viere tiene necesidad para el adorno de su persona, atento a lo mucho y bien que ha servido estas Pascuas a esta Santa Iglesia" (a cassock and cloak of fine cloth from Castilla, a doublet, shirts, undergarments, socks, shoes, a hat, sheets, and whatever else he might see a need for in order to adorn his person, in light of how much and how well he served this Holy Church this Easter).[87] Just as in the example of his diet, this instance illustrates that Barreto received certain privileges in exchange for his service to the cathedral. Furthermore, the singer's clothing reflected his considerable value and thus served as a visual signal of the church's wealth, not unlike the lavish vestments that some priests donned or the extravagant textiles that adorned the altar.[88] Barreto's rich clothing was also a sign of his objectification, inasmuch as it casts the singer as just one more fine object in church inventories. Gloria Fraser Giffords highlights the importance of such excess in New Spanish churches: "to instill pride among the congregation and to encourage reverence for the 'temple of God,' great care was taken in the selection and maintenance of furnishings. Indeed, some friars felt that rich furnishings and decorations and impressive architecture would help create the splendor, drama, pomp, and mystery needed to draw new converts to the Faith."[89] Fraser Giffords' reading amplifies a perplexing dissonance that arises with Barreto's costuming, if we can call it that. As a symbol of personal status, the performer's dress signals a standing that outstrips his race and enslaved stature.[90] As an object of the church, however, Barreto's visual appearance reinforced efforts to assimilate non-Europeans, including members of his own community, to religious and political systems that subjugated them.

Indeed, luxurious clothing most certainly drew attention to Barreto's figure. As an example of Baroque visual rhetoric an enslaved Afro-descendant who "sings like an angel" and dresses as a gentleman becomes as an anamorphic device.[91] On stage, the musician's dark skin, a sign of sin and also of his lower social status, contrasted with his elegant appearance and exemplary voice. Thus, the presentation of Luis Barreto and other Black singers as sophisticated and esthetically appealing beckoned audience participation in order to resolve the tension that arises when dressing one of society's most humble members in elegant finery. For all of this, Barreto's instrumentalized body is a carefully curated vehicle for his voice, inasmuch as his visual presence informs and performs his auditory one. The enslaved man's clothing is excessively European, and in the listening imagination, such garb embodies Western vocalities.

While it is easy to construe such presentation as the imposition of the cathedral council and other authorities concerned with preserving the church's integrity in choosing representative musicians, interpretations must also account for Barreto's agency and self-determination in creating his image. Indeed, even in the context of enslaved Africans and Afro-descendants and their commodification (or instrumentalization), the self-fashioning—albeit within the limits that slavery imposed—should inform any reading of his presence and career. Along these lines, Daniel Stein's discussion of the dissonances that surface in Louis Armstrong's self-representations is useful. Stein observes that "being hypervisible and hyper-audible as an artist of color but invisible and inaudible as a black social being, Armstrong uses excessive self-presentation as a dramatic marker of difference that counters the notion of lack (of consciousness, intelligence, white skin color, and so forth) while heightening it at the same time."[92] For Stein, Armstrong's written, embodied, and vocal expression signifies his illegibility within Eurocentric epistemologies. Because of his talent, the African American trumpeter and vocalist dominated stages at social gatherings where skin color might have been a reason to deny him entry. As a result, Armstrong's voice percussed against the limits of his race.

As an Afro-descendant singer with a prominent cathedral position, Barreto similarly challenged socio-political constructions, audience reception, and ideals of spiritual exemplarity. From this perspective, it is possible to read Luis Barreto's clothing as a response to his audibility, inasmuch as it embodies the celestial voice and also amplifies it with rich adornments. Such ornamentation made Barreto's body the focal point of liturgical celebrations in which he participated, simultaneously drawing attention away from his Blackness but also intensifying its audibility through conspicuous costuming. To be certain, the musician would not have been the only Afro-descendant at mass or in festivals, for colonial authorities encouraged people from all ethnic backgrounds to take part in Catholic worship and attend religious ceremonies. Nonetheless, Barreto's position as a chapel singer would have been unusual, at least insofar as extant records make race explicit. During his time, many cathedral performers were clerics who would have needed to prove blood purity in order to become ordained.[93]

### FUGITIVE VOICES

While Barreto's privileges were extensive, they did not offer the one thing that the performer presumably desired most: freedom and autonomy to shape his own life and career. The singer's 1601 escape attempt and his manumission in 1615 lend insight into this longing and further illustrate how vocal commodification impacted his life. First, Nava Sánchez details Barreto's thwarted flight in 1601, when he left the cathedral for the Veracruz port and attempted to board a ship bound for Spain. Disappointingly, Barreto never made it to his destination. A bounty hunter captured the singer at the harbor and returned him to the cathedral.[94] In New Spain, runaways like Barreto were an additional liability for their owners, who generally had to pay for traders or bounty hunters to escort them back from the Veracruz port. Sierra Silva notes that many masters opted to sell runaways rather than absorb the costs of their return.[95] In order to discourage such behavior, urban slaveholders meted out harsh punishments to escapees. Some offenders suffered facial branding and others were sold to plantations, far away from their families and support networks.

For all this, the archive tells us little about the reasons for Barreto's escape. Indeed, in this and other cases, records offer limited insight into the mindset of maroon men and women themselves. Sierra Silva observes that "the archival silence surrounding escaped slaves presents a number of challenges to historians attempting to understand runaways' motivations, successes and failures."[96] From this perspective, Barreto's escape attempt is similar to others, for scholars can only speculate about the motives behind the performer's flight. While most enslaved men and women fled to maroon communities near Veracruz to escape extreme mistreatment, records indicate that church authorities spared Barreto from harsh treatment or physical deprivation on account of his voice. Furthermore, the singer did not take refuge in an Afro-descendant settlement like San Lorenzo de los Negros but instead headed straight for the port. For these reasons, Nava Sánchez hypothesizes that Barreto's ambitions underlay this decision and suggests that he sought to better his career with a post in the royal chapel or an important Spanish cathedral.[97]

Ordinarily, Barreto would have suffered severe consequences for his transgression. However, since the church council was eager to protect their prize singer, they needed to avoid physical punishment. Nava Sánchez observes: "al parecer, el cabildo pensó que el mejor castigo para su intento de fuga consistía en quitarle, por algún tiempo, los privilegios a los que estaba acostumbrado el afrodescendiente" (so it seems, the council thought that the best punishment for his escape attempt was to revoke, for a time, the privileges to which the Afro-descendant was accustomed).[98] Nava Sánchez goes on to explain that officials reduced the performer's clothing and food allowance for a time after his attempted escape.[99] These details further evidence the worth of Barreto's voice as well as its impact upon his lifestyle.

Cathedral authorities opted for a punishment that protected his valuable instrument. The limits that they placed upon Barreto's living stipends illustrate that he enjoyed greater privileges than most enslaved men and women.

Eventually, Luis Barreto realized his dream of freedom. Nava Sánchez recounts the episode. With financial assistance from chapelmaster Juan Hernández, the enslaved singer raised 1,500 pesos, an amount equal to his original purchase price. Then, Barreto petitioned the church council to purchase his liberty.[100] The council consulted with archbishop Juan Pérez de la Serna and met several times to discuss the matter. While the archbishop supported Barreto's manumission, others, including the dean Pedro de Vega Sarmiento, were opposed. They argued that the cost of the singer's upkeep and the value of his voice in the chapel far exceeded the 1,500 pesos that the cathedral had paid some years before.[101] After much debate, the council decided to accept the sum that Barreto offered in exchange for his freedom, provided that the singer also committed himself to an additional six years as a chapel musician. In 1615, Luis Barreto became a free man, with the autonomy to make decisions about his own life and career.[102]

Barreto's flight and purchase of freedom lend a fugitive tone to the story. Even if the singer did eventually achieve liberty through legal means, both events illustrate his negative response to enslavement. Moten returns to the concept of fugitivity time and again in his Black avant-garde philosophy. The aural underpinnings of enslaved, Afro-descendant peoples' longing for escape particularly intrigue the author. From Moten's perspective, Black sound and fugitivity are inextricably linked. The moment of refusal occurs when the commodity voices its first "no," and the ghostly echo reverberates across generations as extra-linguistic and extra-musical interventions. In a characteristic riff on jazz's Black performativity, Moten likens fugitivity and rebellion to "what Miles Davis came to understand as an ineluctably 'social' music whose perceived disharmony and arrhythmia operates as an enactment of surreptitiousness and flight, a harmonic and rhythmic reorganization, if not disorganization, reconstruction if not destruction."[103] For Moten, Black voice is an echoic longing for freedom that repeatedly unshackles itself from the Western forms of being that once reduced the Afro-descendant speaker to a voiceless commodity. In a gesture that aligns voice's philosophical and auditory dimensions, Moten frames unscriptable Black aurality as a metaphor for the unrealized fantasy of narrative and subjective unity.[104] Indeed, he underscores Aunt Hester's shrieks as a sign of collective refusal in Frederick Douglass's autobiography, and he teases out Du Boisian whistles or murmurs that interrupt the written account's reproduction of oppressive forms "like a scar in and on the body of the voice."[105]

Within this context, the particular commodification of Barreto's voice strains against the idea of Black sonority as disruptive to the objectification of enslaved men and women as mere entries in financial ledgers. In almost every context in which the archive inscribes the singer's voice, his instrumentalization stands out in records of physical and vocal upkeep, performances, and payment. Written registers thus muffle vocalic resonances of refusal that recording technologies or phonographic writing might make audible. Alas, scholars have not recovered an account of what Barreto or Vera's voices sounded like, although the next chapter will put forth some ideas for gaining a better understanding of the two singer's abilities. Instead, the minutes from council meetings and correspondence among church officials ascribe value to the singers based upon the cathedral chapel's need for sopranos. Extensive training and possible castration shaped these performers' voices, and archival accounts rarely offer specific details about individual artistic expression through which fugitivity might become audible.

Nevertheless, I argue that this careful adherence to dominant sound cultures in New Spain is precisely what makes Vera and Barreto's song fugitive. From positions of limited agency, the performers perfected their craft and gained access to spaces, supporters, and material privileges that would not otherwise have been available to them. The fragmented portraits of Barreto and Vera that today's scholars reconstruct with archival records are similar to the post–World War II passport photos of the Afro-Caribbean population of Birmingham, England, that Tina Campt has examined. Attentive to the portraits' serial nature, Campt observes "they are archetypically quiet photos, yet they are photos that ruminate loudly on practices of diasporic refusal, fugitivity and futurity."[106] To be certain, the passport photo is a genre that codifies sitting subjects according to their national identities. Among working-class immigrants and Afro-descendants in Birmingham, however, such "images . . . strive to enunciate respectability and aspiration."[107] Precisely, the passport photos register the sitters' desire to exercise agency to visit family or build a better life by moving across political borders. The price of such freedom is to don a nondescript suit and pose before the camera with an impersonal, prescribed posture. For Campt, it is within this unremarkable ordinariness that fugitive voices resound.

With this theoretical context in mind, written details about Barreto's path to becoming a free man complement his vocal commodification and amplify his fugitive voice. Indeed, it is clear that the singer hoped to leverage his talents for a more promising future. Nowhere is this desire more salient than in the enslaved man's written petition for freedom, redacted by an official scribe.

50    AMPLIFICATIONS OF BLACK SOUND

> Luis Barreto, músico y criado de vuestra señoría, en la causa de libertad que tengo pedido, digo en conformidad de lo últimamente proveído por Su Ilustrísima, del señor arzobispo, y de vuestra señoría—por información ante el provisor de este arzobispado—, de la utilidad que, de dárseme la dicha libertad, se consigne a la Fábrica de esta Santa Iglesia la cual, vista, da licencia y facultad para que vuestra señoría otorgue en mi favore escriptura y carta de libertad, en forma como consta de los autos originales que sobre ellos se hicieron y están en poder del presente secretario—de que si necesario es, hago presentación y, así mismo, la hago de esta carta de pago de Lorenzo de Burgos, mayordomo de la dicha Fábrica, del entrego que se le hizo de los mil y quinientos pesos que por mi libertad ofrecí—. Atento a lo cual, a vuestra señoría pido y suplico se sirva de mandar otorgar, y otorgue en mi favor, carta de libertad en forma—o cometiéndolo a quien fuere servido, para que en su nombre la haga—, que yo estoy presto de hacer la obligación de servir a esta Santa Iglesia de músico, tiempo de seis años, con el salario que vuestra señoría fuere servido señalarme, en que recibiré merced con justicia. Luis Barreto.[108]

> Luis Barreto, musician and servant of your honor, in the case of my request for freedom, I state that in conformity with the latest statement supplied by His Grace, the esteemed archbishop, and your honor—because of the evidence before the Auditor of this archdiocese—about the payment that, upon awarding me the aforementioned freedom, will be made to the Treasury of this Holy Church, whereas, the aforementioned grants the power and authority so that your honor might favor me and award me a letter of freedom, consistent with the original degrees that were given and are in the possession of the current secretary—for which if necessary, I appear before the court with this letter of payment from Lorenzo de Burgos, administrator of the aforementioned Treasury, which certifies the receipt of the 1,500 pesos that I offered in exchange for my freedom—. With respect to which, I humbly request that your honor graciously favor me with a letter of freedom—or consign the task to whomever might be of service so that he redacts it in your name—, whereas I am disposed to serve this Holy Church as a musician for six years, with the salary that your honor sees fit to award me, in which I will receive mercy and justice. Luis Barreto.

In this document, Barreto declares his longing for freedom in the first person. Furthermore, he takes ownership of the transaction that results in his manumission by referring to the "1,500 pesos that I offered in exchange for my freedom." There can be no stronger refusal of objectivity, no shriller scream than this. Here, the enslaved man not only speaks but does so in a legal declaration, where he takes charge of his own fate and demands freedom. Luis Barreto's fugitive voice rings out loud and clear in his petition for liberty, and it hums quietly beneath his instrumentalization as a cathedral singer.

CHAPTER 2

# Musical and Lyrical Rememberings of Black Male Sopranos

A two-foot-tall, vellum choirbook adorned with stunning decorative features preserves several polyphonic jewels from the Mexico City cathedral's seventeenth-century repertoire, including Mexico City chapelmaster Antonio Rodríguez Mata's four-part *Passio secundum Matthaeum*.[1] Like most responsorial passions from the *more hispano* genre, Rodríguez Mata's piece combines plainchant with polyphonic sections that generate drama and emotion.[2] In all likelihood, the chapel performed *Passio secundum Matthaeum* in the cathedral on Palm Sunday or during Holy Week. Indeed, the liturgy incorporated up to four sung passions during this time period, and church officials expected all members of the chapel to participate in the musical celebration of one of its highest holidays.[3] A cleric and skilled contralto, Rodríguez Mata was a key figure in the cathedral's music scene from the early 1600s until his death in 1643. As his predecessor Juan Hernández aged, Rodríguez Mata increasingly took on duties that normally fell to the chapelmaster, including rehearsals, organ repairs, and more. In 1618, he composed his first *chanzonetas* for the cathedral's Christmas festivities, and by 1625, the council had named him chapelmaster.[4] Rodríguez Mata's early years of influence in New Spain's most powerful church coincide with the peak of Luis Barreto's career. Thus, it is likely that the chapelmaster penned at least some of his compositions with the soprano's voice in mind, including, perhaps, *Passio secundum Matthaeum*.

Matthew Grey Brothers has transcribed Rodríguez Mata's *Passion according to St. Matthew* and extensively studied it, particularly as an example of the New World transformation of the Spanish-style passion. He observes that for the most part, the piece is musically conservative. Indeed, today's scholars can encounter more daring rhythms or text settings in extant examples of passions by Puebla's Pedro Bermúdez or organist Luis Coronado, who became the Mexico City cathedral chapelmaster after Rodríguez Mata.[5] Regardless, Brothers underscores the surprisingly developed interventions of women's voices in Rodríguez Mata's work, where tiple and bass duets juxtapose high and low voices and offer textural contrast with the *cronista*'s sung plainchant. Brothers draws specific attention to the musical role of a servant maid who appears before Peter in Matthew 26:69–72 to identify the apostle as one of Jesus's followers. He remarks that "the duet settings of the speeches of the servant maids (*Passio secundum Matthaeum*, mm. 408–12 and mm. 417–23; *Passio secundum Lucam*, mm. 290–93) also stand out due to the wide tessitura of their tiple parts—both of which reach d" [d5], a pitch rarely attained elsewhere in Rodríguez Mata's settings—and the elevated rhythmic and melismatic activity of both voices."[6] Given such anomalies, Brothers speculates about the unusual emphasis on female utterances in Rodríguez Mata's passions. He notes that the composer's expressive choices in these passages could have heightened listeners' emotional reaction to certain sections of the Gospel. Additionally, he maintains that performance conditions could also have influenced unusually florid settings of female voices in Rodríguez Mata's passion and in other sixteenth-century examples of the genre. Along these lines, Brothers argues that the composer's emphasis on these parts reflects their use in women's communities, specifically, the Convento de Nuestra Señora de la Encarnación, where a copy of the *Passio secundum Matthaeum* evidently circulated.[7]

Brothers' observation is astute, and it opens new avenues for understanding the roles of women's voices in New Spanish music culture. As a complement to these ideas, I would like to put forth a different hypothesis. Given Barreto's prominence in the cathedral chapel during the early days of Rodríguez Mata's influence, it is also possible that the composer wrote the segments that feature women's utterances in such a way as to showcase the male soprano's voice. This explanation clarifies the broad range upon which Brothers remarks, particularly if Barreto was a capón singer, for much of the part falls in the range of the castrato voice.[8]

In lieu of recordings, speculative readings of extant scores can lend insight into how Barreto and Vera's song might have sounded. Despite the potential fruitfulness of this line of inquiry for hearing Afro-descendant voices from colonial Mexico, scholars often overlook liturgical pieces like the *Passio secundum Matthaeum* as sources because of their connotations with the white or European music canon. Instead, research tends to debate the "authenticity" of Afro-descendant song in New Spanish villancicos, where it particularly underscores stereotypical portrayals of Black sound that distance it from Eurocentric traditions and offer a limited perspective.[9] Regardless of these shortcomings, however, imaginings of Afro-descent in villancicos can shed light on the cultural construction of Black voices as a product of dark-skinned bodies. Like Noémie Ndiaye has affirmed in her reading of racemaking in seventeenth- and eighteenth-century theater from France, England, and Spain, "the scripts projected onto the material techniques used by white actors—professional and amateurs—in various loci of early modern European performance culture shaped new habits of the mind, new ways for spectators to think of the Afro-diasporic people who lived or could live in their midst."[10] Precisely, Ndiaye argues that racialized tropes in writings and performances featuring Afro-descendant characters contributed to codified representations of Blackness that originated in the early modern period and persist today.

There is little doubt about the distance between imagined Blackness in early modern cultural production and the day-to-day lives of Afro-diasporic people who lived in New Spain, other parts of the Americas, and Europe. With Ndiaye's comments in mind, this chapter is the first of several to focus on phonographic renderings of Afro-descendants in musical scores and lyrics from seventeenth-century New Spain. While I concur with Ndiaye's observations about how these works established links among skin color and physical, sentimental, intellectual, and sonic traits, on the rare occasions when scholars have information about early modern performers of African descent, it is possible to think about how non-European singers and actors shaped scripted imaginings of Blackness. The cases of Luis Barreto and Juan de Vera therefore provide fruitful opportunities to reread racial themes in music that these figures would have performed as indexes of New Spanish representations of Blackness and also as phonographic archives of the two sopranos' voices. Indeed, an exploration of imagined Afro-descendant voices in pieces written by composers who worked with Vera and Barreto draw out stark contrasts among the highly trained voices of cathedral singers, music written for professional singers of African descent, and representations of Black vocality as bizarre and far outside of the European tradition.

Villancicos are my primary source for this chapter's exploration of Afro-descendant soprano voices in New Spain's liturgical sound culture. These musico-poetic works formed extravagant song cycles that resounded in the great cathedrals of New Spain and its colonies. They were popular throughout the early modern Spanish-speaking world, and by the seventeenth century, the genre had generated a production industry that featured collaboration among some of the most important composers and poets of the day. Based on the liturgical hours and divided among three "nocturnes," villancicos consisted of eight- or nine-piece sets that complemented mass on feast days. Their purpose was to transmit sacred themes to diverse publics in New Spain and elsewhere in the Spanish-speaking world, and as such, they drew upon a surprising variety of voices and musical forms in order to transpose Christian doctrine to a popular register.

Throughout the Spanish-speaking world, villancicos accompanied religious feast days, especially Christmas and Corpus Christi. They blend popular musical, lyrical, and dance forms with church doctrine and humor to appeal to diverse audiences. Within the genre, *villancicos de remedo*, or "ethnic villancicos," are especially noteworthy. These pieces rework Peninsular literary tropes as buffoon-like portraits of rural Spaniards, Indigenous figures, gypsies, Portuguese, Africans, and more. Of all the caricatures, stylized representations of Afro-descent in the Black villancico were the most popular. Pseudo-dialects, "ethnic" dance forms, embodied racial tropes, and stereotypical cultural references feature prominently throughout the subgenre. Furthermore, intersections of performance and performativity are crucial to constructions of race in Black villancicos. More often than not, when narrators announced the entrance of an African or Afro-Mexican character, a white actor—possibly in blackface—voiced the role. In some cases, topsy-turvy musical accompaniment and references to affected song heighten Black performers' absurd contrast with Castilian counterparts.

Black villancicos and other ethnic works therefore prompt important questions about how the early modern Hispanic world imagined race, particularly in diverse areas like New Spain. For some, the pieces offer a glimpse into the region's cultural plurality, and they challenge the strident racial boundaries that colonial authorities sought to enact.[11] For others, the ethnic villancicos perpetuate socio-political hegemonies and imagine diversity through reductive categories like "Indian" and "Black."[12] There is little doubt that colonial elite perspectives resonate deeply in these pieces. Nevertheless, as I argue here, they can also offer valuable insights into the voiced presence of marginalized peoples and resonate more fully with contemporary audiences.

Although scholars have long thought that Creole and Peninsular singers performed Afro-descendant villancico roles in blackface, Morales Abril rightly points out that Juan de Vera likely sang these parts in Puebla chapelmaster Gaspar Fernández's works. He emphasizes the composer's use of a soprano voice in pieces like "Andrés do queda el ganado" or "Negrinho tiray vos" and suggests that the composer penned them with the famed singer in mind.¹³ Morales Abril concludes that "no es difícil imaginar el efecto magnificente producido por Juan de Vera al cantar las negrillas compuestas por Frutos de Castillo, Pedro Bermúdez, Gaspar Fernández e incluso las suyas, representando lúdicamente a su propio grupo racial, con su voz de niño, pero con la potencia, agilidad y madurez expresiva de un adulto"(it is not difficult to imagine the magnificent effect produced by Juan de Vera in singing the negrillas composed by Frutos de Castillo, Pedro Bermúdez, Gaspar Fernández, and even his own, playfully representing his own racial group, with the voice of a child, but with the power, agility, and expressive maturity of an adult).¹⁴ Whether or not Vera was a capón singer, his soprano voice certainly provoked some dissonance with his adult, male body, even in a time period when men singing high was commonplace. To this end, Alisha Lola Jones observes that constructions that aligned the castrato's song with angelic tones also distanced the singer from his gender identity, for in early modern culture, angels were androgynous.¹⁵ In terms of race, Vera's rigorous technique was surely striking when he performed *chanzonetas* or villancicos that poked fun at Black voices through linguistic, timbral, and other references.

Examples of the tendency appear in repertoire that coincides with Vera and Barreto's heydays. For instance, Puebla chapelmaster Gaspar Fernández's five-voice *chanzoneta* "Negrinho tiray vos" (Epiphany, 1610) features a tiple *negrilla* solo that Juan de Vera would likely have performed.¹⁶ The *estribillo* opens with playful banter between a Portuguese man (tenor) and a Black person (tiple). First, the Portuguese singer bets that one of the three kings who visits the baby Jesus is Portuguese. Minims or half-note values dominate the composer's ternary setting of this tenor solo. Spirited *sesquialteras* (hemiolas) momentarily shift the solo from triple to duple meter in measures 1–2 and 3–4. While these rhythmic fluctuations lighten the mood, the overall declamatory effect of the Portuguese man's solo is rather serious. In contrast, the tiple solo has a jocular tone. Before the tenor even finishes his final note, the Black singer jumps in and rebuts the Portuguese man's opening statement. He declares: "Güi-güi-ri-güi que negrito es" ("Blah, blah, blah, he's a Black baby!").¹⁷ The solo begins with a minim on C5, relatively high in male sopranos' general tessitura, and then descends with a lively pattern of semiminims (quarter notes), twice as fast as the tenor's opening line. Together, the falling melody and quick rhythm create a topsy-turvy effect, almost as if the Black person is tumbling into the scene while he interrupts the Portuguese singer. To be certain, Vera's powerful soprano voice alone would have created a striking effect as he sang these lines. Furthermore, the opening of this solo line would have fallen within the most powerful part of

**2.1.** Gaspar Fernández, "Negrinho tiray vos." *Cancionero de Gaspar Fernandes*, vol. 1, transcribed, edited, and with an introduction by Aurelio Tello and in collaboration with Juan Manuel Lara Cárdenas (Instituto Nacional de Bellas Artes / Centro Nacional de Investigación, Documentación e Información Musical Carlos Chávez: Mexico City, 2001), 76–77, m. 1–13.

a singer like Vera's range, where he could have projected fully. In this way, the composer's knowledge of the performer's voice may well have influenced his composition choices, for he set the Black person's interruption in such a way as to showcase Vera's conspicuous vocal presence.

If Vera and Barreto were capones, questions about the reception of their racialized and gendered bodies become even more intriguing. Indeed, their singing may have been particularly inspiring for audience members. Early modern concertgoers and composers celebrated castrati for their vocal agility, as well as for brilliant timbre and unmatched breath control. Martha Feldman compiles qualities of castrati stars in the seventeenth- and eighteenth-century Italian opera industry, for which there is considerably more documentation from the listener perspective. She notes that

> in their various skills, castrati counted as first among equals in attaining ideas of singing that were broadly shared until about 1840 . . . they included beautiful unobstructed vocal sound, pure vowels, excellent diction, perfect intonation, light and rapid passagework, legato singing ("on the breath"), smoothly joined registers, evenness of timbre, and improvisational skill (cf. Wistreich 2002; Foreman 2006). Nevertheless, scores, treatises, and anecdotes make clear that castrato singing, while it differed vastly from individual to individual (like all singing), was marked by abilities rarely shared by contemporaneous females or tenors.[18]

To be certain, it is impossible to determine whether these characteristics are a product of the castrato's unique vocal anatomy, his intensive training or simply his enormity within the popular imaginary. Nevertheless, Feldman's description of the voices of Italian eunuch singers can shed light on New Spanish preferences for well-trained male sopranos in sacred and secular festivals.

Given the robust industry for creating and educating male sopranos and especially castrate singers with legendary vocal technique, Morales Abril's reading of Juan de Vera as inspiration for Gaspar Fernández's Black villancicos opens unexplored interpretative terrain, just as my reading of "Negrinho tiray vos" demonstrates. In what ways did the presence of African and Afro-Mexican singers shape the Spanish American Black villancicos? Morales Abril's remarks about Gaspar Fernández's Black villancicos offer a preliminary response, upon which this chapter will expand. Morales Abril maintains that Gaspar Fernández's use of a soprano soloist distinguishes his pieces from those of Puebla's next chapelmaster, Juan Gutiérrez de Padilla.[19] Nevertheless, there are also soprano solos for Black male characters in Gutiérrez de Padilla's repertoire. The detail is noteworthy, especially since Nava Sánchez underscores Luis Barreto's presence in the Puebla cathedral from 1621 through 1626, a period that coincides with Gutiérrez de Padilla's early years in the city.[20] Although it is possible that Gutiérrez de Padilla's villancicos simply follow a tradition that his predecessor established for musical imaginings of Black voices, it is also plausible that they recall Barreto's vocal presence in the Puebla chapel long after his departure.

This context beckons a closer examination of the musical and textual construction of Afro-descendant men's high voices in both Fernández and Gutiérrez de Padilla's Black villancicos. First, given Vera's role in the Puebla cathedral chapel at the time Fernández's works were penned, musical details underscore the singer's fame and lend insight into the shape of his voice. Moreover, lyrical references to timbre, accent, and other vocal qualities combine with male vocal lines in the upper register and shed light on racialized representations of Black voices, sound, and bodies. These constructions stand out against Vera and Barreto's Eurocentric training and technical skill and underscore the role that cultural conditioning plays in imagining links between dark-skinned bodies and Black sound. For all this, phonographic re-readings of Fernández and Gutiérrez de Padilla's Black villancicos draw out the complexities of imagining and listening to race in New Spain.

### VILLANCICOS AS VOCAL ARCHIVE

The scripting of Black voices into New Spanish villancicos has long troubled scholars, who often approach the problem through an interpretative lens that privileges villancicos' written lyrics over other expressive and epistemological modes. Furthermore, prior readings often look for non-Western evidence of "Blackness" and thus perpetuate essentialism that can be a barrier to more inclusive canons.[21] For example, some experts have sought to recover the contours of African or Afro-Mexican language in these pieces. The studies of John Lipski, Glenn Swiadon Martínez, and Claudio Ramírez Uribe are illustrative in this regard. On one hand, analyses from this perspective can lend insight into sonorous contours of the Western imagining of African and Afro-descendant voices. On the other, however, they also imagine that all Black Mexicans spoke "Africanized" Spanish, even well into the seventeenth century, when many Afro-descendant families were several generations removed from their *bozal* ancestors. In contrast, Baker argues that the villancico texts feature mere caricatures of Blackness that reproduce the stylistic codes of *habla de negros* and transmit the ideologies of New Spain's lettered elite.[22] Although Baker rightfully attends to the villancico's underlying aim to harmonize different factions of New Spanish society, he leaves little room for polyphonic readings that draw out Afro-descendant, Indigenous, and other non-Western voices.

In response to interpretative limits like these, scholars like Ireri Chávez Bárcenas, Caroline Egan, and Nick Jones have sought to reposition villancicos as syncretic products of New Spain's Indigenous, African, and Spanish inheritance. Chávez Bárcenas has argued that Gaspar Fernández's *Cancionero musical*, a polyphonic songbook from the Oaxaca Cathedral, incorporates Nahua performance traditions that would have been familiar to his multiethnic audience.[23] For her part, Egan incorporates a nuanced understanding of the alignment of music, dance, and poetry in Aztec philosophical tradition in order to situate Sor Juana's rendering of Indigenous figures within the longstanding practice of attending to "indigenous language and its lyric tradition [. . . in New Spain as] objects of sustained study for the purposes of appropriation and evangelization."[24] With respect to how villancicos engage with New Spain's Black and African inheritance, Jones draws upon dual expertise in early Hispanic literature and culture and Africana studies to read Sor Juana's representation of Afro-descendant figures. He maintains that "Sor Juana's *habla de negros* is an African linguistic trope rendered visible for those who wish to see it, although it has been transformed and adapted by her New World subject position as colonial, Creole, and woman."[25] In this way, Jones enables Sor Juana's scripting of Black voices to move beyond subaltern readings that view these characters as mere objects of the perspective that her position in colonial society affords.

Considering such developments, how might scholars continue to advance current understanding of the Black and African sounds that inform imaginings of Afro-Mexican voices in villancicos? One solution is to distance Black villancicos and other colonial Latin American sacred genres from interpretations that privilege Spanish and Creole voices as dominant in musical canon. Indeed, as historical evidence for Black and African musicians as well as Indigenous ones has shown, the music industry was far more diverse than scholars previously surmised. In this chapter, I will develop a reading of Black villancicos that underscores Afro-descendant musicians as co-creators of the genre, thus reimagining the canon by underscoring the impact of non-European voices. Specifically, I will focus on the documented presence of Black and African sopranos in New Spanish cathedrals and hypothesize about the ways their extraordinary voices shaped the villancico repertoire and also offered opportunities for Afro-descendant singers to gain audibility, seemingly within the constraints of social hierarchies that marginalized them.

## SHOWCASING AFRO-DESCENDANT SOPRANOS IN GASPAR FERNÁNDEZ'S PASTORAL VILLANCICOS

Morales Abril's supposition that Juan de Vera inspired some of Gaspar Fernández's villancicos is well-founded and merits analytical development. During a tenure as Puebla chapelmaster that spanned more than twenty years, the composer penned a significant liturgical corpus, including numerous villancicos.[26] Today, some 270 of those works are preserved in the *Cancionero Musical de Gaspar Fernández*. Fernández's legacy is one of the earliest and most extensive surviving collections of scores by a New Spanish chapelmaster, and it offers significant insight into the production of church music. In addition, as Chávez Bárcenas has shown, villancicos from the *Cancionero* can also illuminate how these compositions harmonize Puebla's diverse sound cultures. She focuses on intersections with Nahua-Christian ritual and argues that "Fernández's 'villancicos en indio' show a deliberate attempt to create an Indian affect, aided by specific musical devices that suggest the sonority of native performative practices."[27] Chávez Bárcenas's reading is sensitive to the *Cancionero*'s underlying resonances with social and racial hierarchies that privilege native-born Spaniards and Creoles of pure Castilian descent over other castes. Nonetheless, she also attends to the rich acoustical context of New Spain's City of Angels and makes a compelling case for its influence upon the composer's musical imagination.

In a similar gesture, I extend Morales Abril's supposition that Fernández penned Black soprano solos from the *Cancionero* with renowned singer Juan de Vera's talent in mind. My argument is that in some pieces, the chapelmaster framed individual treble lines in a way that distinguishes them from other Afro-descendant voices and thus underscores their vocalized authority. These parts present key liturgical messages in a simple, declamatory form, eschewing the cacophonous onomatopoeia and boisterous rhythms that characterize Black villancicos. Frequently, a "Guinean" or "Angolan" chorus responds with textual, melodic, or rhythmic echoes. In contrast with the rowdy musical portraits of Afro-descent that scholars often emphasize in Black villancicos, the works that I study here adopt a subdued, idyllic tone, inspired in part by the pastoral novels of such authors as Jorge de Montemayor and Lope de Vega. Chávez Bárcenas has highlighted this subgenre's prominence in early works from the *Cancionero*, especially around 1610 and 1611. She notices that Fernández's pastoral villancicos incorporate shepherds and shepherdesses from a variety of cultural backgrounds, including Portuguese, Indigenous, and Afro-descendant characters. Furthermore, they "are often the most theatrical ones, as a result of the prominent use of dialogues and exhortative phrases to portray the shepherds recounting the details of the Annunciation of the Nativity, inviting others to join in the trip to Bethlehem or in the celebration."[28] Like Chávez Bárcenas argues, these pieces constitute local reimaginings of both the Biblical scenes that they stage and the genre from which they borrow.[29] Such figures resonated with Puebla's diverse listening public and, as I will argue here, vocalize subaltern authority in a way that challenges scripted and social limits.

Just as Luis Barreto's clothing echoed his vocal exemplarity with visual symbols of beauty and high status, so Fernández's pastoral settings of Black soprano solos imbue the voices that perform them with a dignity that stands out among villancicos' often irreverent imaginings of Afro-descent. Since I concur with Morales Abril about the likelihood of Juan de Vera taking on these roles, at least during Fernández's early years in the cathedral, I read such influence in relation to celestial resonances and the affective potency of the Black soprano voice. In Fernández's pieces, Afro-descendant male tiples take advantage of their powerful voices to transmit liturgical knowledge to their peers. In this way, the vocal presence of Juan de Vera and other high-voiced male singers emerges as central to Black villancicos' performance of Black and African evangelization. Far more than mere curiosities or symbols of the cathedral's wealth, I contend that these musicians actively shaped the repertoire they performed. The problematic nature of Afro-descendants performing stereotypes intended to demean and marginalize them aside, my interpretation amplifies the actual Black and African voices that villancicos encode.

In support of this reading, I will examine two pieces from the *Cancionero*: "Andrés do queda el ganado" ("Andrés, where are the cattle," Christmas, 1610) and "Fransiquiya donde bamo" ("Francisquiya, where are we going," Corpus Christi, 1610). Each example features a tiple 2 soloist who sings in *habla de negros*, imparts important messages about the day's liturgical content, and then leads a Black chorus in song. Along with Morales Abril, I maintain that Fernández wrote the solos for Juan de Vera. The dates coincide with the singer's heyday in Puebla's church music scene, and it thus seems likely that the composer knew exactly who would perform in those roles. If we accept this position, then it is possible to interpret these pieces as windows into Juan de Vera's vocality and presence.

To begin, "Andrés do queda el ganado" announces Jesus's birth through a musical dialogue between the tenor and tiple 2 voices. First, the tenor addresses the featured soloist and asks, "Andrés, ¿do queda el ganado?" (Andrés, where are the cattle?) His interlocutor replies, "Puru cieto que no lo sé, / que se apantaro, bona fe" (To tell the truth, I don't know / they got scared, in good faith).[30] The tenor is not satisfied with the shepherd's response and asks him to elaborate: "¿Y por qué?" (And why?)[31] The soprano answers:

| | |
|---|---|
| Dizque viro un angelito, | Apparently, they saw an angel |
| bolandito | flying by |
| y cantava tan bonito, | and singing so prettily, |
| y deciva lo patocito | and he told the humble pastors |
| que Jesucrito | that Jesus Christ |
| aquesta noche nacé, | was born that night, |
| y se apantaro, bona fe.[32] | and they got scared, in good faith. |

Here, the soloist narrates the angels' annunciation of Jesus' birth to the shepherds. The sweet, modest voice part allows the lyrics to shine and emphasizes this villancico's didactic tone. The moderate rhythm of minims and semibreves is consistent throughout the opening section and does not distinguish one voice part from another. Likewise, the tiple 2 solo has a relatively small range—less than an octave—and there are no large leaps or prolonged high notes to showcase vocal dexterity. Along the same lines, Chávez Bárcenas highlights a surprising lack of word painting and remarks that Andrés "does not even burst out singing when he refers to the angel's song."[33]

For all this, the solo's deliberate simplicity offers intriguing insight into how Fernández might have imagined the affective power of the tiple 2 voice. Indeed, the shepherd's straightforward vocalization aligns with the exemplary, pastoral humility that Chávez Bárcenas has signaled in New Spanish villancicos.[34] In fact, Andrés echoes this portrayal in the *copla* when he asserts "Yo, pobre neglo pastó" (I, poor black shepherd).[35]

Of course, it is plausible that a skilled singer like Juan de Vera would have added tasteful ornamentation to the plain vocal line. In this case, a display of vocal dexterity would have provided rich contrast with the lyrics' meek portrayal of the shepherd. Moreover, in an echo of the angel chorus, underlying consonances of the singer's highly trained voice would have allowed the audience to appreciate celestial harmony. Assuming that the tiple 2 possessed extraordinary vocal training and talent, like that of Juan de Vera, a performance of this ilk certainly would have echoed heavenly song. Without recordings or firsthand accounts, it is impossible to know how a singer might have interpreted the *Cancionero*'s score. Nevertheless, one subtle detail suggests that Fernández may indeed have written the tiple 2 part with Juan de Vera's voice in mind. Like Chávez Bárcenas observes, the phrases in Andrés' opening solo are progressively longer, with slower note values. In addition to showcasing the richness of the singer's tone and his

**2.2.** Gaspar Fernández, "Andrés do queda el ganado." *Cancionero de Gaspar Fernandes,* vol. 1, transcribed, edited, and with an introduction by Aurelio Tello and in collaboration with Juan Manuel Lara Cárdenas, (Instituto Nacional de Bellas Artes / Centro Nacional de Investigación, Documentación e Información Musical Carlos Chávez: Mexico City, 2001), 284, m. 1–13.

unique timbre, this setting would also flaunt the exceptional breath control of a well-trained performer. Castrati were especially renowned for this trait. Taking everything into account, "Andrés do queda el ganado" aligns the Afro-descendant soloist with the angel who announces Jesus' birth. The opening lines' lyrical content amplifies this function, for in the context of the villancico's performance, Andrés takes on the seraphic role and tells the shepherds and audience of the Nativity. While the Afro-descendant shepherd may well have been among Puebla society's lowest-ranking members, his vocal interventions in the villancico's Biblical discourse resonate with the highest of heavenly beings.

"Andrés do queda el ganado" is not the only villancico from Fernández's early days as chapelmaster to treat Black tiple voices in this way. "Fransiquiya donde vamo" similarly assigns vocal and narrative authority to an Afro-descendant soprano soloist. In this piece, a band of Afro-descendant shepherds queries the female leader, Fransiquiya, about the enigmas of the eucharist. In the *coplas*, the tiple 1 and alto parts direct a series of questions to Fransisquiya. Straightforward, homophonic declamation whose rhythms align with the 3/2 beat and tertian harmony underscore the childlike innocence of inquiries like "¿Cómo harta la criatura, bocarita, decí vozo?" (How does such a small mouthful fill up the little one, what do you say?)[36] In turn, Francisquiya's replies offer straightforward, if simplistic, interpretations of Corpus Christi. Dotted rhythms playfully contrast with her interlocutor's solemn interrogations, and polyphonic repetition of the shepherdess's lyrical and musical motifs underscore her vocal authority.

When the curious chorus's questioning becomes overwhelming, in the second *copla a duo*, Francisquiya's discourse breaks down:

| | |
|---|---|
| —Si no cabe lo lo cielo, | —If it does not fit in the heavens, |
| ¿cómo cabe lo lo pan? | how does it fit on bread? |
| —Cómelo lo que lo dan, | —Eat what you're given, |
| que lo demás no entendelo.[37] | for you don't understand the rest. |

Here, the pastoral leader responds with a Baroque rhetorical silence that disrupts the major voice of the liturgy. As a closing punch line, Francisquiya's reply opens itself to audience interpretation. Is the shepherdess so well-versed in Christian teachings that she anticipates the material's incomprehensibility before her audience? From this perspective, the singer's refusal to answer upholds the eucharistic mystery as a pinnacle of Catholic faith. Conversely, does Francisquiya's silence merely signal the limits of her own capacity to understand church doctrine, perhaps in an echo of popular representations of Afro-descendants as brutes with inferior intellect?

In some ways, the tiple 2 soloist's vocal and discursive authority in "Francisquiya donde vamo" parallels Andrés's alignment with the celestial proclamation of Jesus's birth in "Andrés do queda el ganado." In both pieces, treble-voiced soloists recount central tenets of Christianity in the "Africanized" voice of *habla de negros*. While the male shepherd's singing resonates with the heavens and thus performs his salvation, Francisquiya influences the earthly realm. The shepherdess's voice drives "Francisquiya donde vamo" both musically and lyrically, for her companions echo the singer all throughout this Corpus Christi work.

Gender lends an additional layer to my reading of vocal authority in Fernández's pastoral rendering of Afro-descent. First, the female leader of Black shepherds in "Francisquiya donde vamo" had distinctive social resonances among Afro-descendant communities in New Spain. Indeed, as

**2.3**. Gaspar Fernández, "Francisquiya donde vamo." *Cancionero de Gaspar Fernandes*, vol. 1, transcribed, edited, and with an introduction by Aurelio Tello and in collaboration with Juan Manuel Lara Cárdenas, (Instituto Nacional de Bellas Artes / Centro Nacional de Investigación, Documentación e Información Musical Carlos Chávez: Mexico City, 2001), 76–77, m. 1–13.

Nicole von Germeten has argued in her study of Afro-Mexican confraternities, Black women assumed positions of authority to a much greater degree than Spaniards or Creoles. Von Germeten speculates that the prominence of female leaders in Afro-descendant lay organizations is a vestige of African traditions that privileged female authority.[38] Fernández's villancico reproduces these persistent, gendered hierarchies by centering a female voice in "Francisquiya donde vamo." Nevertheless, if Juan de Vera had taken on this character's role, then his masculine body would have been absurdly at odds with the woman character, even if he were a castrato with a feminized appearance. Such dissonance would have heightened the villancico's jocularity and thus destabilized Francisquiya's narrative authority with humor. At the same time, it may also shed light on Spanish and Creole impressions of Afro-descendant women's leadership within their communities, for the practice was discordant with European gender roles. By imagining a high-voiced Afro-descendant singer as Francisquiya, Fernández's portrayal aligns the Black shepherdess with the *mujer varonil* or "manly woman" archetype.

In sum, the representation of Afro-descendant voices in Gaspar Fernández's pastoral villancicos challenges interpretations of these characters as one-dimensional products of European stereotypes about Black and African people. By imbuing the composer's scores with the vocal presence of Juan de Vera, Puebla's celebrated Afro-descendant soprano, my readings generate new possibilities for hearing non-Western contributions to New Spanish sacred music. As I have shown, the privileged status of enslaved male sopranos destabilizes assumptions about Blackness and also opens itself to new registers from which to voice Afro-descent. In the next section, I will attend to the persistence of these figures in a villancico by Fernández's successor, Juan Gutiérrez de Padilla.

### REMEMBERING JUAN DE VERA IN JUAN GUTIÉRREZ DE PADILLA'S "AL ESTABLO MÁS DICHOSO"

Beyond Gaspar Fernández's work, later villancico references to high-voiced male singing among Afro-descendant characters suggest that the presence of Black male sopranos in urban cathedral ensembles persisted in the musical and literary imagination of New Spanish artists. One telling example of this tendency is from Gutiérrez de Padilla's 1652 Christmas set for the Puebla cathedral. This grouping includes an *ensaladilla* (little salad) titled "Al establo más dichoso" (At the happiest stable). A subgenre of villancico, the *ensalada* or *ensaladilla* combines popular voices, song, and dance forms in a clever quodlibet. It was often the last piece in an eight- or nine-work set, a gesture that we might interpret as the symbolic harmonization of disparate social factions. To this end, Gutiérrez de Padilla's piece loosely adapts pastoral themes to imagine Puebla's popular classes. It features four characters or groups of characters: shepherds, a drunken muleteer, Indigenous farmers, and a raucous band of "Angolans." For this reason, Andrew Cashner underscores the performativity of "Al establo más dichoso" and argues that the piece "puts the social hierarchy of New Spain on display" through its imagining of divine order.[39] Cashner undertakes a skillful reading that sets the villancico's musical and poetic texts against early modern musical thought, their social background, and the newly rebuilt Puebla Cathedral, the space for which it was composed. His interpretation accounts for all aspects of the villancico's performance and is a model for additional work on this understudied genre. Here, I extend Cashner's reading of Minguelillo, the Angolan protagonist in the *negrilla*.

As in customary in multivoiced *ensaladillas*, Gutiérrez de Padilla's *negrilla* opens with an introduction in which neutral narrators situate the characters.

| El Angola Minguelillo | Little Miguel the Angolan, |
| acaudillando su tropa, | marshalling his troop, |
| no quiere ser postrero | does not wish to be the last one |
| en la fiesta que se goza. | at the party that is being enjoyed. |
| | |
| Dejando el tumbacatumba | Leaving the "tumbacatumba" |
| y gruñendo a lo de Angola | and grunting like the Angolans do |
| desenvainó con la voz | he unsheathed his voice, |
| de su tizón | like pulling a sword from his |
|    La Tizona. |    charred log.⁴⁰ |

The anonymous poet's lyrics represent Minguelillo's vocal presence with surprising detail. Cashner highlights the insight that these references can offer into how colonial listeners heard Afro-descendant voices:

> *Tumbacatumba* is apparently a nonsense word referencing both the mythical perpetual drumming of Africans and the sound of their Bantu languages, such as Kikongo.... The narrators describe Minguelillo's singing as "grunting" or "groaning"—like an animal sound—and they associate the vocalization with a stereotypical Angolan identity, *a lo de Angola* (in the Angolan manner). Playing on the image of Minguelillo as leader of a "troop," they compare the act of singing to that of unsheathing a sword. The wordplay on *Tizona/tizón* heightens their mockery: *La Tizona* was El Cid's famous sword, while *tizón* was a charred log. By saying that he has to pull his voice out of a log, they are characterizing Minguelillo's voice as deep, gravelly, produced with difficulty, and as black in sound as the color of the skin on his muscular, log-like throat.⁴¹

While Cashner insightfully draws out Bantu and Peninsular resonances in the introduction, he overlooks the playful sexual jibe that the author elaborates. "Tumbacatumba" is indeed an imagined onomatopoeia meant to imitate Kikongo or other African languages. However, it is impossible to overlook the root "tumbar." According to the *Diccionario de Autoridades*, this word means "caer rodando, ò dando vueltas" (to fall head over heels, or rolling around). In this sense, "tumbacatumba" might describe Minguelillo's unruly body movement, as well as the sound of his voice.

In addition, "tumbar" can refer to a stinging insult: "por analogía vale sorprehender con algun chasco, ò zumba à alguno, corriendole, y avergonzandole desuerte, que se sienta, y se pique" (by analogy it means to surprise someone with a snappy jibe or insult, making fun of someone and embarrassing him so that he feels the biting humor). Sonorous and tactile imagery stands out in this definition. For instance, the *Diccionario de Autoridades* defines "chasco" as follows: "Vale tambien burla, chanza, cantaléta ò engaño jocóso y de passatiempo, de hecho ù dicho, que se hace à otro. Díxose assi por semejanza del chasco de la honda ò látigo, respecto del susto, temor, desasossiego, y alteracion que este causa en el que oye su estampído, aunque no le llegue à herir" (It also means taunt, joke, insulting refrain, or playful and entertaining deceit that is directed at another through words or gesture. It is said in this way because it is similar to the snap of a slingshot or whip, regarding the fright, terror, unease, and anger that this causes in the one who hears its roar, although it may not cause injury). Along the same lines, "zumbar" describes a joke and also refers to buzzing. The *Diccionario de Autoridades* definition highlight's sound's impact upon the listening ear: "hacer ruido, ò sonido continuado, y bronco, al modo del que se siente en los oídos, quando se ha introducido en ellos algun viento, ò vapor" (to make continuous, out of tune noise or sound in such a way that one feels as if some wind or vapor has entered in the ears). Taken together, all of these definitions enable a reading of "tumbacatumba" as an example of how Afro-descendant voices burble out as illegible within the authority of Western writing.

The apparently playful description of Minguelillo's chaotic entrance has one more resonance to explore. Indeed, the etymological relationship with "tumba" or "tumbar" conjures up graveyard imagery and also recalls lying down as an allusion to the sexual act. Through "tumbacatumba," the philosophical linkage between death and climax crystallizes in Minguelillo's soprano voice. First, the term's topsy-turvy underpinnings recall the gleeful dancing skeletons that pepper Renaissance visual art as memento mori or reminders of death.

From these reminders of mortality, it is a short leap to the lascivious overtones of "tumbacatumba," especially in combination with the introduction's description of Minguelillo drawing his "charred log." Read from this angle, the introduction aligns with hypersexualized representations of Afro-descendant subjects and also with the erotic allure of high-voiced male singers, and particularly castrati.

The conflation of sex and death in the introduction to Gutiérrez de Padilla's *negrilla* recalls early modern linkage of the two concepts. Often, women were the scapegoats of *la petite mort*, imagery that arose from the belief that ejaculation sapped men of their vigor and shortened one's life. Beth Ann Bassein argues that in early modern Western culture, "women served as memento mori to men in at least three ways: sexual experiences with her

2.4. Wenceslaus Hollar, "Me & te sola Mors separabit." *Mortalitum nobilitas*, 1680. Courtesy of Wenceslaus Hollar Digital Collection, The Thomas Fisher Rare Book Library at University of Toronto Library.

took their strength and brought on early death; she represented lust and for the sinner was the destroyer of the afterlife; and she was simply a rotting piece of matter already putrefied as she moved about adulterating the 'more clean.'"[42] In addition, Bassein observes that popular and moral works tended to relate women to physical and spiritual uncleanliness, vestiges of their supposed association with Eve's disobedience, the transmission of sexual diseases, and of course, menstruation.[43] For all this, Minguelillo's connection to "tumbacatumba," with its connotations of death, lust, and memento mori, feminizes the character and ironizes the metaphoric reference to his genitalia. The introduction's emphasis on his dark member recalls the singer's skin tone and also aligns him with bodily discharge and excrement.

Perhaps not unsurprisingly, Eidsheim has drawn out similar resonances in media framings of United States jazz singer Jimmy Scott. Scott was afflicted with Kallman syndrome, a congenital disorder that delayed puberty, in his case, until age thirty-eight. As a result, the singer's physical features and high-pitched voice remained ambiguous within Western codes of gender. Scott's African American heritage heightened discord among his vocal and embodied identities. Eidsheim asks: "Why did listeners find Scott's voice incoherent in relation to social and cultural expectations of normative masculinity and, specifically, of normative black masculinity?"[44] In similar fashion, Licia Fiol-Matta's reading of Afro–Puerto Rican contralto Ruth Fernández highlights an equally hazy approach to the singer's physical presence and her resonant, low-pitched voice. Like Minguelillo's representation in "Al establo más dichoso" illustrates, then, these troubling entanglements of voice, gender, and race are not limited to genres traditionally associated with Afro-descent, nor even to the recorded era. Indeed, New Spain's Black male sopranos audibly and visibly challenged the limits of embodiment and, to some degree, of their enslaved condition.

Chromatic imaginings of the Afro-descendant sexualized body and high voice also stand out in "Al establo más dichoso" and deepen Minguelillo's alignment with sex and death. The colorful description of the singer's genitalia serves as a chiaroscuro that underscores his dusky complexion as worthy of mention and notably different from lighter pigments. Scholars of early modern visual culture have pointed to racial and spiritual overtones in the juxtaposition of black and white that frequently occurs in depictions of Afro-descendant subjects. Erin Kathleen Rowe has argued that whiteness in the iconography of Afro-descendant saints and other religious figures highlights their purity and redemption.[45] Fracchia associates such representations with "the whiteness of the African's soul," a characteristic that becomes manifest upon passing.[46] She cites visual examples like the frontispiece to Alonso de Sandoval's 1647 reedition of *De instuaranda aethiopum salute* (1627, rev. 1647), the first history of the transatlantic slave trade written in the Americas, as well as literary cases like Spanish villancicos. Within this context, the pigmented construction of Minguelillo's phallus in "Al establo más dichoso" evokes the character's depravity and places him at odds with both purity and whiteness. This representation is significant to the *negrilla*'s culminating alignment of Mingeulillo's band with an angelic choir, a transformative moment whose performance of Angolan salvation is fundamental to the *ensaladilla*'s ideological underpinnings.

First, however, there is one more symbolic layer to the "tizón" metaphor that bears mention. Like Cashner notes, the metaphor compares Minguelillo's voice to Castilian war hero El Cid's famous sword.[47] Cashner underscores the significance for imagining the singer's vocal timbre; however, he overlooks phallic symbolism that aligns with "tumbacatumba's" sexual overtones.

Indeed, Michael Horswell argues that the influence of El Cid's emblematic masculinity persists well into the colonial period. He maintains that

> here [in *El poema de mio Cid*] we have a most suitable example of how gender is not an essential characteristic of personhood, but how it must be iterated and reconstructed, imitated and reinvented in each specific cultural moment. The Cid steps into his cultural moment with a potency that reinforces the masculine gender ideal for an entire culture. This new identity is "performed" through explicit bodily gestures and through gendered acts. The body becomes a site on which those new values are inscribed, and the Cid's specific body becomes the dominant figure in a homosocial gender system whose influence will reach the Andean colonies hundreds of years later.[48]

For Horswell, the hero's famed weapon and iconic beard symbolize his gendered military prowess. Gutiérrez de Padilla's *negrilla* inverts the formula and directs a gendered barb at Minguelillo. One of the opening metaphors compares the singer's voice to La Tizona, El Cid's iconic sword. While not obvious at first, the association's absurdity becomes clear the moment Minguelillo sings in dulcet, high-pitched tones. Furthermore, the description of the singer "unsheathing" his voice contributes to the sexual overtones of "tumbacatumba" and also underscores the male soprano's erotic appeal.[49]

In all of these ways, the introduction to the *negrilla* in "Al establo más dichoso" sexualizes Minguelillo and leaves his gender ambiguous. When the Angolan choir begins to sing, the piece's musical characteristics muddy the waters even further, for Minguelillo's voice is not that of a typical adult man. Rather, the composer writes his solo for a soprano. After all of the military references and hypermasculine imagery that stand out in the introduction's depiction of Minguelillo, his high voice would have therefore been totally unexpected, inasmuch as women naturally sing in the upper register. Cashner draws attention to this humorous characteristic, and he underscores the musical setting's role in portraying the Black character's song as ridiculous: "The soloist representing Minguelillo sings irregular patterns composed from uneven groupings of *sesquialtera*, dotted patterns, and short-long groups with forced accents on weak final syllables. His melody moves repetitively within a narrow range in awkward skips and hops with clipped phrase endings. The music portrays a character that is clownish and grotesque, but perhaps also endearing, even cute."[50] In this analysis of the musical and poetic symbolism of "Al establo más dichoso," Cashner shows how Minguelillo and his troop are out of tune with the sonorous, urban, and social harmonies the piece performs. Here, I extend his reading to consider what Gutiérrez de Padilla's riotous Angolan choir might reveal about timbral imaginings of Afro-descendant voices and how they relate to resonances of capón singers like Juan de Vera in the New Spanish auditory imaginary.

The vocal texture of Minguelillo's first entrance heightens the jarring effect of the Black singer and military leader's high-pitched voice. Indeed, following the four-voice introduction, the soprano and bass open the Angolan chorus' part with a duo:

| | |
|---|---|
| Diga plimo donde sa? | Tell me, cousin, where is |
| la niño, de nacimenta | the baby who was born? |
| pulque samo su palenta | for we know his relatives |
| y la venimo a buscá. | and we come to seek him.[51] |

The sparse vocal arrangement in this section breaks off from the full-bodied introduction and underscores the difference between the two singers' registers. Furthermore, the soprano and bass parts move in perfect rhythmic unison, a characteristic that enables listeners to imagine them as a single voice. In this way, the *negrilla*'s opening duo contributes to the gender slippage that is consistent in representations of Minguelillo. The bass sounds as a ghostly double of the Black soprano, intensifying his voice's surprising register through contrast and brimming with auditory masculinity that exceeds Minguelillo's range.

The accompanying lyrical reference to "la niño" deepens this section's muddied imagining of masculine and feminine themes. Although Lipski observes that mistakes in gender agreement were a common feature of *habla de negros*, in the context of "Al establo más dichoso," the erroneous coupling of a feminine article with a reference to the baby Jesus echoes Minguelillo's ambiguous gender identity.[52]

As Cashner notes, the *negrilla*'s musical text reflects the broken, absurd *habla de negros*. Given the staged contexts of villancicos, it is also possible to read the uneven rhythms in Gutiérrez de Padilla's piece as an echo of frenetic bodily motion, possibly meant to imitate the "African" dance styles that these pieces invoke.[53] Such undisciplined motion, along with Minguelillo's sexual cavorting and feminized voice all contrast sharply with military references in the *negrilla*'s opening verses. Throughout the sixteenth and early seventeenth centuries, violent uprisings among New Spain's Black and African population worried colonial officials. In 1537, a group of enslaved Africans in Mexico City elected a king, and authorities interpreted their action as rebellious. Then, around 1570, Kongo-born leader Gaspar Yanga and his

**2.5.** Juan Gutiérrez de Padilla, "Al establo más dichoso." *Villancicos about Music from Seventeenth-Century Spain and New Spain*, edited by Andrew Cashner, Web Library of Seventeenth-Century Music, no. 32 (2018) 206–7, m. 153–71.

band of *cimarrones* formed a Maroon community near Veracruz and terrorized the region until viceroy Luis de Velasco attempted intervention in 1609. Just a few years later, a 1612 conspiracy among confraternity members resulted in the brutal public execution of some thirty-five leaders from the Afro-descendant community.

Viceregal authorities sometimes responded to these threats with measures that tempered Black masculinity, including castration. For instance, in 1579, shortly after the first archival mention of Juan de Vera, viceroy Martín Enríquez de Almanza asked the Council of Indies for permission to reinstate capital punishment for workers in bondage and servants found in possession of unsanctioned weapons. While the viceroy sought to whip offenders, references to castration in his correspondence cause Nicolás Ngou-Mve to suggest that the practice continued in the region, despite the king's ban.

[Enríquez de Almanza] también recordaba que en la época de los virreyes Mendoza y Velasco (1535–1550, 1550–1564, respectivamente), e incluso años después de que él mismo había iniciado sus funciones, la pena infligida a estos negros era simplemente la castración, cosa que los aterrorizaba. Pero a la supresión de ese castigo por orden del propio rey, ya no se encontraba forma de atemorizar a los negros y, el número de sus víctimas aumentaba, la mayoría eran indios, quienes se manifestaban como débiles y sumisos.[54]

[Enríquez de Almanza] also reminded the Council that during the times of viceroys Mendoza and Velasco (1535–1550, 1550–1564, respectively), and including years after he himself had begun his duties, the punishment inflicted upon these *negros* was simply castration, which terrified them. But after the suppression of this punishment by order of the king himself, there was no longer any way to intimidate the *negros*, and the number of their victims rose, the majority of whom were *indios*, who appeared as weak and submissive.

Ngou-Mye's reading of Enríquez de Almanza's epistle underscores physical abuse as a response to the threat of Afro-descendant uprisings. This interpretation particularly illustrates how, in the imaginary of the New Spanish elite, partial or full removal of the male sex organs tamed enslaved Black and African people. Penal castration was not limited to enslaved Afro-descendants. In fact, Touba Ghadessi observes that throughout early modern Europe, the punishment was meted out for crimes like rape or sodomy. She argues that "the removal of the testes signified the removal of sacred symbols of divine and masculine power" and affirms that the practice stripped criminals of gender identities, reproductive capacity, and even the legal authority to "testify."[55] In the case of enslaved people who already endured limits on their rights and personhood, castration or even complete ablation further debased their subjugated bodies and also impeded procreation. Incidentally, the latter consequence responded to New Spanish authorities' fears that the Afro-descendant population might become too large to control.

The document that Ngou-Mve recovered is not the only evidence of race-based castration penalties in New Spain during the second half of the sixteenth century. Yari Pérez Marín underscores Alonso López de Hinojosos's description of the surgical procedure in his *Summa, y recopilacion de chirvgia, con vn Arte para sangrar muy vtil y prouechosa* (Summary, and compendium of surgery, with a very useful and beneficial guide to bloodletting, 1578). The surgeon highlights his own experience performing the operation and affirms "if authorities ever ordered removing the testicles, that it should be done in this manner."[56] Significantly, this reference links castration to order and obedience. Furthermore, in light of the doctor's subsequent affirmation that he had experience with the procedure, an overview of his career can elucidate race's intersections with these themes. Hinojosos arrived in New Spain in 1564 and spent much of his career at the Hospital Real de los Naturales, an institution long thought to serve the Indigenous population of Mexico's urban center. Nevertheless, osteological, ethnohistorical, and genetic analyses of three skeletons uncovered at the site suggest that the Hospital Real de los Naturales also treated Africans and Afrodescendants during Hinojosos's tenure.[57]

Gutiérrez de Padilla's *negrilla* prominently staged the emasculated Black body some seventy-five years later. The humorous depiction of the unruly Angolan further emasculates the character and tames the dark history that his body remembers. For Spaniards and Creoles, the Black capón was a reminder of the threat of revolt among New Spain's Afro-descendent population. For Africans and Afro-Mexicans, he was an ominous warning to remain within the bounds of colonial hierarchies.

One last detail of "Al establo más dichoso" beckons attention in my analysis of how the villancico constructs race and gender through its Black soprano protagonist. At the height of the piece, Minguelillo hushes his companions, and his tenor counterpart announces the arrival of a celestial choir, poised to sing the Gloria in Excelsis Deo:

| | |
|---|---|
| Caya, caya, mila no panta | Hush, hush, look, don't startle him |
| que duelme la siguetito. | for the tiny boy is sleeping |
| Sesú, Sesú, que bonito, | Jesu, Jesu, how lovely, |
| scuchá, que cantamo lo angelito: | listen, for we are singing [like the] angels.[58] |

Cashner interprets "cantamo lo angelito" (we are singing [like the] angels) as a comparison between the Angolan choir's voices and seraphic song. An astute reading of a musical change supports his argument. The musicologist observes: "Just after Minguelillo says they will sing like the angels, the bass drops out and two voice parts enter that have thus far been silent: the two highest boys' voices of the second chorus, apparently representing the angels" (166). Cashner goes on to describe the polymetric exchange that makes this piece's Gloria singular within villancico repertoire of the time. Instead of following the same rhythmic structure for all parts, the composer sets the Angolan choir in triple meter (three beats per measure) and the heavenly one in duple (two beats per measure). Despite apparent metrical dissonance, imitative counterpoint, a compositional technique in which different voices sing variations on a melody with different timing, yokes the Afro-descendants to the angels, and the group sings in impeccable harmony. Cashner argues that in combination with the heavenly and Angolan singers, this section's complex rhythm makes worldly and sacred harmony audible and aligns Minguelillo and his followers with St. Michael the Archangel and his forces.[59] Continuing, Cashner details this section's rhythmic features and situates them within the music philosophy of the day. His analysis shows how score and lyric work together in villancicos to perform celestial harmony, which, in turn, resonated with New Spain's urban and sacred spaces, socio-political hierarchies, and more.

For all of these merits, however, Cashner overlooks the extended symbolism of the relationship that the piece establishes between Afro-descendants' vocal register to high-pitched celestial voices. Just as the Gloria's rhythms assimilate Angolan voices to Christian ideals, the soprano and alto doubling of the angelic choruses reinforces the two group's associations. As a castrato, Minguelillo's seraphic resonances would have been the strongest of the group. Murcian writer Francisco Cascales' letter to Gerónimo Martínez de Castro defending this vocal tradition clarifies:

> fuera de todo esto el oficio que [los hombres castrados] tienen en este mundo, es oficio de angeles, es cantar con la dulzura de los candidos cisnes, con los passages de los dulces ruiseñores, con la harmonia del celeste movimiento. ¡O tres veces felices i bien afortunados, a quienes naturaleza os dotó de una voz suave, regalada, subtil, graciosa música que nos arroba los sentidos, i hurta las almas!⁶⁰

> besides all of this the place that [castrated men] have in this world, it is the role of angels, singing with the sweetness of innocent swans, with the sweet passaggios of nightingales, with the harmony of celestial motion. ¡O thrice blessed and of good fortune, those who nature gifted with sweet voice and gentle, measured, elegant music that enchants the senses, and steals away souls!

Here, Cascales underscores inherent tensions in constructions of castrati, particularly in early modern culture, where vestiges of the music of the spheres persisted. In a subtle linkage of their deformed genitals and an adolescent or feminine lack of self-control, the emasculated bodies were associated with sexual excess.[61] And yet, the singers' well-ordered voices and striking beauty resonated with celestial harmony and aligned them with the highest spiritual planes, just as Cascales argues in his letter.[62] Such tensions deepen when it comes to enslaved, Afro-descendant capones. On one hand, early modern culture sometimes expresses racial inferiority through animalesque tropes. For instance, in a reading of villancicos from Peru and New Granada, Larissa Brewer-García has drawn out the mouth as a prominent site of beastly imaginings of Blackness.[63] On the other hand, however, depictions of castrati like in Cascales' epistle relate these singers to the highest beings by suggesting that their voices echo seraphic harmony. In sum, there is irreconcilable dissonance between the Afro-descendant eunuch singer's highly trained, angelic voice and his racial and gender ambiguity.

Minguelillo is ideal for appreciating these contradictions. Indeed, the opening description of his base, corporeal appetites and violent nature seem at odds with his angelic song. Cultural stereotypes about Afro-descendants' boisterousness and lasciviousness as well as their tendency toward rebellion heighten these dissonances and also become essential to the villancico's performance of Minguelillo's salvation. Precisely, the soprano soldier's voice transcends the worldly limits of his disabled, racialized body and aligns him with the heavens. Brewer-García frames gestures like this as part of the villancicos' evangelizing function: "the presence of black musicians in the performance of the villancicos would instantiate Christ's promise to save *all* the world, including the black men and women of the Americas."[64] Although Brewer-García refers to the immediate presence of Afro-descendant singers as co-creators of the roles that Spanish and Creole writers imagined for them, her observation usefully draws out the harmonization of actual capón voices (or their cultural memory) with heavenly accord in "Al establo más dichoso." The performance enacted the salvation of Minguelillo, his band, and the Afro-descendants that they represented and also underscored the enormous value of the Black castrato voice. As an instrument fashioned to the highest level of perfection, the Afro-descendant castrato sounded the possibility of tuning even the lowest bodies in the social hierarchy so that they might resonate with celestial harmony. From this position, it is easy to see how Luis Barreto, Juan de Vera, Juan Marín, and others might have been able to take advantage of this position in order to exercise new forms of agency within the constraints of dominant social hierarchies.

For all this, it is clear that "Al establo más dichoso" features a particular representation of Afro-descendant voices. Given this chapter's engagement with how embodied performance (or Taylor's repertoire) influenced the archive, a significant question remains about Gutiérrez de Padilla's composition: who were the performers, specifically in the *negrilla* section? Through meticulous archival work, Cashner has recovered the identity of many singers at the first staging of "Al establo más dichoso." Records indicate that a prepubescent Francisco Rodríguez played the role of Minguelillo, and Cashner indicates that, in fact, "the performers of the Puebla Cathedral ensemble in 1652 were apparently all men and boys of Spanish descent and high social standing, to judge from the names in a 1651 roster in the cathedral chapter acts."[65] If the observation is indeed correct, Minguelillo's treble part is nevertheless noteworthy. More than just a conventional trope of Blackness within the genre, Minguelillo's feminized voice recalls the earlier practice of training Afro-descendant sopranos as cathedral singers. The introduction's hypersexual portrayal of the Angolan heightens this vestige. Reading Black villancicos in this way is a significant advancement for understanding the ways Africans and Afro-Mexicans shaped New Spanish culture, and specifically, villancicos. Indeed, both the compositional practice of situating male Afro-descendant voices in unusual registers and timbral references throughout surviving villancico texts suggest that audiences expected the thrilling allure of a high-voiced male singer. Even if there were few enslaved capones by 1652, when Gutiérrez de Padilla penned the "Al establo más dichoso," the (blackface) boy soprano who played the Angolan is an echo of the Black voices who might have held the role some thirty to fifty years earlier.

As I have shown throughout this chapter, oblique readings of the music written for these voices can stand in for the embodied hums and breaths that a recording would capture. By relating actual Afro-descendant singers to auditory imaginings of Blackness in the texts and lyrics of New Spanish villancicos, my readings embody the acousmatic voices of musical scores and trace a history of mutual exchange between performer and genre. Just as the works of Fernández, Gutiérrez de Padilla, and others helped codify Afro-descendant sound and shaped the listening positions of their audiences, so they also responded to real, embodied singers whose voices informed the villancico's development in New Spain. Although the archive does not offer immediate access to the presence of Juan de Vera, Luis Barreto, or Juan Marín, attending to the absence of glossolalic disruption in their musical scores makes the imposition of a unified sonic narrative audible and highlights the dampened whispers and snorts that vocalize experiences beyond the archive's textual limits.[66]

### AFRO-DIASPORIC RESONANCES

Although we can only speculate about the sounds of the Afro-descendant voices that Black villancicos encode, examples from the post-recording era can offer some insight. For instance, Fiol-Matta's account of one of the first recordings to feature Afro–Puerto Rican contralto Ruth Fernández shares common themes with Morales Abril's suggestion that Gaspar Fernández composed Black roles with Juan de Vera's voice in mind. Among other resonances, Fernández's example can aid in imagining the powerful vocal presence of singers like Juan de Vera or Luis Barreto.

A trailblazer in Puerto Rican music, Ruth Fernández's stardom during the 1940s through the 1960s was comparable to that of Libertad Lamarque or Olga Guillot. Her performance venues range from the high-class Puerto Rican clubs where she performed with Mingo and His Whoopie Kids to a solo debut at Carnegie Hall (1960), and she appeared on radio throughout Puerto Rico and the United States, on the silver screen, and in the debut of Gonzalo Roig's operetta *Cecilia Valdés*, based on Cirilio Villaverdes's 1882 novel, which examines race relations in Cuba. Throughout the singer's career, voice, race, and gender were intimately linked to attempts to situate her within the canon. Fiol-Matta notes that Fernández was the earliest woman to front a Puerto Rican band and the island's first Black musical icon.[67] From these positions, her deep, distinctive voice, broad nose, and dark skin became emblems of Afro–Puerto Rican women's sound and symbols of a career that intermittently responded to and challenged audio-racial stereotypes.

Like Fiol-Matta argues, perceived distance between Fernández's rich contralto and her physical presentation as a Black woman opened fertile terrain for auditory reimaginings of gender and race. Within this context, Fiol-Matta maintains that the singer was not a mere observer, "mouthing racist descriptions," but rather an active agent in the construction of her own image.[68] Fernández capitalized upon her voice's unintelligibility within the cultural codes of the day and created a space from which to intervene in the island's changing political and artistic landscape. Fiol-Matta observes that

> listeners belonging to multiple publics regarded Fernández's voice as masculine, at a disjuncture or dissonance with her body. Fernández narrated how, when she was singing with Los Hijos del Arte (Art's offspring) on the radio, circa 1935, Domingo Colón, the bandleader of Mingo and His Whoopee Kids, heard her on the street an asked, "What is that? Is it a young man? Is it a woman?" The newly hybrid colonial society naturalized her deep voice with its mighty volume as one appropriate for a black woman, establishing an insidious connection between vocal register, race and beauty.[69]

In other words, incongruencies between Fernandez's female body and her bassoon-like voice made it possible for listeners to reconcile her sound and physical presence within existing cultural filters. In the Puerto Rican imagination of the 1930s and '40s, the singer's race tempered her discordant corporeal and vocal identities and opened new registers in a society that sought to redefine itself in the shadow of US imperialism.

Fernández negotiated her career from an identity perspective that can seem troubling or even conflicted. Fiol-Matta's reading of how the singer used her voice to disrupt racialized discourse, even while she appeared complicit in its perpetuation, can be useful for thinking about how the auditory and embodied presence of New Spain's Afro-descendant male sopranos resisted dominant racial narratives, albeit while singing from a subordinate, enslaved position. In 1941, Fernández recorded "Y tu abuela onde etá," Domingo "Mingo" Colón's setting of one of Fortunato Vizcarrondo's *negrista* poems. Fiol-Matta argues that the recording contributed to Afro-sonic imaginings of the star: "this is no small detail since the poem's speaker is masculine, resonating with his initial confusion as to whether Fernández's voice was masculine. Colón explicitly linked Fernández's voice to Black sound, using the acoustic coordinates supplied by Afro-Caribbean poetry to implant this identification."[70] Nevertheless, Fiol-Matta remarks upon Fernández's extra-linguistic interventions, including "phrases such as 'mi bien' (my sweet) and sonorous elements such as humming, snickering."[71] Like de Certeau's glossolalia, the singer's embodied presence vocalizes itself here and transgresses the "major voice" of Vizcarrondo's poem and Colón's musical imagining. In this instance, Fernández's song exists as pure voice, fully embodied and freed from discourse's lingual discipline.

Despite geographic and historical distance, I maintain that Fernández's story can resonate with the experiences of singers like Luis Barreto and Juan de Vera. In the context of these seventeenth-century singers, the written archive stands in for recordings that would allow present-day listeners to appreciate their immense vocal dexterity and power. To be certain, lettered accounts of Black sopranos capture the major voice and consequently mute what de Certeau calls glossolalia: "the cracks of ordinary conversation: bodily noises, quotations of delinquent sounds, and fragments of others' voices [that] punctuate the order of sentences with breaks and surprises."[72] Indeed, official records inventory expenses associated with the singers and index their performance. Consequently, Afro-descendant voices emerge as commodities and instruments, and scholars have little access to the actual sounds of these well-trained singers.

## CONCLUSION

In his reading of "Al establo más dichoso," Cashner argues: "The *ensaladilla*, taken by itself, is a window into Spanish attitudes, not a record of subaltern voices. If anything, it is a document of how the Spanish *suppressed* those voices, by speaking for them and controlling their representation."[73] In response, the musicologist has situated Gutiérrez de Padilla's piece more fully within the social and cultural fabric of seventeenth-century Puebla de los Ángeles by presenting the piece's diverse characters as echoes of real Black and Indigenous figures with whom the composer had contact, including his *indio* apprentice Pedro Martín and his own Afro-descendant slave Juan Angola. In this chapter, I extended Cashner's historical contextualization to argue that in addition to subjects with whom Gutiérrez de Padilla and other artists had direct contact, their works are valuable records of colonial listening positions that can lend insight into audio-racial constructions of Afro-descent in New Spain and beyond. By attending to these resonances, scholars can relate musical characteristics in villancicos and other pieces to the presence of Afro-descendant musicians in sacred ceremonies. Such insights push colonial Latin American musicology and cultural studies in new directions. Instead of listening to Blackness through the sonic filter of an African "other," a tempting practice to which musicologists like Robert Stevenson and performers like the San Antonio Vocal Arts Ensemble have fallen prey, my analysis hears the rich and significant contributions of Black and African voices in cathedral sound culture and thus challenges Eurocentric readings of this tradition.[74]

To be certain, none of this helps us to escape the problematic nature of villancico representations of Afro-descent. Nevertheless, deliberately silencing these pieces within our musical and cultural canons is not an adequate response to the challenges that they present. Instead, Cashner argues that "both scholars and performers have an ethical responsibility to try to understand the work these pieces did in colonial society and to assess the work they can do when unleashed in our communities."[75] From the perspective of music and cultural scholarship, oblique readings like this chapter presents illustrate how these sources contribute to our understanding of Afro-descent in New Spain and elsewhere. As I have shown, careful consideration of the actual voices that persist in pieces like "Andrés do queda el ganado" or "Al establo más dichoso" can highlight how Black, African, and other marginalized figures shaped these genres and thus frames them as co-creators of an embodied, percussive text that disrupts the dominant narratives of the lettered archive. In this way, my reading in this chapter opens new interpretative pathways for attending to Afro-descendant presence within New Spain's cultural and social hierarchies.

CHAPTER 3

# Harmonizing Blackness in Urban Political Ceremonies

One of the cosmopolitan centers of the Spanish empire, seventeenth-century Mexico City was a nexus of transatlantic exchange among Europeans, native Americans, Africans, and other travelers who passed through the region along the Manila Galleon trade route. While such diversity was a hallmark of the vibrant, bustling cityscape, it also challenged European ideals of urban accord. This spatial and socio-political model had roots in neo-Platonic harmony, a philosophical approach that viewed musical, physical, spiritual, or interpersonal consonance as a product of perfect, mathematical ratios. In *Viaje a la Nueva España* (1699), Italian explorer Giovanni Francesco Gemelli Careri describes the city's harmonious form.

> La ciudad está fundada en un casi perfecto plano, cerca o mejor dicho, en medio de la laguna, y así sus fábricas, por la poca firmeza del terreno, están medio sepultadas, a despecho de los habitantes, que procuran hacer bastante sólidos los cimientos. Su figura es cuadrada, y parece un tablero, a causa de que sus calles son rectas, y así mismo largas, bien empedradas, y están puestas hacia los cuatro vientos cardinales: por lo cual no solamente desde el centro, como Palmero desde su fortaleza, mas desde cualquiera otra parte se ve casi toda entera. Su circunferencia es de dos leguas, y cerca de media su diámetro, pues casi forma un perfecto cuadrado.[1]

> The city is built with a nearly perfect design, close, or rather, in the middle of the lake, and thus its buildings, because of the land's instability, are half buried, in spite of the inhabitants, who are able to build fairly solid foundations. Its shape is square, and it looks like a chess board, because its streets are straight, and at the same time long, well paved, and are placed toward the four

cardinal points: for this reason not only from the center, like Palermo from its fortress, but from any other point the city can be seen in its entirety. Its circumference is two leagues, and close to half of its diameter, thus, it almost forms a perfect square.

The geometric space that Gemelli Careri outlines responds to ideals of spatial and civic harmony. Renaissance humanists inherited such concepts from Antiquity thinkers like Plato and Hippodamus and applied them to urban planning in the Americas. The result was what Ángel Rama calls "the ubiquitous checkerboard grid," a quadrangular arrangement of physical space (*urbs*) that was intended to encourage social order (*civitas*).[2]

Mexico City's symbolic layout reinforced hierarchies of race and class and visually buttressed Spanish authority. The cathedral and viceregal palace loomed over the *zócalo* (central square), the heart of civic gatherings and commerce. There, they served as twin nuclei and reminders of political and ecclesiastic power. Wealthy convents and the homes of Spanish noblemen and -women filled the surrounding neighborhoods. Farther afield, on the urban outskirts, Indigenous and Afro-descendant citizens made their homes in separate communities. As we shall see, colonial officials frowned upon extensive contact among these groups, and numerous prohibitions cautioned against intercultural exchange. In all likelihood, such decrees are a manifestation of anxiety about rebellion among the lower castes, for Black, African, and autochthonous people, and their descendants, far outnumbered New Spain's Spanish and Creole population. Gemelli Careri himself estimates "tendrá México cerca de cien mil habitantes; pero la mayor parte negros y mulatos, ya por los muchos esclavos que son llevados allí" (Mexico must have close to one hundred thousand inhabitants; but most are *negros* and *mulatos,* because of how many slaves are taken there).[3] Whether or not his population estimates are accurate, Gemelli Careri's emphasis on the region's large Black and African community aligns with Herman Bennett's affirmation that by the mid- to late seventeenth century, Afro-descendants and their culture were entrenched prominently throughout New Spain.[4]

While maps and official documents imagine Mexico City's physical and social organization as highly stratified, in everyday life, residents from all walks of life came into contact in the *zócalo* and other communal areas. Ignacio Martínez argues that

> it would be a misrepresentation, however, to suggest that European elites physically dominated the center of the colonial cities. Quite the opposite. While it was true that they preferred to live closest to the main plaza, the plaza

was daily filled with Indians, blacks and mixed raced people who could be seen working, buying goods for themselves or their masters, getting drunk in taverns and engaging in romantic liaisons.[5]

Within this diverse cityscape, Martínez observes that the arrangement of diverse bodies in public spaces further reinforced social hierarchy. The sequence of participants in a procession, style of dress for religious holidays, or the seats that a particular group occupied at mass were visual symbols of position and rank.

Scholars of colonial Latin America often consider urban space in visual terms, in part because maps and written representations of sixteenth- and seventeenth-century cityscapes lend themselves to such analyses. Rama's paradigm of the "lettered city" further solidified the privileging of inscribed constructions of urban space over oral ones. He wrote: "in Latin America, the written word became the only binding one—in contradistinction to the spoken word, which belonged to the realm of things precarious and uncertain."[6] To be certain, New Spain's lettered elite sought to exercise control through written decrees, correspondence with Peninsular authorities, and indeed, the imposition of a writing system to which native Americans, Africans, and other marginalized groups had less access. In this sense, script's timelessness and its proximity to *logos* offered a certain advantage, for in Western philosophy, they were tied to concepts like rational thought, law, and truth.

In contrast, orality, speech, music-making, and other sonic interventions were ephemeral expressions whose very sonority eluded lettered authority. Precisely because of this distance, the auditory offered a means by which subaltern figures in New Spain and other colonial Latin American regions could reinforce community identities and preserve cultural memory. Indeed, as the next two chapters will show, Black and African people in New Spain found ways to sound Afro-diasporic traditions from within Euro-sonic codes that the colonial elite imposed. In written accounts, these audio legacies do not stand out as "different," like one might expect. Rather, they resonate in harmony with dominant expectations about the role of Afro-descendant voices in urban New Spain.

I continue with a simple but noteworthy observation. Seventeenth-century Mexico City was not the silent, rhetorical map that Gemelli Careri inscribes in his journal. Rather, it was a noisy, clamorous space, filled with multiethnic voices that rang out in consonance or dissonance with the city's harmonic grid and its accompanying sounds. As I noted in the introduction, Baker attends to neo-Platonic concord's importance for understanding how resonant imaginings of Mexico City relate to lively performances that took place throughout the viceregal capital. Precisely, he hears the urban setting as an audible grid whose resonances harmonize the city. Inasmuch as architecture and urban planning enacted an ordering of the cityscape and all of its residents, so music-making and performance in the civic space endeavored to harmonize New Spain's Indigenous, Black, and African population with elite ideologies via sonic ritual. This concept guides my interpretations of the civic and ideological resonances of Afro-descendant harmonies in lettered accounts.

In the next two chapters, the sonic filter of harmony enables an appreciation of how the trope figured sociopolitical relationships among different factions of New Spanish society and also amplifies the ways Afro-descendants performed in accord with elite expectations. In his reading of the role of Catholicism in the formation of Afro-Atlantic identities, Jeroen Dewulf maintains that "the adoption of Iberian cultural elements by Africans, as such, should be understood not as a sign of friendship, but rather as a conviction that siding with the powerful created new opportunities, increased one's prestige, and made one less vulnerable in a world where only the strongest survived."[7] Along similar lines, I read the apparent concord of the Afro-Mexican performances with European traditions that the next few chapters examine as examples of how the region's Black and African people negotiated from within established hierarchies to create audible spaces for themselves.

As part of New Spain's urban sound culture, ecclesiastical and political authorities endorsed performances that served as audible counterpoint to inscribed hegemonies. These included commercial theater as well as staged productions in convents and the viceregal court, lavish civic celebrations that commemorated the entry of prominent political and ecclesiastical leaders. Among other elements, these festivities included the staging of villancicos. While written and painted representations lend insight into performances and festive practices, the perspectives of the lettered elite who pen these sources can muddle their portrayal of popular or marginalized cultural expression. Taylor draws out the epistemological distance between inscribed records (the archive) and embodied performance (the repertoire). She maintains that facile dichotomies of power/repression condition scholarly reception of these materials and mute their polyphony.[8] In response, scholars like Dewulf, Cécile Fromont, Jones, Ndiaye, Valerio, and Lisa Voigt have attended to intersecting forms of agency and meaning-making in early Atlantic rituals and performance traditions long considered through Eurocentric lenses.

Here, I complement their work with a focus on Afro-descendant presence and its accompanying sounds in political ceremonies (Chapter 3) and religious ones (Chapter 4), largely held in Mexico City and Puebla, two of New Spain's largest urban centers. At first hearing, the sonic interventions of Black and African performers in these settings appear to harmonize with European-derived traditions and expectations. Nonetheless, I will argue that such concord is actually the result of complex negotiations undertaken in order to preserve Afro-descendant cultural expression by aligning it with dominant sonorities.

## THE POLITICS OF REPRESENTING AFRO-DESCENDANT SOUND

For scholars of sixteenth- and seventeenth-century New Spain, there is no shortage of evidence that Black and African residents intervened in the region's sonic practices. Indeed, these people were far from silent. They sang, made music, and danced in public and private settings. Dance troupes performed at political ceremonies and in the homes of noble families, and by all accounts, Afro-descendant horsemen were star performers in equestrian ballets. Confraternities hired horn players, singers, and other musicians to accompany their processions on feast days like Corpus Christi or during Holy Week. In contrast with these sanctioned displays of devotion, Inquisition cases and official decrees suggest the prevalence of popular religious practices featuring music and dance, including clandestine oratorios. While participants from a variety of social and racial backgrounds took part in these colorful celebrations, some records pinpoint Black hosts and guests.

For all this, the persistence of African sound traditions in New Spain seems inevitable. Indeed, early performers must have drawn upon forms of musical and oral expression from their countries of origin and passed such knowledge on to their descendants. Nevertheless, primary sources offer scant evidence for how such music might have sounded. Indeed, surviving descriptions of Afro-descendant sound in New Spain are etic accounts, whose authors lack the language or cultural knowledge to articulate the nuances of non-European sound traditions. While such lacunae are frustrating, it is important to bear in mind that the archive is not at all silent before Black and African sonorities in New Spain. On the contrary, tropes of consonance and dissonance guide imaginings of Afro-descendant sound and lend insight into how it resonated with or threatened the order of the urban imaginary.

Representations of Black and African song and dance frequently relate to the underlying ideology that frames their source. For instance, in a hagiographic biography of Bishop of Puebla Juan de Palafox y Mendoza, Gregorio de Argaiz underscores music-making as a symbol of Black and African residents' devotion to the bishop:

Son los negros, (como lo conocen y saben todas las naciones de Europa), las criaturas más alegres que entre las racionales ha creado Dios, y perdidas por la música, sea de cualquier instrumento. Había en la Puebla grande número de ellos, que eran el regocijo de la ciudad en los días de fiesta; porque como en los demás sirven como esclavos, en las fiestas descansan y se ocupan en danzar y bailar al son de instrumentos de cualquier género que sean; llegando a tanto que traen por la cintura colgadas muchas calabacitas pequeñas, porque tocándose unas con otras cuando anda, y moviéndolas ellos con los dedos, como quien toca una ginebrilla, se satisfacen y alegran con aquel ruido a falta de otra música. Pues amaban tanto a don Juan de Palafox, que desde el día que faltó de la Puebla, no se oyó música de negros en las plazas y calles, ni instrumento suyo; no se vio negro que danzase ni bailase ni cantar. Y preguntándoles la justicia seglar que por qué no alegraban la ciudad y las fiestas, como solían, respondían que como habían de cantar y tañer, cómo alegrarse faltando su padre *Jan de Calajós*. Con esta tristeza, silencio y melancolía pasaron en todos los cinco meses más alegres del año en aquellas partes, diciendo con el rostro y semblante lo que con las palabras.[9]

The *negros* are (just as all European countries know), the happiest rational creatures that God has created, and music of any kind makes them lose their senses. There were a lot of them in Puebla, and they were the joy of the city on festival days; because since they serve as slaves on other days, on festival days they rest and occupy themselves dancing to the sound of whatever kinds of instruments they have; they wear small gourds around their waists because they bump against each other when they move around, and they also move them with their fingers, like someone playing a ginebra [a simple percussion instrument made of sticks], they are satisfied and happy with that noise when there is no other music. They all loved Juan de Palafox so much that since the day that he left Puebla, no *negro* music was heard in the plazas and streets, nor any of their instruments; and no *negro* was seen dancing or singing. And when the magistrate asked them why they did not liven up the city and festivals like they used to, they responded, asking how could they dance and play music, how could they be happy without their father Jan de Calajós. In these parts, they all passed the five happiest months of the year in sadness, silence, and melancholy, with their faces echoing the sentiments they uttered.

To be certain, this passage offers a positive view of African and Afro-Mexican performers in New Spain's urban spaces. The enslaved, Afro-descendant musicians that Argaiz imagines happily participate in the city's ritual sound practices, resting on Sundays and feast days, just as *poblano* mandates indicated. Presumably, they take part in performances that harmonically reinforce the political and ecclesiastical ideals of the elite patrons who funded such spectacles.

The passage offers scant musical details, and the performer's crude instruments resonate with their construction as impoverished, non-European subjects whose uncontrollable love of song and dance is safely contained as part of "official" festival culture. However, Argaiz's portrayal of Afro-descendant music is more than a proto-ethnographic account. The chronicler's depiction draws upon neo-Platonic concepts of political accord, which imagine a leader's moral composure as internal harmony (*musica humana*) with the capacity to provoke sympathetic reactions within his or her subjects.[10] Interpreted through this lens, Argaiz's biography depicts the joyful Afro-Mexican music that distinguishes Puebla's sonic environment as a resonance of the bishop's balanced governance and accompanying social harmonies.

In contrast with the favorable portrayal of Afro-descendant music in the previous passage, other references use auditory tropes to describe the disruptive presence of Black and African people. There is a representative example of this tendency in a 1596 document titled "Consulta del consejo de las Indias sobre los servicios personales de los indios" (Guidance from the Council of the Indies about the personal services of the *indios*). Among other recommendations for the positive treatment of Amerindians, a passage near the end discourages contact with free Afro-descendants. Precisely, the text counsels against idleness among lower castes, who are prone to drunkenness and excess. In addition to Indigenous people, rampant vice among "los negros libres, mulatos y zambahigos que turban la paz y quietud de la república con sus vicios y malas costumbres" (free *negros*, *mulatos* and *zambaigos* that disturb the peace and quiet of the republic with their vice and bad habits) also threatens social order.[11] Continuing, the enquiry suggests that segregating Amerindians from Black and African people can diminish the immoral influence of Afro-descendants. The contrast between Argaiz's representation of Black music and disparaging remarks about disorder in the 1596 *consulta* illustrates a salient relationship among harmony, social order, and urban space that resonates with representations of Afro-Mexican sound in seventeenth-century New Spain.

As the examples in this chapter will illustrate, Afro-descendants living in New Spanish cities took part in ceremonies that performed political authority and reinforced social hierarchies. Although music-making and dance were important parts of such spectacles, primary accounts offer few details about exact sounds or choreography. Close readings of these sources can lend some generalized insights, particularly when compared to examples of Afro-Mexican sound in other seventeenth-century political festivals. Regardless of whether Black and African people presented Euro-descendant, diasporic, or even Indigenous genres at these events, elements from their performance harmonized voices and bodies as some of the lowest in the region's social order. As I will argue here, such marginal imaginings contrasted with the manner in which political celebrations centered Black performance in key public spaces. Just as in the case of cathedral singers, this dissonance enabled Afro-descendants to negotiate spaces of audibility within a setting of consonant performance. In this context, it was possible for singers and dancers to preserve elements of their sonic heritage. Indeed, subtle references from primary sources suggest that they did just that.

### HARMONIC BODIES AND VOICES IN *FESTÍN HECHO POR LAS MORENAS CRIOLLAS DE LA MUY NOBLE Y MUY LEAL CIUDAD DE MÉXICO . . .*

One of the most noteworthy examples Afro-descendant performance in a political context is the dance that a troupe of *morenas criollas*—free Black women—from Mexico City performed for the newly appointed viceroy, Don Diego López Pacheco Cabrera y Bobadilla, marquis of Villena, duke of Escalona. In 1640, cities and villages throughout New Spain organized a two-month series of performances to pay tribute to López Pacheco as he entered the territory. The nobleman was one of the highest-ranking dignitaries to lead New Spain, and by all accounts, the region's inhabitants were enthusiastic about his appointment. According to Dalia Hernández Reyes, Felipe IV designated an official of López Pacheco's stature to lead New Spain with the expectation that his authority would ease political and economic tensions.[12] In light of the viceroy's unprecedented standing, his arrival was met with great anticipation. The spectacles that commemorated López Pacheco's entrance were some of the grandest events that the region had ever seen, and in 1640, all of the accompanying texts and accounts of performances were published as a *Sammelband*, or composite volume, called *Viage de tierra, y mar*. The anthology opens with Christóbal Gutiérrez de Medina's account of López Pacheco's journey, *Viage de tierra, y mar*, which detailed the nobleman's transatlantic voyage and the municipal celebrations organized in his honor. Following Gutiérrez de Medina's account, the collection includes the accompanying text for a triumphal arch that honored López Pacheco, a set of virtues, a *loa* that the Compañía de Jesús performed, Creole author María de Estrada Medinilla's festive verse, and cleric Nicolás de Torres' description of a danced homage that featured a group of free, Afro-descendant women.

The poems, scripts, and descriptions contained in *Viage de tierra, y mar* offer a window into the Mexico City celebrations for López Pacheco, and Gutiérrez de Medina's *relación* narrates political spectacles that welcomed the new viceroy as he traveled through other New Spanish cities. Indeed, during a two-moth journey from the Veracruz port to his residence in the viceregal capital, López Pacheco was treated to lavish festivals with vibrant displays of local color and aspirations of political harmony. These spectacles included military processions, bullfights, mock equestrian battles known as *juegos de cañas*, floats, fireworks, music, and courtly and Indigenous dance. In an echo of Argaiz's description of Palafox y Mendoza's influence upon Black music-making in Puebla, Gutiérrez de Medina frequently underscores participants' jubilant merrymaking during López Pacheco's entry as a sign of their obedience to Spanish authority. For example, his description of the nobleman's passages through Tlaxcala begins with a reminder of the city's historical importance in the region's conquest:

> Es obligacion precisa de los Virreyes, el pasar por esta Ciudad de Tlaxcala, y priuilegio suyo, por auer sido la Cabeça deste Reyno, y auer ayudado particularmente sus Naturales a su conquista, y por esto es costumbre venir aqui todos los Tribunales de Ciudades, Inquisicion, Cabildos de Iglesias, Tribunales de Cuentas, y Oficiales Reales a dar la bienvenida a los señores Virreyes como la dieron a su Ex.[13]

> Passing through Tlaxcala is a Viceroy's essential obligation and privilege, for having been the Capital of this Kingdom, and because its Citizens aided in its conquest, it is customary that all of the City Courts, Inquisition, Church Councils, Courts of Auditors, and Royal Officials come here to welcome Viceroys, just like they did his Excellency.

Here, Gutiérrez de Medina refers to the Tlaxcalan alliance with Spain in order to defeat the Mexica inhabitants of Tenochtitlán, with whom they had a longstanding rivalry. In *Viage de tierra, y mar*, the chronicler's allusion to these events highlights López Pacheco's authority before the region's Indigenous population.

In a subsequent description of the city's welcoming procession, Gutiérrez de Medina emphasizes the joyful response of autochthonous groups and portrays their exuberant song and dance as an outward expression of happy obedience.

los Indios nobles no dexaron de mostrar a su vsança la alegria que sentían, con vn castillo de chichimecos, que desnudos salían a pelear con fieras, haciendo tocotines, y mitotes, que son sus saraos antiguos con muchas galas a su vsança, y muchas plumas preciosas de que forman alas, diademas, y aguilas que llevan sobre la cabeça, y desta suerte en tropas cantando en su idioma estauan todo el dia sin cansarse en su sarao dançando.[14]

the noble *Indios* did not cease to demonstrate in their way the happiness that they felt, with a float of Chichemecas, who came out naked to fight with wild beasts, performing *tocotines*, and *mitotes*, which are their ancient dances in a very elegant style, and many precious feathers that form wings, diadems, and eagles that they wear on their heads, and they spent the whole day in this manner without tiring, singing in groups in their language and dancing their sarao.

These lines frame the persistence of Indigenous traditions as a sign of native devotion to the viceroy. At first glance, tropes of barbarian representation stand out, like, for instance the nude performers, whose fierce combat is just one step removed from the wild brutes that they battle. In contrast, the author characterizes the Chichimecas' dance as refined and graceful. His use of the word *sarao*, a courtly dance form that often took place in Spanish civic celebrations, lends a political significance to traditions like the *tocotín* and *mitote* and frames them as a response to López Pacheco's authority. This apparent opposition is noteworthy, for the transformation of Indigenous bodies from uncontrollable to refined performs the taming of the region's disparate social factions at the incoming viceroy's hand. The description's musical context is relevant to this chapter's discussion of urban concord, and it beckons a reading of Gutiérrez de Medina's text as a means of harmonizing New Spain's diverse bodies and voices. Furthermore, the incorporation of native sound traditions in the viceroy's entry hints at the possible incorporation of Afro-descendant sonorities as well.

Themes of political consonance are salient throughout *Viage de tierra, y mar*. Their relationship with Afro-descent is especially relevant for this book's discussions. Indeed, links among harmony, Blackness, and performance stand out in one of the last sections of Gutierrez de Medina's *relación*: *Festín hecho por las morenas criollas de la muy noble y muy leal Ciudad de México al recibimiento, y entrada del Excellentísimo Señor Marqués de Villena, Duque de Escalona, Virrey de esta Nueva España* (Celebration performed by the *morenas criollas* of the most noble and most loyal Mexico City for the reception and entry of the Most Excellent Señor Marquis of Villena, Duke of Escalona, Viceroy of this New Spain, 1640). Cleric Nicolás de Torres authored this festival text, which describes the performance that a group of Afro-descendant women gave to honor López Pacheco. The event took place in the semi-private viceregal palace, likely with sacred and secular officials in attendance. It featured a troupe of twelve dancers, who were dressed in lavish costumes of gold-threaded cloth. They carried banners with emblems on one side and poetry on the other and knelt before the viceroy to present them. For all this, *Festín*'s harmonious description of Afro-descendant performance offers intriguing counterpoint to depictions of Black and African people as dissonant within New Spain's concordant settings.

*Festín* is notable for its detailed account of Black women's performance, a rarity among seventeenth-century sources. Dalia Hernández Reyes highlights the singularity of Torres' *relación* among other textual inscriptions of Afro-descent in the New Spanish archive.

> La omisión frecuente [de la presencia afrodescendiente] en la oficialidad del impreso refleja quizá el lugar que la comunidad negra tenía en la sociedad novohispana: el más bajo debido a su condición de esclavos, pues aunque sus descendientes (mulatos, morenos, criollos y castas) o ellos mismos lograran obtener su libertad, lo cierto es que el estigma de la esclavitud siempre estuvo presente en la mentalidad del estrato social dominante. Por otra parte, las características físicas y lingüísticas, así como muchas de las costumbres de este grupo étnico fueron vistas—muchas veces con el propósito de justificar la esclavitud—como señal de inferioridad intelectual y de acusada inmoralidad.[15]

> The frequent omission [of Afro-descendant presence] in official print perhaps reflects the role that the Black community occupied in New Spanish society: the lowest due to its enslaved condition, even though community members themselves or their descendants (*mulatos*, *morenos*, *criollos*, and *castas*) were able to obtain their freedom, the truth is that the stigma of slavery was always present in the mentality of the dominant social class. Furthermore, their physical and linguistic characteristics, like many of this group's traditions were seen—often with the goal of justifying slavery—as signs of intellectual inferiority and the immorality of which they were accused.

As Hernández Reyes alludes here, Torres' text offers rich contrast with the derogatory and patronizing representations that abounded in other staged representations of Blackness, including villancicos, which I will discuss presently. Consequently, *Festín* offers valuable counterpoint that can help to understand diverse inscriptions of Afro-descent. As we shall see, such scriptings do not always appear as stilted caricatures but nevertheless often respond to the social and political perspectives of New Spain's elite. Furthermore, as a historical document, *Festín* can lend insight into Afro-descendant participation in the region's extensive festival culture.

Torres' text describes a procession of Afro-descendant Creole (American-born) women who staged a performance to celebrate the dignitary's arrival. Through music, dance, elaborate costuming, poetry, and emblems, the women told the story of the Queen of Sheba's encounter with the Israelite King Solomon. As the Biblical history goes, a beautiful female monarch heard intriguing stories of the monarch's sagacity. Laden with gifts of jewels and spice, the queen traveled from her wealthy kingdom of Saba—situated in present-day Yemen or Ethiopia—to Jerusalem in order to meet the leader and learn about his wisdom. During her visit, the Sabean ruler tested Solomon's knowledge with a series of riddles about his theological convictions. His responses impressed the queen so much that she adopted Judaism and spread the faith throughout her own kingdom. In some interpretations, notably the Ethiopian epic *Kebra Nagast*, the Queen of Sheba's devotion is spiritual and sexual, for the monarch offers her body to Solomon. Together, they bear a son, Menelik, who became the first ruler of the Solomonic dynasty of Ethiopia.

For Valerio, *Festín*'s engagement with the Queen of Sheba was not happenstance. Indeed, he relates the Queen of Sheba to the performers' agency and argues that by linking the Biblical figure to the Afro-descendant performers, *Festín* emphasized the Black and African community's inheritance of Christian faith and also highlighted the women's physical beauty and leadership within their communities.[16] The observation is sharp, and Valerio's comments underscore the rich polysemy of Baroque performance, which can give voice to a variety of perspectives. From another perspective, however, *Festín* also suggests the queen's submission to Solomon. Indeed, bodily gestures and postures and references to the viceroy's authority as a harmonizing force underscore the performers' obedience to New Spain's new leader. While it would be easy to criticize such a perspective as narrow-minded or accuse it of muting the dancers' agency, like I argued in Chapters 1 and 2, this conformity with the social and political expectations of the ruling class is a significant aspect of Afro-descendant negotiation of audible spaces. Precisely, it is this apparent concordance that allows for such prominent staging of the Afro-Mexican consciousness that Valerio underscores.

Like many Baroque festive practices and the texts or visual art that record them, the 1640 performance to honor New Spain's new viceroy invites readings from various angles, particularly in light of the performers' African heritage. Linda Curcio-Nagy reads the piece as a mechanism for reiterating the role of marginalized subjects within colonial hierarchies. She explains that

> the participation of representative Native American and Afro-Mexicans in the festivals reaffirmed the official vision of an idealized colonial polity that was both hierarchical and unified.... In this case, different groups participated as separate entities but were joined by their acceptance and recognition of Spanish superiority. The message embedded in the festivals suggested that to do so would benefit spectators personally. In this fashion, participants were put forth as a type of colonial "success story." They represented select and privileged groups who through their participation bolstered their own positions, solidified patronage ties to the city councilmen and the viceroy, and earned the esteem of their own ethnic groups.[17]

In an echo of Maravallian guided culture, which channeled Baroque marvel and excess into vehicles for disseminating elite interests, Curcio-Nagy underscores *Festín* as an example of the socio-political harmonization of Afro-descendants. Although this analysis compellingly resonates with the alignment of power and spectacle in New Spain, it leaves little room for considering how marginalized groups confirmed or resisted the identities that such works performed.[18]

In contrast with Curcio-Nagy's remarks, Valerio draws attention to the ways that *Festín* afforded the dancers agency. While it is difficult to determine the degree to which the performers took part in the creative and administrative details of their staged welcome, he compellingly suggests that Torres penned the dance's accompanying script, and the Afro-descendant women themselves organized the choreography, props, and other details, possibly in conjunction with a confraternity.[19] Furthermore, he suggests that the women supported the publication of Torres' text, perhaps even financially, as a means of gaining visibility.[20] For all this, Valerio maintains that the women's participation in the welcoming celebrations for López Pacheco and their potential role in the publication of Torres account were strategies for increasing personal visibility, and perhaps, that of the lay organization to which he argues that they belonged.

> In sum, both the women's performance and Torres' text constitute an invaluable testament to Afro-Mexican women's social agency in colonial Mexico, especially seventeenth-century Mexico City. Not only did they manage to

perform before the highest authority in the land, but they may have also sponsored the publication of the text that immortalized their performance—to borrow Torres' allegory, a Herculean feat given the oppressive sociohistorical context in which they lived. In their performance, the women put in motion their cultural awareness. They selected a legendary feminine figure that allowed them to perform their sexuality within an acceptable signifier—loyalty to the viceroy and everything he represented. Their dance included cultural elements that underscored their Black creole identity—a syncretism of African, European, and American cultural elements, such as the black hand charm, the phoenix, and the eagle. In the end, then, the women did not perform vassalage, as Curcio-Nagy contends, but rather sexuality, cultural identity, and power—demonstrating, through it all, a good grasp of Hispanic baroque culture.[21]

Valerio's reading echoes Chapter 1's discussion of how cathedral high-voiced singers amplified their audibility through exemplary performance that corresponded with dominant political and spiritual ideologies. His remarks here highlight three interrelated modes of agency: writing, visual symbolism, and embodied performance. Like the symbols that Valerio highlights, this hybrid political spectacle is also a product of syncretism that responded to the pluricultural audience of New Spain's capital. Indeed, the women's multimodal presentation resonates with diverse methods for performing authority and historicizing the past. Among others, these include Europe's lettered tradition as well as the political spectacles that were popular during the time, Amerindian pictographic chronicles, and West African griots.

Here, I complement Valerio's observations by considering how Torres' description inscribes the Black performers as resonances of urban and political harmonies. In particular, my interpretation focuses on *Festín*'s concordant inscription of Afro-descendant bodies and voices. This section's central claim is that such representations intersect with sonorous imaginings of political power in early modern culture. From this perspective, I read the women's inscription as consistent with López Pacheco's authority not only as a resonance of Spanish officials' desire to assuage social tensions in the region but also as a strategy for harmonizing Afro-descendant bodies and voices in agreement with dominant expectations so as to support their participation in these important celebrations. The dancers' embodied and vocal harmony—inasmuch as the text and emblems they carried inscribe their voices, albeit from a dominant perspective—amplify the performers' presence in a venue to which they may not otherwise have had access. In this way, the *Festín* dancers echo the Afro-descendant capones that Chapters 1 and 2 examined. Through exemplary consonance with the harmonic structures that undergird *urbs* and *civitas*, the dancers perform their obedience to the viceroy and also gain an opportunity to center their bodies and voices in a prominent venue.

With respect to *Festín*, it is first important to consider the performance's physical context and its sociopolitical resonances. The event took place in the viceregal palace, in a semi-private setting before an audience of the capital's elite. Given this setting, Valerio comments that the performance elements were tuned for the high-ranking members of New Spanish society who were in attendance.[22] Consequently, *Festín* beckons a reading that accounts for the multiple perspectives that it encodes. Voigt reflects upon how scholarship on plurivocity challenges reductive dichotomies of power and margin. She notes that

> more recent studies, mine included, have found multiple non-hegemonic motives and meanings in festivals and their accounts, not so much by uncovering a "hidden transcript"—disguised or out of view of the powerful—but by showing how non-elite groups participated in public celebrations and even the publication of festival accounts in ways that served their own purposes, even if they did not necessarily subvert those of the elite.[23]

Along the same lines, an interpretation attuned to textual polysemy can reveal that Torres' account not only represents the perspective of the elite, lettered class but also illustrates how marginalized groups like *Festín*'s Afro-descendant protagonists worked within established cultural codes to heighten their visibility in some of New Spain's most prominent venues. Valerio's careful analysis of *Festín*'s relationship with Black women's authority is the first approach to this text that attends to such features. Here, I extend his observations with an interpretation that focuses on links among harmony, socio-political space, and Afro-descent.

For all this, it becomes important to consider how Torres's text inscribes Black bodies and voices, especially within the urban political harmonies that Baker signals. Prior research has debated the significance of Afro-descendant women's embodied presence in *Festín*, particularly with respect to the connections between danced expression and race. Curcio-Nagy contends that Afro-descendant women's danced expression in religious and civic rituals was not singular to the festivities for López Pacheco's entry. She observes that despite a lack of detailed documentation, Black and African performers took part in civic and religious ceremonies from the viceroyalty's earliest days. In fact, she remarks that Afro-descendant woman dancers regularly took part in public and private processions, and one group even won a monetary award for their performance in the 1583 Corpus Christi parade.[24] Furthermore, beyond the embodied presence of female dancers in ceremonies, it is also important to consider the persistence of sub-Saharan traditions in popular dances that were an important part of the transatlantic cultural exchange.

For all this, research has debated interpretative perspectives on the dance that *Festín* describes. Dichotomies of Western/non-Western or European/African shape these readings and challenge contemporary engagement with lettered accounts of the *morenas criollas*' embodied presence. For instance, Hernández Reyes inserts the women's performance within the European tradition and argues that it was a *sarao*, a courtly dance form with music, poetry, and elaborate costumes that often accompanied political processions. Within this context, she notes that

> la peculiaridad de esta pequeña fiesta radica en el origen africano de las ejecutantes. Puesto que la población negra ocupaba el último lugar en la jerarquía social novohispana, y debido a los estereotipos degradantes que sobre ésta se generaron a partir de la descalificación moral provocada por la incomprensión de sus costumbres y creencias nativas, llama la atención que se haya incluido en esta magna celebración una danza de negras.[25]

> the peculiarity of this little festival consists in the performers' African origin. Since the Black population occupied the lowest place in New Spanish social hierarchies, and due to degrading stereotypes that were generated about this group based on an impression of corrupt morals provoked by a lack of comprehension of their native customs and beliefs, it is noteworthy that a black women's dance was included in this great celebration.

Hernández Reyes' observations respond to the dearth of archival resources for studying Afro-descendant presence in New Spanish performances. From this perspective, her reasoning is sound, particularly in light of the distinction she underscores between the nomenclature for refined, formal dance forms—*danza*—and that of popular traditions—*baile* or *fandango*.[26] Nevertheless, Hernández Reyes' supposition about the exclusion of Black and African subjects from the region's musical and theatrical traditions is indicative of misguided assumptions that challenge the study of Afro-descendant expression in "white" or "European" cultural contexts. Indeed, as I argue throughout this book, highly skilled performers of African origin or heritage took on central roles in some of New Spain's most celebrated music traditions, many of which derived from longstanding European practices. Contemporary scholarship tends to approach these artists through a lens of difference that regards Black participation in European and Creole cultural practices as exceptional.

For his part, Valerio situates the dance within a tradition of Afro-Iberian performance. He argues that "while the women's performance did take place within a courtly context before an audience of 'people of esteem and hierarchy,' it is unlikely, in my view, that they would have performed a European-inflected courtly dance, since there was already a long-standing tradition of 'bailes de negros' (Black dances) in the Iberian world."[27] Instead, Valerio underscores possibility that the performers presented a dance with African roots. His remarks are intriguing for considering *Festín* as Afro-Mexican repertoire. Given the evidence this book presents for the persistence of African sound traditions in urban New Spain, I largely concur with Valerio's argument. Alongside this astute observation, however, it is important to consider how the dancers' consonant performance of their role in Mexico City's sound culture and its associated order enabled the possible staging of diasporic music and dance in a politically significant space. Attending to Black resonances with dominant cultural practices can lend insight into how these subjects negotiated their roles in colonial society to create opportunities for cultural expression and community memory. My readings here thus consider how sonorous references in *Festín* harmonically imagine the *morena criolla* performers' voices and bodies as resonances of the viceroy's authority. I argue that this political concordance is essential for understanding the staging and reception of Black voices and bodies and the Afro-descendant dance they might have performed in honor of López Pacheco.

To support his interpretation of *Festín* as an example of Afro-descendant dance, Valerio argues against Hernández Reyes and points out that the *sarao* did not reach its heyday until the eighteenth century. Nonetheless, Lynn Matluck Brooks has examined the genre's presence in Sevillian civic performances from the same time period. She notes that elaborate costumes and graceful motion were central elements, and she also highlights recurring celebrations of ethnic diversity in *saraos*:

> A frequent theme for those dances entitled *saraos* was the presentation of diverse nationalities together in one dance. Although the documents do refer to the diverse groups as "nations", this word must [not] be understood in its contemporary definition. Gypsies, Negroes, Moors, and Spaniards of other provinces were included in the *saraos* as members of different nationalities. The word "nations" then, in these documents, identified a population group

which had a culture markedly distinct from that of Seville or Castile—distinct enough to be demonstrated and recognized in that group's clothing, music, and dance.[28]

Continuing, Matluck Brooks describes how *sarao* performers' dress and the instruments that they carried helped audiences to imagine their cultural identity. She remarks that the festive genre often featured groups of ten to twelve dancers and "noisy" accompaniment that might include percussion, brass, fifes, and bells worn on performers' costumes, along with a variety of other instruments.[29] Matluck Brooks underscores the wide range of instruments included in early seventeenth-century Sevillian *sarao* contracts, and she cites at least one case in which a piece's instrumentation correlated with the racial identities that it purported to present.[30] For all this, the *sarao*, much like the villancico, is an example of the curious juxtaposition of aural tropes that differentiate Afro-descendant sounds from European ones with references that underscore these subjects' resonances with viceregal society.

The opening of Torres' text harmonizes the dancer's bodies within New Spain's festive sound culture: "De instrumentos sonoros, y dulce turba en preuenida dança, se dispuso vn corto numero de Negras, Estrellas, que produzidas en este Indiano suelo, solicitauan la predominación de su *influencia*: y lleuadas de la mayor grandeza que ha visto esta Monarquia, se preuinieron para vn celebre festin" (With sonorous instruments, and the sweet disorder of a well-prepared dance, a small group of *Negra* women organized themselves, Stars, born in this Indian soil, they sought the favor of divine *influence*: and carried away by the highest grandeur that this Monarchy has seen, they rehearsed for a reverent *festín*).[31] While Valerio focuses on the description's insistence upon the women's Black Creole status and what it means alongside "contemporary discourse of the greatness of the Americas," I draw attention to how Torres' opening lines circumscribe the women's act in harmonic terms.[32] In stark contrast with boisterous representations of Afro-descendant music in villancicos, the cleric's text draws out the act's dulcet tones and highlights the dancer's skill and preparation, that is, bodily motion consonant with the accompanying music and its surroundings. Through use of "influencia," he relates the women's performance to celestial harmonies. Among other definitions, *Diccionario de Autoridades* explains that the term "significa tambien la virtud y calidad de los Astros y cuerpos celestes, con que ocasionan varios efectos en los cuerpos sublunares, por medio de su luz y su calor" (it also means the virtue and essence of the Stars and celestial bodies, which provoke various effects on the sublunar bodies, by means of their light and heat). Thus, the persistence of the music of the spheres in early modern thought enables a reading that relates the "influencia" that the Afro-Mexican dancers sought to the musical medium of the performance itself. Given the underlying sonorous context of Torres' opening descriptions, the phrase's final reference to a political celebration frames the women's staged praise for the viceroy in moral terms by heightening their performance's resonance with social order.

Within the context of this book, one of the most interesting features of the *morenas criollas*' tribute is the relationship among their bodies and voices and the poetry and emblems that they presented to López Pacheco. Like Hernández Reyes notes, Torres's text does not indicate whether the dancers recited or sang the maxims that they carried.[33] Whether or not the Afro-descendant performers vocalized their concordant loyalty to the viceroy, however, many of these inscriptions notably harmonize the women within New Spain's urban settingthrough gesture and writing.

For example, *Festín* narrates the troup leader's entry: "La Capitana que en acorde concierto lleuaua vn estandarte de lama de plata" (The Captain who in concordant order carried a shield of silver-threaded cloth).[34] In agreement with this account, the woman moves into the performance space with grace and decorum ("acorde concierto"). She carries a cloth banner threaded with silver and decorated with silk and gold. On one side there is an emblem with the viceroy's coat of arms. On the other, King Solomon's throne visually announced the performance's underlying Biblical theme. The accompanying verse explained the allegory:

| | |
|---|---|
| Saba su cetro enajena | Sheba cedes her throne |
| por prudente a Salomón, | to Solomon for his wisdom |
| y hoy con toda su nación, | and today with all of her nation, |
| se le rinde al de Villena, | she obeys the rule of Villena, |
| por ser mejor Girón.[35] | for he is the finest Girón. |

Here, the text and emblem liken López Pacheco to Solomon. It aligns the performers with an obedient Queen of Sheba, and the third line suggests that they are representatives of all Africans and Afro-Mexicans. The dancers' kneeling posture is a further indication of their submissive position. In this way, choreographic, written, and graphic elements of the presentation all perform the women's loyalty.

The rest of the performers follow the leader, and each carries a board painted in the same style as the banner. On one side, there is an emblem, and on the other, a written text. Just like Torres's representation of the first performer, his description of subsequent women illustrates their accord with social hierarchies through body position: "Las que como á sol de azabache seguían sus rayos de abalorio, lleauan distintos geroglificos, que hincadas de rodillas, con la deuida reuerencia los offrecian á su Excellencia, con ayroso desenfado" (Those who followed like beads from a jet-black sun carried different hieroglyphics, that, kneeling with due reverance, they offered to his Excellency with graceful aplomb).[36] Here, Torres employs the term "airoso" to depict the women's aspect. Etymologically, the comparison relates their physical refinement to air's gentle motion and further heightens *Festín*'s harmonic rendering of the *morenas criollas*' bodies. These elegant and graceful depictions imagine an Afro-Mexican femininity whose obedient—but confident—deference and consonance inscribe the dancers within imagined social order.

From one perspective, sonorous imaginings of the performers' embodied presence align with Curcio-Nagy's argument that "officials utilized the rituals at their disposal to present a submissive and loyal Afro-Mexican vassal to the audience and sidestep the society's very real racial tensions."[37] Nevertheless, just like in Campt's readings of Afro-diasporic identity photos, it is also possible to attend to the women's inaudible resistance. I return here to the example of Afro-Caribbean passport photos from Birmingham, England, that I likened to Luis Barreto's exemplarity as a cathedral singer and longing for a better future at the end of Chapter 1. Campt describes the sounding registers of the identification portraits. She observes:

> Neither silent nor inaudible, these photographs resonate just below the threshold of hearing. They do not speak, but they are not mute. Both honorific and repressive, these portraits are command performances of a very specific kind—performances dictated by crown and country of their subjects and citizens.... They are photographs that engendered new circuits of movement, relation, and dwelling that reshaped the post-war culture of the Black Atlantic. They are some of the least audible and, for many, most ordinary of photos. To me, these sublimely quiet images enunciate an aspirational politics that are accessible at the lowest of frequencies—frequencies that hum and vibrate between and beyond the leather binding and governmental pages to which they were intended to be affixed.[38]

Here, Campt considers how the inaudible sonorities of photography disrupt the dominant gaze and lend insight into the sitters' quiet performance of a just future for Afro-diasporic people. The lens that she develops here is especially apt for moving beyond the textual and visual dimensions of the 1640 performance in order to attend to sounds and vibrations that unsettle the elite perspectives with which the dance appears to conform. To this end, Valerio has discussed the tribute's Afrofuturist themes, especially with respect to the Queen of Sheba as a symbol of Black women's agency.[39] I extend these ideas and specifically attend to the Afro-descendant vibrations that subtly disrupt the imagined harmonies of New Spanish society and thus imagine an order that centers their (feminine) voices and bodies within the urban setting and its sociopolitical resonances.

Like Valerio observes, *Festín* inscribes the women within the mystic tradition in a way that aligns their loyalty to the new viceroy with exemplary femininity but also enables the performers to center female sexual desire vis-à-vis their association with the Queen of Sheba. With respect to the text's suggestive framing of the performers' devotion to López Pacheco, Valerio argues that "the women's purpose of performing loyalty functioned as an acceptable signifier that permitted this highly erotic embodiment of patriotic love—that is, love of land, king, and his representatives: in other words, the women's declared affection for the viceroy and everything he stood for— the Spanish king and his empire."[40] In counterpoint with the embodied allegiance that Valerio describes, *Festín* aligns the women's voices with the mystic devotion, where they simultaneously harmonize with López Pacheco's authority and sound feminine agency.

Allusions to Teresa of Ávila, canonized just a few years earlier in 1622, amplify the performance's ecstatic overtones and relate the performers to the female saint. For instance, Torres sonorously portrays the second dancer's placard: "lleuaua la primera en una tarja pintada al Cerubin Teresa, que en acordes consonancias *animaua* el Instrumento del clarin, Rey, y Propheta musico, y qual siguero de los cielos refería este mote" (the first dancer carried a round board painted with the Cherubim Teresa, who in consonant accord *filled* the Instrument of the trumpet, King, and musical Prophet, and the heavenly goldfinch to which this maxim alluded).[41] These lines liken Teresa's voice to spiritual sonorities of note and thus underscore the Carmelite visionary's spoken or sung authority. First, the trumpet sounds divine power in several Biblical accounts. Among these, well-known examples include Exodus 19:16–19, when it heralds God's appearance before Moses atop Mount Sinai and Revelation 8–11, where seven angel trumpeters announce the advent of the Apocalypse. A subsequent reference to David recalls how the ruler's music was powerful and harmonious enough to act upon listeners' souls, a talent that stands out when he plays the lyre to heal Saul (1 Samuel 16:14–23). Finally, the "heavenly goldfinch" is a moniker for one of Teresa's best-known students, Juan de la Cruz. *Festín*'s description of the performer's shield highlights the nun's impact upon each of these figures, for the verb *animate* means "to give life" or "to fill with breath." In this way, Teresa's voice becomes a sign of female agency that complements the Queen of Sheba's embodied wisdom and power.

Following Torres' explanation of the placard, a sonnet imagines Teresa singing and inscribes her vocalization as a resonance of López Pacheco's harmonic influence:

| | |
|---|---|
| Canta el Cisne Imperial de Palestina, | The Imperial Swan of Palestine sings, |
| En dulce lyra, en metro sonoroso | In sweet lira, in sonorous verse |
| Las grandezas de aquel, que en si glorioso, | The glories of him whom, glorious unto himself, |
| Exercitos de Archangeles destina. | Armies of Archangels appointed. |
| | |
| No cessa, no, porque a su voz diuina, | It does not cease, no, because his divine voice, |
| El contrapunto lleua numeroso | Provokes harmonious counterpoint [with] |
| Aquel Carmelo, que en virtud frondoso, | That Caramel, who in leafy virtue, |
| con el cielo se abraça, y se auezina. | approaches the heavens and embraces them. |
| | |
| Cante Teresa, que a su ardiente vuelo | Let Teresa sing, for her ardent, Immortal flight prepares the |
| Inmortal se preuiene la corona; | crown; |
| Leuante el punto, que obligado el cielo | Let the tonic resound, in heavenly obligation |
| | |
| A el honor de Villena la eslabona, | Chained to honor Villena Triumphant celebration of his |
| Gozando el lauro su diuino zelo, | divine zeal, |
| De Patron suyo, y gloria de Escalona.[42] | of its patron, and the glory of Escalona. |

Here, the Carmelite saint raises her voice in celestial accord to join heavenly choruses that celebrate López Pacheco's appointment. In an echo of mystic devotion, Teresa pledges her voice to the viceroy, just like the dancers offer their bodies, ardent with desire, in the tradition of the Sabean queen. For all this, female voice stands out as a sign of agency in *Festín*. Indeed, in this piece, Teresa's voice is necessarily powerful so as to underscore López Pacheco's harmonic influence. It is possible to read the saint's vocalic influence as an amplification of the dancer's corporeal presence, for they carry cards that inscribe the saint's song. Consequently, even as *Festín* sounds the Afro-descendant women's obedience and submission to colonial authorities, it also performs their desire for self-determination and audibility.

Complementary to sonorous imaginings of power like these, *Festín* also draws the performers' embodied presence into its extended metaphor of concord. Indeed, the text associates the Black dancers with celestial elements and thus underscores their concordant relationship to López Pacheco. The text regularly likens them to stars and depicts the viceroy as the sun. For instance, the second dancer carries a placard that reads:

| Y en regiones extrañas, | And in foreign regions, |
| Adora tu arrebol, | My dark cloud |
| Mi negra nube, | Adores your rouged clouds, brilliant |
|    por luciente sol: |    from the setting sun: |
| recibe de Guinea | receive from Guinea |
| Este pebete, que en tu luz | this incense, which glows in your |
|    humea[43] |    light |

These lines juxtapose the performers' dusky aspect with the viceroy's/sun's glowing light. They set up the performance of loyalty that occurs in the last line, when the women offer a stick of incense, which burns brightly in the official's light. The image of the black women burning with devotion for López Pacheco abounds in *Festín* and heightens the solar metaphor of the viceroy's influence. As Valerio notes, references like these can be read as erotic symbols and also in the context of mystical devotion, where ardent desire for union with Christ is a sign of female exemplarity.[44] The opening reference to Teresa of Ávila heightens such connections. From a mystic perspective, language of desire likens the viceroy to Christ and draws upon imagery that likens both political and religious leaders to the sun. Sara Gonzalez observes that association is especially prevalent in imaginings of monarchal power in Habsburg Spain. She argues that "identification with the main astral body recreated the idea of the divine order of the heavenly spheres, and especially the need of updating and preserving it within the state in consonance with God's plan."[45] By portraying López Pacheco's power in this way, the women's performance reminds the audience that the viceroy represents the Spanish Crown's authority. Furthermore, the celestial imagery draws out themes of social harmony that undoubtedly resonated with musical elements and dance in the performance.

Beyond the textual inscription, the dancer's costumes extend the solar metaphor. As Hernández Reyes points out, metallic threads in the cloth that the dancers wear and the banners they carry reinforce their resonance with López Pacheco.[46] Indeed, if the viceroy is the brilliant sun, then the glittering threads that adorn the women and their props reflect his rays. The contrast with the dancer's dark skin would have been particularly stunning, as chiaroscuro references throughout the text seem to indicate.

As a complement to this chromatic symbolism, Hernández Reyes makes a thoughtful observation about another way the performers' embodied presence resonates with celestial harmony.

> A lo largo del texto, Nicolás de Torres nombra a los personajes de la danza como estrellas, pero por el número (doce) se puede proponer asimismo que en realidad simbolizaran a los signos zodiacales o tal vez a los planetas; en cualquiera de los casos cuerpos celestes. En este sentido es pertinente comentar que la elección de astros como los personajes simbólicos de esta danza haría quizá eco a la revaloración renacentista de la danza cortesana, sustentada en la creencia de que la danza reflejaba el movimiento armonioso y perfecto de las esferas celestes, que producía una música celestial, de acuerdo con la tradición pitagórico-platónica, que planteaba [según Margaret Rich Greer] "un cosmos divinamente ordenado, a la vez fijo y en constante movimiento."[47]

> Throughout the text, Nicolás de Torres refers to the characters in the dance as stars, but because of their number (twelve), one might propose that in reality, they symbolized the zodiac signs or even planets; heavenly bodies, in either case. In this sense, it is relevant to comment that the choice of stars as this dance's symbolic characters might echo the Renaissance revaluing of courtly dance, rooted in the belief that dance reflected the perfect and harmonious movement of the heavenly spheres, which produced celestial music, in agreement with the Pythagorean-Platonic tradition that posed [according to Margaret Rich Greer] "a divinely-ordered cosmos, at once fixed and in constant motion."

Hernández Reyes' observation is astute, and the women's performance of embodied concord with the "sun" (López Pacheco) merits further development, especially given my argument that *Festín* harmonizes the Afro-descendant dancers' with the New Spanish imagined city.

Torres closes his account with a conclusion that summarizes many of the themes I have drawn out here: "Con esto dieron discreto fin curiosas consonancias admiración a los ojos, aplauso a los oydos, tan conforme assumpto; festejo corto para tanto Príncipe; audacia grande en tan pequeña humildad; corta pluma para tan alto vuelo" (With this, delicate consonances came to a modest end, beauty for the eyes, applause for the ears, such well-proportioned poetry; a brief celebration for such a Prince; great intrepidity in such extreme modesty, a small feather/pen for a flight of such heights).[48] Several aspects of this passage are notable. First, allusions to visual and auditory affect draw attention to the multimodal celebration, and harmonic descriptors underscore the underlying proportion of sounds, visual art, and poetry. These tropes highlight the dancers' skill and also illustrate their resonance with the viceroy's political influence, imagined here in concordant terms. In addition to this feature, the phrase closes with a series of *chiaroscuro* references that contrast Villena's prominent standing with the performers' lower place in New Spain's social hierarchies. The contrasting figures emphasize the *morenas criollas'* modesty and also draw attention to the viceroy's capacity to harmonize even those elements of society that are farthest removed from his stature.

For all this, the closing passage of Torres' *Festín* illustrates how the Black women's bodies and voices perform political power. Both the texts that the dancers carry and their corporeal positions suggest their obedience before the new viceroy. Celestial and aural themes emphasize Villena's influence and attune the performers with harmonic imaginings of order among New Spain's diverse inhabitants. Sadly, Torres' account offers little insight into the tribute's musical context, but there is little doubt that it further reinforced these ideas. Despite the apparent prevalence of a colonial elite perspective that imagines Afro-descendants as submissive, it is also important to recognize the audibility of the female dancers. Indeed, just like the Black high-voiced singers that Chapters 1 and 2 discussed, the women who participated in the festivities to celebrate Villena's entrance performed deference to Spanish authority and thus gained access to a privileged and politically significant stage. In this way, contrary to directives that might mute or obscure Black and African presence in New Spain, the performers negotiated a space that would allow them to be heard.

## AFRO-MEXICAN WOMEN'S PERFORMANCE AND CONTEMPORARY REPERCUSSIONS

*Festín* is not the only example of Afro-descendant women dancers performing in the residence of a high-ranking Mexico City official. In *Viaje a la Nueva España*, Gemelli Careri describes a party he attended at the home of Don Felipe de Rivas y Angulo, assayer of the Royal Treasury. "El mismo día fui a casa de D. Felipe de Rivas, invitado por él para ver festejar a doña Antonia, su mujer. Encontré allí muchas señoritas que bailaban y cantaban muy bien, al uso del país. Vinieron poco después cuatro mulatas y bailaron lo que llaman sarao, moviendo los pies con gran ligereza; y luego otras seis, con hachas encendidas en las manos bailaron otro sarao" (The same day I went to the home of D. Felipe de Rivas, who invited me to see the celebration of his wife, doña Antonia. There I found many young women who danced and sang very well, in the style of the country. A bit later, four *mulatas* came and danced what they call the *sarao*, moving their feet with great agility; and later another six women, with lighted candles in their hands, danced another *sarao*).[49] Given the multicultural context that Matluck Brooks outlines in her description of the *sarao*, it is plausible that Gemelli Careri uses the term in reference to a non-European dance for which he has no other name. The explorer describes two dances: a performance with rapid, nimble steps and another in which the women carry candles.

Although Gemelli Careri offers scant details, it is possible to speculate about the dances he described and their resonances. The quick movement of the first relates to descriptions of Afro-descendant dance as frenzied and wild, a topic that Chapter 5 will address in greater detail. Furthermore, it loosely recalls the *zapateado* in contemporary *son jarocho* practices. In this genre, dancers perform rhythmic steps atop a *tarima* or wooden stage. More than just a visual or decorative touch, the tapping of participants' feet becomes the pulse that underlies this communal form of music-making.

The second dance that Gemelli Careri mentions could be a "torch dance" (*danza de uma hacha*), a choreographic form that Louise Stein affirms concludes all *saraos*.[50] Nonetheless, popular or even Afro-descendant readings of the account are also possible. For instance, the candles that the women carry are reminiscent of a present-day *son jarocho* called "La bruja." One of the most distinctive choreographic features of this piece is that the female dancers place a glass, bottle, or lit candle on their heads as part of the dance.[51]

Additionally, Gemelli Careri's description is also reminiscent of *cumbé*, often considered a flirtatious predecessor of Afro-Colombian *cumbia*. Leonardo D'Amico describes present-day *cumbia*.

> From the choreographic perspective, cumbia is a Spanish-like court dance that is characterized by a lover's duel, in which movements simulate a game of repulsion and attraction between the two dancers (the *cumbiaberos*). A couple dancing in a counterclockwise circle around a group of musicians

performs it. As it is usually performed at night, the woman carries a bundle of lit candles that she uses to push away the man, who pursues her by circling her with open arms. with the other hand, the woman holds the tip of her long skirt (*pollera*), and in a standing position, swings her hips and takes small steps, all while trying to remain untouched by her partner. The man dances around the woman with a hat (the traditional *sombrero vueltiao*, a staple of the Colombian Caribbean) in his hand, which he tries to place on her head as a symbol of amorous conquest.[52]

Naturally, additional research is necessary in order to tease out the seventeenth-century roots of *son jarocho*, as well as its Latin American or transatlantic derivatives. Nevertheless, Afro-descendant resonances like I have drawn out here usefully supplement the observations that scholars like Rafael Figueroa Hernández and Antonio García de León and Liza Rumazo have made about the African origins of one of Mexico's most iconic dance forms.[53]

### DANCING COWBOYS

While *Festín* offers one of the most extensive and detailed accounts of Black performance at a New Spanish political celebration, other records suggest that the *morenas criollas*' presence on the civic stage was not singular. Equestrian ballets are another festive practice in which Afro-descendants participated. Popular throughout the early modern world, these lavish political spectacles featured horsemanship, music, and elaborate costumes and scenery. In equestrian ballets and their derivatives, which have roots in medieval military exercises like jousting, riders guide their mounts through choreographed movements set to courtly music. The display must have required extensive rehearsal in order to maintain harmony with the animal and keep time with the music.

These equine spectacles accompanied political events throughout seventeenth- and eighteenth-century Europe and beyond. Like Kate van Orden has proposed, their "mutable geometry" relates to French court ballet as a spatial and kinetic inscription of bodily resonances with universal harmony.[54] Given the relationship among consonance, space, and social order, I maintain that such significance would have been even stronger in New Spain, where corporeal harmonization with the urban stages where the ballets took place likewise attuned the performer and audience to dominant social hierarchies. Despite its importance, however, the equestrian ballet is understudied, especially in the Hispanic world. Most scholarship on the topic focuses on Italy, France, or Germany.[55] Nonetheless, references to these displays in the Hispanic world are ripe for further investigation. In Spain, Stein's description of a 1605 *máscara a caballo* (equestrian masque) to commemorate Philip IV's birth offers details about the event and its accompanying music. She notes that the masque "was announced by a corps of forty trumpets and drums," and she cites the performance of both popular tunes and *música alta*. Singers participated in the event, along with lutists, sackbut and shawm players, harpists, and more.[56]

For her part, Cristina Bordas Ibáñez details equestrian performances that took place in Prince Carlos IV's court at Aranjuez, from 1770 to 1788. With respect to earlier periods, she offers a brief history of horse displays in Spain, including bullfights, military displays, and other derivatives of the equestrian ballet. Bordas Ibáñez includes some musical details that can be helpful for imagining the sounds of the New Spanish display:

> las descripciones de las carreras de Parejas parecen indicar que en ellas los pasos se ejecutaban con acompañamiento de clarines y timbales, esto es, toques marciales, marchas o música de ritmo marcado, mientras que en los juegos o «funciones» de Parejas, más próximos a los ballets ecuestres, las evoluciones se hacían con ritmos cortesanos, como contradanzas, también marchas y otros como gigas o galops.[57]

> descriptions of the races of Pairs appear to indicate that in these performances, steps were executed to an accompaniment of drums and bugles, that is, military tunes, marches, or music with a marked rhythm, while in the games or "performances" of Pairs, closer to equestrian ballets, movements were executed to courtly rhythms, like contradanzas, as well as to marches, jigs, or gallops.

Using research based largely in eighteenth-century practices, Bordas Ibáñez notes that while the *carreras de pareja* (races of pairs) included military instruments like trumpets or drums, *juegos de pareja* (games of pairs) featured animated courtly rhythms. Given the proliferation of Spanish-language terms that appear in seventeenth-century documentation of such events, it can be difficult to distinguish among performance subcategories. Here, I will use "equestrian displays" or "equestrian ballets" interchangeably as general terms for performances that featured horsemanship, music, and choreography. In all forms related to this genre, as Bordas Ibáñez's remarks illustrate, the musical accompaniment formed part of a tradition of political displays that underscored the authority and military prowess of Hispanic nobility. Performers undoubtedly responded with lively and perhaps acrobatic movements that would have dazzled audiences.

In New Spain, travelers' descriptions suggest that equestrian ballets flourished in political events, albeit with an exotic twist. Among other elements, chroniclers remark upon the astonishing skill of Afro-descendant horsemen in New Spain's equestrian displays. For example, Gemelli Careri describes a performance that he witnessed in Acapulco, a city whose prominent Black and African population captures the explorer's attention.

> El domingo, día 17, por ser el primero del carnaval, después de comer corrieron parejas a caballo los negros, mestizos y mulatos de Acapulco, en número de más de cien, con tal destreza que me pareció sobresalían en mucho a los grandes que había yo visto correr en Madrid; aunque los de Acapulco solían ejercitarse en este juego un mes antes. Sin mentir, puede decirse que aquellos negros corrían una milla italiana, cogidos unos por las manos y abrazados otros, sin soltarse un momento, ni descomponerse en todo aquel espacio.[58]

> On Sunday the seventeenth, as it was the first day of Carnival, after eating, the *negros*, *mestizos*, and *mulatos* of Acapulco put on an equestrian display, numbering more than one hundred [riders], with such skill that it seemed to me that they well exceeded the great displays that I had seen in Madrid; although those of Acapulco tended to train for the event a month before. Without lying, it could be said that those *negros* ran an Italian mile, some joined by the hand and others embracing, without letting go for a single moment nor separating from one another in all of that space.

From all appearances, Gemelli Careri witnessed a large equestrian ballet in which a troupe of Afro-descendants on horseback performed choreographed movements that matched accompaniment with courtly and military resonances. He remarks upon the performers' skill, and favorably compares the event to displays he had seen in Madrid.

Gemelli Careri's enthusiastic description is not the only reference to equestrian performance among New Spain's Black and African residents. Gregorio Martín de Guijo tells of a similar event that took place in Mexico City as part of the birthday celebrations of viceroy Luis Enrique de Guzmán, marquis of Villaflor and count of Alba de Liste. He relates:

> Martes 3 de septiembre y algunos días antes de éste, después del día de San Luis, celebró el virrey cumplimiento de sus años con toros, que se lidiaron

en el parque, con tablados que se armaron, y dieron los toros los condes de Calimaya y Orizaba, y Fr. Gerónimo de Andrada, provincial del orden de la Merced, y del día referido y el siguiente hicieron los mulatos y negros de esta ciudad una máscara a caballo con singulares galas.⁵⁹

Tuesday, September 3 and a few days before, after the feast of San Luis, the viceroy celebrated his birthday with bulls, who fought in the park on stages that were armed, and the counts of Calimaya and Orizaba and Father Gerónimo de Andarada, superior of the Order of the Merced, and on that day and the next, the *mulatos* and *negros* of this city performed an equestrian display with singular elegance.

Like Gemelli Careri, Guijo highlights the Afro-descendant performers' elegance and skill. Just as in *Festín*, here the commemoration of the viceroy's birthday becomes an opportunity to perform social harmony through the prominent staging of Black and African bodies. Indeed, the performers' well-executed choreography, perfectly in time with the music, reflected both their skill and their loyalty to Guzmán.

The prevalence of Afro-descendant horsemen in New Spanish equestrian ballets invites reflection. To be certain, Gemelli Careri and Guijo's emphasis on the riders' race in their discussions of the practice may reflect the absence of Black performers on horseback elsewhere in Europe. While this may be true, it still begs the question: were there more Afro-descendant riders in New Spanish equestrian ballets than in other countries? If so, why?

First, it is possible to relate Afro-descendant performers in the ballets to a tradition of Black horsemanship in the early modern Hispanic world. Valerio offers astute observations about the presence of Afro-descendant knights in New Spain, beginning with Bernal Díaz del Castillo's description of an Afro-descendant procession that took place in 1539 as part of regional festivities to commemorate the signing of the Truce of Nice (*Historia verdadera de la Conquista de la Nueva España*, 1632). He contextualized Black horsemanship in this spectacle by comparing it with other Afro-Hispanic and Afro-Luso-Brazilian performances from the sixteenth through eighteenth centuries. Valerio notes that the animal's prominence in these displays "may point to Afrodescendants' use of horses as markers of status."⁶⁰ Along similar lines, J. Arturo Motta Sánchez has examined the broader importance of bulls, horses, and cattle ranching among Africans and Afro-Mexicans from the seventeenth century onward. He even cites the case of a *mulata* rider who appeared in a bullfight in 1700.⁶¹ Like Valerio, Motta Sánchez remarks upon the social symbolism of these activities. He is especially attentive to the position of a rider's body, which rose above crowds (or animals) on foot in a position of dominance: "Obvio entonces fue el papel del caballo: símbolo a la vez que manifiesta contundencia del poder y, por analogía, la de su montura ya fuera hijodalgo o un infamado negro o mulato" (Thus, the role of the horse was obvious: it was a symbol that manifested strength and power and, by extension, that of its rider whether he was a knight or an unrenowned *negro* or *mulato*).[62] For all this, as a complement to the social meaning of horses among Black and African people in New Spain and elsewhere on the American continent, their role in performance is intriguing and merits further attention.

Beyond the significance of equestrian ballets as part of a longstanding Afro-Hispanic performance tradition, it is also important to consider Black participation in these musical events from a perspective of harmony, broadly construed. Here, as elsewhere in this book, I propose that the staging of Black and African bodies in politically and spiritually significant spaces responds, in part, to elite concern about uprisings among the lower castes. Given this context, the presence of Afro-descendant riders in an art form derived from military exercises seems out of place. Nevertheless, Bordas Ibáñez discusses an emblem from Juan de Solórzano Pereira's *Emblemata regio politica* (Madrid, 1653) that can clarify.[63] This image and its accompanying commentary present a cautionary tale about Sybarus, a wealthy Greek city whose overindulgent citizens had taught their horses to respond to music. While the diversion may have been entertaining, it turned out to be a poor military tactic. The Sybarites lost their city when rivals from nearby Croton played music during battle in order to distract the cavalry. Paradoxically, then, equestrian ballets were symbols of political authority and also of military weakness.

For all this, the presence of Black and African performers is especially meaningful. First, just as in the case of the dancers in *Festín*, the Spanish courtly tradition that underlay equestrian ballets harmonized Afro-descendant riders' corporeal presence as part of a Euro-descendant sound tradition. Within the broader, audio-political imaginary of these displays, the consonance among music, steed, and horseman resonated with the harmony among the New Spanish authorities the events celebrated and those they governed. Second, by supplanting a military exercise with dance motions, equestrian ballets effectively "tamed" their riders and thus countered any inclination toward violent rebellion. Kate van Orden remarks that in equestrian ballet, "music projected refinement across equitation, harmonizing the relationships among riders, 'civilizing' a martial art, and bringing a new political dimension to horsemanship."[64] Indeed, in equestrian ballets, including those that featured Afro-descendant performers in New Spain, the physical response of animal and human performers to the accompaniment was a visual symbol of musical and, by extension, social order. Along the same lines, the geometric movements of the choreography traced neat courses for the Black bodies carrying out the movements and harmonized their physical presence with the well-ordered New Spanish city.

## CONCLUSION AND REPERCUSSION

To be certain, the spectacles that this chapter has discussed served to harmonize Afro-descendants within a social hierarchy that imagined them as subservient. Nevertheless, it is also important to bear in mind that by performing consonance with these expectations, the Black and African people who took part in these celebrations created spaces for the preservation of cultural memory or the creation of new, syncretic traditions that blended European, Indigenous, and African forms of expression. Echoes of the practices discussed here persist in present-day Mexico. For example, Motta Sánchez notes that in the Costa Chica region, an area of Mexico's western coast with strong Afro-Mexican presence, residents continue to participate in equestrian displays with music. Specifically, he cites horse shows that take place in San José Estancia Grande to commemorate the Feast of St. James and also calls attention to the *danza de los vaqueros* (cowboy dance), whose choreography, while devoid of horses in contemporary representations, mimics the capture of a bull.[65]

By relating these present-day practices to New Spanish festive traditions, Motta Sánchez is able to draw attention to their possible African roots. He remarks:

> en ese mismo sentido es que también resulta factible encuadrar el espíritu general de la casi totalidad coreológica de la danza de los Diablos, pues sin desconocer que algunos de sus elementos característicos puedan ser originarios del golfo de Guinea, en África, no obstante resultan plenamente constitutivos de este mulato novohispano discurso escenográfico del hacer vaquería.[66]

> in the same sense it is also viable to frame the general spirit of the almost complete choreology of the dance of the Devils, without failing to recognize that some of its most characteristic elements could originate in the gulf of Guinea, in Africa, nevertheless, [these elements] turn out to be fully constitutive of this New Spanish *mulato* staged discourse of horsemanship.

Indeed, it would be a mistake not to recognize that vestiges of Black performance or sound culture exist in these contemporary traditions. In the next chapter, I will develop these ideas further, by showing that another early source of Afro-Mexican performance offers tantalizing connections with contemporary sound practices. Some of these traditions lie at the heart of genres with strong ties to Mexican identity. Their resonances with sixteenth- and seventeenth-century Afro-descendant sound culture beckon a re-evaluation of the country's national music as a product of its tripartite Indigenous, European, and African inheritance.

CHAPTER 4

# Harmonizing Blackness in Popular Religious Settings

Son prácticas ancestrales indígenas, pero también de la tercera raíz, la africana (. . .). La gente quiere tirarse pa la parte española. ¿Por qué? ¡si [sic] somos morenos!

They are ancestral Indigenous practices, but they also come from the third root, the African one. (. . .) People want to align themselves with the Spanish part. Why? Yes, we are *morenos*!

—**Anonymous leader of Blanca Flor**, a Veracruz prayer group devoted to La Santa Muerte, in an interview with Kali Argyriadis, "'Católicos, apostólicos y no-satánicos'"

Just as Afro-descendants in New Spain performed concord with the dominant socio-political order in urban spaces by taking part in political ceremonies, so they also participated in spiritual demonstrations that occurred in public and private spaces. Sound was a key element in these activities, although it can be difficult to pinpoint exact musical details in paraliturgical celebrations. There are few extant scores, and musical references from account ledgers often just list the instrument that an organization hired and the musician's fee. Drew Edward Davies observes that in lieu of more traditional primary sources, scholars of music and sound must rely on "early ethnographic description, payment records of professional musicians, knowledge of performance practices and contexts, and occasional clues from the notated repertoires and ecclesiastical documents."[1] In addition, as this chapter will show, travel writing and Inquisition records can also be important indexes of New Spanish sound culture. Among other themes, the difficulty of musically accounting for the region's diversity stands out in Davies's remarks. In fact, his observations rightly underscore the importance of attending to non-European voices by using a variety of materials to account for sonorities that exceed the limits of written records.

Such methodologies serve as my starting point here. In order to draw out the ethno-sonic richness that Davies describes, I will show that Black and African people marched in processions for feast days, organized private oratories with music and dance, and even sold their services as mediums and fortune tellers. For the most part, these practices harmonized with Christian tradition by expressing devotion to Catholic doctrine. I argue that such resonances were strategic on the part of Afro-descendant practitioners, for they created a space from which to articulate and preserve syncretic traditions with ties to their countries of origin. Although the archive offers scant details about the exact sights and sounds that took place in these ceremonies, by placing diverse sources in dialogue, it is possible to attend to echoes of African and Afro-diasporic sonorities that once resounded as an integral part of urban New Spain.

## CONFRATERNITIES AND URBAN RELIGIOUS FESTIVALS

Chapters 1 and 2 examined professional Afro-descendant musicians who performed in New Spain's most important cathedrals. Records of such figures are scarce, at least during the seventeenth-century, and the dearth of written evidence suggests that Afro-descendants took on audible roles in churches with less frequency. As a complement, this chapter begins by considering a religious space in which Black and African voices were much more prominent: confraternities, or lay brotherhoods. Dating back to the thirteenth century, these organizations played an important role in the sacred and social fabric of cities throughout Europe and the Americas. Members often devoted themselves to works of piety or charity, and their exemplary faith served as a model for other community members. In New Spain, clerics like archbishop Francisco de Aguiar y Seijas especially promoted the formation of lay brotherhoods among people of Indigenous and African descent, for they believed that these religious societies promoted Christian ideals and doctrine among those newer to Catholic faith. As a result, confraternities with particular ethnic affiliations emerged as spiritual and community centers. Nicole von Germeten identifies nine Black and African lay organizations established in Mexico City between 1599 and 1706. Recent research has pinpointed four more, although scholars have yet to determine a founding date for some.[2]

Among other activities, confraternities attended to the spiritual and physical needs of their brothers and sisters after death by taking care of funeral arrangements. They also organized processions and other celebratory demonstrations for feast days, a practice that afforded prestige and visibility to the organization. Members elected leadership from within the group, and these representatives negotiated with church and city fathers in order to ensure an organization's place in large public ceremonies, like those that commemorated Corpus Christi or Holy Week. Securing a better (more visible) position depended upon a society's reputation as devoted and obedient Christian servants. Orderly and harmonious decorum was one characteristic that could earn a confraternity good standing. For example, during the 1670s, the Afro-descendant lay brotherhood the Preciosa Sangre de Cristo (founded in the parish of Santa Catarina Mártir) petitioned to maintain their spaces in the processional order. Confraternity members alleged that "algunas personas pretenden perturbar la procession y lugar de la preferencia que le toca a la antigüedad y dignidad de dha cofradía quitándole el lugar que en los concurssos y actos públicos a tenido lo qual es de molestia y perjuicio para dha cofradía pues siembre a goçado el lugar ynmediato al estandarte de la cofradía de la Sanctissima Trinidad" (some people try to perturb the procession and place of preference given because of the seniority and dignity of said confraternity, taking away the place that it has had in displays and public acts, which is bothersome and detrimental to said confraternity since it has always enjoyed the place next to the standard of the confraternity of the Most Holy Trinity).[3] This complaint, along with its supporting documentation, illustrates the importance of how lay organizations and other religious groups were distributed in ceremonial space. Terms related to order stand out here and show the manner in which processions resonated with harmonic imaginings of urban space.

The document affirms that the confraternity of the Preciosa Sangre de Cristo's privileged place in processional order was due, in part, to the protection of the archconfraternity of San Juan de Letrán de Roma. Additionally, supplementary documents that defend the petition highlight the group's orderly composure as a strong reason for maintaining their position. Spaniard Bernardo de Reiros, a supporter of the group, remarks that "en la possession de dho lugar los a visto estar y persseverar quieta y pacificamente sin contradiction de persona alguna" (in the possession of the aforementioned place, I have seen them conduct themselves quietly and peacefully, without anyone's contradiction).[4] Sebastian Diaz, another witness, makes the exact same assertion, and his testimony includes two separate remarks about how lay brothers from the Preciosa Sangre de Cristo confraternity carried out their duties "quieta y pacificamente" (quietly and peacefully).[5] For all this, the significance of social and spatial concord among confraternal members stands out. In addition to their affiliation with a more powerful organization, members of the Preciosa Sangre de Cristo needed to reflect civic and religious harmony in order to maintain processional privileges. In addition to a calm demeanor, the confraternity's appearance, the rhythm of their movement, and sounds that accompanied their passage through city streets all performed exemplary concord.[6]

Complementary to orderly composure, confraternities also strengthened their reputation through displays of faith. At times, these bordered on excessive, particularly among Afro-descendant sodalities, who had a reputation for fervent self-flagellation. With respect to such practices, Valerio and Javiera Jaque Hidalgo argue that "the penitent character of many of the ceremonies that linked . . . [lay brotherhoods] to mendicant orders may be both related to the pious example of the passion of Christ as well as a validation of practices employed by marginalized subjects looking for a way of becoming visibly legitimized by the dominant culture."[7] In other words, lay organizations performed heightened displays of Christian faith as a strategy of gaining recognition and acceptance in a society that otherwise disregarded them.

Just as Valerio and Jaque Hidalgo's observation illustrates, scholars tend to focus on the visual presence of Afro-descendant confraternities in religious festivities in New Spain. Nevertheless, music and other sonorous practices were also important among these groups' religious customs, and financial ledgers and firsthand accounts include passing references to dances, musical instruments, and other sonic materials. Despite such evidence, however, the topic has received little scholarly attention. In part, this lacuna arises from primary source descriptions that are lacking in specific auditory details that might enable scholars to reconstruct Afro-descendant sound traditions and pinpoint their diasporic connections. Although I cannot shed additional light on the exact customs in which sodalities took part, in this chapter, as elsewhere in *Amplifications of Black Sound*, I will show how Black and African people performing in concord with spiritual and civic sound practices that the colonial elite imposed also created spaces for the rearticulation and syncretic reimagining of cultural traditions from their ancestral homes.

Since participation in religious processions was one of the most important functions of confraternities, leaders put great effort into attending to every detail. Account books can lend insight into various ritual elements that accompanied these displays, including flowers, special food and drink, costumes, and musicians or ensembles hired for the occasion. Among Afro-descendant sodalities, who often had fewer economic resources than their Creole and Spanish counterparts, there are scant records of instruments that lay organizations hired to accompany their celebrations. Still, ledgers and other archival documents can offer some idea of the musical activities that took place. For instance, I consulted seventeenth-century account books for the confraternities of the Coronación de Christo de Señor Nuestro and San Benito de Palermo. Both include lists of the expenses associated with Holy Week processions. Trumpets appear with some frequency in these records. The instrument has rich auditory symbolism, especially in early modern cities. Its loud, brazen cries alerted passersby to the presence of royal and political figures, town criers, militias, and more. Within a religious context, trumpets sound the seven apocalyptic events in the Book of Revelation (chapters 8–11). Surely, the horn's significance in confraternity processions was twofold, for both its civic and religious meanings undoubtedly resonated with the listening public. In sum, references like these clarify some of the instruments accompanied festive practices in the Mexico City streets, and they illustrate that lay organizations indeed took part in the audio-spiritual fabric of New Spain's urban areas.

While such details offer general insight into the sounds that might have accompanied Afro-descendant confraternities as they processed, accounts of specific celebrations can offer insight into how their musical practices fit within the broader festive setting. Corpus Christi is perhaps the best-known example of an urban religious festival that invited members from all social and racial backgrounds to participate. This feast day celebrates the doctrine of transubstantiation, whereby the consecrated bread and wine become the body and blood of Christ. It often includes a Eucharistic procession during which the consecrated host is carried through city streets as a public symbol of faith. Just like Corpus Christi parades in Europe, the New Spanish display generally featured a colorful array of performers and costumed figures. Among others, there were elaborately dressed giants; *cabezudos*, or big heads—entertainers who walked with oversized heads; dancers whose performances recalled diverse popular and ethnic identities; an array of floats; and the dazzling *tarasca*, an enormous dragon that led the procession.[8] Collectively, these elements made for a lively and expensive spectacle. Indeed, in colonial Mexico City, Corpus Christi was one of the most lavish public ceremonies. The city council, rather than the church, organized and funded the activities. Curcio-Nagy notes that by the early seventeenth century, Corpus Christi expenses accounted for about one fifth of the municipal budget.[9]

The procession had both civic and religious symbolism, for representatives from all of the city's communities took part in it. Curcio-Nagy remarks that the Mexico City Corpus Christi display performed social and racial order as Spanish and Creole leaders imagined it. Nevertheless, she also notes that the celebration united the diverse urban space's many factions: "This unique festive space encouraged integration and identification with a larger community, beyond one's ethnicity, social status, guild, confraternity, or ecclesiastical affiliation, and could thereby stir a sense of civic pride."[10] In this way, the Corpus Christi festivities reinforced social and racial hierarchies beneath the umbrella of a unified civic identity. Just like in the Preciosa Sangre de Cristo's petition that I previously discussed, the order of diverse individuals and lay organizations in Corpus Christi parades harmonized the marching bodies with the imagined concordance of urban space.

The Corpus Christi festival performed civic harmony in other ways as well. For instance, Indigenous, Afro-descendant, and European troupes paraded through the city on well-adorned floats and performed dances before eager crowds. Just like in political processions, it is likely that these festivities staged musical traditions that were representative of the ethnic groups that performed. To this end, Valerio cites direct evidence for the performance of Afro-descendant dance at the 1664 Corpus Christi celebrations in Veracruz. He notes that "five groups of Afrodescendants were paid twelve pesos each to perform five different 'national' dances for the city's Corpus Christi procession: these were congos, matambas, lobolos, and bendos or bandos."[11] While Mexico City records for the ceremony are less specific, it is plausible that Black and African performers who took part in these urban rituals also staged diasporic customs. Like the *morenas criollas* who performed for Diego López Pacheco's entrance or the Black horsemen whose equestrian skills dazzled audiences, African and Afro-Mexican dancers whose music, steps, or body motions recalled traditions from their countries of origin performed Afro-descent in a setting that harmonized their embodied and envoiced presence within imagined social, spatial, and spiritual hierarchies. Precisely, concordance with these ideals enabled participants to display their heritage publicly and thus created spaces for the preservation of cultural memory.

Members of Afro-descendant sodalities took part in other religious processions and celebrations as well. For instance, Rosa Elena Rojas has examined the role of the Confraternity of Santa Veracruz Negra (Coyoacán) in the district's Maundy Thursday procession. Rojas notes that the members of this group define themselves as "mestizos, mulatos y morenos de esta villa [de Coyoacán]" (*mestizos, mulatos,* and *morenos* from this district [of Coyoacán]).[12] Despite the apparently marginal status of the confraternity's members, the group successfully petitioned to lead the Maundy Thursday parade in 1638 and continued to head this and other religious processions for years after.

It is striking to think that such an important religious display was headed by Black and African people who held domestic positions or worked in the *obrajes*, textile factories that took advantage of forced, slave, and criminal labor to fuel the New World economy. Rojas describes the spectacle:

> La procesión de sangre que abría el desfile nocturno era organizada de común acuerdo con la de los españoles: salía del convento dominico de San Juan Bautista y recorría las principales calles aledañas en un despliegue fúnebre de flagelantes, hermanos de las tres naciones, que al toque de campanillas, desplegaban sus emblemas.... Conforme sus finanzas, producto de las aportaciones en metálico y en especie, se iban incrementando, el fasto de la procesión iba en aumento, siempre a semejanza de la centenaria Cofradía de la Santa Veracruz de la Ciudad de México; la música y la presencia de un religioso revestido cerraban el paso.[13]

> The Holy Blood Procession that opened the nocturnal parade was organized in mutual agreement with that of the Spaniards: it departed from the Dominican convent of San Juan Bautista and traversed the principal neighboring streets in a funerary display of flagellants, lay brothers from all three races, who to the sound of bells, displayed their emblems.... As their finances increased, thanks to contributions of silver and spice, the procession's pomp became more developed, always reflecting that of the hundred-year-old Confraternity of Santa Veracruz of Mexico City; music and the presence of a cleric in full vestments ended the display.

With an ear attuned to this description's sonic details, the bells that accompanied the procession stand out. Bells were important auditory symbols of ecclesiastical authority in New Spanish urban centers. They rang throughout the day, marking canonical hours; alerting worshippers to the goings-on within the walls of convents, within which the spiritual activities of cloistered men and women played an important role in cities' spiritual health; and finally, calling citizens from all walks of life to worship. As subsequent chapters will show, the last use stands out in the *villancicos de negros*, where Afro-descendant characters' entrances frequently respond to the tolling of church bells. In Rojas' description of the Maundy Thursday celebration, it is easy to imagine marchers slipping into a communal rhythm, as regular chimes guide their way through the geometric grids of city streets. From this perspective, the sound of the bells harmonizes Black and African bodies with the urban harmonies that they traverse. In part, the sonic order that this ceremony imposed upon subjects who the dominant class considered unruly in other contexts might help contemporary scholars to understand the Confraternity of Santa Veracruz Negra's position at the head of the procession.

In addition to the symbolic order that bells imposed upon the processions, confraternities also organized music and dance to accompany the spectacles. The Confraternity of Santa Veracruz Negra's account books lend insight into the objects used in the Maundy Thursday display. Rojas takes note of particularly rich entries between 1715 and 1722 that include food, music, dance, candles, and costumes. She details several paid performers and instruments, including a harpist, singer, drums, trumpets, and bugles. In general, Afro-descendant and Indigenous lay organizations were of lesser means than Creole and Spanish sodalities. Therefore, they often went to great lengths to rent instruments for important celebrations, just as Rojas observes. While ledgers like that of the Confraternity of Santa Veracruz Negra offer mere echoes of the actual sounds of the festivities that Afro-descendant confraternities organized, references to instruments in their records illustrate the importance of music in these festive contexts. In response to this archival dearth, representations of Black and African festivities in villancico lyrics and other literary texts can complement confraternity account books with more detailed musical descriptions, just as I will argue in the next section.

### IMAGINING BLACK SOUND IN "COMO TIENEN LOS MORENOS"

Although documentation of musical practices among Afro-descendant confraternities can be sparse, villancicos and other imaginings of Black and African sound offer useful material for thinking about what festive practices might have sounded like. At the same time, such representations also intersect with this book's discussion of how New Spanish artists, chroniclers, and listeners harmonized Black bodies and voices within the region's urban settings. In this regard, chapelmaster Mateo Tollis de la Rocca's eighteenth-century Christmas piece "Como tienen los morenos" is an excellent example of the insight that villancicos can lend. While Marín López remarks that "Como tienen los morenos" requires no more than a small ensemble of violins as accompaniment, the villancico's text describes much more elaborate musical festivities, and it relates particular practices to *blanco* and *moreno* bands that take part in the celebration. These sonic depictions are thus useful for delving into the New Spanish audio-racial imagination and may also deepen understanding of the sonic atmosphere of the region's festivals.

Notably for this section's analysis, the *estribillo* for "Como tienen los morenos" includes a distinctive description of "white" music, narrated by a "brown" audience:

Ay, cosa más resonara, branco es una salvajera,
qué fiesa hace lo branco, la bajona, la culneta,
ólgana, chilimingola, alapa, violona, y seisa,
alto, contralto, tenole, villancica de maestla,
músico con gargantía, olganista con pulsela,
sochantle voza goldare, tipre que echia en garguera[14]

Ah, what a resonant thing, white people sure can carouse,
what a party the white people have organized, bassoon, horn,
organ, shawm, harp, violin and guitar,
alto, contralto, tenor, a first-rate villancico,
a musician with pipes, an organist with rhythm,
a sochantre with a happy, burbling voice, and a soprano who
sings like a bird

Among other features, these lines are especially notable for their description of the ensemble. Indeed, it reads almost like an inventory that one might expect to find among cathedral expenses.

In contrast, the relative poverty of instrumentation among the *moreno* band resonates with the sparse musical instruments listed in seventeenth-century confraternity account books:

| INTRODUCCIÓN | INTRODUCTION |
|---|---|
| Como tienen los morenos | Since the *morenos* have |
| gigante y giganta negra, | a Black giant and giantess, |
| los han pedido esta noche | they have asked for them tonight |
| para hacer su negra fiesta. | to throw their Black party. |
| | |
| 2.Como es de | Since the son is a descendant |
|    David el hijo |    of David |
| gigantes al Niño llevan, | they bring giants to the Child, |
| que si el padre venció a uno, | for if the father defeated one |
| el Niño a otros mucho venza. | may the Child defeat many more. |
| | |
| ESTRIBILLO | REFRAIN |
| —Entle, ah, siolo giganto, entle la giganta beya, | —Come on in, Mr. Giant, come in, pretty lady giantess, |
| venga, siola, la gitana, repicando castañeta. | Come on, Mrs. Gypsy, ringing her castanets, |

—Entle. —Entle que entle. —Venga. —Come on in. —Come, come on in.
—Venga que venga. —Come on. —Come, come on.
—Danza. —Danza que danza. — —Dance. —Dance up a frenzy. —
Vuelta. —Vuelta que vuelta. Turn. —Turn about in circles.
—Venga salao, glavetona, con la —Come to the sarao, slaves, with
cotiya beyena, the court of Bethlehem,
toca guitarra y sonaja, pa li tocay play the guitar and rattle, play the
la rabela. rabel for him.
—Entle . . . —Come on in . . .
—¿Van entrando lo giganto? —Sí, —Are the giants coming in? —Yes-
siolo, turo entla. sir, they're coming in.
—Pues bese lo pe al Niño Jesú. — —Then kiss the Baby Jesus' feet. —
Cu, cusumbú, cusumbú. Cu, cusumbú, cusumbú.
—¿No entla lo cascabele? —Sí, siolo, —Are the bells coming in? —Yessir,
turo entla.[15] they're coming in.

In these lines, the "gigante y giganta negra" (Black giant and giantess) dance and whirl to the sound of popular instruments: castanets, bells, a guitar, a "sonaja," (shaker or rattle) and a "rabela" (rabel or rebec).

For the most part, Tollis de la Rocca's description of the *moreno* band references percussion instruments. The details can be useful for imaging the sounds and body movements of the dances that accompanied the band. Rhythmic instruments like these correspond with the frenetic motions and lightness of feet that stand out in representations of Black and African dance in the early modern Hispanic world. Furthermore, Tollis de la Rocca's description suggests a strong presence of percussion in Afro-Mexican musical practices, which may well have incorporated ankle rattles like those used among West and Central African groups. Indeed, throughout the region, ornamental idiophones fashioned from a variety of materials accompany ceremonial dances. Ndiaye calls attention to the tradition's persistence among Afro-diasporic people living in the Hispanic world. Indeed, accounts of *guineo* dancing during Brazil's Corpus Christi festival describe bells on the dancers' legs.[16]

Finally, I would be remiss not to point out that the Spanish lyrics might encode other styles of African-derived instruments as well. For example, "rabela" could refer to a Spanish folk fiddle that early modern music and literature often associate with shepherds or other rural figures. Nevertheless, it is also possible that here, the term describes a West African stringed instrument for which the lyricist had no other word, like, for instance, the pluriarc, a bowed or plucked lute that indigenous African groups from the west, central, and southern African coast use in ceremonies. Like Rogério Budasz summarizes, such instruments often accompany healing and religious rituals, where they sometimes induce trance.[17] Budasz details the strong presence of pluriarcs in accounts of Afro-descendant music in Brazil, beginning in the late eighteenth century.

Elsewhere on the African Atlantic's American shores, Kristina Gaddy has traced the history of lute-like instruments, which she argues are predecessors of the contemporary banjo with African roots. At their most basic, these objects feature a hollowed-out body that musicians seem to fashion from available materials, such as a gourd or the shell of another fruit, for instance. A neck protrudes from the instrument's body, and strings of animal hair or other organic material allow for strumming or bowing. Often, carvings decorate the neck or resonator. Gaddy relates instruments like these to West and Central African traditions. She compiles evidence for their use among enslaved people in various parts of the Black and African diaspora, where they sometimes appear alongside descriptions of danced performances with ankle rattles.[18] Although her remarkable detective work does not extend to the Spanish-speaking world, the lutes' prevalence in contexts like seventeenth-century Jamaica or Martinique make it plausible that Afro-descendant musicians in New Spain incorporated similar objects into their musical practices. In line with this hypothesis, the description of Black music at a festival in Tollis de la Rocca's villancico could be evidence for the presence of Afro-diasporic lutes in New Spain, particularly given its resonances with Gaddy's research.

While the *blanco* ensemble performs with a four-part choir and a full orchestra, a rich array of dances characterizes the *moreno* procession. Indeed, the narrators underscore distinctive aspects of their own festival: "tocando lo salambeque, gallalda y palaleta, / que no lo sabe lo branco, aunque son muy buena pieza" (playing the *sarambeque*, the *gallarda*, and the *paradeta* / songs that the white people don't know, even though they are very good pieces).[19] The dances described here poke fun at the performers and inscribe their bodies within a kinetic, Afro-descendant tradition whose characteristic movements are rhythmic, light, and highly energetic. First, the gallarda is a Spanish courtly dance that the *Diccionario de Autoridades* describes as "mui airosa" (very elegant). The reference may be humorous, for the idea of Black performers knowing the piece and not white ones would have been out of tune with the expectations of the day.

The graceful *gallarda* offers sharp contrast with the other kinetic forms mentioned in Tollis de Rocca's villancico. Continuing, the *paradeta* is linked with the peasant dance known as the *villano*. The imagery of Afro-descendants performing this genre would have harmonized with their low status in the social hierarchy and also echoed musical references to rural instruments like the rebec. Moreover, K. Meira Goldberg links the word to convulsions, a reference that underscores the frenzied motion often associated with Black dance and duplicated here in the rhythmic instruments.[20]

Lastly, the *sarambeque* was an Afro-descendant dance of notable popularity in the Spanish- and Portuguese-speaking world. Peter Fryer discusses its evolution.

> In Minas Gerais, were danced the *quimbete*, another variant of the samba, and the *sarambeque*. The latter dance came from Mozambique, where it was known in the Chuablo language as *saramba*, which means "dance featuring swaying bodies and hips accompanied by amorous gestures to the rhythm of small bells and rattles," and also "the small bells and rattles used in this dance"; the Nyungwe (Wangongwe) call it *sarama*, the Yao *salamba*, with the same meanings. In the first half of the seventeenth century it was popular in Portugal (where Francisco Manuel de Mello advised husbands that for a wife to know about this dance, and to carry castanets in her pocket, were sure signs of licentiousness), and, as the *zarambeque* or *zumbé*, in Spain (where dictionaries defined it as "Very gay and rowdy strumming and dancing, which is very frequent among the blacks").[21]

The instrumentation that Fryer describes—castanets, rattles, and strummed instruments—align with the music that the Afro-descendant band plays in "Como tienen los morenos." The frenzied, lascivious movements that he associates with the *sarambeque* deepen these resonances. Such connections illustrate how imaginings of Afro-descendant dance as well as its accompanying sounds can complement each other.

Finally, no reading of "Como tienen los morenos" would be complete without considering the Black giants that form part of the procession. Although giants are a hallmark of Corpus Christi celebrations throughout western Europe and the Americas, scholars have not yet connected them to Christmas parades. Nonetheless, there is evidence that giants appeared in processions other than Corpus Christi. For example, Matluck Brooks notes that a 1671 display for the Feast of San Fernando in Seville included giants and a dragon.[22] Likewise, Edward Muir underscores the incorporation of giants in a variety of celebrations. He observes that these larger-than-life representations sometimes took their inspiration from popular or religious figures, including Gargantua and Goliath.²³ In "Como tienen los morenos," it seems likely that the giants relate to Goliath, for the final lines of the introduction mention David slaying the Philistine behemoth. Accordingly, giants in the Afro-descendant procession visually support the poetic reference to the conflict between David and Goliath. In the context of the well-known battle, they recall Jesus' lineage and also signify the magnitude of his power.

In addition to the giants' possible incorporation in a Christmas celebration, the figures' overt racialization in Tollis de la Rocca' villancico also merits reflection. While Curcio-Nagy notes that Afro-descendants often carried the giants and made them dance along the route, the inclusion of Black or other racially marked figures has garnered less scholarly attention.²⁴ Nevertheless, there is evidence of dark-skinned giants in Spanish processions. First, Nicolás de León Gordillo's "Mapa del Orden con que se haze la Solemne Procesión del Corpus Christi en la Sta. Metropolitana y Patriarcal Iglesia de Sevilla en 1747" (Map of the Order of the Solmen Process of Corpus Christi in the Holy Metropolitan and Patriarchal Church of Sevilla in 1747) includes a seven-headed dragon, *cabezudos*, and an array of giants, two of whom are Black.²⁵ Likewise, Valerio draws attention to a female giant with Afro-descendant features who appeared in the 1657 Corpus Christi procession in Madrid. He asks: "Did Mexican *tarascones* share in this racialized aesthetics? If so, by whose design? These are important questions that future research may be able to answer."²⁶ From my perspective, it seems likely that New Spain also featured Black and other non-European giants. Indeed, Curcio-Nagy takes note of a 1722 festival where the costumed Goliaths "represented the four parts of the world."²⁷ It is easy to imagine that such a display might have inspired racialized imaginings of the four figures. In light of such evidence, Tollis de la Rocca's representation of Afro-descendant festive practices in his early eighteenth-century villancico can further support hypothesis about the incorporation of Black giants in New Spanish processions.

For all this, "Como tienen los morenos" illustrates cultural exchange among African, European, and Indigenous cultures. Nevertheless, such a reading also generates tension that resonates with contrasting approaches to Afro-descendant sound elsewhere in the archive. Indeed, the lyrics establish a clear division between *moreno* and *blanco* celebrations, and the striking difference between the two musical ensembles underscores their dissonance. Here, as in other villancico imaginings, like the next few chapters will show, Afro-descendant characters intervene in the festive setting with their own sonic customs which, though disruptive, are integral to the process of harmonization that takes place when otherwise disorderly sounds affectively respond to spiritual and political authority.

### FUNERALS

Beyond the processions associated with feast days, confraternities took part in New Spanish auditory culture through their participation in funerals. There are limited mentions of musical instruments and other sound objects in confraternity records of funeral expenses. One notable exception is free African Juan Roque's will, which includes instructions for a sung requiem.[28] While Roque's testament offers remarkable detail, it is important to bear in mind that his burial reflected his social standing as a free, property-owning member of the Zape community, which von Germeten explains is a New World group with ties to Sierra Leone.[29] Other members of his community would have made arrangements for simpler celebrations. Nonetheless, even at the funerals of less prominent individuals, it seems likely that in the very least, singing would have taken place at these ceremonies, perhaps with accompaniment using whatever instruments those in attendance had on hand. Like the other forms of Afro-Mexican religious expression discussed in this chapter, undoubtedly funeral processions offered opportunities for performing cultural identity and ancestral memory.

There is some evidence that ceremonial dance was part of early seventeenth-century burial displays that Black and African confraternities organized. Von Germeten draws attention to a 1611 incident where more than 1,500 Afro-descendants gathered for the funeral of an enslaved woman whose mistreatment led to her death. She observes that

> clerics from the confraternity's church [Confraternity of Blacks of the Monastery of Nuestra Señora de la Merced] could not control the dances and ceremonies that took place in connection to the funerals. According to some Portuguese informers who understood the slaves who spoke in the language of Angola, the next step was a violent attack on Spaniards during the extensive processions in the week before Easter.[30]

The original documents surrounding this uprising can lend insight into the dances to which von Germeten refers. Luis Querol y Roso transcribed one of the reports in his 1931 or '32 article "Negros y mulatos de Nueva España (Historia de su alzamiento en Méjico en 1612)" (*Negros* and *mulatos* from New Spain [History of their uprising in Mexico in 1612]). The account frequently underscores gatherings among members of the Afro-descendant community as opportunities for planning revolts like those of 1608 and 1612. As a result, this and related documents, including Nahua chronicler Chimalpahin's telling of the same histories, can be key resources for understanding early Afro-Mexican festive culture as well as its relationship to resistance, as Valerio shows.[31]

To be certain, the ideological stance of written accounts like the one that Querol y Roso includes rings loud and clear. Their underlying goals were to condemn the uprisings and draw attention to the unrest that troubled all levels of New Spanish society at the time. Nevertheless, when approached from a perspective that accounts for their plurivocity, just like in Cécile Fromont's polyphonic readings of nineteenth-century travelers' visual representations of Afro-Brazilians, it is possible to attend to important ethnographic details that the reports encode.[32] Indeed, there is no escaping the fact that despite the emic perspective and prejudices of the reports' authors, to some degree they capture the daily life of real subjects, who do not often speak for themselves in the archive.[33] For instance, the document that Querol y Roso transcribes includes noteworthy accounts of funeral practices. After the 1611 death of the abused woman that von Germeten referenced, the informer observes that "los negros con mucha furia y alboroto arrebataron el cuerpo de la difunta y salieron con el por las calles de la ciudad por partes de tarde a la ora que auia de ser el entierro dando vozes y gritos lo lleuaron a las casas Reales de Palacio en que el Arçobispo residia" (with great frenzy and noise, the *negros* snatched away the body of the dead women and marched with it in the city streets during parts of the afternoon at the time when the burial was to be with loud cries and shouts they carried it to the Royal houses of the Palace in which the Archbishop resided).[34]

Later that year, when Pablo Brioso, an elected official from the Black Confraternity of the Monastery of Nuestra Señora de la Merced, became ill and passed away, members of the group organized his burial. The report describes: "se juntaron muchos negros con ceremonias y rritos barbaros usados en su nacion de alaridos cantos y danças lacearon y regaron el cuerpo con vino y aseite, y lo mismo la sepultura, metiose uno viuo en ella y auiendole echado tierra y vino se leuanto furioso con una arma en la mano" (many *negros* got together with ceremonies and barbaric rituals used in their nation with shrieking songs and dances they bound and washed the body with wine and oil, and they did the same to the tomb, a live participant climbed in it and having tossed in earth and wine he stood up furiously with a weapon in his hand).[35] Despite their problematic tone, the accounts of funeral practices in these documents offer important insights into Afro-Mexican customs. In lieu of explanations written by the participants themselves, outsider portrayals can offer significant details. To this end, Joan Bristol observes that the descriptions have resonances with funerary practices from Africa's west coast.[36]

In addition to these connections, auditory tropes stand out in reports of the slave revolts under viceroy Luis de Velasco y Castilla and his successor Fray Francisco García Guerra that illustrate the importance of sonorous tropes in dominant imaginings of Black and African people. Indeed, in all of these examples, there is a clear connection between Afro-descendant sound and violence. Along similar lines, María Elena Martínez observes that around the time of the 1612 uprising, "even the sound of hogs squealing made . . . [the Spanish elite] imagine themselves as targets of colonial uprisings."[37] This perception of Black sonorities as threatening is striking, and it recurs in accounts from seventeenth-century New Spain. The trope invites speculation about why the sonic presence of Afro-descent so disturbed observers. Juxtaposing fearful descriptions of Black sound in funerals and other public ceremonies with the imposition of order through bells and imagined harmony can provide a partial response. Indeed, unregulated sound cannot be dampened easily, particularly in large groups. Thus, unruly Black sonorities threatened the social and political concord that governed urban space and also disturbed the rituals intended to perform order.

In addition to attending to the burial rites of confraternal brothers and sisters, members of these organizations sometimes took part in processions to honor the death of important politicians or dignitaries. For instance, Guijo notes the presence of Black and Indigenous musicians from Mexico City's numerous confraternities at interim viceroy Marcos de Torres y Rueda's 1649 funeral rites. He relates: "salió la procesión, que se compuso de todas las cofradías de indios, negros, mulatos y españoles, y tras ellos las religiones; salieron de palacio, vía recta por la calle de Porta-Cœli y las demás por donde estaban las posas, donde en cada una se le cantaba su responso" (the procession began; it was composed of all of the confraternities of *indios*, *negros*, *mulatos*, and Spaniards, and behind them the clerics; they proceeded from the palace, on a straight route through the Porta-Cœli Street and the others where the *posas* were, where at each stop a response was sung).[38] Funeral processions in colonial Latin American included a series of *posas*, or stations where mourners paused with the body to sing responses. The practice formed part of an ecclesiastical musical economy that exceeded cathedral walls and harmonized urban space with the spiritual imaginary. Moreover, the *posas* were a status symbol. Martina Will de Chaparro notes that "priests had been paid for each posa they made, and people measured the social standing of the deceased in part by the number of stops."[39] Like in other festive contexts, New Spanish funerals became important opportunities to display one's standing in social hierarchies. Given the connections between the size of a funeral procession and the importance of the deceased in New Spanish society, visible and audible participation of lower castes in the funerals of church officials and politicians reinforced civic order.

For all this, the confraternities' presence was twofold. First, they raised their voices in celestial harmony to accompany the dead on their journey heavenward. In this way, Afro-descendant processors and, indeed, all ritual participants, performed celestial sounds. Through song, they vocalized the angelic harmonies that awaited the deceased. The heavenly choruses that await the dead in paintings like Gaspar Conrado's *Muerte de San Francisco Javier* (c. 1650–70, Pinacoteca de la Profesa, Templo de San Felipe Neri) and Miguel Jerónimo Zendejas' *Entierro de San Ignacio* (1780s, Colegio de las Vizcaínas) are useful visual complements for imagining this concept. Beyond their spiritual symbolism, the presence of Black, African, and Indigenous confraternities in funeral ceremonies for New Spanish leaders is a sign of devotion, similar to the political examples of Afro-descendant sound that Chapter 3 explored. The sung responses that confraternities performed at each of the *posas* rang out as resonances of heavenly concord and also harmonized their voices with the deceased subjects' authority. For this reason, Afro-descendant confraternities' participation in funerals can be read through a harmonic lens that attends to the concept's political and spiritual significance.

## POPULAR RELIGIOUS PRACTICES

Beyond these sanctioned activities, New Spain's Black and African inhabitants also organized their own gatherings where music and dance were prominent. Extant documentation of these festivals rarely offers insight into the exact sights and sounds that took place. Nevertheless, the private setting of these events, in combination with their guise as Christian festivities, created spaces to preserve resonances of Afro-descendant sound. Curcio-Nagy maintains that in general, "popular religious rituals and beliefs were flexible, spontaneous, and open to other religious traditions present in the colony."[40] As we shall see, examples of religious syncretism have strong resonances with existing Catholic practices, and they often heighten the devotional tone. Such concordance with Christian ideals made it possible to interpret Indigenous or Afro-descendant traditions carried out in these settings as exemplary and thereby created a framework within which to preserve cultural memory and customs that would have disrupted urban harmony in other settings. In the remainder of this chapter, I will explore some of these devotional practices and the sounds that accompanied them.

Like Curcio-Nagy rightly points out, popular expressions of faith offered opportunities to reaffirm community identity, and participants often belonged to the same caste or social class. Since colonial officials were concerned about uprisings among marginalized groups, these gatherings provoked suspicion. Descriptions of them frequently signal large, disorderly crowds as a key element, and sonic tropes heighten representations of the groups as threatening. For instance, Guijo describes altars in private homes and neighborhood processions that took place during the 1650 Christmas Eve celebrations in Mexico City.

> Dicho día, Noche Buena, todos los vecinos de esta ciudad pusieron en las ventanas de sus casas, cual un bulto de Nuestra Señora, y otras pinturas de su Majestad en lienzos, de particulares devociones, y adornaron de muchas luces, con que siendo la noche muy oscura estaban las calles muy claras, y fue de mucha devoción; y se juntaron mulatos, negros, mestizos e indios en las cruces de esta ciudad, y a voces rezaban el rosario de nuestra Señora, de rodillas, y por las calles iban haciendo lo mismo los muchachos en cuadrilla mucha cantidad de ellos, y personas de todas edades, y hubo cuadrillas por las calles gobernadas de algunos sacerdotes que los seguían.[41]

> That day, on Christmas Eve, everyone who lives on the outskirts of this city placed in the windows of their homes: an effigy of the virgin Mary, and other canvas paintings of her Majesty, of specific Marian devotions, and they adorned [their windows] with many lights, so that the streets were very bright in the very dark night, and [the atmosphere] was devout; and *mulatos, negros, mestizos*, and *indios* in the corners of the city, and they loudly prayed the rosary of our Lady, on their knees, and gangs of children traversed the streets in great numbers doing the same, along with people of every age, and there were gangs in the streets, guided by some of the clergy who followed them.

Guijo's description relegates this popular practice to the urban periphery, which primarily was home to members of the city's lower castes. He marvels at the religious fervor of participants in the ceremony and also makes note of the vast number of worshipers as well as their noisy, disruptive presence.

Just one year later, Guijo refers to a 1651 document that cautions Mexico City inhabitants against such celebrations. The edict specifically prohibits praying the rosary in public spaces:

Domingo 15 de dicho [año], se hicieron edictos en los púlpitos de las iglesias de esta ciudad, despachados por el ordinario, en que prohíba que no saliesen clérigos, ni otras personas eclesiásticas ni seglares, así hombres como mujeres, rezando por las calles, como lo habían hecho y acostumbrado desde la Noche Buena el rosario de nuestra Señora, ni en las cruces, sino que lo rezasen en sus casas e iglesias.[42]

Sunday, the fifteenth of that [year], edicts were read in the pulpits of the churches of this city, executed by ordinary jurisdiction, which prohibited clerics, other ecclesiastical and laypeople, both women and men, from going out to pray the rosary of Our Lady in the streets and corners, like they had done regularly since Christmas Eve. Instead, they were to pray in their homes and churches.

The edict does not take issue with the devotional practice itself. Rather, it responds to two specific elements: large gatherings and noise. Indeed, even when raised in worship, the sounds of Afro-descendant, *mestizo*, and Indigenous crowds disrupted urban order.

Guijo's description resonates with the apparently widespread practice of organizing private gatherings to celebrate religious holidays or venerate particular saints. Throughout the early 1600s, edicts were issued to curb these oratories. For instance, a 1643 document forcefully discourages popular religious festivities.

Nos pareció el señor Doctor Don Antonio de Gauiola Promotor Fiscal, de este Sancto Officio, y nos hizo relación, q en acuesta dicha Ciudad de México, y en otras Ciudades de acueste nuestro districto, se ha introducido de algún tiempo a esta parte, por perniciosa, e intolerable costumbre, entre todo genero de gentes, con notable escándalo del pueblo Christiano, el haber en sus casas Oratorios priuados, de particulares devociones, haciendo nacimientos de nuestro Saluador y Redemptor Iesu Christo, y Altares a la santíssima Virgen Maria nuestra Señora, su Madre, y a otros Santos, y Santas de su devoción, poniendo en dichos Altares cierto número supersticioso de candelas encendidas, y algunos retratos de personas que murieron con opinion de virtud, con resplandores, y señales de gloria, sin determinación de la Santa Sede Apostólica, y contra lo por ello determinado, congregándose para tales celebridades, en las partes donde se hazen los dichos Oratorios, hombres y mujeres, a comer y beber demasiadamente, a jugar, cantar, y baylar con gran deshonestidad, e indecencia.[43]

> Dr. Don Antonio de Gauiola, Prosecutor of this Holy Office, appeared before us and told us that in this the aforementioned Mexico City, and in other Cities in our district, a pernicious and intolerable custom that is notably scandalous to Christians has been popular for a long time in these parts, among people of all classes, who have in their homes private Oratories to venerate particular devotions, like the birth of our Savior and Redeemer Jesus Christ, or Altars to the most holy Virgin Mary our lady, his Mother, and to other male and female saints, putting in these Altars a superstitious number of lit candles, and portraits of people who they opine died with virtue, with brilliance, and with signs of glory, without the determination of the Holy Apostolic See, and against that what has been determined by it, they congregate for such celebrations, in places where the Oratories are assembled, men and women get together, to eat and drink too much, to play, to sing, and to dance with great impurity, and indecency.

The directive specifically addresses song and dance, and it underscores the illicit nature of the music that accompanied popular devotional practices. In particular, the authors condemn the mixing of men and women in partner dances. The detail lends a sexual tone to their description that resonates with the lasciviousness attributed to popular dances elsewhere in Inquisition files. In particular, such descriptions aligned with imaginings of Afro-descendant dance. Marín López explains that

> the public spaces of the city, ideal for the display of identity and collective ceremonial expression, also provided the natural setting for the proliferation of licentious dancing. . . . The presence of these dances can be considered a form of political critique and religious satire, ranging from the comical to the openly erotic; all in all, they attacked colonial power and, at the same time, provided a form of entertainment with its roots in popular culture.[44]

While Marín López's study focuses on street music, his framing also applies to the vehement condemnation of song and dance in decrees that prohibited oratories. Indeed, the music and other forms of expression that took place in private spaces threatened church authority and provided opportunities to blend religious and popular practices, as well as European and non-European customs.

Continuing, the 1643 edict prohibits private devotions, specifically, dance and music: "no hagáis, no consintáis hazer en vuestras casas, los dichos Nacimientos, y Oratorios públicos, en que intervengan indecencia de lugar, banquetes, juegos, musicas, bayles y juntas" (you will not organize, or allow to be organized in your homes, the aforementioned Nativities, and public Oratories, in which indecency of place, banquets, games, music, dance, and gatherings all come together).[45] In addition to music and dance, the edict's authors also underscore the "indecency" of such gatherings. In this case, the term refers to a secular setting that is not fitting to venerate saints or carry out other religious ceremonies. This emphasis on place suggests a certain anxiety among New Spanish officials about spiritual gatherings that took place behind closed doors, where the Christian traditions that they sought to impose might mix with expressions of African or Indigenous faith. Moreover, resonances among "indecency" and concepts like blood purity and race, like those discussed in Chapter 1, enable the edict's reader or listener to imagine private oratorios as pagan assemblies, where non-Christian practices abounded.

Within this context, sonorous interventions would have been particularly disruptive. As Inquisition case records show, these auditory signs of "indecency" drifted out the open windows of unsanctioned gatherings and alerted passersby to activities that were otherwise concealed, save for a lighted window with the image of the Virgin Maria or a saint. Such sounds were dissonant with the devotional sounds of urban areas like Puebla or Mexico City. Illicit rhythms, laughter, and the sounds of men and women mingling all contrasted with the sonic order that church bells or the criers who read edicts and decrees imposed in order to maintain the cities' spiritual health. Given the persistence of African religious traditions in other private contexts, as the next section will show, it is plausible that diasporic music traditions formed part of oratories that Afro-descendants attended.

By all appearances, the directives that New Spanish officials published did little to quell the popular religious celebrations that took place in the homes of citizens throughout Mexico City. Guijo cites a similar mandate from 1652: "En este mes de diciembre se leyeron edictos en esta ciudad y fuera de ella, despachados por el Dr. don Pedro de Barrientos, provisor de este arzobispado, prohibiendo las danzas y músicas y los altares, y postular limosna con imágenes de devoción por las calles" (In this month of December, edicts were read in this city and outside of it, executed by Dr. don Pedro de Barrientos, ecclesiastical judge of this archbishopric, prohibiting dance and music and altars and seeking alms with devotional images in the streets).[46] Among other activities in Guijo's description, music and dance stand out. Although the reference does not lend insight into the musical styles performed or their accompanying body movements, it illustrates how officials imagined them as disruptive to the city's spiritual and social order. Within the context of urban harmony, colonial officials' perception of these sonorous practices as disturbing or even threatening to ideals of concord is notable. In addition to the examples I discuss here, Curcio-Nagy cites edicts from 1626, 1684, and 1704 that forbade devotional gatherings in private homes. She rightly argues that the number of mandates suggests a proliferation of popular religious festivities in the capital throughout the seventeenth century.[47] At the same time, a poignant question beckons attention: what was it about such festivals that so disturbed New Spanish officials?

One possible response is that private oratorios created spaces for social and racial mixing, as some of the edicts affirm. In a religious context, the possibilities of miscegenation stood out in stark contrast with the hierarchical organization of space in cathedrals and public processions. This spiritual and social disordering threatened Peninsular and Creole dominance, and perhaps also made Christian participants vulnerable to the influence of more recently converted Indigenous and Black participants, who may have maintained spiritual practices from their own cultural traditions. Guijo's discussion of the 1652 mandate does not offer details about who was involved in the private oratories and popular processions. Nonetheless, given his emphasis on the participation of Mexico City's *mestizo*, Indigenous, and Afro-descendant population in his previously cited description of Christmas Eve practices, it is possible to infer that such activities were prominent among lower castes, and also, perhaps, among Creole and Peninsular inhabitants. In addition, the 1643 edict's reference to drinking, games, and lascivious dancing where men and women mixed echoes descriptions of Afro-descendants as thieves and licentious drunkards.

While linguistic and musical parodies of Afro-descendant dance as well as its representation in Inquisition cases obviously respond to dominant imaginings of Black culture as hypersexual and uncontrollable, they may offer windows into the broader underpinnings and influence of such traditions. For instance, Jones relates the "hyperkinetic, provocative movements" associated with the *zarabanda* to trance, a central feature in some African and Afro-diasporic religions, including Brazilian *candomblé* and Cuban *lucumí* (popularly known as Santería and sometimes referred to as Regla de Ochá).[48] In cultural production of the day, he notes that the dance "received harsh backlash for its presumed lascivious nature and sensuality."[49] In contrast with disparaging descriptions, Jones convincingly argues that Peninsular *teatro breve* performed the transatlantic spread of Angolan dances like the *cumbé* and *paracumbé*.[50] Since attitudes like these, or at least some semblance of them, presumably made their way to American soil, it is informative to consider the disruptive song and dance that took place in private oratories in dialogue with the tension that Jones observes.

While Jones focuses on secular representations of Afro-descendant sound and dance, performances at private oratories, some of which I hypothesize featured Black and African cultural expression along with practices from other cultural traditions, can be juxtaposed with lyrical references to such forms in villancicos. The next few chapters will consider the genre in detail. In this instance, as in Chapter 3's discussion of Afro-diasporic presence in New Spanish political ceremonies, it is notable that while non-European sound was tolerated and even celebrated in contexts that permitted its harmonization with urban order, in other instances, it was scorned and prohibited.

As a complement to official edicts, Inquisition cases can shed light on the form, participants, and persistence of these festivities. Curcio-Nagy considers extant records through a lens of gender and maintains that they can lend insight into the devotional habits of everyday women, whose lives and expectations differed from those of their cloistered sisters.[51] Nevertheless, she hypothesizes that Inquisitorial mandates designed to curb the practices responded to the ruling class's anxieties about civil unrest, particularly among non-European castes. "Perceiving a certain precariousness to the established order, Spanish colonists and authorities expressed feelings of unease, which proved to be well founded as riots and rebellions shattered illusions of peace and prosperity in seventeenth-century Mexico. Most important, this emergent multiethnic society meant a mixing of cultures which affected religious mores and practices, forcing the inquisitors to a keener scrutiny of popular religious forms."[52] In the next few pages, I will extend Curcio-Nagy's observations about the role that race might have played in the perception of these parties as threatening. References to mingling among castes, along with emphasis on the disruptive and unruly nature of such gatherings, suggest that political and ecclesiastical authorities perceived the oratorios' disorder through a harmonic lens.

Just like the decrees that prohibited private altars and the accompanying celebrations, Inquisition processes related to them often highlight music, dance, and drink as significant and disruptive elements. For example, the denunciation of a 1663 oratorio, presented before inquisitor Antonio de Peralta, includes detailed descriptions of festive elements at the event. The witness was passing by a home in Puebla, when animated music called his attention. He relates that "en una casa baxa auía oydo una mussica de Arpa y visto Luces encendidas y llegando mas cerca rreconosio un Altar con un frontal morado y quatro Luces encendidas y que al son del Arpa estaba baylando una mujer y el Altar tenia diferentes ymagines de bulto y de pincel" (in a one-story house having heard the music of a Harp and seen Lights burning and coming closer he recognized an Altar with a purple façade and four Lights burning and a woman was dancing to the tune of the Harp and the Altar had different devotional images, both statues and drawings).[53] Further in the proceedings, another witness names the musicians: "un indio que dixo llamarse Simon de la Crus que estaba tocando una harpa y que assitia y a otro indio que dixo llamarse Nicolas [sic] que tocaba una guitarra" (an *indio* who said his name was Simon de la Cruz said that he was playing a harp and that he attended and another *indio* said his name was Nicolas [sic] played a guitar).[54] Throughout the case, informants implicate the guitarist and the harpist as essential to the party's atmosphere. The inventory of belongings found in the establishment includes these instruments and thus confirms their presence.[55] The specific description of the harp and guitar, along with the reference to a woman dancing to the music—a lascivious presentation by the day's standards—is singular among the oratorio cases that I have consulted. Indeed, most accusations simply reference "music and dance." Something about the particular sounds in this setting must have caught the attention of passersby. Since the majority of participants at the 1663 oratory were Indigenous, I hypothesize that the harp and guitar were characteristic of a popular dance with autochthonous roots. If the dance was widely known, then by referencing this detail, witnesses would have drawn attention to the performance of non-European music in an unsanctioned setting.

Among extant cases of New Spanish inhabitants prosecuted for hosting private oratories, one record merits discussion within this book's inquiry into connections among Afro-descent, sound, and popular religious practices in the region's urban areas. Manuel Apodaca Valdez cites the 1649 case of Mariana de la Cruz, a free *mulata* from Puebla who hosted a private party in her home. He notes that there were a number of free and enslaved Afro-descendants among the participants named.[56] To some degree, this detail suggests that gathering in private devotional celebrations served to reinforce community ties, particularly among Afro-descendants. Apodaca Valdez underscores the importance of music and dance in this festivity and notes that descriptions of the event "recuerda[n] las velaciones de santo de las religiones afrocaribeñas de la diáspora" (are reminiscent of the venerations of saints in Afro-Caribbean religions from the diaspora).[57] His observations are astute. Although the Inquisition files themselves give scant details about the sonic practices that took place at Mariana de la Cruz's parties, I contend that intersections among the participants' Afro-diasporic origins and emphatic constructions of the party's sounds as licentious invite a reading of their disruptive dances as forms of cultural expression connected to the performers' heritage.

In the case against Mariana de la Cruz, Lucas Pérez de Ribera charged her with the following:

> La suso dha pusso en las cassas de su Morada un horatorio de la Santa Cruz haciendo novenario que se acabo a los diez y siete de este presente mes para el qual enbido a muchas personas de su sequito y devoción repartiéndoles un dia a cada una de los de dho novenario para que zelebrasen la fiesta abiendo escandalo general en el por los muchos Bailes mussicas y danças que introduxo en los dhos nuebe días.[58]

> In the houses where she dwelt, the aforementioned held an oratory of the Holy Cross that took place during nine days and ended on the sixteenth of the present month in which she invited many people from her community and cult distributing among them one of each of the days of the novena so that they would join in the festivities, where there was general scandal because of the many dances and music that were played during the aforementioned nine days.

Here, the accusation directly relates the "general scandal" that the gathering causes to music and dance. The disordered representation resonates with harmonic imaginings of *urbs* and *civitas* by underscoring sound as the site of disruption. Furthermore, the allegation that Mariana de la Cruz invited members of her community and "devoción" (cult) suggests that the host belonged to one of Puebla's Afro-descendant confraternities. If, indeed, this is the case, then the gender of the accused is significant for understanding the event's preservation of African heritage. Like von Germeten has argued, Black women's agency and leadership in Afro-Mexican confraternities is distinctive and echoes matrilineal systems of kinship in sub-Saharan Africa. She argues that "the highly visible participation of confraternity sisters is an illustration of the ways Afromexicans negotiated with colonial authorities to maintain a distinctive spiritual space in New Spain."[59] From this perspective, it is possible to read Mariana de la Cruz's leadership in her community as a symbol of her Afro-diasporic heritage, particularly given the possibility that the event was connected to a confraternity.

Continuing, the record notes that commissioner of the Inquisition Juan Bautista de Urquiola y Elorriaga found it necessary to take action against Mariana de la Cruz "por lo desonesto y profano con que se acian dhas musicas Bailes y dancas" (because of the lascivious and irreverent nature in which the music and dances were performed).[60] Although the description does not clarify details about the musical activities that took place in Mariana de la Cruz's oratory, the portrayal of "lascivious and irreverent" dances resonates with representations of Afro-descendant dance that have arisen elsewhere in this chapter. Given these similarities, I propose that it is likely that participants in Mariana de la Cruz's festival performed dances from the same genre.

One of the witnesses in the case, a free *mulato* named Miguel de Comilla, offers additional details about the gathering. It included "un altar puesto muy bien aderessado con forma de altar muchos velas de cebo y muchas flores y ramilletes en el qual ubo muchos bayles y musicas todo el tiempo que estuvo dicho novenario" (an altar set up and very well decorated in the form of an altar, with many tallow candles and many flowers and bouquets in which there were many dances and much music all throughout the aforementioned novena).[61] Colmilla is not the only witness to describe an image decorated with flowers and candles as central to the festival. Thus, in addition to the disruptive sonic elements that Mariana de la Cruz's gathering featured, visual aspects of the oratory also disturbed the city's sacred order. In private homes, symbols of sacred rituals like those described in the cases against Mariana de la Cruz undermine the authority of clergy and other ecclesiastical figures. Furthermore, their juxtaposition with Afro-descendant dance and music that was imagined as racy and immoral in other contexts undoubtedly unsettled passersby and church officials alike.

While Curcio-Nagy notes that the consequences of hosting an oratory were often light, Mariana de la Cruz was imprisoned, and Inquisition authorities seized her belongings.[62] Although the present example refers to a single case, her uncharacteristic sentence beckons speculation. On one hand, the *mulata*'s imprisonment could suggest that oratory hosts from lower castes received more severe punishments. On another, perhaps there was something about the party that merited heavier penalties. The dance forms most certainly perturbed Inquisition authorities. Furthermore, the first document in the files states that "añadiendo delicto a delicto" (adding one crime to another) Mariana de la Cruz told partygoers that she had permission from the commissioner of the Holy Office "para que se congregase mucha gente al dicho novenario como se congrego y junto" (so that many people would attend the aforementioned novena, just as many came together and attended).[63] This note offers a possible explanation for Mariana de la Cruz's harsh sentence but it also illustrates how the oratory's organizer manipulated ecclesiastical codes in order to create a space for festive gathering within her own community. Regardless, audio-racial descriptions in this particular case offers strong evidence such gatherings were, indeed, the site of Afro-Mexican music and dance, and there is little doubt that some of the practices that took place behind closed doors preserve the cultural heritage of those present, even if they took a syncretized form.

## HOLY VENTRILOQUISM

From public processions on feast days to home altars and private oratories, it is clear that Afro-descendant sonorities resounded in the spiritual practices of urban New Spain. At times, participants performed longstanding Catholic traditions and voiced their role as marginal and obedient within the region's social hierarchies. Often, the distribution of Black bodies in city streets and ritual spaces mirrored these harmonies. Sometimes, public ceremonies incorporated Afro-descendant song and dance, framed as a resonance of sacred and secular authority so as to harmonize this sector of society within imagined concord. In private settings, New Spain's Black and African residents adopted Christian practices with fervor, for doing so afforded them a space to gather and reinforce community ties. Based on descriptions of these gatherings, it seems likely that worshipers sometimes performed songs and dances with African roots. In this way, private oratories offered opportunities to preserve diasporic cultural heritage in a form that aligned with dominant Catholic ideals.

Afro-descendants also participated in sonic spiritualities that were more distant from Christian ritual. One notable example is a practice that New Spanish Inquisition cases refer to as "hablar por el pecho," or "speaking from the chest." This term refers to a form of divination in which practitioners offer divine insight by speaking in tongues, in a voice that observers affirm seems to come from their chest. If Inquisition documents are representative of the custom, these fortune tellers were almost exclusively women of African descent. The apparent prevalence of diviners among this ethnic group beckons a reading of the practice that relates it to African traditions, just as Javier Villa-Flores has skillfully done. Here, I will extend Villa-Flores's analysis to consider the specific role that the disembodied voices played in disrupting urban harmonies and also enabling the fortune tellers to vocalize authority.

For the most part, the enslaved women who were prosecuted for oracular ventriloquism were classified as "bozal" (not Hispanicized) or by their African origins as "conga" or "angola." The detail suggests that the practice was common among newly arrived enslaved women and beckons a reading that accounts for its resonances with diverse cultural traditions. Indeed, "speaking from the chest" is a complex example of how contact among European, Indigenous, and African people gave birth to polyvalent practices that resonated differently among ethnic groups. As Villa-Flores affirms, ventriloquist fortune telling has both Christian and West African roots. In the Bible, accounts of oracular ventriloquy disrupt links between voice and identity. From this perspective, the ritual lends itself to an open-ended question:

"Who is speaking?" In New Spain, inquisitors responded by condemning "speaking from the chest" as witchcraft, and they affirmed that the women who practiced divination in this way communicated with familiars or evil spirits. In contrast, autochthonous groups from Congo and Angola viewed prophecy and possession as a means of communicating with their ancestors and revered the wisdom that practitioners gained from bodily and vocal connections with other realms.[64]

Men and women from all walks of life visited the oracles to consult with them about their love lives, seek advice for weighty decisions, and more. With some regularity, the diviners—or their owners, in the cases of the enslaved—charged for these services. Consequently, oracular ventriloquism created a space in which Afro-descendant women could earn money and also assume a position of authority before those seeking their consult. Villa-Flores remarks that

> los archivos criminales y de la Inquisición del siglo xvii revelan . . . que las esclavas buscaban contrarrestar su marginalidad social recurriendo al cimarronaje, la rebelión, la blasfemia y la adivinación. De todas estas prácticas, sólo la adivinación las dotaba de autoridad y prestigio social en la Nueva España, y su uso por parte de mujeres esclavas ofrece una oportunidad única para analizar la relación entre tácticas de resistencia y políticas de identidad en un entorno colonial.[65]

> criminal and Inquisition files from the seventeenth century reveal . . . that enslaved women sought to counteract their social marginalization by turning to plots to flee, rebellion, blasphemy, and fortune telling. Of all of these practices, only divination provided them with authority and social prestige in New Spain, and its use by enslaved women offers a unique opportunity to analyze the relation between tactics of resistance and identity in a colonial setting.

Put another way, Inquisition files capture Afro-descendant women's longing for freedom, better living conditions, or higher social stature.[66] Nonetheless, just as with the capones who sang in New Spain's urban cathedrals, in the case of these Black and African fortune tellers, we find what Villa-Flores refers to as a "calle de dos sentidos" (two-way street).[67] He observes that on one hand, the women's divination afforded them authority and audibility. On the other, they depended on their owners to provide access to various ethnic groups. With some frequency, these slaveholders stood to gain financially from the practice, whose popularity was widespread enough that masters or employers could charge a fee for fortune tellers' services. "Speaking from the chest" thus illustrates the complex negotiations that Afro-descendants and their masters undertook within the established institutions and racialized order of New Spanish society.

For all this, it is informative to examine how voice and marginal gendered and racial identities intersect within the tradition. Indeed, oracular divination vibrates with the quiet hum of practitioners' aspirations for a better future; their disembodied vocalizations literally give voice to such yearnings. And yet, the sounds that one experienced as part of these fortune-telling rituals were far from human, and they seemed disconnected from the embodied presence of the diviner. Witnesses described the women's voices as thin and otherworldly, and they were shocked that the fortune tellers seemed to vocalize from spaces other than their mouths. Villa-Flores describes:

> las esclavas respondían a las preguntas con una voz "delgada" y apagada cuyo sonido comparaban los asistentes a las reverberaciones de un silbato suave, el quejido distante de un conejo en agonía, o incluso el sonido de un "títere ronco." La mayoría de los testigos identificaban al pecho como la fuente de la voz ultraterrena, pero otros creían que emanaba de una de las axilas o los costados de las esclavas. Lo que los asistentes encontraban más sorprendente, por supuesto, era el hecho de que las ventrílocuas se hubieran borrado como sujetos de enunciación.[68]

> the enslaved women responded to questions with a "thin" and muted voice whose sound attendees compared to the reverberations of a soft whistle, the distant groan of a rabbit in agony, or even the sound of a "hoarse puppet." The majority of the witnesses identified the chest as the source of the supernatural voice, but others believed that it emanated from one of the armpits or the ribs of the enslaved women. What attendees found most surprising, of course, was the fact that the ventriloquists seem to have erased themselves as speaking subjects.

Continuing, Villa-Flores also notes that some of the women who "spoke from the chest" were capable of imitating sounds from the natural world, and witnesses suggested that they even moved objects through sound.[69] Details like this underscore the skill and detail with which the ventriloquists carried out the practice, and they also illustrate sound's capacity to unsettle even the most dubious listener when it strays from the norms of culturally specific auditory contexts.

In instances of ventriloquism among enslaved women, the separation of self and voice enabled divination practitioners to disassociate themselves from their natural identity and adopt a position of authority that they might not otherwise possess. Precisely, Villa-Flores remarks that "al hablar con la voz de otro, o permitir que un ente sobrenatural hable a través de ellas, las mujeres intentaban superar su exclusión de otros canales de expresión establecidos y así hacerse de autoridad y prestigio" (by speaking with the voice of another, or allowing a supernatural being to speak through them, the women tried to overcome their exclusion from established forms of expression and in this way gain authority and prestige).[70] As Villa-Flores signals here, one of the most notable details of the practice is that Afro-descendant women disembodied their voices in order to gain influence and audibility that their Black corporeal existence might not otherwise afford.

The manner by which ventriloquist fortune telling enables these enslaved women to acquire a position of authority is twofold. First, given the long history of possession in African religions as well as observer descriptions from Inquisition files, it is impossible to discount the possibility that trance plays a role in rituals where practitioners "hablar por el pecho." Erika Bourguignon explains that "possession trance, as a psychological state, involves alternations of consciousness of personal identity, and some bodily changes, as well. In the ritual context, it includes the shared belief that such changes result from the takeover of the body and person of the actor by another entity—a spirit, an ancestor, another living person, or even an animal."[71] Such distance between everyday identity and the possessed self creates a state of ritual liminality in which a practitioner might behave in ways that would be otherwise far afield of his or her personality. From the gendered perspective that is commonly associated with trance—particularly among African and Afro-diasporic practices—Bourguignon maintains that "women's possession trance must be understood as a psychodynamic response to, and expression of, their powerlessness. It is not an attempt to gain power for its own sake, but, rather, an attempt to gratify wishes whose satisfaction is ordinarily denied the women, wishes rooted in their situation."[72] Along these lines, it is possible to read possession among enslaved Black and African women from New Spain as a response to limits placed upon them. Indeed, the practitioners' dual marginalization in viceregal society was a product of both their race and gender. Just like the Afro-descendent sopranos that Chapters 1 and 2 explored, the fortune-tellers' heightened vocal presence afforded them authority and audibility.

While this broad explanation offers some insight into the art of "hablar por el pecho," however, the women's ability to disguise or throw their voices beckons a more nuanced analysis. To this end, Adriana Cavarero's discussion of Afro-diasporic music, language, and voice can address the female diviners' affected vocalities. Cavarero remarks upon the changes that languages undergo in colonial contexts. She notes that

> languages have a sensibility all their own with respect to the acoustic experience of the environment.... There is no universal sonority that is equal for all languages, for all mouths or all ears. The voice is not only sound; it is always the voice of someone as it vibrates in symphony with the natural and artificial sounds of the world in which she or he lives. Language imitates the sonority of the environment; it is attuned to its music.[73]

For Cavarero, the voice and its communicative modes are archives of cultural memory. While contact, displacement, and exchange may alter voices, the original gesture of envoicing one's place in the world persists across space and time. When we examine Inquisition accounts of "speaking from the chest" through this lens, another possibility vibrates just below the surface of written accounts, perturbing their very authority. Perhaps the women were not practicing ventriloquism at all. Instead, is it possible that the women spoke in their native tongues, and onlookers interpreted something about the pitch or tone as ventriloquism? Methods in historical linguistics of African languages, perhaps in interdisciplinary conversation with Hispanic or Mexican studies, could shed light on the subject.

Finally, it is important to situate the African roots that Villa-Flores draws out in divination rituals within the broader Black Atlantic. The undertaking leads us outside of Mexico City and Puebla, to 1620s Acapulco, where Diego Javier Luis has recovered the case of Cathalina Gonzalez de Santiago, a free *mulata* who incorporated dance into her divination ritual. Luis notes that "the testimony does not reveal the dance's purpose, but the Afro-Atlantic context suggests spirit mediumship."[74] Indeed, there are strong resonances between Cathalina Gonzalez de Santiago's performance and contemporary Afro-diasporic practices, like, for example, *lucumí* ritual in Cuba. This syncretic religion derives from Catholic practices and those of the enslaved Yoruba, brought to Cuba from Nigeria. Today, *lucumí* practitioners gain spiritual wisdom, *aché*, through *toques de santo*, ceremonies that invite their spirits, or *orishas*, to become present through music and carefully choreographed dance. Sacred *batá* drummers open the ritual with special rhythms, or *toques*, for each orisha (*oru del igbodú* in *lucumí*), and ceremonial singers (*akpwón*) later accompany the *batá* with speech-like praise songs known as *oriki*. In this way, music-making welcomes the orishas and encourages them to become present or embodied through highly choreographed dance movements that the mounted dancer or *caballo* performs.[75]

To be certain, many questions remain to be answered before drawing conclusions about the relationship between Gonzalez de Santiago's seventeenth-century New Spanish divination and present-day *lucumí* possession. Nonetheless, commonalities among the two rituals—specifically, links among sound, dance, and divine wisdom—offer a firm foundation for drawing the practices of Gonzalez de Santiago and the oracular ventriloquists of New Spain into a broader, Afro-Atlantic web. Perhaps by viewing these acts of popular spirituality through a diasporic lens, scholars can glean a fuller understanding of Afro-Mexico, both in terms of its colonial roots and their persistence in contemporary practice.

## CONCLUSION

As this chapter has shown, Black and African people living in New Spain's urban spaces played official and unofficial roles in the region's spiritual landscape. Through confraternal processions and other paraliturgical activities, Afro-descendants gained visibility and audibility while responding to imposed sonorous and social orders. In contrast with these public celebrations, private spaces seemed to offer greater freedom of expression. Indeed, the Holy Office's prosecution of fortune tellers or the conveners of religious gatherings illustrates how these practices threaten established order, particularly inasmuch as sonic practices concealed from the public ear reinforced community ties and offered spaces for the preservation of Afro-descendant cultural heritage. By all appearances, syncretic devotional practices offered important opportunities for Black and African people in urban New Spain to articulate and transform their diasporic identities. While civic and ecclesiastical officials sought to impose order and harmony through public religious ceremonies, inevitably, out-of-tune voices, off-kilter rhythms, and uncontrollable bodies challenged the imagined concord between non-European practitioners and Christian ideals.

## REPERCUSSION

Beyond urban New Spain, a better understanding of Afro-descendant sonorities and other forms of expression in devotional practices during the viceregal period can also prompt re-readings that attend to the Black and African roots of contemporary traditions. For instance, the contemporary folk saint La Santa Muerte is venerated in Mexico and beyond. In today's popular culture, as Kali Argyriadis' affirms, this popular image forms part of a fetishized web of violence that links narcotrafficking, Cuban Regla de

Ochá, and devotion to La Santa Muerte. Popular culture, Mexican journalism, and even the television series *Breaking Bad* prolong these connections.[76] Nevertheless, the figure's history is much more complex. With medieval European roots and a New Spanish presence that dates back at least as far as the seventeenth century, La Santa Muerte generally takes the form of a robed, female skeleton.[77] Images and statues imitate Catholic iconography, and La Santa Muerte frequently appears with a crown of flowers or attributes like a globe, a heart, or a scythe. Beyond these Christian resonances, practitioners associated her with pre-Hispanic cults of death that strongly resonate in Mexico's national identity, just as Argyriadis's fieldwork in Veracruz shows. Nevertheless, in this coastal region, once home to the port through which enslaved Africans entered New Spain and also known for *cimarrón* (Maroon) communities like Yanga, La Santa Muerte's Afro-descendant roots run deep. While Argyriadis's informants identify the saint's Blackness with the influence of Afro-diasporic forms of spirituality like Brazilian *candomblé* or Cuban Santería, I maintain that it is also plausible that the figure is a legacy of the Afro-Mexican Catholic practices that this chapter has drawn out.[78]

Complementary to these Afro-diasporic resonances, Argyriadis's description of celebrations that honor La Santa Muerte bear a remarkable resemblance to the private oratories that so plagued New Spanish authorities.

> Los grupos de rezo, encabezados por un líder (en general el dueño del altar en cuestión o de la estatua principal), organizan rosarios en casa o tiendas particulares, desbordando a veces en el espacio callejero, en los cuales se recitan el Padre Nuestro y el Ave María, numerosas oraciones católicas, . . . transformando en particular las oraciones a la Virgen en oraciones a la Santa Muerte. . . . Pero a diferencia de los rosarios católicos, se dedica también gran parte del ritual a actos de purificación y curación (limpias), operados bajo un espíritu formal y con fuentes de inspiración múltiples. Finalmente, es frecuente observar que se prolongue la ceremonia con una fiesta, donde se come, se toma, se canta, se baila, se intercambian regalos e informaciones, en fin donde se refuerza el sentimiento comunitario. A nivel íntimo, también a diferencia del uso oficial que se le da a las imágenes católicas, la Santa Muerte es solicita para trabajos de magia, inclusive trabajos ofensivos llamados de "magia negra," aunque no todos sus devotos acepten o reconozcan hacerle este tipo de peticiones.[79]

> Prayer groups, headed by a leader (in general, the owner of the altar in question or of the main statue), organize rosarios in homes or local shops, spilling over into the streets at times, in which the Our Father and the Ave Maria are

recited, along with numerous Catholic prayers, . . . especially prayers to the Virgin transformed in litanies to the Santa Muerte. . . . But unlike Catholic rosaries, a large part of the ritual is also dedicated to acts of purification and healing (spiritual cleansing), carried out with a formal spirit and with multiple sources of inspiration. Finally, observers frequently note that the ceremony can be extended with festivities, where participants eat, drink, sing, dance, exchange gifts, and converse, in sum, where a sense of community is reinforced. On an intimate level, in contrast with the official use ascribed to Catholic images, the Santa Muerte is asked for acts of magic, including offensive acts called "black magic," although not all of her devotees accept or recognize making such petitions to her.

The ritual elements that Argyriadis describes echo those found in seventeenth-century clandestine celebrations, including the assembly of altars in private or local spaces, community identity, the recitation of Catholic prayers, music, dance, food, and even witchcraft or popular magic. To be certain, these traditions are common to sacred ceremonies from a number of cultures, and therefore, we can only draw a tenuous line from colonial devotional practices to present-day ones. Nonetheless, the resonances should prompt scholars to take another look at this tradition, with eyes and ears attuned to the conceivable persistence of early Afro-Mexican religious practices. Are the ties between La Santa Muerte and devotional expression among Black Cubans as close as researchers have long believed, or do the voices of enslaved and free Afro-descendants who were once integral to New Spain also echo in this and other contemporary examples of popular Catholicism? Furthermore, by entertaining the prospect that such resonances exist, is it also possible to attend to other contemporary devotional practices in Mexico with greater awareness of similar rituals' significance as spaces from which seventeenth-century Black and African people performed diasporic identities and cultural memory?

CHAPTER 5
# Harmonizing Blackness in *Villancicos*

> Polque pala sel cantola
> E menestel la solfeona
>
> For to be a singer
> One must sing in tune and follow the beat
>
> —**Unknown composer**, "El negro Maytinero"

Complementary to Afro-descendants' actual participation in religious festivals, the music, texts, and other forms of cultural expression that accompanied these ceremonies performed the social and spiritual roles of Black and African people living in New Spain. Black villancicos are the most prevalent of such representations. On one hand, the portrayal of Afro-descendant characters responded to the low social position that the dominant class imagined for them. Stylized speech, affected vocalities, crude instrumentation, and unruly dancing all circumscribed Afro-descendants as outsiders who disrupted civic concord. Despite these dissonances, however, villancicos also harmonized Black subjects with Christian ideals. From a sonic perspective, they frequently portray Afro-descendant song and dance in resonant devotion, even though the characters have a simplistic or erroneous understanding of Catholic doctrine. Such tensions show how representations of African and Afro-Mexican sound in New Spain responded to the harmonious framework that undergirded spatial, social, and spiritual relationships. In this chapter, I will examine lyrical representations of Afro-descent in villancicos by focusing on two separate but interrelated aspects: vocalic and bodily imaginings.

My specific focus is how villancico lyrics harmonize Afro-descendant sounds and bodies within New Spain's imagined sociopolitical harmonies. I avoid overreliance on the dominant/marginal binary that privileges elite perspectives and instead approach these works as polyphonic festival sources that encode diverse sounds and identities. I draw out tensions that emerge between how Afro-descendant subjects harmonize with the urban and ritual spaces in which they move and dissonant representations of their song and dance. Often, villancicos portray Black musical expression as awkward motion and cacophony that are clumsily dissonant with New Spain's sociopolitical sounds but joyfully resonate with Christian ideals. For this reason, I will argue here that representations of Afro-descendant performance in villancicos record a listening positionality that responds to the pieces' evangelical bent. A reading from this perspective sheds light on how the genre scripts Black sonorities in order to perform spiritual conversion. Furthermore, it invites speculation about the Afro-diasporic traditions that villancicos might encode.

First, lyrics are notable aspect of these pieces' racialized discourse. Written representations of Afro-descendant speech are rooted in a Spanish literary style known as *habla de negros*, or blackspeak, a stylized pseudo-dialect that Francisco de Quevedo codified in his *Libro de todas las cosas* (1631). Spanish authors including Lope de Vega, Pedro Calderón de la Barca, and Luis de Góngora drew upon these written and auditory constructions of Afro-descent to codify Blackness in poetry and theater alike.[1] The use of *habla de negros* was widespread in Spain and the Americas, and writers like Sor Juana Inés de la Cruz and many anonymous poets adapted the subgenre to the colonial context.[2]

John Lipski has cataloged common features of early modern blackspeak from the Spanish-speaking world. In addition to the much-cited example of exchanging /1/ for /r/, he also mentions errors in agreement, nasalization, and extra vowels that appear at the end of words.[3] Beyond these linguistic characteristics, abundant laughter often punctuates villancico portrayals of Black and African speech. Like Deborah Singer argues, the trope sometimes imagines Afro-descendants as jovial, and other times, it imparts a mocking tone.[4] Moreover, textual or musical references to timbre and vocal quality further distance Black voices from supposedly normative Western vocalizations. Finally, blackspeak also features vocables like "gulungú" or "menguiquilá" that seem to imitate African words. On one hand, scholars emphasize the manner in which these near-indecipherable phrases contribute to the marginalization Afro-descendant characters.[5] On the other, Glenn Swiadon Martínez offers a linguistic perspective that convincingly relates them to African languages.⁶ Swiadon Martínez's work illustrates that it is possible to read *habla de negros* as the inscription of Western ears listening to African sounds. For all this, regardless of its faithfulness to the actual sounds of Black and African speech, it is clear that *habla de negros* imagines Afro-descendant Spanish speakers as different. The extensive and deliberate manner in which the trope scripts the sonorities of Black characters intends to codify them as non-Hispanic before New Spain's diverse listening public.

Complementary to caricatures of Black and African speech, the body in motion was also important for Black villancicos' imaginings of Afro-descent. Indeed, references to so-called "Guinean" dance and related forms, motifs of Black beauty rooted in Song of Songs 1:5 "soy negra, pero (y) hermosa" ("I am Black, but [and] beautiful"), and Christian antithetical tropes that contrasted white purity with Black skin all formed part of a canon for representing Black bodies on stage.⁷ References to Afro-descendant dance often include descriptions of wild, uncontrollable movements and lively motion, including quick footsteps and jumping. Sometimes, they eroticize the characters with allusions to twirling hips and buttocks. To this end, Marcella Trambaioli remarks that the "convulsión, soltura y bullicio que caracterizan los gestos y los pasos del baile de negros, además de aludir a lo sensual, evocan el mundo infernal trazando una implícita ecuación entre africanos y seres demoníacos" (the convulsions, unbridled movement, and noise that characterize the gestures and steps of Black dance, in addition to sensual allusions, evoke the infernal world, tracing an explicit link between Africans and demons).⁸ Trambaioli's comments about devilish associations with Afro-descendant sonorous expression are especially telling in a context like that of villancicos, for evangelization is one of their many functions.

These disorderly portrayals of Black dance may indeed have some roots in Afro-Hispanic reality, as Jones and K. Meira Goldberg maintain.⁹ Complementary to Jones' observations about how Spanish theater contributed to the popularization of Afro-diasporic dance forms, Goldberg draws out the transatlantic influence of early modern Afro-Hispanic dances. She connects historical descriptions to later traditions in Cuba, Martinique, Brazil, Peru, Argentina, Spain, and more.¹⁰ For her part, while Ndiaye recognizes the value of "read[ing] black dances recorded in white archives as instances of authentic Afro-diasporic dances evidencing a retention of African aesthetics and subjectivity," she distances herself from this interpretive framework and instead underscores wild movement as a form of embodied autonomy.¹¹

Despite provocative links with agency and cultural memory, I am concerned with the politics of representation that underlies villancico renderings of Black dance. On one hand, such imaginings portray Afro-descendant bodies as disruptive elements that vibrate beyond harmonic order. From this perspective, Black and African dancers in villancicos sharply contrast with lay brothers and sisters who decorously march in religious processions. Nevertheless, on the other hand, lyricists and composers often find ways to harmonize Afro-descendant characters' kinetic commotion by depicting it as a performance of their Christian faith. Consequently, villancicos' representations of Afro-diasporic dance draw upon themes of evangelization to tame Black bodies' otherwise-uncontrollable motion.

For all this, scholars have drawn upon connections between body and voice to link blackspeak and dance in readings of villancicos. Trambaioli loosely underscores the relationship between the round, rhythmic vocalizations of *habla de negros* and the names that Hispanic authors give to Afro-descendant dances.[12] Jones situates the theme within broader discourses of literacy, orality, and race. He turns to Black studies scholars

> to challenge Western epistemic illiteracy in the field of black sound—or, at least, the sounds emitted not only by black mouths but also by the dances and sonic Blackness of habla de negros speech forms' grunts, hums, musicality, and vocables. Appearing in the baile, entremés, and mojiganga subgenres of the teatro breve, the variety of black dances explored herein represent most vividly instances in which Black communication and expression manifest in early modern Spain.[13]

Jones's analysis of how written records encode Blackness as non-lexical sounds and corporal movements is intriguing. Here, I extend the observation by showing how harmony guides representations of Afro-descendant bodies and voices.

It is impossible to consider imaginings of Afro-descendant dance without also thinking about their musical accompaniment. Musically, villancicos do not imagine Blackness in the ways a contemporary listener might expect. Although it is easy to associate lively rhythms or the sometimes-exotifying accompaniment that contemporary recordings use with "Africanness," scholars problematize facile readings of such sounds. With respect to Spanish guitarist Santiago de Murcia's "Cumbées" (1732), Mario Ortiz remarks that "no es sino un producto de la imaginación europea del sujeto africano; una imaginación que quedó grabada en un artefacto cultural que 300 años después lo usamos como puente epistemológico para crear nuestra propia imaginación del mismo sujeto" (it is nothing more than a product of the European imagining of African subjects; an imagining that was recorded in a cultural artifact that, some three hundred years later, we use as an epistemological bridge to create our own imagining of the same subject).[14] Like the musicologist rightly observes, it is important to account for historical distance and the listening ear of present-day audiences when discussing and programming these works. Along the same lines, Baker questions contemporary performances that overemphasize the Black villancico's "African" roots.[15]

Although it is unlikely that villancicos musically encode African traditions, there is a strong relationship between textual and musical representations of Blackness. Singer remarks that "there are syncopation, onomatopoeias and different rhythmic combinations that, on the one hand, seek to generate a lively sound and, on the other hand, project the idea that black men and women have a 'natural inclination' towards music and dances."[16] These connections merit attention in the context of how villancicos represent Afro-descendant sound. Indeed, for those pieces with extant scores, it is important to account for how the musical language might heighten or extend textual themes. In addition to Singer's observations, Chapter 2 also showed how musical imagining of Afro-descendant voices constructs racialized characters through compositional technique. Here, I complement such readings by examining lyrical allusions to Black sounds in villancico texts.

### PERFORMING BLACK VOICES, UNMASKING BLACK FACES

To begin, Juan Gutiérrez de Padilla's Black villancico for the Puebla cathedral's 1651 Christmas celebration features stereotypical Afro-descendant tropes that are characteristic of the genre. For example, the opening lines of the *estribillo* introduce a Black chorus that happily dances and sings unintelligible lyrics in celebration of Jesus's birth:

| | |
|---|---|
| Atentos al bayle, | Attentive to the dance, |
| la nación morena, | the *moreno* nation |
| también, se convida, | also joins in, |
| y todos se alegran, | and they all become happy, |
| esdrújulos cantos | proparoxytonic verse |
| en sus medias lenguas, | in their pidgin languages, |
| que ni ellos se entienden | that not even they understand |
| ni ay quien | nor is there anyone who |
|    los entienda.[17] |    understands them. |

In these lines, linguistic references frame the Afro-descendant choir as non-European and situate their "Otherness" in the sound of their voices. First, the musical group's provenance is not a specific area like "Angola" or "Congo," as is often specified in other villancico lyrics and even historical documents. Instead, the reference to "la nación morena" (the *moreno* nation) highlights the Afro-descendant group's ethnic diversity and also underscores the importance of phenotypical markers in racial constructions.[18] The subsequent description of their "pidgin languages" heightens this allusion, for newly arrived *bozales* from various African regions likely compensated for their lack of lingua franca with a mixture of Spanish, Portuguese, and native African languages. Finally, the lyric voice draws out rhythmic differences that distinguish Afro-descendant verse or song from its European counterparts. Although there is no extant score for this villancico, it is likely that playful hemiolas and other rhythmic variations in the musical setting heightened this poetic representation.

Continuing, the introduction imitates the Black voices that praise the infant. Here, tautonyms like "roro" and "mumu" imagine the Afro-descendant choir's song as childish and incomprehensible. The narrative voice incorporates some blackspeak characteristics, including inconsistencies in article-noun agreement and the replacement of /r/ with /1/.

| A la roro y | To the sound of "shh-shh" and |
|---|---|
| a la mumu, | "hush, hush," |
| a la roro y a la nene, | to the "shh-shh" and "baby," |
| y a la tutulutu, | and to the hubbub,[20] |
| que no duelme[19] | he doesn't sleep. |

"Roro" and "mumu" are more than just nonsense syllables that reinforce the narrator's insistence upon Afro-descendant incomprehensibility. Indeed, the *Diccionario de Autoridades* classifies "rorro" and "mu" as words used to soothe a sleeping child. The allusion provides striking—and humorous—contrast with the happy dance that the *estribillo*'s opening lines describe. In the *coplas*, subsequent references to lively dance and a "horde" of Black worshipers amplify the distance between the lullaby that the *estribillo* suggests and the Afro-descendant choir's noisy din. The absurd juxtaposition of genres reinforces stereotypical associations of Black and African people with excessive parties and also accentuates their voices as loud and disruptive.

The *coplas* of Gutiérrez de Padilla's piece feature the voices of Afro-descendant characters themselves. The lyrics develop auditory and linguistic themes from the *estribillo* and further portray the Afro-descendant characters as disruptive and outside of Eurocentric norms.

| | |
|---|---|
| 1. Quelemo ser lo su guéspele<br>pala daye mucho pésigo,<br>una cameya de dátiles<br>y uno borrica de alvéchigos. | 1. We want to be his guests<br>in order to give him many peaches,<br>a camel carrying dates<br>and an ass bearing peaches. |
| 2. Aquí samo tanta cáfila,<br>carregadito con cuébano,<br>que les hablamo en arábigo<br>y en vascueço respondémolo. | 2. Here we are in a big horde,<br>weighted down with baskets,<br>we talked to them in Arabic<br>and responded to them in Basque. |
| 3. Mucho de plisa venímole,<br>plu q[ue] sa neglo colélico,<br>de Monicongo con plátano,<br>y de Castiya con nuégaro.[21] | 3. We came to him quickly,<br>because the *negros* are in a mad frenzy,<br>[we come] from Kongo with bananas,<br>and from Castilla with nougat. |

These verses feature a jumble of cultural themes that make the singers' ethnic identity difficult to ascertain, despite the typical blackspeak that sounds their Afro-descent on stage. It is not common for villancico lyrics to blend racialized tropes in this way, and the anomaly enables a metadramatic reading of Gutiérrez de Padilla's villancico. Indeed, throughout the *coplas*, the Black actors draw attention to race's performative underpinnings by adopting diverse ethnic identities.

In the first strophe, the characters bring gifts of peaches and dates. Both foods are associated with the Middle East and the Islamic world and indicate the group's origin. Here, the lyrical attitude is stately and gracious, for the choir members wish to be guests of the Holy Family. The tone changes in the second verse. In these lines, the visitors describe themselves as a "horde" carrying a number of baskets. They speak in both Arabic and Basque, references that suggest the singers' Spanish origin. Although both languages relate to Spain's cultural roots, it is important to note that neither is the region's national tongue. Consequently, one might imagine the choir members as unintelligible to each other as well as to their New Spanish audience. The continued use of blackspeak further disrupts linguistic codes in these lines.

The third *copla* draws in tropes of Blackness that would have been familiar to early modern audiences in Spain and the Americas. Here, the choir takes on an Afro-descendant role that matches their voice. The performers arrive at the Nativity with frenzied motion that mirrors typical representations of Black dance, and they bring gifts of Castilian nougat and Kongolese bananas. The alignment of African and Spanish products in this strophe blurs the singers' origin and leaves the audience wondering whether they hail from Europe or a sub-Saharan land. Additionally, while the banana's association with the Kingdom of Kongo certainly reflects racial stereotypes, particularly in light of the *estribillo*'s classification of the choir as the "*moreno* nation," it is also possible to read it as a symbol of cultural pride, just like Spanish *turrón*, or nougat, whose popularity persists today.

From a perspective of contemporary Afro-descendant performance, the Kongolese bananas in Gutiérrez de Padilla's villancico evoke Miguel Luciano's 2006 print *Plátano Pride*. This image of a young, Black boy sporting a platinum-encased plantain on a chain graces the cover of Raquel Z. Rivera, Wayne Marshall, and Deborah Pacini Hernandez's edited volume *Reggaeton*. Marshall and Rivera argue that *Plátano Pride*, along with two other images in Luciano's series, "suggests some poignant readings of reggaeton style by juxtaposing charged cultural symbols, bringing the plantain's evocation of field labor, racial and class stigmas, and national and/or Caribbean pride together with contemporary connotations of platinum as a glorification of conspicuous consumption."[22] The historical and geographical distance between Gutiérrez de Padilla's villancico and Luciano's print notwithstanding, it is pertinent to wonder if the Pueblan composer or some of his multicultural audience might have envisioned the banana through a similar lens. After all, poetically, the African fruit's juxtaposition with Castilian nougat aligns the two as equally prized gifts.

For all this, the first three *coplas* of Gutiérrez de Padilla's villancico substantiate the *estribillo*'s affirmation that Afro-descendant speech is impenetrable. The hodgepodge of cultures and stereotypes that these *coplas* blend is reminiscent of the *ensaladilla* except for a pair of significant differences. Whereas the *ensaladilla* inscribes ethnic difference by imagining various dialects, each character grouping in Gutiérrez de Padilla's play-within-a-play voices its intervention in blackspeak. This distinguishing feature suggests that Black actors take on all of the ethnic roles. Though the villancico's storyline is fictitious, it is not difficult to imagine it as a parody of Afro-descendant performers who took on "white" parts in villancicos, particularly given Gutiérrez de Padilla's contact with Luis Barreto.[23] Without documentary evidence of other Afro-descendant performers in the Puebla cathedral chapel, a reading from this angle is purely speculative. Nonetheless, the composer's curious framing of Afro-descendant voices in the Black villancico from his 1651 Christmas set raises questions about performance practice and casts doubt on hypotheses about Euro-descendant actors' prominence on stage.

Against this backdrop, the final *coplas* of the Black villancico from Gutiérrez de Padilla's 1651 Christmas set literally unmask the performance.

| | |
|---|---|
| 6. Tlaemo tanto de títere<br>pala habra de mistelio<br>q[ue], aunq[ue] cantamo lo mángulu,<br>tambén savemo retruécano. | 6. We bring many puppets<br>so that there will be mystery<br>for, although we mángulu are singing,[25]<br>we also know wordplay |
| 8. Venimo con unos páxalos<br>a pediye, pues es mérico,<br>que quitamos las calátulas<br>o ponemo branco el évano.[24] | 8. We came with some birds<br>to ask him, because it is fitting,<br>that we take off our masks<br>or whiten the ebony. |

Here, the choir reveals that their ethnic caricatures have been part of a show, complete with puppets and actors in costume. The last two lines of the eighth strophe reveal a plot twist, for when the players remove their masks, they expose light skin beneath dark masks. This reversal of a blackface performance alludes to the spiritual purification that takes place during Christian worship—a literal "whitening" of the soul.[26] In this way, Gutiérrez de Padilla's play-within-a-play performs both the racialization and the evangelization of Puebla's Afro-descendant population. When the characters reveal white faces at the piece's conclusion, they remind spectators that the costumes, movements, and speech patterns that mark them as Black in the performance are representations of a racial identity that the villancico brings into being.

### RACIALIZING TIMBRE

I opened this chapter's lyrical analyses with a discussion of how Gutiérrez de Padilla's 1651 Christmas villancico disrupts ideas about Afro-descendant marginalization in public performances in order to distance subsequent interpretations from the notion that Euro-descendant actors would have taken on these roles. Indeed, just like Luis Barreto, Juan de Vera, and the dancers who performed for López Pacheco's entrance into Mexico City have hinted, Black artists had a more prominent role in New Spain's music and theater scene than historical narratives allow. This context conditions my subsequent readings of villancicos from New Spain and elsewhere in the Spanish empire, for I maintain that actors from a variety of ethnicities could have performed the roles.

Although prior scholarship privileges language's phonemic and grammatical contents as key sites for distinguishing Black and other non-European voices in villancicos, sonorous references also contribute to the racialized vocality that these pieces establish. For example, the seventh villancico from Sor Juana's attributable set for the 1678 Christmas liturgy in the Puebla Cathedral (*Villancico* xvi) includes a vocal representation of Afrodescent that exceeds linguistic imaginings of voice. It opens with an echoic dialogue between two Black characters:

| | |
|---|---|
| —¿Ah, Siñol Andlea? | —Ah, Señor Andrés? |
| —¿Ah, Siñol Tomé? | —Ah, Señor Tomé? |
| —¿Tenemo guitarra? | —Do we have a guitar? |
| —Guitarra tenemo. | —We have a guitar. |
| —¿Sabemo tocaya? | —Do we know how to play? |
| —Tocaya sabemo. | —We know how to play. |
| —¿Qué me contá? | —What are you telling me? |
| —Lo que ve.[27] | —What is seen. |

Here, the reflective structure causes the listener to wonder if Siñol Andlea truly knows how to play the guitar or if his affirmation is an inverted echo of Siñol Tomé's query, a simple refraction of sound. Lyrical echoes in the villancico allude to a phonocentric process of meaning-making that exists beyond language's semantic limits. In this way, Sor Juana's villancico text uses echo as a rhetorical tool for hearing beyond the bounds of Western epistemology. The trope resonates with similar themes elsewhere in her oeuvre.

For example, in *Romance* 8, one of Sor Juana's three "Lyrics for Singing," the nun reflects upon the experience of voice and self-hearing. The poem recounts the tale of Narcisa, a feminized Narcissus. At first, Narcisa's vocalizations are a sign of her agency, for they are powerful enough to harmonize the sun, stars, and all cosmic elements.[28] Nevertheless, when the subject's song reflects back to her, the results are fatal.[29] Precisely, hearing one's own voice echoed as acousmatic sound disrupts several foundations of Western subjectivity: the distinction between self and other as well as tentative links between voice and identity.[30] The result is an endless chain of re-signification that underscores the vocal utterance (and by extension, the self it represents) as a performative event whose echoic residue opens to transformation.

While Narcisa may not have fared so well, *Romance* 8 illustrates how sonic resonance can amplify voices beyond the textual bounds of the poetic self, particularly in sung pieces. In *Villancico* xvi, Siñol Andlea and Siñol Tomé describe their musical contributions to the Nativity celebration. They commemorate Jesus' birth with "guitarriya y paderiyo" (guitar and tambourine) and also take part in the festivities through song.[31] Despite this apparent assimilation to Christian practices, however, Sor Juana's text contrasts the figures' musical interventions with "white" harmonies. The Afro-descendant characters negatively describe their own singing and affirm: "—Sando ronca y resfrïara, / cantalemo mal, siñole" (We sound hoarse, like we have a cold, / we are singing badly, ladies and gentlemen).[32] Later, Siñol Andlea and Siñol Tomé distinguish their voices from European and Euro-descendant counterparts: "De los branco no guardemo, / que tosemo a lo billaco" (We stay away from white people / because we have a wicked cough).[33] Consonant with the humorous tone that often distinguishes the "ethnic" villancicos, the singers suggest that their hoarse technique is the result of tobacco use.[34] Tobacco had multivalent meanings, all associated with the lower castes. It was produced on large plantations in Veracruz, which depended on the labor of numerous African and Afro-Mexican workers. Furthermore, it was also an Indigenous product that Europeans associated with laziness and sloth.[35]

This timbral reference is not unique to Sor Juana's lyrics but rather appears as a trope that imagines Black voices throughout American and Peninsular repertoire. To give one example, Vicente Sánchez's *ensaladilla* "La fama de que es Dios hombre" (The news that God became man) similarly underscores husky timbre as a distinguishing feature of Afro-descendant vocality. Like Sor Juana's *Villancico* xvi, Sánchez's lyrics highlight the Black singers' hoarse, gruff tone. Furthermore, just like in the nun's text, "La fama de que es Dios hombre" attributes this characteristic to illness. The first singer invites the second, Dominga, to participate in Epiphany festivities. Unfortunately, though, Dominga has a cold.

While Mandinka pleads with her friend to take part in Epiphany musicmaking, Dominga protests that she cannot sing because of her cold. She sneezes all throughout the piece and fears that the "white" attendees ("la brana") will make fun of her:

| [Negro 1.] Que cantemo. 2. No polemo, polque catarrara zamo, y si negla eztolnudamo, la brana, que ez zucarrona burla halá de la plezona, ¡Hachú! 1. Jezuz.[36] | [*Negro* 1.] Let's sing. 2. No, we can't, because we have a cold, and if we sneeze, and sing hoarsely, the white people will make fun of us Achoo! 1. Bless you. |

Although there is no extant score for Sánchez' text, it is easy to imagine a loud and boisterous musical interruption every time Dominga sings "hache," an onomatopoeia that imitates sneezing. While Dominga protests, the first singer offers her a lozenge and tries to convince her otherwise. Alas,

Dominga replies to her friend that her throat is fine; the constant sneezing is her most disruptive symptom.

| | |
|---|---|
| [Negro 1.] Mala está, tome, plimiya, caramela y pelandiya. 2. La galaganta está bitarra, que no zentimo el catarra, sólo eztonudá zentimo.³⁷ | [*Negro* 1.] You're awfully ill, take this, cousin, a lozenge with a bit of candied almond. 2. My throat isn't the problem, we don't even notice the cough, we are only suffering from the sneezing. |

Finally, the two characters settle on a solution. Mandinka resolves that "si tú dises hache y yo digo Jezúz" (if you say ach- I'll say bless you).³⁸ Every time that Dominga sneezes, her companion will reply with a devotional phrase, and no one will be any wiser about her illness.

Complementary to representations of Afro-descendant voices as a result of illness, writers also likened them to animals or musical instruments. For instance, Sor Juana's *Villancico* 232 likens the *bozal* singer's piercing, nasal sound to a trumpet: "¡Huye, husico ri tonina, / con su nalís ri trumpeta!" (Away with you, dolphin-singer / with your trumpet-like nose).³⁹

Sor Juana was not the only lyricist to compare Afro-descendant song to brass instruments. Mexico City cathedral sacristan and poet Gabriel de Santillana includes similar references in his villancico set for the 1688 Nativity of the Blessed Virgin Mary. In the second villancico on the third nocturne, a Black choir compares their voces to a tromba marina:

| | |
|---|---|
| —Pues las nenglu tuque su tlumba malina que tlumba las nenglu tene en su fosica.⁴⁰ | —So the *negros* play their tromba marina because the *negros* have a trumpet in their snouts. |

Despite its name and comparison in the poem, the tromba marina that is central to Santillana's play on words here is not a wind instrument. Rather, the term references a chordophone whose use dates to the Middle Ages. The tromba marina was a massive string instrument with a triangular body and one or two cords. Players bowed the tromba marina quite high on the neck and fingered below the bow. This technique is different from what performers use for other string instruments. For instance, a violinist draws his or her bow across the resonating box and fingers the neck. The tromba marina's unique playing position emitted a particular sound. Suzanne Lord describes, "instead of the normal tones, the tromba marina instead produced sounds known as harmonic overtones, which sounded abnormally

**5.1.** Filippo Buonanni, "Tromba marina." *Gabinetto armonico pieno d'istromenti sonori.* Rome: Nella Stamperìa di Giorgio Placho, 1722, 103r. Courtesy of the Smithsonian Libraries and Archives. https://doi.org/10.5479/sil.744616.39088011251444.

high and rather ethereal. As if that weren't enough, the bridge over which its string was stretched was left intentionally loose on one end so that when the string vibrated, the bridge would also vibrate against the instrument face and produce a rasping sound."[41] Based on Lord's description, by likening Black voices to the tromba marina, Santillana underscores the nasal, hoarse quality of their song. Furthermore, the instrument's physical shape surely related to the racialized imagining of Afro-descendants' overly large noses. Despite these representations of Black and African people as different from Euro-descendants, the tromba marina metaphor in Santillana's lyrics aligns dark-skinned performers with the Virgin Mary, even as it distances them from other ethnic groups. Like Lord affirms, the instrument's name has nothing to do with the sea. Rather, it is a Marian reference that recalls its longstanding use in convents. By comparing Afro-descendants' noses to the tromba marina, then, Santillana's representation embodies the singers' faith and makes it visible for all to see. In this way, the reference performs Black Christian devotion and simultaneously underscores racial difference. I will return to these ideas in Chapter 6.

References like these highlight vocal timbre as a marker of racial identity, echoing one of the main constructions that Nina Sun Eidsheim interrogates in her study of conflations of voice and race. Indeed, the scholar discusses how subjective listening positions inform vocal imaginings of racialized bodies, even in acousmatic contexts. Eidsheim's insights underscore cultural tendencies to associate immaterial auditory interventions with an unseen, racialized sounding body. Under these circumstances, personal and cultural listening positions condition the auditory imagination to hear particular sounds as embodiments of ethnicity, gender, or other identities. When we isolate sonic interventions from both the sounding vocal apparatus and the listening ear, they become uncanny echoes whose formlessness unsettles registers of audio-symbolism and the embodied politics that the imply. Eidsheim observes that

> the *symbolic* position is concerned with the ways in which vocal sound presentations are interpreted. Broadly described, this position considers how dynamics (of power, for example) are played out through the acceptance of meaning-making.... Whether voice is read and understood as sound, as text, or even as implicated with the body, this analysis assumes that the power and impact of voice take place only on the symbolic level. In other words, for voice to have a different meaning, it is the symbolism that must be changed. However... the voice becomes so intimately associated with whatever symbolic position is taken that considering the connection between the thick event of the voice and the given symbolism as a true choice becomes challenging.[42]

For Eidsheim, Western constructions of voice are so deeply entrenched in a dialectics of identity and embodiment that it is difficult (and perhaps inappropriate) to examine the concept through a purely sonorous lens. Therefore, she sets out to amplify the politics of racial difference that conditions the listening ear and influences the way that bodies make and listen to (interpret) sound.

In contrast with pejorative imaginings of Afro-descendant voices, some villancicos offer more positive counterpoint. For instance, Oaxaca chapelmaster Tomás Salgado's "Que tambén somo gente la nengla" ("We *negros* are people too," Christmas, early eighteenth c.) exalts the sounds of an Afro-descendant chorus that lends joy to religious festivities.

| | |
|---|---|
| Que tambén somo gente la nengla | Since we *negros* are people too we are going to sing to Jesus of Nazareth |
| al Dioso nasiro hemo de cantá | |
| y en nuevo tuniyo alegle y de gusto | and in a happy new tune and with gusto |
| cun turo plesiso, | and with a lot of percussion, |
| Golgeos, tinaros y sus golguritos. | turns, trills, and mordents. |
| —Blabamente discurrimo, | —Boldly singing the tune, |
| —La tipre a yegaro, | —The soprano has arrived, |
| la Baja a veniro | the Bass has come in |
| essa tura junta | everyone is gathered |
| que canta cunmigo.[43] | who sings with me. |

The villancico's opening stanza relates the first line's affirmation about Black personhood to the Afro-descendant singers' musical capacity. Unlike disorderly representations of non-European song that I have discussed in other contexts, Salgado's piece describes the Black musicians' performance as "alegre" (happy) and "cun turo plecisio" (with much precision). In the musical score, a tenor solo sings the majority of this section. The musical setting is largely declamatory; however, melismas on words like "alegle" (happy) and "gusto" stand out and heighten these words' emotional impact. Here, the characters' joy resonates with the festive occasion and therefore performs their faith. Furthermore, Salgado set "golgeos, tinaros y sus golguritos" (turns, trills, and mordents) to a series of runs and trill-like figures in the tenor solo section. In this way, the singer's line illustrates the vocal technique he describes and also offers an opportunity for the Black performer to demonstrate his expertise.

The discussion of the singers' "plecisio" and musical and lyrical allusions to refined techniques like the trill merit attention, for these references underscore the singers' skill. Indeed, the *Diccionario de Autoridades* describes "precisión" as "particularidad o distinción en las cosas" (special talent or refinement in something). It is possible to read Salgado's lyrics from two perspectives. From one angle, descriptions of the Afro-descendant singers' dexterity might brim with genuine appreciation for a well-trained musical group. In this case, it is not too far a leap to hypothesize that in addition to the sopranos from Chapters 1 and 2 or the equestrian ballet performers from Chapter 3, other Afro-descendant singers carried out their craft with a dexterity that defied crude stereotypes about Black music. From another angle, however, the value that Afro-descendant narrators ascribe to their own music might also contrast humorously with their performance,

**5.2.** Tomás Salgado, "Que també somo gente la nengla." *Neglo celeblamo, Pañolo burlamo: La negrilla en España y en América*, vol. 2, edited by Leonardo Waisman, (self-published, 2021), 599, m. 17–34.

especially if singers peppered their roles with deliberate errors.

Subsequent lines support a reading from the second perspective, for they give the impression that, in its enthusiasm, the Afro-descendant choral group performed at a tempo they could not manage:

| | |
|---|---|
| cantemo ya uniro, | we are all singing together, |
| gualdando las pausas | attentive to the rests |
| en el villancico, | in the villancico, |
| y a compás que veloses, | and to the quick rhythm |
| a la turu seguimo, | that we all follow, |
| una, dosa, quatlo, cinco.[44] | one, two, four, five. |

Here, although the group affirms that they followed all of the villancico's rhythms and rests, their count in line 23 skips right past the third beat. This omission suggests some irregularities in other parts of their performances and weakens the opening declaration of their talent. The musical setting of "una, dosa, quatlo, cinco" (one, two, four, five) further caricatures the performers' clumsiness. On the heels of a section in strict triple meter, when the chorus begins to count the rhythm, they begin each number on an off-beat. Furthermore, the tenor solo line leaps in intervals of fourths and fifths. The melodic anomaly furthers these two sections' ungainly tone.

In sum, just like Sor Juana's *Villancico* xvi or Sánchez's "La fama de que es Dios hombre," representations of Afro-descendant voices in "Que també

**5.3.** Tomás Salgado, "Que tambén somo gente la nengla." *Neglo celeblamo, Pañolo burlamo: La negrilla en España y en América*, vol. 2, edited by Leonardo Waisman, (self-published, 2021), 601, m. 77–82.

somo gente la nengla" respond to their performance of harmony. In this case, the joyful song responds to Christmas celebrations, and the narrators highlight their own skill in terms from the European music tradition. Even so, inconsistencies in the second stanza suggest otherwise. Here, as in the previous two examples, villancico lyrics imagine Black voices in jubilant consonance with the Christian themes they celebrate but dissonant with other cultural and musical codes.

### HARMONIZING BODIES

From a bodily perspective, the happy (dancing) slave offers intriguing counterpoint to the joyful, off-key strains of Afro-descendant singers. The topic has garnered more scholarly attention than questions of voice. For example, Baker sees the alignment of dance and elation as a manifestation of villancicos' overtones of social and spiritual assimilation, tendencies of the Maravallian Baroque. He emphasizes stereotypical underpinnings and suggests that "the association of Negroes with music and dancing reduced their role in society to that of mere entertainers of the white populace."[45] Larissa Brewer-García further develops these links and imagines the double-performativity that Afro-descendant singers and dancers might imply in villancicos:

> black musicians would have been invoked as stereotyped caricatures *and* the musicians performing the music. In such performances, the black caricatures

of the Christmas *villlancicos* would Index the successful spread of Christianity by presenting New World black men and women as obedient and joyful pastoral rustics receiving the Christian message and playing entertaining music. The presence of black musicians in the performance of the *villancicos* would instantiate Christ's promise to save *all* the world, including the black men and women of the Americas. It would also include them as a means of celebrating the successful Iberian expansion of the project of Christian salvation from Africa into the Americas.[46]

Brewer-García's remarks here frame the villancicos' imaginings of Afro-descent as a continuation of Reconquest ideology, a topic that scholars like Bennett and Gwendolyn Midlo Hall have addressed.[47] Along these lines, it is interesting to note that some *villancicos de negros* associate southern Spanish musical styles and instruments—some of which have Moorish roots—with Afro-descendant musicians.[48]

Untamable and exuberant dance is a recurring theme in representations of Afro-descent in villancicos and throughout the early modern Hispanic world. In these imaginings, rapid accompaniment, punctuated by rhythmic percussion, popular song, and laughter underscore Black bodies in motion. At times, lyrical references to drumming or even bells and castanets dangling from the dancer's bodies provide sonic contours for their movement. Representations of Afro-descendant dance frequently incorporate themes of lasciviousness or drunkenness, portraying non-European celebratory practices as decadent.

While such characteristics draw upon numerous cultural and artistic motifs, one concept is particularly useful for examining links among the musical, moral, and spatial underpinnings of Black and African dance in the early modern Hispanic imaginary: neo-Platonic harmony. Here, I explore rhythmic geometries of Afro-descendant dancers in villancicos through this lens, underscoring the subjects' tumultuous relation to the colonial city's sociopolitical and spiritual harmonies. For early modern theorists, harmony and rhythm had shared mathematical roots. Each was understood as a manifestation of universal accord, itself a product of planetary motion, and thinkers like René Descartes, Athanasius Kircher, and Marin Mersenne explored music's physical and affective impact upon the human microcosmos.

In villancicos, disorderly corporeality pairs with off-key song to sound Black characters' dissonance and heighten resonances of depravity. In a study of French *ballet du cour*, Kate van Orden attends to the "rhythmic ethos" of early modern bodies in motion and underscores "dance as a moral practice relevant to the civilizing process."[49] Along these lines, portrayals of

Black dancers as clumsy or arhythmic circumscribes them at odds with the harmonies that inform the villancicos' musical accompaniment, New Spain's urban grid, and even norms of social decorum. The apparent disruptions notwithstanding, such dissonances are crucial to representations of Afro-descendant dance in works like villancicos, for they enable the performative harmonizing of non-European bodies and voices with the racial ideologies of the Peninsular and Creole elite.

In some villancicos, Black participation in Christian ritual through song and dance was central to the primary message. For example, the *coplas* from the eighth piece of an anonymous, Mexico City cathedral set of *chanzonetas* for the 1672 Feast of St. Peter gives voice to an Afro-descendant troupe who wants to take part in the religious ceremony.

| | |
|---|---|
| Ya essá encendiro luz velaz, | The votives are lit, |
| y el curo cantando essa, | and the priest is singing, |
| chanzoneta a noso Parre, | a *chanzoneta* for our Father, |
| al sun del fa, fa, rafa. | to the sound of fa, fa, ra-fa. |
| *Tod.* Ha, ha, ha, | *All.* Ha ha ha, |
| que bincandome za. | I am jumping about. |
| | |
| Luz siñole Pribindalo, | The gentle Prebendaries |
| can zibela magesta, | with civil majesty, |
| luz Bribiarias en las manos | their Breviaries in their hands |
| a turus eromplu da | are an example to everyone. |
| *Tod.* Ha, ha, ha, &c. | *All.* Ha, ha, ha, &c. |
| | |
| Luz Capellana de curu, | The chaplains, |
| Monasillo, y Sacritá, | monks and sacristans |
| cun lu decias de la Iglesia | with the church choirboys |
| turu contenta essará. | will all be content. |
| *Tod.* Ha, ha, ha, &c. | *All.* Ha, ha, ha, &c. |
| | |
| Proz, també luz Neglo quele | Well, the *Negros* also want |
| cantar cumu luz demaz, | to sing like the others |
| | |
| que no importa la color, | color doesn't matter, |
| que a todos recibirá. | for He will receive everyone. |
| *Tod.* Ha, ha, ha, &c.[50] | *All.* Ha, ha, ha, &c. |

The Black singers' description of ritual participants and objects lends these lines an ethnographic or even didactic tone. They, too, want to raise their voices in song, and in the last strophe, the choir affirms that the Catholic church opens itself to people of all skin colors.

For all of their enthusiasm, when the Afro-descendant performers join the solemn ritual, it erupts in merry pandemonium. The *estribillos* emphasize the Black men and women's acrobatic dance, and their choral interventions in the "todos" (all) sections are onomatopoeic approximations of laughter or musical instruments. The semantic content of these sections' lyrics contributes little in terms of spiritual knowledge.

| | |
|---|---|
| 1. He, he, he, he, he, | He, he, he, he, he, |
| que solga mi alma, | my soul is leaping with joy, and |
|    y me come lo pé. |    my feet are itching to dance |
| He, he, he, he, he, | he, he, he, he, he, |
| | |
| 2. Frasiquiyo ¿qué tené? | 2. Francisquiyo, what is ailing you? |
| | |
| 1. He, he, he, he, he, | 1. He, he, he, he, he |
| pulque es de Perro la fiesta, | because the party is for Peter, |
| a que biejo fafarón. | that old braggart |
| *Tod.* Ho, ho, ho, ho, ho, | *All.* Ho, ho, ho, ho, ho |
| que lindo que za, | how beautiful it is, |
| ha, ha, ha, ha, ha, ha. | ha, ha, ha, ha, ha, ha. |
| | |
| 1. Essa noche en las Mastine | 1. Tonight at Matins |
| a lo biejo cantalemo, | we'll sing for the old man |
| que es honrado en bona fee. | so he is honored in good faith |
| *Tod.* He, he, he, he, he, he, | *All.* He, he, he, he, he, he |
| ho, ho, ho, ho. | ho, ho, ho, ho. |
| | |
| 2. Puz bamo luz tambó, | 2. Well, let's go there with drums, |
| que aya ruydo con son. | so there will be noise with rhythm. |
| *Tod.* Ton, ton, ton, ton, ton, | *All.* Ton, ton, ton, ton, ton |
| que lindo, que bueno, ¡válame Dios! | so pretty, so good, oh my God! |
| Ton, ton, ton. | Ton, ton ton. |

| | |
|---|---|
| 1. Tambe llevamo zonaxa, | 1. Let's bring shakers too, |
| ulqui toros se hagan raxas. | so that everyone does it right. |
| *Tod.* Chiz, chiz, chaz, chaz, chiaz, | *All.* Chiz, chiz, chaz, chaz, chiaz, |
| ha, ha, ha. | ha, ha, ha. |
| | |
| 2. Y turu cun castañeta, | 2. And everyone with castanets, |
| pala haz mil zapateta. | so there will be thousands of *zapateos*. |
| *Tod.* Chaz, chaz, chaz. | *All.* Chaz, chaz, chaz. |
| Puz baylemo, saltemo, y corramo, | Well let's dance, jump, and run, |
| cun la son de luz instrumenta, | to the sound of the instruments, |
| ha, ha, ha, ha, he, he, he, he | ha, ha, ha, ha, he, he, he, he, |
| vchihá, ha, ha, vchihé, he, he, he, | *vchihá*, ha ha, *vchihé*, he, he, he, |
| si en bona fee, | yes, in good faith, |
| que bincándome essá | I am jumping, |
| pul hazé cabliolas, | to cartwheel, |
| de allí pala aquí, | from here to there, |
| de acá, pala ayá, | from there to here, |
| ha, ha, ha, ha, ha, ha.[51] | ha, ha, ha, ha, ha, ha. |

While the 1672 *chanzoneta* depicts Afro-descendants taking part in mass, their role is reduced to that of mere entertainers. The representation distances the Black singers' expressions of faith from the serious worship that ecclesiastical officials carry out in the *coplas*, and it reflects the privileging of Euro-descendants in church hierarchies. To be certain, the *chanzoneta* does not exclude the Afro-descendant characters from the celebration, even if their interventions are at odd with the occasion's solemnity. Indeed, the troupe affirms that their feverish motion and exuberant song is the result of an external, affective force ("que solga mi alma, y me come lo pé" [my soul is leaping with joy, and my feet are itching to dance]). In this way, the lyrics harmonize the festive disruption with spiritual and social expectations, for the dancers' performance is a resonance of their Christian devotion.

Within this context, the Black performers' imitative interventions in the choral are especially noteworthy, for it is possible to read them as indicative of Afro-Christian ritual. Throughout the *estribillo*, the singers associate instruments like drums, rattles, and castanets with dance. Percussive vocalizations like "ton, ton, ton" or "chiz, chiz, chaz" mimic the instruments' sounds. At first glance, the *chanzoneta*'s sonorities seem to reflect the reductive privileging of rhythm in Afro-descendant music. Nonetheless, I contend that the audio-lyrical representation beckons a more nuanced analysis. In his research on Black villancicos, Swiadon Martínez has remarked upon rich intersections of poetic and danced rhythm in the villancicos' representations of Afro-descent. In particular, he draws attention to resonances among African cosmologies and the pieces' depictions of drumming, dance, and joy:

> En resumen, en los villancicos las palabras *sanguaguá, gurumbé* y *tumba* parecen relacionarse con los nombres de los tambores, la música de los tambores, un baile y un sentimiento general de alegría. Los tambores y la alegría son manifestaciones de la fuerza vital, según la cosmovisión africana. Esta fuerza vital, presente en los bailes de origen africano que observaban los españoles en la Península y en América durante las festividades religiosas, pasó a los villancicos.[52]

> In summary, in the villancicos, the words *sanguaguá, gurumbé,* and *tumba* appear to be related to drum names, drum music, a dance, and a general feeling of happiness. Drums and happiness are manifestations of the life force, according to African cosmology. This life force, present in the African dances that Spaniards in the Peninsula and in America observed in during religious festivals, became part of the villancicos.

These links are a fruitful and relevant strand of analysis for villancicos like the 1672 piece for San Pedro. Indeed, the *estribillo*'s alignment of percussion, vocalization, dance, and ecstatic expression is reminiscent of contemporary Santería ritual. Possession trance and dance are important parts of *lucumí* ceremony, and ritual *batá* drums are essential for provoking such states. Contemporary *batá* players often describe their craft as "making the drums speak" and thus highlight the conflation of voice and percussion in this Afro-diasporic tradition. Katherine Hagedorn frames Regla de Ochá's speaking-drumming connections as "utterance" and explains how it conditions movement.

> First, the *batá* drums on which the Ochá rhythms are performed "speak" Lucumí, the Afro-Cuban liturgical language prevalent in Ochá ceremonies (Villepastour 2010). For example, a combined open-stroke/closed-stroke drummed phrase played on the larger head of the lead *batá* drum, *iyá*, is heard as "Di de, Di de, Di de," which is commonly understood to be Lucumí for "arise" or "get up" from the *morforibale* position, for which one lies on the floor to salute the *orichas*.[53]

In essence, in Regla de Ochá ceremony, the *batá* drums signal to performers (or tell them) how to move their bodies. Danced motion follows a related script, and different movements indicate which *orisha* (deity) has mounted or possessed practitioners. The lyrical linkage among percussion, speech, and dance in the 1672 *chanzoneta* provocatively resonates with present-day Regla de Ochá ritual. Similarities between the two suggest that the *chanzoneta*'s *estribillos* offer insights beyond Afro-descendant marginalization in liturgical celebrations. Additional research on Afro-Christian ceremony in New Spain would shed further light on the topic; however, few primary sources describe such practices.

Complementary to the harmonization of Afro-descendant dance and Catholic ritual in the 1672 set for the Feast of St. Peter, other *villancicos de negros* resolve Black dancers' hectic motion by depicting the joyful frenzy as a sympathetic response to religious spectacle and its underlying Christian values. Joyous representations of song and dance also stand out in Sor Juana's *Villancico* 258, from her 1679 cycle for the Mexico City Cathedral's celebration of the Feast of the Assumption:

> A la voz del Sacristán,
> en la Iglesia se colaron
> dos princesas de Guinea
> con vultos azabachados.[54]

> At the Sacristan's voice,
> two Guinean princesses
> snuck into the Church / whitened themselves in the Church
> their effigies of jet-black stone / their coal-blackened faces.

Like in so many sorjuanine villancicos, this introduction circumscribes the musicians' voices and movements within the urban space of Mexico City. The section's opening lines invoke the sacristan's voice as it calls city-dwellers to worship. While this auditory symbol of ecclesiastical authority leads the female characters into the church; however, it is not solemn ceremony, but rather, a spectacular party that captures their attention:

> Y mirando tanta fiesta,            And seeing such a party,
> por ayudarla cantando,             in order to join in with song,
> soltando los cestos, dieron        they tossed aside their baskets,
> albricias a los muchachos.[55]     and gave the crowd the happy news.

Here, the lyrics perform the villancico's intended affective response. Music, verse, and spectacle all act upon the "Guinean princesses," who respond in a joyful, uncontrollable outpouring of song and dance.

The *estribillo* inscribes the women's festive reply, complete with several common tropes for imagining Afro-descent in villancicos and beyond:

| | |
|---|---|
| Negr. 1—¡Ha, ha, ha! | Negr. 1—¡Ha, ha, ha! |
| 2.—¡Monan vuchilá! | 2.—¡Monan vuchilá! |
| ¡He, he, he, | ¡He, he, he, |
| Cambulé! | Cambulé! |
| | |
| 1.—¡Gila coro, | 1.—Spin around, choir, |
| Gulungú, gulungú, | Gulungú, gulungú, |
| Hu, hu, hu! | Hu, hu, hu! |
| 2.—¡Menguiquilá, | 2.—Shake it, |
| ha, ha, ha![56] | ha, ha, ha! |

Here, Black voices sound via *habla de negros*, and the singer's laughter—perhaps doubled in the non-extant musical score—punctuates near-onomatopoeic imitations of Africanized Castilian. Words like "gila" ("gira" or "to turn") and "menguiquilá" (loosely related to "menear" or "to shake") bring to mind whirling, frenetic motion that is all but impossible to contain. These pulsations shake the villancico's text and amplify the authorial act of self-hearing that inscribes *Villancico* 258's Afro-descendant voices. Precisely, tympanic vibrations become manifest in the dancers' swaying hips. Attending to the corporeal movements and the staccato laughter that keeps the beat enables listeners to engage with the fluid identities that come into being as the sounds of another percuss the self's auditory threshold. From this perspective, the *estribillo* is more than just an unintelligible vocal caricature. It is a reckoning with the very alterity of self-presence and a disruption of the process of "othering" that resonates with post-Cartesian thought. In a nutshell, percussive themes lay bare the artificial construction of Black voices in *Villancico* 258, and their illegibility underscores the impossible remembering of Afro-diasporic histories.

Despite these challenges, Sor Juana's lyrics can lend insight into how representations of Afro-descendant dance respond to the villancicos' spiritual and ideological functions. The women dance the "gulungú" ("gurujú"), one of several "African" dances that recur in early modern Hispanic poems and theater. In the New Spanish context, frenzied, near-ecstatic representations of dance like in *Villancico* 258 produce surprisingly tension with the apparent desire to contain Black bodies within particular spaces and social positions. While wild, dancing bodies might seem like a puzzling paradox against this social backdrop, I maintain that their disorderly motion is, in fact, a key element to the villancicos' performance of social order. Set against the consonant grid of urban space, the bombastic movements of Black dancers create dissonance with social order and reinforce the non-European performers' "outsider" status. At the same time, the musicians' euphoric, involuntary responses are suggestive of a sympathetic reaction. Precisely, the celebration's music acts upon the Afro-descendant participants and harmonizes them with divine concord. Their gyrating bodies thus become an outward symbol of spiritual transformation, and their dance performs evangelization.[57]

## PERFORMING HARMONY

Beyond their religious overtones, some villancicos also parody New Spain's social hierarchies and perform the civic harmonies that authorities hoped to instill in the multiethnic region. For instance, a 1657 Christmas villancico set from the Mexico City cathedral includes a villancico that takes the form of a dialogue between an impertinent Black character and an overbearing Spanish one who appears to be his master. When the pair arrives in Bethlehem to celebrate Jesus's birth, the Spanish man orders his servant to bale the hay. The Afro-descendant gives a saucy reply, and his interlocutor threatens to punish him for insolence. Still, the servant does not yield to his master, and their argument intensifies.

| | |
|---|---|
| 1. Negro hablemos con mas tiento, mira que me nojaré, guarda que te pringaré, por el santo Nacimiento | 1. *Negro* let us speak with caution, lest I become angry, take care or I'll punish you, I swear on the Holy birth. |
| 2. Mal año pala los blanca, que lo niño que a veniro, para tulos ha naciro, y a lo negro hacemos franca. | 2. It is a bad year for the white people, for the child that has come was born for all of us, and he frees the *negros* and loosens our tongues. |
| 1. Calla, calla, por la Virgen de la Estrella. | 1. Quiet, quiet, for the love of the Virgin of the Stars. |
| 2. Vaya, vaya vuese con ella: y digame vuesance, ¿qué quele? que tenemo tanto pico.[58] | 2. Go on, go on with it then: And tell me Master, what do you want? for we are itching [to do it]. |

There is little doubt that scenes like the one that the 1657 villancico describes were commonplace in New Spanish streets, where enslaved men and women frequently suffered physical abuse. Inquisition files can shed some light on the subject, for there are numerous cases against Afro-descendants for blasphemous utterances during punishment. In this villancico, however, it is the exasperated Spaniard who curses, not the Black man whom he threatens.

At this point, the master is at his wits end. In order to put an end to the argument, he asks the enslaved man to sing a villancico in honor of Jesus's birth.

| | |
|---|---|
| 1. Pasito, quelito, | 2. Slowly and tenderly, |
| que yo cantalé | I'll sing, |
| que yo tañelé, | I'll strike, |
| que yo tucalé | I'll beat |
| mi tambolilico, | my little drum, |
| la sonaja, | my rattle, |
| y cacambé, | and my gourd, |
| y cantando lo gugulugú, | and singing the gugulugú, |
| y tañendo lo gutulugué, | and striking the gutulugué, |
| y baylando lo gugulugá, | and dancing the gugulugá, |
| lo branco, y lo negó se aleglalá: | the white people and the *negros* will be happy: |
| que ya junta essá, | for they are together, |
| que lo niño a naciro[59] | and the child has been born. |

Just as Christ brought harmony to the world and freed humans from sin, so the Black singer's music tempers social discord. Even though the musician performs an African piece on crude percussion instruments, the song has a peaceful effect on listeners because it is a resonance of the player's Christian faith. In this way, the anonymous villancico illustrates music's capacity to perform spiritual and civic harmony, regardless of the genre.

As my reading of the 1657 Christmas piece from the Mexico City cathedral showed, although villancicos often portray Black music as crude in comparison with the European tradition, they do not necessarily marginalize or even devalue it. The *ensaladilla* from Sor Juana's attributable set for the Mexico City cathedral's 1677 celebration of the Feast of the Assumption (*Villancico* ix) also explores dissonances and consonances of Afro-descendant dance. This piece celebrates Black song and dance as vibrant, syncretic products of European and African cultural contact. The *ensaladilla* features a chorus of Afro-descendant characters whose festive practices pay tribute to the Virgin's heavenly ascent. The lyrics indicate that the underlying dance rhythm is a *canario*, an early modern dance associated with the Canary Islands:

> El *Canario* que suena festivo,
> pagado y contento de buenos pasajes,
> se comienza (que en eso está el toque)
> metiéndolo a voces la música, tate[60]
>
> The Canario that/who sounds festively,
> paid off and happy in its/his journey,
> begins (and here's the proof/rhythm)
> giving voice to music, tate

At first glance, these lines establish the villancico's musical and festive contours—an intriguing possibility for the poet's knowledge of music theory if we consider the mutual collaboration between composer and writer in the production of villancicos.[61] Due to the fluidity of terms like "moro" and "africano" in sources describing the dance, its non-European origins are difficult to pinpoint, although Samuel Charters links the form to the transatlantic slave trade.[62] Sor Juana's villancico plays with these resonances, and it is unclear whether the "canario" to which the lyrics refer is a dance—commissioned as part of the festival—or an enslaved Afro-descendant whose music-making belies his contentment.

Continuing, the *coplas* contrast the narrators' angelic song with the frenetic motion of "Perico" and the Afro-descendant dancers:

> La fuga sonora, que suena lucida,
> escrita en latín y dicha en romance,
> de las voces que Angélica suenan,
> su triunfo glorioso, es sólo el *tu-autem*.
>
> Aunque gorrón en danza me meta
> la dulce armonía que suena en los aires,
> por decirla bailando de gusto
> delante de todos, estoy *casi, casi*.
>
> Prosigue la Introducción
> Perico, con otros Negros,
> dando de contento brincos,

aunque los estribos pierda
no ha de perder su estribillo.⁶³

The sonorous fugue/flight, a splendid sound,
written in Latin and sung in romance,
from the Angelic voices that sound,
her glorious triumph, is only the tu-autem.

Although clumsy, let the sweet harmony
that resounds in the air urge me to dance,
let me say it by dancing with gusto
before everyone, I am almost, almost.

The introduction continues
Perico, with other *Negros*,
happily leaping,
though he might lose his wits
he will never lose the refrain.

Similar to *Villancico* 258, this example depicts Afro-descendant dance as a wild, uncontrollable, ecstatic response to the sweet harmonies of the Angelic chorus that carries Mary heavenward.⁶⁴ The Black characters' unwieldy leaps and bounds contrast sharply with the heavenly "fuga sonora" (sonorous fugue/flight), and the metaphor of an unsteady rider on horseback, along with the accompanying play on words, heightens the imagined, rhythmic chaos of Afro-descendant dance. In these lines, the word "fuga" stands out, perhaps as an ironic challenge from poet to composer. As a reference to a Baroque musical form, the term invokes order and harmony. Nonetheless, as an indicator of the rapid-fire speed often associated with imaginings of Black dance, "fuga" suggests a disordered and chaotic accompaniment. Although there are no extant seventeenth-century scores for Sor Juana's villancicos, audio-racial allusions like this one can help us to imagine how the piece's musical text might have contributed to constructions of Afro-descent.

Beyond their significance for harmonizing Black and African bodies with New Spain's urban and social order, dance references like the *canario* in Sor Juana's *ensaladilla* underscore a rich, transatlantic musical exchange. Swiadon Martínez has drawn attention to this tendency in other pieces as well.⁶⁵ A particularly intriguing example is José Pérez de Montoro's Christmas cycle (Cádiz Cathedral, 1688). In Pérez de Montoro's lyrics, Afro-descendant musicians debate which dance to perform in honor of Jesus' birth. The finally settle on the *tocotín*, an Aztec dance from New Spain:

> 4. Vaya é soneciyo
> de una rinda ranza
> que ha venido en frota
> de la Nueva España,
> y en Chapurtepeque
> la señaron a mí.
> 1. Y ¿cómo se yama,
> pala lo seguí?
> 3. El tocotín, tocotín, tocotín.[66]

> 4. My, what a sound
> of a beautiful dance
> that has come on a ship
> from New Spain,
> and in Chapultepec,
> they taught it to me.
> 1. And what is it called,
> so that we can follow it?
> 3. The tocotín, tocotín, tocotín

Like Sor Juana's piece, Pérez de Montoro's lyrics capture the musical syncretism that results from Contact among Europeans, Indigenous Americans, and Africans.[67] Both writers underscore the creative potential of the liminal, watery Atlantic. While there is little doubt about the villancicos' resonances with discourses that we would consider racist by today's standards, representations like these offer another perspective. Indeed, in the face of attempts at racial segregation within urban space, Sor Juana and Pérez de Montoro's lyrics celebrate the new artistic products that emerge as a result of intercultural exchange.

## CONCLUSION

This chapter has examined Afro-descendant song, dance, and language in villancicos from New Spain and elsewhere in the Spanish-speaking world. My re-readings here offer important counterpoint to interpretations that emphasize villancicos' denigration and negative portrayal of Black characters and beckon a careful, nuanced approach to these themes. While the racist overtones of such depictions are undeniable and prolong stereotypical ideas about dark-skinned people, some *villancicos de negros* can shed light on Afro-descendant practices and customs that other archival sources do not record. Other villancicos feature favorable representations of Blackness and the syncretism that emerged from African, European, and Indigenous encounters. Altogether, this chapter illustrates the need for interpretative frameworks that attend to villancicos as products of a multicultural imaginary. Overwhelmingly, this plurivocal perspective privileges Spanish and Creole ideals, but it also draws upon Black and native traditions in order to affect a diverse audience.

CHAPTER 6

# Black Women's Performance in Sor Juana's *Villancicos*

To be part of an audience is to experience audentia, a hearing and a listening, and every audience, whether for theatre, opera, cinema, television, video, webcams, and even media that may be "inaudible," such as written texts, painting, sculpture and site-specific installations, is a listener or eavesdropper.

—**David Toop**, *Sinister Resonance*, 83

If the visual and auditory spectacles of seventeenth-century Mexico City performed its ordered urban identity, like the previous chapter showed, then Sor Juana Inés de la Cruz was a particular kind of spectator. As a cloistered nun, she spent her life within the walls of the forbidding Hieronymite Convent of Santa Paula, where church authorities only granted permission to leave under exceptional circumstances. Although the poet received frequent visitors in the *locutorio* and corresponded with scholars throughout the Spanish empire, her physical presence in the city was veiled. Though unable to attend popular festivals and celebrations, Sor Juana penned dozens of pieces for civic and religious events, including the triumphal arch *Neptuno alegórico* (Allegorical Neptune), plays, *loas*, and villancicos. In this way, the nun's lyric voice became a synecdochic form of participation in Mexico City's lively urban space.

In Western literate culture, scholars tend to understand the poetic voice as a metaphorical construction that is largely separate from the physical act of vocalization. Eidsheim explains this dichotomy as distance between the material and figurative realms: "within these two camps—the measurable and the symbolic—the voice has been formulated as two entirely different objects, and because of this there have been no grounds, reason, or purpose for their scholars to interact."[1] Despite the two approaches' dissociation, however, each closely intertwines with the politics of identity. Like signing one's name, the poetic voice inscribes both speaker and—to an extent—lyric subject while vocalization emanates from the physical body as an extension of the self. These intersections of written and audio-corporeal identity are useful for examining musico-lyrical works like villancicos, where the stage embodied Sor Juana's authorial voice and rendered it audible. Though physically cloistered, I argue that the nun commits an act of poetic ventriloquism by "throwing" her voice and transferring it to the characters she invents, who are imagined bodies themselves. Performances of Sor Juana's musico-poetic works thus enact a complex politics of sounding and listening to intertwined "marginal" identities that merit theorization as part of Mexico City's sound culture.[2]

With all this in mind, this chapter considers Sor Juana's poetic representations of Afro-descendants in Black villancicos.[3] From a perspective of race, the pieces are notable for their complex entanglement of Spanish poetic traditions and New Spain's diverse ethnic fabric. Prior scholarship richly debates the degree of transposition and the extent to which it reflects the nun's attitude toward enslaved Black and African people. In a classic reading of the theme, Baltasar Fra Molinero distinguishes between "los villancicos con protesta social" (villancicos with an overtone of social protest) that sympathetically respond to racial inequalities in the poet's environment and mere demonstrations of lyrical prowess that flaunt the *habla de negros* style.[4] For his part, Baker understands Sor Juana's villancicos as an echo of the racial tensions that threatened colonial order.[5] And yet, representations of this ilk nearly always exceed neat subject/object or empire/colony dichotomies. In a reading that situates Sor Juana's *villancicos de negros* within Black Atlantic paradigms, Jones maintains that imaginings of Afro-descent intertwine colonial ideologies of race and faith with an intersectional politics of identity that allow the poet to "align herself with black African slaves."[6]

Complementary to questions of representation, I am interested in the insights that Sor Juana's *villancicos de negros* can lend into constructions of Blackness as a product of New Spanish sound culture. In terms of audible historical authenticity, Black villancicos offer little insight into the exact sounds of Black and African speech and music-making and instead tell us much about the genre's role in imagining colonial hierarchies. To this end, Baker remarks: "The caricature linguistic deformity . . . was a means of harnessing a popular stereotype to an élite project."[7] Despite such limitations, however, *villancicos de negros* can be useful for delving into what one might call the Afro-Hispanic auditory imagination, as well as its contemporary resonances. While a number of prior studies explore the general racial politics of Sor Juana's representations of Afro-descent, few have considered connections among ethnic identity, imagined sonorities, and the stage's audibility. These lacunae beckon further attention, particularly in light of recent scholarship that more fully attends to Black and African presence in New Spanish popular culture as well as an emerging canon of research on Afro-diasporic sound.

In a preliminary approach to the topic, Ortiz asks poignant questions about how "African" sounds in Peninsular and colonial music encode a politics of racial identity: "¿Cómo imaginaba él [seventeenth-century Spanish composer Santiago de Murcia] al sujeto colonial africano? ¿Cómo fue este sujeto imaginado por sus contemporáneos peninsulares o coloniales? ¿Cómo lo imaginamos hoy a partir de las imaginaciones coloniales que nos quedaron?" (How did he [seventeenth-century Spanish composer Santiago de Murcia] imagine the colonial African subject? How was this subject imagined by his Peninsular or colonial contemporaries? How do we imagine him today based on the colonial imaginings that remain?)[8] Ortiz's astute observations highlight the need for a more comprehensive study of sonic Blackness in early modern Hispanic music and related genres. Furthermore, they serve as the entry for this chapter's exploration of Sor Juana's Afro-auditory imagination and its resonances with sounds from seventeenth-century Mexico City's harmonic order.

### HEARING AND RE-SOUNDING RACE IN MEXICO CITY: A THEORETICAL APPROACH

First of all, Black villancicos' emphasis on race as an audible quality relates this musico-poetic subgenre to Eidsheim's concept of "acousmatic blackness."[9] The term underscores cultural tendencies to associate immaterial auditory interventions with an unseen, racialized sounding body. Under these circumstances, personal and cultural listening positions condition the auditory imagination to hear particular sounds as embodiments of ethnicity, gender, or other identities. When we isolate sonic interventions from both the sounding vocal apparatus and the listening ear, they become uncanny echoes whose formlessness unsettles registers of audio-symbolism and the embodied politics that they imply. Following Eidsheim, the previous chapter argued that Western constructions of voice are deeply entrenched in a dialectics of identity and embodiment that make it is difficult (and perhaps inappropriate) to examine the concept through a purely sonorous lens. Therefore, it is important to amplify the politics of racial difference that condition the listening ear and influence the way that bodies make and listen to (interpret) sound.

Here, I place Eidsheim's observations into dialogue with embodied sounds of Blackness in Sor Juana's *villancicos de negros*. I understand the poet's ear as a subjective listening position shaped by the sounds encountered through first- and second-hand audition as well as cultural attitudes and affective responses that shape reception. My premise is that the poet's auditory imagination informs such representations, a symbolic filter conditioned by her inheritance of Peninsular literary traditions as well as her particular engagement with a rich and diverse sonic environment that lay just beyond the convent walls.

As part of the Mexico City setting that Sor Juana heard, performances endorsed by ecclesiastical and political authorities served as audible counterpoint to inscribed hegemonies. Nevertheless, like this book has shown, streets echoed with a rich auditory culture that exceeded harmonic, plotted, and written bounds. Marín López contrasts this unregulated auditory fabric with the tightly controlled cathedral harmonies. He notes Peninsular and Creole musicians dominated music-making in sacred spaces while non-European ethnicities were more prominent in popular music traditions that, unsurprisingly, are less prevalent in the written archive.[10] Nevertheless, anxiety before popular dissonances in official records, particularly as expressions of collective identity, illustrates the pervasiveness of non-European sounds. For example, both Mark Pedelty and Marín López underscore Indigenous, Chinese, Black, and African musicians as Inquisitorial targets whose frequent presence in case records suggests that "ethnic" music was a compelling popular force.[11] Along the same lines, Ortiz cites an evocative 1618 ordinance that regulates sonic Encounter between Black and Indigenous populations by superimposing auditory and ethnic boundaries on urban space: "que no aya juntas de negros y mulatos en las plaças y calles Reales ni en los barrios de los yndios y que no hagan bayles danças juegos ni otros entretenimientos y ruidos de que an resultado y resultan riñas enemistades e riñas muertes y otros daños . . . que ni anden de noche tirando piedras a bentanal ni haciendo ruidos ni dando musicas"[12] (let there be no assemblies of *negros* and *mulatos* in the plazas and Royal streets or in the *indio* neighborhoods, and that they do not perform dances or games or other diversions and noises that have resulted in and lead to quarrelsome animosities and deadly arguments and other damages . . . let them not go out at night throwing rocks at windows or making noise or music). Here, attempts to order ethnic sounds within the harmonic cityscape relate to deep apprehension about interracial mingling. Despite colonial authorities' best efforts, however, bodies are more easily contained than the immaterial sounds they produce. Conspicuous references to audible performances of ethnicity throughout sixteenth- to eighteenth-century legal and Inquisitorial documents illustrate their unsettling effects on urban concord and deepen acousmatic constructions of race.

These intersections of space, sound, and ethnicity in the auditory imaginary guide my reading of Sor Juana's villancicos in relation to Mexico City sound culture. For all this, it is important to bear in mind that the poet's listening positionality is unique, not only for the intersectionality implied by a female, American poetic imagining Black and African sounds, but also because of how the cloister shaped her auditory engagement with urban space. Indeed, the material architecture of the Santa Paula convent walls—tightly regulated visual barriers with contrasting acoustical porosity—conditioned Sor Juana's encounter with Afro-Mexican popular culture. Using Puebla de los Ángeles as an example, Rosalva Loreto López has commented upon the significance of convent sonorities within New Spanish urban landscape. She focuses in particular on the bells and other sounds of religious ceremony as audible symbols of ecclesiastical authority and a limited means of "eavesdropping," so to speak, on the daily routines of cloistered nuns.[13]

Drawing upon Loreto López's observations about the convent's significance in New Spanish urban settings, I approach sonic exchange from the opposite perspective, whereby open windows and eyewitness accounts of correspondents or visitors to the *locutorio* engaged inhabitants with syncretic auditory cultures as listening subjects with a heightened acousmatic position. Like the eavesdropper in David Toop's reading of seventeenth-century Dutch painting, the cloistered poet adopts an uncanny position, threatening to reveal the secrets that resonate in her hidden ear at any moment.[14] If New Spain's official sound culture sought to enact an audio-ethnic biopolitics, Sor Juana's disembodied eavesdropping disrupts the process by breaking down sound's imagined corporality. In this context, auditory interventions are released from the symbolic order of sounding and listening bodies. They vibrate freely in the air between the two, connecting the sonic source and its recipient via minute fluctuations that contrast with the perfect harmonies and neat grid pattern that defined Mexico City's physical space.

This uncanny chain does not end with the eavesdropper herself. Indeed, Sor Juana translates urban sounds into the public realm of villancicos and makes the imagined dimensions of sonic embodiment audible for all who choose to "listen in." This entreat to aural participation is an essential characteristic of Sor Juana's villancico lyrics. For instance, *Villancico* 230 from the 1676 cycle for Conception calls the public to take part in the spectacle: "¡Oigan, miren, atiendan / lo que se canta" (Listen up, look, pay attention / to what is sung!).[15] Similarly, in the 1690 set for the Feast of Saint Joseph, the *ensalada* (*Villancico* 299) beckons musical engagement:

> Los que música no entienden
> oigan, oigan, que va allá
> una cosa, que la entiendan
> todos, y muchos más.[16]
>
> Those who do not understand music
> listen up, listen up, here goes
> something else, let it be understood
> by everyone, and many more.

These lines underscore music's importance for "harmonizing" colonial order, for it is a force that will attune listening subjects to social and religious hierarchies. Paradoxically, they also highlight the *ensalada* as an "illegible" genre whose combination of forms—the Spanish *jácara* as well as sections titled "Indio" and "Negro"—only make sense from a collective listening position that necessarily implies a blurring of audio-ethnic boundaries.

By inviting audience members to cock an ear and share in the secret disruption of sonic order, then, Sor Juana as eavesdropper draws the urban public into her auditory imagination. Toop observes:

> Through being enjoined to silence by the eavesdropper, we become a second eavesdropper. The space in which we stand is shared, yet the assumption is that the viewer of the work is hidden from all but one of the characters inhabiting the painting. If we were visible, as we are in actuality in relation to the extended space of the picture, then we would be visible simultaneously to all parties in the house, so exposed as a voyeur.[17]

As earwitness accounts of seventeenth-century Mexico City, Sor Juana's *villancicos de negros* make audible the distance between the sounding body and imagine embodied sound as an index of ethnic identity. These pieces are echoes of the poet's spectral auditing position, and they engage the audience in a process of acousmatic listening that displaces sonic interventions from their physical origin. Precisely, villancicos fracture audio-corporeal links and then restore them through poetic sonorities that amplify acousmatic

Blackness as a product of the auditory imagination rather than an ontological attribute.

In order to tease out resonances of Afro-descent in Sor Juana's auditory imagination, I place her *villancicos de negros* in dialogue with African and Black cultural practices that echoed throughout New Spanish streets and challenged ideologies of sonic homogeneity. Inasmuch as the nun's Black villancicos made Blackness "visible" through stage and written representation, they also made Afro-descent audible in prominent public spaces where it might otherwise be regulated, muted, or dismissed as "noise." As we have already seen, in an ironic gesture, several of Sor Juana's *villancicos de negros* frame Black and African sounds as inferior sonorities (*Villancico* xvi and *Villancico* 241, both discussed in Chapter 5). From one angle, these and other dissonant references portray Afro-descendants as out of tune with colonial order. Nonetheless, by staging these very sounds in a prominent public venue, Sor Juana's *Black villancicos* paradoxically realize the very civic harmonies that they are meant to impose by performing the Afro-auditory register as an integral part of New Spanish society.

## LISTENING TO SOR JUANA'S AFRO-DIASPORIC IMAGINATION

For all this, it is clear that Sor Juana's *villancicos de negros* respond to a complex setting that struggles to harmonize diverse sonorities with the imagined physical and ethnic bounds of urban space. As an example, I will draw out local resonances of Afro-descent in *Villancico* 258, the *ensalada* from the 1679 Assumption set (performed in the Iglesia Metropolitana de México). Baroque polysemy is key to understanding the piece's dual framing of African and Black audio interventions and cultural practices. My argument is that in a staged context, this lexical anamorphism frames the *ensalada* itself, refashioning the Peninsular musico-literary traditions that the poet inherited as syncretic products whose local sounds are only audible to informed listening subjects. In this sense, polysemy in villancicos invites audience members from all walks of life to take part in the polyphonic and multiethnic celebration from various perspectives. David Castillo remarks: "in calling attention to the mechanism that makes the picture work, anamorphic puzzles remind us that meaning contains a kernel of arbitrariness and that *reality* is always tainted by the 'polluting' presence of our own gaze."[18] The very trick of Sor Juana's lyrical stagings of Afro-descent is the manner in which they perform local and racial identities through veiled references that are only legible/audible to the informed audience, in this case, one familiar with the social and cultural fabric of seventeenth-century Mexico City.

Villancico 258 was set for performance by Joseph de Agurto y Loaysa, resident composer of the Mexico City cathedral from 1677 to 1685 and chapelmaster from 1685 to 1688. The *ensalada* includes three sections, each of which imagines a distinct popular voice. It opens with a droll sacristan, who celebrates the Virgin's Assumption with a comical *romance* in macaronic Latin. Martha Lilia Tenorio calls attention to the church officer's verbal potpourri of Spanish and Latin, popular and erudite references, a dissonant babble before finely attuned colonial ears. She reads the juxtaposed registers as a function of the villancico's humorous tone: "Parte del tono burlesco del romance resulta de la conjunción del 'elevado canto' que, en su pedantería, pretende el sacristán con coloquialismos" (Part of the romance's playful tone results from the union of the "elevated song" that the sacristan, in his pedantry, peppers with colloquialisms).[19] For her part, Stephanie Kirk takes the interpretation a step farther and maintains that Sor Juana's skillful remixing of vernacular and scholarly speech took on a position of literary agency on the public stage: "Sor Juana's strategic assumption of authority via the use of Latin in these most public of texts allowed her to challenge the public/private dichotomy to which society confined women through the public and masculine language of Latin."[20] When performed in prominent urban spaces like the Mexico City cathedral, the *ensaladas'* poetic openness becomes a powerful tool for re-harmonizing hierarchies of gender, race, and more.

Following the sacristan's *romance*, a *villancico de negros* features dialogue between two Black female "princesses" / street vendors who abandon their daily activities in order to sing and dance in the Assumption festivities: "*1.— ¡Gila coro, / gulungú, gulungú, / hu, hu, hu!*" (Spin about, choir / gulungú, gulungú / hu, hu, hu!)[21] Like I indicated in my reading of these lyrics in Chapter 5, here, the women sound their Blackness through the affected Castilian of *habla de negros* as well as through popular musical references to the *gurujú*, an imagined "Guinean" dance form that Lope de Vega contrasts with "chaconas de Castilla" (*chaconas* from Castile) in *La isla del sol*.[22] In Sor Juana's villancico, it is difficult to know whether we might read the reference as an authentic representation Black and African dance practices in New Spain. Regardless, it lends important insight into the poet's Afro-auditory imagination by drawing out embodied speech as a key attribute. Marcella Trambaioli explains that the *habla de negros* nomenclature to describe dance forms imitates the sonorous contours of African languages, weaving together speech and bodily movement as racial indices: "En todos los casos recordados, se trata de vocablos que tratan de imitar, o, mejor dicho, evocar de forma onomatopéyica las lenguas africanas, jugando con sus supuestas peculiaridades fonéticas" (In all extant cases, there are vocables that try to imitate, or better said, evoke African languages in onomatopoeic form, playing with their supposed phonetic peculiarities).²³ Beyond the linguistic sounds that these onomatopoeias represent, they also inscribe the dancing Black body. Indeed, words like "gurujú," "zumbé," and "guirigay" sound the sensuous, frenetic movement that authorities so often condemned with deep, closed vowels that bump suggestively against voiced plosives.

In response to the vendors' song and dance, the final section of *Villancico* 258 features cathedral choirboys known as "los seises de la capilla." These singers temper popular festivities with a *juguete* that reviews the feast day's liturgical lesson in an echo of the villancico cycle itself:²⁴

> Los Seises de la Capilla
> en docena con su canto
> se metieron, y dos Seises
> una docena ajustaron.²⁵

> The Six Choirboys
> butted in with
> their song, and two groups of Six Choirboys
> numbered a dozen.²⁶

The verb "ajustar" is the crux of the *juguete*'s complicity with harmony as an auditory and civic representation. According to the *Diccionario de Autoridades*, the term implies a return to balance, imagined mathematically: "Hacer o poner una cosa iguál, y tan medída, y proporcionada, que nada le sobre ni falte" (To arrange or adjust something equally, and so measured, and so proportioned, that there is nothing left over or lacking). An additional definition for "ajustar la vida" (to live in equilibrium) draws out its moral resonances: "Vivir christiana y prudentemente, reglando las costumbres conforme à las reglas moráles y honestas" (To lead a Christian and prudent life, aligning one's habits with honest and moral principles). Within the context of the *ensalada*'s performance of Mexico City sound culture, with all of its popular dissonances, the *seises*' closing *juguete* thus restores order via the harmonizing force of New Spain's "official" music culture.

Having overviewed the three parts of *Villancico* 258 in dialogue, I now return to the blackspeak section. Like other sorjuanine compositions in this style, it blends auditory and visual tropes of Blackness rooted in the Peninsular stage tradition with resonances of Afro-descent in the urban American setting. In true Baroque fashion, lexical ambiguity and plays on words obscure meaning and lend themselves to multiple interpretations.

The *villancico de negros* begins with an introduction that circumscribes Afro-descent:

> A la voz del Sacristán,
> en la Iglesia se colaron
> dos princesas de Guinea
> con vultos azabachados.
>
> Y mirando tanta fiesta,
> por ayudarla cantando,
> soltando los cestos, dieron
> albricias a los muchachos.[27]
>
> At the Sacristan's voice,
> two Guinean princesses
> snuck into the Church / whitened themselves in the Church
> their effigies of jet-black stone / their coal-blackened faces.
>
> And seeing such a party,
> in order to join in with song,
> they tossed aside their baskets,
> and gave the crowd the happy news.

Line 35's allusion to "princesas de Guinea" ("Guinean princesses") evokes the Afro-Mexican confraternity practice of naming ritual royalty to reign over feast days and other important celebrations.[28] Prevalent throughout the Spanish and Portuguese empires, Black brotherhoods provided a space for articulating collective popular identities within ecclesiastical hierarchies. In *Villancico* 258, female protagonists of Afro-descent dominate the festival space and underscore women's agency as distinctive to Black and African confraternities.[29] Von Germeten observes: "there is very little evidence of a strong female role in Spanish confraternities or in any position of religious leadership outside convents. Spanish confraternities were male-dominated organizations. In contrast, women of African birth were active sisters. The leadership roles black and mulatto women held . . . linked them to the traditions of rural Indian confraternities and perhaps to gender roles in Africa."[30] It is thus possible to read these characters as a resonance of the gender politics that shapes Sor Juana's canon. In this sense, the empowered Guinean princesses embody the nun's poetic voice, and their shared feminine condition exceeds racial difference. By staging Black and African women's religious practices in a prominent venue, *Villancico* 258's imagining of lay sisterhoods therefore harmonizes both Afro-descent and women's agency with the "official" Mexico City sound culture.

*Villancico* 258's reference to "Guinean princesses" is just one example of how Sor Juana's *villancicos de negros* encode the urban presence of Afro-descent through a Baroque polysemy that veils local references. The verb "colar" in line 34 is another instance of this tendency. First, it underscores the princess's outsider status within the Catholic church by indicating that they needed to "colarse" or "sneak in" to the ceremony ("passar o ser admitida a una cosa que no debía, por ser falsa o de mala calidad" [to enter or be received where one does not belong, for being dishonest or of poor quality], according to the *Diccionario de Autoridades*). This "outsider" status appears rooted in both racial and Christian hierarchies, for a subsequent definition of "colar" suggests that participating in the Assumption ceremony "whitens" the faces of the Black subjects, just as one bleaches clothing. The *Diccionario de Autoridades* explains the practice: "COLAR LA ROPA. Ponerla en la canasta de mimbres, y echarle la lexía, para que colando y passando por los agujeros, que forman los mimbres, se límpie y blanquee" (TO BLEACH CLOTHING. To put clothing in the cane basket, and put lye on it, so that by straining it and passing it through the holes, that the canes form, it is cleaned and bleached). The metaphor is notable for its suggestion that the church lightens the Afro-descendant performers' dark skin. Line 36's reference to the women's "vultos azabachados" (coal-blackened faces) deepens this imagery by evoking the stage tradition of darkening one's face, and thus destabilizes notions of embodied Blackness by portraying it as a mere costume.[31]

The concept of spiritual "whiteness," particularly where Black and African people are concerned, has roots that extend well beyond *Villancico* 258. Fracchia has drawn attention to Sor Juana's insistence upon the purity of Afro-descendant souls and underscores their recurring association with light and whiteness throughout the poet's oeuvre. The scholar relates the trait to beliefs about salvation, which figuratively and literally lightens dark bodies. Furthermore, Fracchia observes that early modern racial and spiritual discourses extended these themes by relating redemption to freedom.[32] Alongside the promise of divine liberty Fracchia draws out, it is interesting to note the persistence of a seemingly paradoxical trope that celebrated exemplary devotion to Christian ideals. Complementary to Fracchia's position, Sor Juana's lyrics for the 1679 Assumption festival underscore the Black, female characters' obedient responses to the sacristan's voice in a way that is reminiscent of the expectations for cloistered women.

Indeed, the penultimate *copla* in *Villancico* 258 elaborates on spiritual freedom that Christian devotion can offer enslaved followers:

| | |
|---|---|
| 1.—Ésa sí que se nomblaba | 1.—Yes, that one was called |
| escrava con devoción, | a devoted slave, |
| e cun turo culazón | and with all of her heart |
| a mi Dioso servïaba: | she served my God: |
| y polo sel buena Escrava | and for being a good Slave |
| le dieron la libertá! | they gave her freedom! |
| ¡Ha, ha, ha! &[33] | Ha, ha, ha! & |

Here, the narrator explains that since Mary served God with her whole heart, she earned freedom. The nucleus of this verse's devotional message is a dual synecdoche that relates the heart to both (enslaved) body and spiritual affect, of which the heart is the seat. Accordingly, and somewhat paradoxically, the Virgin placed her corporeal and sentimental self at Christ's service and gained freedom in return. These resonances burble up from the verse as a voiced longing for freedom, which the villancico lyrics frame in terms of the soul's spiritual liberty. This representation brims with significance, for it fulfills expectations about the proselytizing language that lyrics directed to Afro-descendants should incorporate but also identifies with Black subjects' desire for liberty, in all forms.

Continuing, *Villancico* 258 develops the chromatic tropes that stand out in the text and links them to enslaved people's yearning for freedom. In line 40 of the introduction, "albricias" (coins given in tribute) deepens the references and adds an emotional layer. According to the *Diccionario de Autoridades*, "albricias" describes

> las dádivas, regálo, ù dones que se hacen pidiéndose, o sin pedirse, por alguna buena nueva, ò feliz sucesso à la persona que lleva ù dá la primera notícia al interessádo. Covarr. aunque no lo afirma, dice que algunos son de sentir que esta palabra viene de Albícias, porque el que trahía nuevas de alegría entraba vestído de blanco, como al contrario el que vá à dár pesame con capa negra de luto.

> the donations, gifts tributes that are made, solicited or unsolicited, to recognize some good news or a fortunate deed. [They are given] to the person who brings or announces the news to the interested party. Covarrubias,

although he does not affirm it, says that some believe that this word comes from Albícias, because he who brought happy news entered dressed in white, and on the contrary, he who is going to express condolences came with a black mourning cloak.

In the same way, the implied spiritual transformation of *Villancico* 258's Afro-descendant performers colors their affective response. Indeed, contrasting references to darkness and light throughout the lyrics suggest that the joyful news of Mary's Ascension "whitens" the Black performers. Given the aforementioned connections among the lightening of dark souls (or pigment) and freedom, the women's unbridled reaction relates as much to the feast's religious significance as it does to the promise of liberty through Marian devotion.

For all this, it is clear that through polysemy, Sor Juana's villancico lyrics cipher the dominant perspectives of New Spain's elite classes as well as the nuances of Afro-Mexican experience. In addition to giving voice to the desire for spiritual and earthly freedom, *Villancico* 258 also inscribes festive practices of Black brotherhoods. I return here to "vulto," a term that I previously related to the Peninsular theater tradition of performing in blackface. In addition to this symbolism, other definitions enable a reading of "vulto" as a reference to a ritual object from a confraternal procession. According to the *Diccionario de Autoridades*, "bulto" describes "la Imágen, efigie, ò figúra hecha de madéra, piedra ù otra cosa" (the Image, effigy, or figure made of wood, stone, or another material). Consequently, the word suggests that the festival princesses carried a likeness (or likenesses) of the Virgin or another religious figure. In this context, the reference to a jet-black image or figurine has several interpretative possibilities. First, it could describe the effigy's color and thus suggests that the singers processed with a statue of a Black patron like St. Benedict of Palermo or St. Efigenia.[34] Additionally, the allusion might also refer to the material of which the devotional object is made. If indeed the women carry ritual items fashioned from jet, it is unlikely that the villancico's play on words describes a statue. María Ángela Franco Mata has observed that "las exportaciones de azabache a las colonias eran bastante limitadas en cuanto a variedad de objetos; en concreto, de carácter devocional, se exportaron solamente rosarios y medallones de tipo ovulado, probablemente con representaciones de Crucificados, o con Santos" (the exportation of jet to the colonies was rather limited in terms of the variety of objects; concretely, of those of devotional character, only rosaries and oval medals, probably with representations of the Crucifixion or Saints, were exported).[35] Consequently, the "vultos azabachados" ("effigies of jet-black stone") of *Villancico* 258 might also be devotional medals that adorn the Afro-descendant dancers' necks.

Finally, "vulto" also underscores Afro-descendant presence in New Spanish commercial spheres, for it can refer to black bags ("bultos") that the women carry. A reading from this angle aligns with the *coplas*, which affirm that the two characters are street vendors selling candy and foodstuffs. Indeed, the Black women in *Villancico* 258 peddle amaranth bars and other sweets in the Mexico City streets. In this context, their voices mixed with the urban cacophony:

| | |
|---|---|
| 1.—Flasica, naquete día | 1.—Francisca, on this day |
| qui tamo leno li glolia, | when we are so filled with glory, |
| no vindamo | let's not sell a mishmash |
|   pipitolia, |   of stewed chicken |
| pueque sobla la aleglía | because the joy that the Lady Mary |
| que la Señola Malía | gives to all the world |
| a turo mundo la da.[36] | abounds. |

Here and throughout the *coplas*, food-based plays on words conflate religious and quotidian references and comment on New Spain's racial diversity. For instance, the *Diccionario de Autoridades* clarifies that "pepitoria" (line 54) is a "guisado que se hace de los despojos de las aves, como son alones, pescuezos, pies, higadillos y mollejas" (stew that is made from the leftover parts of fowl, like the wings, neck, feet, liver, and gizzards). In these lines, the Afro-descendant lyric subject suggests that she and her companion sell a more festive dish to mark the occasion. The trope highlights food as a polyvalent sign of the women's social and ritual identities.

The symbolism of "pepitoria" extends well beyond the culinary realm and contributes to the villancico's underlying racial themes. In a 1902 edition of Luis Vélez de Guevara's 1641 novel *El diablo cojuelo* (*The Limping Devil*), Adolfo Bonilla y San Martín explicates the phrase's metaphorical uses. First, he notes that "pepitoria" can describe ethnic variety, like in Fray Alonso Remón's *Entretenimientos y ivegos honestos, recreaciones christianas para que en todo género de estados se recreen los sentidos, sin que se estrague el alma* (Diversions and honest games, Christian pastimes to delight the senses in all states, without corrupting the soul; Madrid, 1623). He quotes from Remón's treatise: "En Nápoles, que és una de las más opulentas y ricas ciudades de Italia, grande mar de población y una como *pepitoria* de diversidad de naciones" (In Naples, which is one of the richest and most opulent cities of Italy, [there is] a great sea of a population, like a *pepitoria* of diverse nationalities).[37] From this perspective, Sor Juana's reference highlights New

Spain's racial diversity. Its opposition with the joy that the Virgin can bring portrays devotion to Mary as an equalizer among the region's different castes.

Complementarily, Cervantes's use of the term in the prologue to his *Novelas ejemplares* (*Exemplary Novels*) adds a literary dimension to the symbolism of "pepitoria." In these self-conscious remarks, the author advises the reader that "de estas novelas que te ofrezco, en ningún modo podrás hacer pepitoria" (you cannot make a fricassee with these novels).[38] Stephen Boyd's comments on the Cervantine allusion can clarify Sor Juana's metaphor. He observes that

> the principal meaning appears to be that, with regard to their content, the stories that follow are not what we might term "pornographic": they do not contain "spicy" descriptions of bodily parts, and are therefore not like a *pepitoria*. A secondary, implied meaning . . . is that, individually and collectively, the stories have the ordered, rational integrity of a complete body: they are works of art written in accordance with reason and Christian principles, not an incoherent mishmash of titillating sex scenes.[39]

While resonances of a certain indecent "spiciness" might seem out of place in this context, they reflect the hypersexual views of Afro-descendant women's bodies in the early modern Hispanic world. Consequently, the lyric narrator's affirmation that "non vindamo pipitolia" (let's not sell a mishmash of stewed chicken) highlights the dancer's feet, "wings," and other body parts as attention-getting but also beckons the audience to attend to the performance with a more solemn attitude. Within the poetic and likely musical context of the villancico, whose *estribillo* peppers the *coplas* with laughter, the direction's irony stands out.

In addition, the allusion relates these women's bodies to the very text that inscribes them. Just as Cervantes insists that his exemplary novels are "ordered" and "rational," so the singer distances her dialogue from "pepitoria" and thus represents Afro-descendant voices as consonant and agreeable within the urban and ritual settings that the piece invokes. From one perspective, this resonance highlights writing as a mechanism for harmonizing racial and social dissonance. From a perspective that considers Sor Juana as an "eavesdropper" into New Spain's bustling street life, however, the concordant rendering of the Black lyric subjects implies that in the quotidian and ceremonial sound practices, their tones are as concordant as any others.

"Pepitoria" is not the only culinary metaphor in *Villancico* 258. In the next line, "aleglía" describes both the women's affective response to Assumption and the goods that they sell. Indeed, the word refers to happiness as well as to an amaranth seed candy that was popular in the viceregal period and continues to abound in today's markets. This seed has an important history among New Spain's autochthonous populations. Esther Katz and Elena Lazos note that "in central Mexico, at the beginning of the sixteenth century, *huauhtli* [the Nahuatl word for amaranth] was a staple and ritual food, as important as maize."[40] Among other uses, pre- and post-Contact Indigenous groups used the seeds in religious settings, where they mixed amaranth with agave to create *tzoalli*, edible idols that participants consumed at the end of spiritual celebrations. Although colonial authorities regulated the practice, Sor Juana clearly was aware of it. Her *loa* to *El divino Narciso* (*The Divine Narcissus*) evokes the tradition when native characters consume a statue of Huitzilopochtli made of maize and blood. Beyond its significance as an example of Baroque syncretism, Amy Fuller argues that the trope enables a performance of debates about how to best integrate autochthonous communities and their beliefs into Christian religion.[41] In a similar fashion, *Villancico* 258's oblique allusion to *tzoalli* and their ritual consumption allows for an anamorphic reading of the first *copla*. On one hand, the Afro-descendant vendors may desire to sell a more festive dish that aligns with the feast day's joyous tone, like I previously maintained. On the other, they may opt to stop selling *pepitoria* because participants will consume the *alegrías* that another merchant (Señola Malía) sells during the Assumption celebrations. This second reading of the "alegría" reference underscores the villancico as an instrument of proselytization. Furthermore, by cloaking the Indigenous practice in Catholic language, the polysemic villancico also performs the very gesture that enabled the persistence of non-Christian spirituality in New Spain. Indeed, as I have suggested throughout this book, the region's Afro-descendant and Indigenous inhabitants adapted their rituals to mimic dominant practices in order to ensure their survival.

One more polysemic food reference from *Villancico* 258 merits attention. Like the examples I previously discussed, the second *copla*'s use of "camote" simultaneously underscores and veils the vendors' ethnic identity.

| | |
|---|---|
| Dejémos la cocina | Let's leave the kitchen |
| y vámoso a turo trote, | and run there as fast as we can, |
| sin que vindamo gamote | without selling any sweet potatoes |
| nin garbanzo a la vizina: | or beans to the neighbor: |
| qui arto gamote, Cristina, | Cristina, there are loads of *camotes* |
| hoy a la fieta vendrá.[42] | coming to the party. |

In his reading of these lines, Swiadon Martínez highlights "camote" as a racial slur rooted in perceptions of the Afro-Mexican diet.[43] From one perspective, the juxtaposition of the garbanzo, a Peninsular dietary staple, and the American sweet potato establishes a contrast between the two. This interpretation particularly resonates with allusions to the opposition between black and white skin tone (sin and purity) that persist throughout the verses.

Indeed, Swiadon Martínez's reading of the "camote" reference in *Villancico* 258 draws out the poet's inheritance of this Spanish literary trope, an important consideration for understanding her engagement with Afrodescent. Nonetheless, inasmuch as Sor Juana's *villancicos de negros* perform Blackness within the fundamentally different context of the New Spanish stage, *Villancico* 258 beckons a contrasting reading. I maintain that alliteration in lines 59 and 60 aligns "garbanzo" and "gamote," thus uniting the seemingly divergent pair in a gesture of poetic *mestizaje*. In a reading that goes beyond the representative politics of Sor Juana's ethnic villancicos, Yolanda Martínez-San Miguel argues that these pieces' plurivocity responds to the epistemological shifts of a multiethnic New Spain:

> Beneath this supposed unification through knowledge of the Catholic faith, the *villancico* executes a process of diversification in the acquisition of knowledge, which unfolds in various successive narrations that use different registers to articulate themselves to the heterogeneous sectors of colonial society. I am interested, therefore, in reading parts of four *villancico* song cycles by Sor Juana in order to trace the articulation of the "intercultural epistemology" these texts indicate through their genetic constitution. In this sense, my analysis does not posit that the gesture of producing new paradigms of knowledge is exclusive to the work of Sor Juana. Rather, it is the result of a colonial or multiracial context that promoted new epistemological and pedagogical paradigm [sic] through intercultural contact.[44]

In this way, *Villancico* 258 makes multicultural knowledge audible through American modulations of a Peninsular poetic tradition. Precisely, lines 59 and 60 transform *habla de negros* into a trope of linguistic creation that exceeds the bounds of "proper" Castilian. Articulated from a position of sonic Blackness, "camote" becomes "gamote," "nin" rhymes with "sin," and "vindamo" shares vocables with "vizina." On one hand, these changes suggest a degree of incomprehensibility that underscores the Black speaker as an outsider. On the other, they phonetically relate symbols of ethnic difference, activating the auditory imaginary to establish likenesses that transcend the lyrics' semantic and metaphorical meaning.

References to the commercial activities of Black and African people like in *Villancico* 258 pepper representations of Afro-descent from both sides of the Atlantic. For Swiadon Martínez, these associations ridicule the poetic subjects that they describe and establish hierarchies of class and race that do not necessarily correlate with seventeenth-century Mexico's social and economic reality.[45] To this end, Valerio has pointed out that some Mexico City Afro-descendants enjoyed lives of considerable means, and a collective political savvy among the region's Black and African inhabitants empowered them to transform New Spanish festival culture into a site for performing Afro-Mexican identity in large-scale public venues.[46] Inasmuch as Sor Juana's *villancicos de negros* make Afro-descent both visible and audible in settings long thought to marginalize people of color, I argue that the pieces amplify Black and African presence in diverse Mexico City contexts, despite their thorny politics of representation.

### THE BLACK VIRGIN OF *VILLANCICO* LVIII (ASSUMPTION, 1686)

Sor Juana's attributable *Villancico* lviii represents Black women's performance by engaging some of the same themes. Like *Villancico* 258, this piece represents the devotional practices of Afro-descendant communities within the context of Catholic rituals. As such, I argue that readings of Sor Juana's lyrics that attend to the underlying percussion of inaudible voices can amplify the Black and African subjectivities that resonate from within the text.

*Villancico* lviii opens with a pair of rural subjects who hail from the province of Valladolid.

| | |
|---|---|
| Con sonajas en los pies | With rattles on their feet |
| dos Patanes han entrado, | two boors have entered |
| de la Provincia que dio | from the Province |
| antonomasia de Payos; | that gave Villagers their name; |
| | |
| y así, con solemne pompa, | and so, with solemn pomp |
| sin estribillo entonaron, | they sang without verse, |
| porque hasta ahora sus pies | because until now their feet |
| de estribillos no han gustado[47] | have not seen a stirrup |

Sonorous references in these lines contrast with their written context. Although the country-dwellers enter "with solemn pomp," the rattles on their feet—like Indigenous ritual dancers—humorously disrupt the somber procession.[48] Furthermore, the opening verses imagine the *patanes* as outsiders in the lyrical tradition, for they sing "sin estribillo," or without metrical verse. Like in the poet's *Villancico* lviii from the 1677 Assumption set, a play on words draws out the polyvalence of "estribillo" ("refrain" and also the diminutive form of "stirrup"). Through this rhetorical figure, the introduction compares the manner in which the rural subjects' song resists the villancico's poetic structure to their uncontrolled movement on horseback. In all likelihood, the reference is prescriptive and also describes the actors' corporeal presence as they move across the stage. For all this, the comparison establishes a relationship between the singers' bodies and their inscribed voices. Although the rural subjects participate in the religious ceremony, the introduction underscores their disruptive presence in lettered forms of cultural expression.

In the villancico's next section, another set of popular characters boisterously intervenes in the ceremony. Here, two Afro-descendant women arrive at the celebration and add their voices to the din. The introduction describes the performers' entry:

| En esto entraron dos Negras | In that moment, two *Negras* entered |
| que dicen las despertaron | and said that they were awakened |
| de los Payos las sonajas, | by the rattles of the peasants |
| no el rumor del campanario.[49] | not the sounds of the bell tower. |

According to these lines, the Black characters arrive at the celebration early in the morning. The church bells announcing the canonical hours did not waken them, though. Instead, the villagers' rattles called them to take part in the ritual. Thus, while the Afro-descendant women participate in the festivities to commemorate Mary's Assumption, they are more interested in the raucous sounds of a party than they are in spiritual matters. Like the peasants from the previous section, these lyric subjects take part in the religious ritual but remain "in the dark," so to speak, about the broader context.

Indeed, the Afro-descendant women do not disrupt the Catholic ceremony. In fact, the next verse elaborates a series of chromatic metaphors that simultaneously integrate the dark-skinned performers into the liturgy but also highlight their presence as out of the ordinary:

| Los Azabaches con alma | The Jet-black Singers, full of spirit, |
| su cántico comenzaron | began their devotional song |
| y novedad fue en Maitines | and what a novelty it was at Matins |
| ver las Tinieblas cantando.[50] | to see the Shadows singing. |

These lines recall chiaroscuro in Baroque visual art by setting up a contrast between the singers' dusky bodies and the lightness of salvation (and their souls, should they accept Christian teachings). The poet refers to the women as "azabaches" or "jet," and she invokes once more the racial slur that links dark pigment to a precious stone. Furthermore, the introduction's second verse compares the performers to the pre-dawn darkness of the hour when Matins is sung. The color-based allusions imagine the women's voices as extensions of their racialized bodies. As we shall see, the villancico's later sections juxtapose the performers' dark skin with the starry heavens. These opposing visual references heighten a key resonance with *Villancico* 258: Afro-descendant freedom through Christian salvation.

Like in the previous example, unbridled joy burbles up from the text in the form of apparently nonsensical vocables and jubilant body motion. From a dominant perspective, the affective response relates to Christian devotion, obedient participation in a Catholic festival, and the "happy slave" trope that Baker underscores as central in Black villancicos.[51] Nonetheless, here, as in *Villancico* 258, the underlying linkage between earthly and spiritual freedom as well as resonances with Afro-Catholic rituals and forms of community-building shake the written script and challenge interpretations that would adopt a unilateral Eurocentric or dominant perspective.

In line with many of the sorjuanine villancicos that this book has examined, *Villancico* lviii inscribes the illegible voices and uncontrollable bodies of Afro-descendant women in the Catholic festival that they join. From this perspective, the characters stand out as dissonant in the consonant imaginaries that guide urban and religious ideologies. The representation is crucial to the villancico's function, for it performs their harmonization through Christian conversion. The introduction's insistence upon the singers' race prepares the *estribillo*, where they sing in apparently impenetrable blackspeak.

| | |
|---|---|
| 1.—¡Ha, ha, ha, | 1.—Ha, ha, ha, |
| buenu va! | It's going well! |
| ¡Cambulé, | ¡Cambulé, |
| gulungué, | gulungué |
| he, he, he! | he, he, he! |
| | |
| 2.—¡Nu va buenu! | 2.—It's not going so well! |
| | |
| 1.—Buenu va, | 1.—It's going well! |
| e si no, la Siñola | And if it's not going well, the Mistress |
| peldonalá![52] | will forgive you. |

Linguistically and structurally, the chorus of *Villancico* lviii relates to *Villancico* 258, and specifically, to the representation of Black and African women's performance that the previous section explored. In both pieces, references to laughter and wild dance punctuate a dialogue between two female singers. The phrases "cambulé" and "gulungú" are repeated, as are references to the jet-black "azabache" as well as the liberty that salvation might offer enslaved people. Likewise, the two villancicos' introductions narrate the Afro-descendant performers' entrance in similar ways. In each instance, the sounds of ecclesiastical ritual attract the women, although both sets of verses insist that general merriment appeals to them more than religious devotion.

Continuing, the *coplas* elaborate on the reason for such festivities—the heavenly ascent of "una Nenglita" (a Black queen):

| | |
|---|---|
| I.—Flacica, turu la Negla | I.—Francisca, all of the *Negras* |
| hoy de guto bailalá | will dance with joy today |
| polque una Nenglita beya | because a beautiful *negra* queen |
| e Cielo va gobelná. | is going to rule the Heavens. |
| Ha, ha, ha, &.[53] | Ha, ha, ha, &. |

In the remaining verses, the singers describe the Assumption in visual terms, with references that loosely relate to the iconography of the Virgin of the Apocalypse. The description's ocular focus is important, for it elaborates a chiaroscuro contrast that draws attention to the whiteness of Mary's spiritual purity before the performers' dark skin. As I will argue here, the lyric narrators' comical inversion of symbols associated with the Virgin of the Apocalypse—specifically, her starry crown—resonates with the chromatic opposition that the *coplas* develop and highlights the characters' "upside-down" affirmation of Mary's Blackness ("una Nenglita" or "a Black Queen").

As an emblem of the night sky as well as a notable element in Marian iconography, the star is one of the most prominent symbols in *Villancico* lviii's *coplas*. Throughout these verses, the Afro-descendant narrators celebrate the heavenly ascent of the "Nenglita" as a journey toward freedom, and she strides across bright stars along the way. The luminous bodies become a sign of liberty, and the singers long for their own stars. Embodied references to the Virgin's path highlight the contrast between her dark feet and the white star upon which they tread. Here, the stellar light stands out as a bright pathway that guides the Black Virgin and her followers on their journey to freedom.

| | |
|---|---|
| 2.— Ay, siñola, lible Negla<br>que estrela pisandi está,<br>dáme una de<br>    la que pisa,<br>pue que a mí me sevilá!<br>Ha, ha, ha, &. | 2.—Ah, madam, free *Negra* queen<br>who is stepping on the stars,<br>give me one of the ones that you are<br>    stepping on,<br>because it will serve me well!<br>Ha, ha, ha, &. |
| 1.—De la luzu que displesia<br>tu pie, la unu dalá<br>polo que sin Ti quedamus<br>e continua eculilá.<br>Ha, ha, ha, &. | 1.—Of the light that your foot<br>scorns, give me one<br>for without You we are stuck here<br>and the light keeps eluding us.<br>Ha, ha, ha, &. |
| 2.—E me envialá la aleglía,<br>pue que mucho tendlá ayá,<br>pala que con ese ayula<br>ganemu su libeltá.<br>Ha, ha, ha, &.[54] | 2.—And send me some happiness,<br>since you will have much of it there,<br>so that with this help<br>we might gain our freedom.<br>Ha, ha, ha, &. |

It is not surprising to see stars featured in Sor Juana's Assumption villancico, for the symbol peppers visual imaginings of the Virgin Mary. In an early Mexican context, the first association that springs to mind may be the starry cloak of the Virgin of Guadalupe, whose image prevalently circulated in the region during the 1600s. However, the Virgin Mary is associated with stars in other visual contexts as well. For instance, Revelation 12:1 describes the Assumption: "a great sign appeared in heaven: A woman clothed with the sun, and the moon under her feet, and on her head a crown of twelve stars."[55] This powerful imagery resonated with visual representations of the Virgin of the Apocalypse or the Virgin of the Immaculate Conception. In these visual imaginings, the Virgin appears standing on a sliver of moon and crowned with twelve stars, one for each of the apostles. Cristóbal de Villalpando's 1685 rendering of this figure for the sacristy of the Mexico City cathedral is a noteworthy example of this iconography, as is *mulato* artist Juan Correa's 1689 *Virgen del Apocalipsis* painting.

Given *Villancico* lviii's 1686 date, it is possible that the piece's engagement with the Virgin of the Apocalypse saluted Villalpando's painting, perhaps in conjunction with a procession by the Afro-descendant confraternity dedicated to the Our Lady of the Conception (founded in 1600 in the Hospital

**6.1**. Cristóbal de Villalpando, *Mujer del Apocalipsis*, 1685. Sacristy, Mexico City Cathedral, Mexico City, Mexico. Waisman, (self-published, 2021), 599, m. 17–34.

**6.2**. Juan Correa, *Virgen del Apocalipsis,* 1689. Museo Nacional del Virreinato, Tepotzotlán, Mexico.

of the Marquis of the Valley).[56] Should this hypothesis prove true, it can lend significant insight into how Afro-descendants participated in New Spain's Catholic festivals by interacting with ceremonial elements like villancicos or visual art. Within the specific context of Afro-Mexican tributes dedicated to the Virgin of the Apocalypse (or the Virgin of the Immaculate Conception), the figure's Reconquest symbolism bears mention. Indeed, as Rosilie Hernández has pointed out, the Virgin of the Immaculate Conception was a female counterpart to St. James the Moor-slayer, Patron of the Reconquest.[57] In New Spain, representations of this figure undoubtedly echoed the Christians' triumphant victory over "heathen," North African Moors. Thus, to some degree, Black and African festival participants performed their own conversion by venerating this figure.

As in other villancicos, however, in *Villancico* lviii, the Afro-descendant singers' faithful narration of Christian doctrine is questionable. Indeed, just as the female performers invert the Virgin's skin tone by referring to her as "una Nenglita," so they also imagine her starry crown as a celestial pathway. Instead of adorning her head, the stars of the twelve apostles support Mary's feet as she climbs heavenward. This humorous reversal resonates with chromatic oppositions throughout the piece, and it centers the distinction between the Black Virgin's dark skin and her starry pathway as the crux of meaning. Here, the Afro-descendant women seek to follow in the Black queen's footsteps so that they too might enjoy the white light of freedom. On the surface, the devotional message easily harmonizes with the evangelization that villancicos are meant to perform. Beneath the surface, however, it also expresses Black and African longing for freedom and the intense joy that enslaved subjects experience before the prospect of liberty.

### CONCLUSION

By way of a conclusion, I would like to turn to an observation that has haunted me throughout the development of *Amplifications of Black Sound*. In a 2021 virtual forum that responded to Miguel Ángel Rosales' 2016 film *Gurumbé: Canciones de tu memoria negra* (*Gurumbé: Afro-Andalusian Memories*), dancer Yinka Esi Graves commented on her sensitivity to flamenco's embodied Blackness: "If you're not told the histories together and have no references, then you're incapable of recognizing gestures in flamenco as Black. It happens because it isn't written through the Western canons of 'Africanness.'"[58] In the same spirit, this chapter proposes a framework that more fully attunes to Afro-descendant themes in Sor Juana's oeuvre and beyond. While previous scholarship reads the poet's inscription of Black and African voices through a lens that privileges writing as a vehicle for expressing dominant perspectives or underscores exotic remnants of West and Central African tongues, here, I argue for reading the nun's renderings of women's performance as indexes of their subjects' quotidian presence in New Spain's urban spaces.

Like I have shown, Sor Juana's representations of Black women's performance underscore Afro-descendant practices in New Spain's social and devotional contexts and also draw out resonances of this social group within dominant spiritual discourses like, for example, the obedience to Christian authorities. To this end, both *Villancico* 258 and *Villancico* lviii notably stage the embodied voices of Black and African women and thus amplify their presence in texts long thought to marginalize non-Western subjectivities.

Furthermore, by inscribing Afro-descendant female performers into Mexico City's festive and quotidian practices, the villancicos discussed here engage with Afro-Mexican experiences by showing how participation in Catholic ceremonies through lay organizations and other means encouraged unity among the region's diasporic subjects and thus led to the development of community identity among diasporic subjects. Along these lines, Rowe explains that

> the claim by black confraternal brothers and sisters to public space and participation in the social life of towns and cities—most of which was organized by ecclesiastical rhythms of feast days and their attendant masses and processions—helped to create distinct spaces for black community members to gather and protect one another. The performance of Christianity, whether from devotion or utility (not that these are mutually exclusive), forced shared public presence even as it could foster group consciousness among African diasporic communities.[59]

From this perspective, Sor Juana's representations of Afro-descendant women in New Spanish religious ceremonies reinforce the Afro-Mexican identity that developed in response to such gatherings.

Finally, my oblique readings of villancicos attend to the quiet resonances that Campt draws out and showcase Afro-descendant perspectives that readings from a binary perspective of dominant/subjugated voices might otherwise dampen. In this way, Chapter 6's analyses resonate with Fromont's polyphonic analyses of nineteenth-century travelers' visual representations of Afro-Brazilians, as discussed in Chapter 4. Here, I propose a framework for attending to Afro-descendant voices in textual sources that frequently are ignored because of their problematic representations of Black subjects or, in contrast, celebrated in excess for their authorial sympathy with these figures. While the latter perspective threatens to marginalize important sources for recovering Black and African presence and customs in New Spain, perhaps the former risks over-interpretation in its embrace of the contemporary alignment of Sor Juana with marginalized subjects, including the Latinx and LGBTQIA communities. I hope that the readings I developed here might lead us to a middle ground that is conscious of villancicos' engagement with seventeenth-century attitudes about race but also recognizes their value as imaginings of the very real Afro-descendant subjects that passed through the Mexico City streets, not all that far from the Santa Paula convent.

### REPERCUSSION

Sor Juana's legacy has strong resonances in contemporary culture, where writers and artists alike have reimagined her in a myriad of ways. Her imaginings of New Spain's Black and African inhabitants are no exception. To illustrate this point, I will examine a creative project that re-sounds Afro-descent in Sor Juana's villancicos: the Mexican sound collective Rak Ric Rack!'s 2008 recording *Tumba La-Lá-La: Los villancicos negros de sor Juana*. This album includes lyrics from the poet's Black villancicos. *Tumba La-Lá-La* samples Sor Juana's poetry with Latin jazz—a notable genre for its African-American and Afro-Latin underpinnings—including bossa nova, samba, and other Afro-diasporic styles. The album closes with a twenty-minute soundscape from Cuajinicuilapa, a town with strong Afro-descendant roots in Mexico's Costa Chica region.

*Tumba La-Lá-La* has received little critical attention, perhaps due in part to the marginalization of Afro-descent in narratives of Mexican nationalism.[60] However, the project recently gained visibility, thanks to references in Jones' reading of Sor Juana as a Black Atlantic writer. Jones interprets *Tumba La-Lá-La* through the lens of *afromestizaje*, maintaining that "it illuminates how both Mexican and Mexican-American rap music *and* the musicalized form of *habla de negros* in villancicos facilitate a blending of cultural influences."[61] Along these lines, he underscores driving polyrhythm, references to dance forms, and the mixture of disparate musical elements as examples of *afromestizaje* that relate to both Afro-diasporic and Baroque cultural expression. I will develop Jones' observations further by reflecting upon how the album re-sounds Black and African voices in Sor Juana's villancicos beyond the limits of the written archive. Echo is a central theme in my argument, for *Tumba La-Lá-La* is filled with reverberations and reflected vocalizations whose echoic nature challenges the listener to hear her own voice among others in the Afro-diasporic remix.

I first began thinking about remixing as a form of scholarly inquiry after reading Myron Beasley's discussion of how a Harlem DJ's "audio palimpsest" of figures like Nina Simone, Langston Hughes, and Zora Neale Hurston amplify writing's spectral engagement with Black identity.[62] For Beasley, Hurston's recorded archive offers sonic counterpoint to the "embodied sensual performances" of her writing.[63] He argues that exploring the two modes' intersections can lead to useful reflections upon Hurston's ethnographic positionality and its relationship to the voices that her work constructs. Remixing draws out the plurivocity of these audio identities and also re-sounds them as echoes of collective possibility, open to new meaning and reinterpretations across space and time. For all this, the technique is useful for re-sounding—or repercussing—non-European voices from the colonial archive.

In *Tumba La-Lá-La*, echo is a useful acoustical lens for understanding how the album re-sounds Afro-descent. The trope is persistent throughout the recording; however, it particularly stands out in the ninth track, "Siñol Andlea Siñol Tomé." This piece reimagines Sor Juana's *Villancico* xvi. Among other characteristics, this sorjuanine work is notable for an echoic dialogue between its main characters, "Siñol Andlea" and "Siñol Tomé." In Chapter 5, I argued that the structure destabilizes language's authority in Western thought. As if riffing on the same theme, Rak Ric Rack!'s remix uses auditory reflections and reverb to amplify the echoic and timbral "othering" that takes place in Sor Juana's lyrics.

"Siñol Andlea Siñol Tomé" opens with clanging church bells, an auditory symbol of ecclesiastical authority in viceregal Mexico. Within seconds, a rapid, heartbeat-like pulse drowns out the bells and resituates the villancico in a different context. The two characters' dialogue follows, set against a percussive background that also features female echoes, laughter, animal-like sounds, song, and unintelligible speech. Stereophonic techniques—achieved by recording sounds in different channels—amplify the text's echoic structure and draw out the overlapping voices that the lyrics encode. In a glossolalian cacophony, Rak Ric Rack!'s heightened uses of reflected voice recall the written archive's marginalization of non-European sounds and also uncover the plurivocity that Western writing and meaning-making suppress.

Re-soundings like in "Siñol Andlea, Siñol Tomé" are a significant part of *Tumba La-Lá-La*'s amplification of Afro-descent in Black villancicos. Their relevance is particularly evident in light of the manner in which echo disorders the linear narratives that underlie Western history. In this track from Rak Ric Rack!'s recording, the acousmatic, reflected utterance disrupts imagined continuity between voice and identity by enabling the speaker to experience her own sonic alterity. Furthermore, as the disembodied, audible remnant of a previous utterance, reverberation evokes Derrida's revenant, a ghostly manifestation that bids us to listen to ourselves listening to the past "by speaking at the same time several times—and in several voices."[64] For Derrida, engaging the revenant is an act of audition that exceeds Western historicization, and its untimeliness enables past and future to coexist in the same moment. The philosopher affirms:

> one does not know if the expectation prepares the coming of the future-to-come or if it recalls the repetition of the same, of the same thing as ghost.... This not-knowing is not a lacuna. No progress of knowledge could saturate an opening that must have nothing to do with knowing. Nor therefore with ignorance. The opening must preserve this heterogeneity as the only chance of an affirmed or rather reaffirmed future. It is the future itself, it comes from there. The future is its memory.[65]

Read through a Derridean lens, echo thus derives meaning from the expectation of its return and the potential for re-sounding. In an album like *Tumba-La-Lá-La*, which manipulates sound to exploit its echoic possibilities, the sonorous asynchronicity of reverberation opens the past to re-signification and thus, to the restitution of voices lost.

In closing, I would like to reflect upon the broader potential of sonic modes of inquiry in text-based disciplines like literature, history, or even musicology. Among other inspirations, my remarks here owe much to artist, curator, and scholar Mark V. Campbell's comparison between the DJ and the archivist. For Campbell, remixing responds to the limits of written records.

> First, the use of DJing techniques honors Afrodiasporic cultures by refusing to disconnect histories of Afrosonic and oral innovation, such as legacies of call and response, improvisation, and repetition.... Second, these performances gesture toward the transparent embedding of Afrodiasporic oral and sonic innovations by curators, archivists, and DJs, not solely as aesthetics, but also as ways to interrupt, undo, and rethink the colonial residues of archives.[66]

Along the same lines, *Tumba La-Lá-La* makes clear possibilities of remixing as a creative and critical mode for attending to Black and African voices in Sor Juana's villancicos. While it may be impossible to access the actual sounds of Afro-descent that Spanish- and Creole-authored writing encode, resampling attends to their affective and cultural contours and also heightens the DJ-historian's awareness of her own listening positionality and its undeniable role in making sense of Afro-descendant sonorities and their echoes.

CONCLUSION

# Black Sounds Echo in New Spanish Waters

The history of the unheard is difficult to write, since so little of it has ever been recorded. It works in the shadows, and while we hear its effects—such as machinic noise, chatter, crickets, music, data sonification, the din of the trading floor, infrastructure networks, transportation, cargo ships—we can only surmise its long-term trajectory. Where it is natural to steer away from these noisy effects, the only opportunity to write a past or future history of the unheard is to attune to these noises as signals of an unheard trajectory.

—**Tobias Ewé**, "The Unheard"

As I have shown throughout *Amplifications of Black Sound*, a nuanced approach to the written archive is necessary for recovering Afro-descendant music, oral histories, and sounds in the Atlantic World. I add my own voice to a chorus of scholars like Baker, de Luna, Ortiz, and Valerio, all of whom underscore the need for new methods if we are to "hear" Black, Indigenous, and other non-European voices in the Atlantic archive. By way of a conclusion, this chapter offers another methodology for attending to the such sounds beyond the silent legacy of written records.

A gesture of restitution lies at heart of efforts to recuperate Afro-descendant sound and other muted subjectivities. Researchers and practitioners alike aim to restore lost voices to their rightful place in cultural narratives and canons.[1] Their indisputable significance notwithstanding, however, such acts of cultural recompense are perpetually unfinished. They reimagine the past by projecting it into a yet unknown future. Jones draws out the uncanny nature of inquiry into marginalized histories. In his discussion of necromancy as a critical mode for revaluing Black subjectivity in the early modern world, Jones describes the twofold gesture of this type of scholarship: "to return, on the one hand, and to animate, on the other hand, an inherent agential voice to the persons bureaucratically filtered, silenced, and regularized in slave owner's inventories and wills as well as dossiers from the Inquisition."[2] Here, restoring voice is key to resituating historical subjects, thus satisfying debt with the past and bringing it to life again so that it might act upon the future.

Taking Jones's remarks into account, the recovery of voices past becomes a critical and ethical act. By attending to extra-archival echoes, we embody sounds at the very margins of writing and make their silences audible in the symbolic realm. As an interpretative archival practice, listening draws attention to processes of subjectification that transcend Western ocular-centrism. With respect to the Black Atlantic visual archive, Campt suggests that engagement with its audible silences gives voice to "the hum of utopian dreams and diasporic aspiration."[3] Consequently, listening to muted echoes is both a historicizing method and a performance that re-sounds longing for Afro-diasporic subjectivity.[4]

For all this, it is important to understand the scholar-listener's role in creating historical narratives out of echoes. Indeed, as Eidsheim has shown, the acousmatic path from voice to vocalizing subject is not as clear cut as one might think, particularly in an audio-racial context. In order to make sense of voice, the listening subject performs an act of sonic embodiment, linking auditory input to a physical form. Eidsheim reads vocal signification as a function of the listener. She argues:

> because a human vocalizer exists and vocalizes within a community, listeners' assessments directly affect and entrain the vocalizer materially and thus sonically.... The assumptions, expectations, and conventions of a given culture, and that culture's impression of who the vocalizer is, are overlaid onto its acceptance or rejection of the vocalizer.[5]

Here, Eidsheim draws out the auditing subject's complicity in constructing imagined vocal identities. From a perspective of ethical-historical scholarship, her remarks underscore the continued need for awareness of our culturally conditioned listening positionalities, even as we strive to give voice to the diverse sonic pasts that do not necessarily jump out at us in archival accounts.

As *Amplifications of Black Sound* has shown, Afro-descendants in New Spain were far from mute. Numerous examples illustrate how Black and African people living in the region's urban settings negotiated audible spaces for themselves through their apparent consonance with sonic traditions that reinforced religious and political order. Harmony is a persistent theme, and dichotomies like dissonance/consonance or disruption/peaceful stand out in records of Afro-descendant sound. By probing these qualifiers and placing diverse sources into dialogue with one another, it is possible to attend to the varied Afro-diasporic sonorities of seventeenth-century Mexico City and other urban spaces. In these areas, Black and African people maintained the audio-cultural memory of their ancestral homes through syncretic traditions that harmonized with the social and religious expectations of colonial elite. These types of sounds were hidden in plain sight. As a result, the sonorities discussed in this book and their contemporary persistence have received limited attention.

To conclude, I will reflect upon how the present-day auditor might harness his or her temporal distance in order to listen to seventeenth-century Mexico City's Black Atlantic resonances. In order to reanimate muted Afro-Mexican sounds and voices from the archive, I employ a critical framework of echolocation. In this process, a human or animal emits a sound and then judges the location of the reflecting object or objects based upon its echo. Jonathan Sterne and Mitchell Akiyama describe echolocation as "a technique for emplacement, for an immediate experience of a space."[6] Through vocalization or its corporeal equivalent, the echolocating subject sonically positions him- or herself before an imagined object. To hear the voice reflected back, however, the echolocator must listen for a past self in order to determine a present location. It is an uncanny act of ventriloquism that enables the subject to hear him- or herself as other. For a split second, the act of hearing collapses physical and temporal distance. Subject and object merge as the echolocator experiences the vibrating frequencies of his or her own voice, freed, as it were, from the sounding body. The audio-spatial experience transcends symbolic dichotomies and makes self and other audible within the same voice. As an interpretative practice, then, echolocation allows the listening subject to engage with the object as a sonic reflection of his or her voice-identity. Understanding historical sound scholarship as a process of vocalization and self-hearing thus shows how contemporary researchers might draw upon their own voices to locate audiotopically sonic identities that the written archive and its imagined sounds mute.[7]

One thread that unifies the chapters of *Amplifications of Black Sound* is the idea of seventeenth-century Mexico City as a sonic mapping of urban space that acts upon the auditory imagination. This concept makes the imposed geometries of the tidy grid plan audible and lends a sonorous dimension to the imposition of civic order. Indeed, urban planning in colonial Latin America responded to harmony's multifaceted construction as a sonic, spatial, and ethical concept. Alongside Baker, I have argued all throughout the book that these resonances among physical space, the organization and conduct of collective bodies, and sound itself to highlight urban sonorities as an audible grid whose resonances harmonize the city.

As part of this setting, ecclesiastical and political authorities endorsed sonic ritual and performances that served as audible counterpoint to inscribed hegemonies. Nevertheless, the bustling streets echoed with a rich auditory culture that exceeded harmonic, plotted, and written bounds. Throughout the colonial archive, however, official attempts to order ethnic sounds within the harmonic cityscape reveal deep apprehension about interracial mingling. Indeed, despite colonial authorities' best efforts, bodies are more easily contained than the immaterial sounds they produce. Like the examples in *Amplifications of Black Sound* demonstrate, conspicuous references to audible performances of ethnicity in seventeenth-century legal and Inquisitorial documents as well in ecclesiastical records and travel narratives illustrate their unsettling effects on urban concord.

In this context, there is at minimum one space that eludes these harmonious constructions. Curiously, non-European sonorities in the canals seem less threatening than in other urban settings, at least according to the descriptions that I will examine shortly. Unlike the straight, ordered streets that stand out in cartographic representations of Mexico City, the waterways wind sinuously through the viceregal capital, especially in the outermost municipalities. As vestiges of the area's Indigenous past, these wet pathways do not conform to the imagined harmonies that underlie colonial principles of urban design. Socially, there are recreational spaces in which all members of New Spanish society convene without the visual signals of social hierarchy imposed in more formal religious or civic settings.

From a sonic perspective, water challenges Western ideas about the organization of sound. Tobias Ewé argues,

> unlike the slow propagation of sound in air, water works at different speeds. The haptic feedback systems of the human body awaken to a more immediate relationship with its milieu. At first you think your ears have been plugged. Unlike earplugs that strip away undesirable frequencies from the audible spectrum, water is not a plug, but an entirely different zone of existence. Soon the sensation of cold, wet, and plugged ears are displaced as the aquatic milieu becomes naturalized. Sound waves move up to four times faster in water than in air, and as you stay under what was previously muffled now attains clarity and precision. The slowness of air, and the mid-range frequencies

evaporate and disperse into the pelagic realm of the unheard. Aeolian sounds ... become unheard sounds. Striated space gives way to smooth space until that again reaches a point of striation. The unheard moves outside of time.[8]

For Ewé, listening underwater affords a more intimate sonic experience that transcends the temporal distance of listening through air. Ewé explains that listening always entails a social or physical filter that leaves some audible material just beyond the listeners' reach. He continues by clarifying that "the unheard is not a transcendental *out there* that can never be grasped due to hard-coded human biosensory or audiosocial limitations; the unheard exists in an immanent outside that *can* be transformed into audible material through the act of unhearing. Either with the right technological (ne/a)ural-enhancements, sono-stimulants, or bodily (de)tuning."[9] In this conclusion, I ask the listening reader to accompany me and "unhear" Black sound in the New Spanish archive. The task is to submerge one's metaphorical ear in the murk of Mexico City's canals. There, where terrestrial frequencies are muted and water closes the temporal gap between sounding object and auditor, it is possible to attend to sounds that land drowns out. As a stranger in a new sonic environment, the listener is displaced from hearing as an embodied experience of self. The higher frequencies of sonorities that might otherwise go unnoticed become amplified, and new auditory perspectives emerge.

Ayesha Hameed's audio-visual essay *Black Atlantis* can offer insights to help listeners capture Afro-descendant echoes in the watery sound culture of New Spain. In this piece, Hameed beautifully reflects upon water as a symbol of the Black Atlantic and its enduring legacies. She frames the aquatic as a means of situating Black bodies and juxtaposes historical accounts of the Middle Passage with sonic and visual records of migration across the very same waterways. The ocean is a central medium, and Hameed observes: "What wetness brings back to the table is a sense of the haptic, the sensory, the bodily, and the epidermal. What below-the-water, and Atlantis brings back is the bottom of the sea, the volume of the water, the materiality of the space of the ocean, and other protagonists that inhabit the sea."[10] For Hameed, engagement with the Black Atlantic is the product of historical inquiry as well as the corporeal, sensory archive. The observation can complement the disembodied "unhearing" that takes place in the watery depths of the canals. Indeed, once separated from auditory perception as an experience of her own physical presence and capacity for meaning-making—positions that respond to the self/other binary in Western contexts—the listener can attend more fully to other sonic histories and bodies in the same space.

Beyond the transport and commerce of captive laborers, scholars also draw attention to the Atlantic Ocean's important role in facilitating the exchange of ideas and cultures. For example, with respect to the musical cross-pollination that had Spanish, Portuguese, American, and African ports at its center, Jones remarks that "many dances of African influence appeared almost simultaneously at different points of the so-called Atlantic triangle, a region that comprised coastal cities of the Congo-Angola, Iberian Peninsula, and Latin America. As these contacts took place across the sea, sailors and dockworkers played an important role in this cross-fertilization between the sounds and rhythms of three continents."[11] In this observation, the watery Atlantic crossing becomes a symbol of intertwining sonic histories whose cultural roots can be difficult to pinpoint.

Mexico City's canals stand out in primary descriptions of the city, and they frequently intersect with audio-racial themes. For instance, the multicultural Mexico City sound culture stands out in Bernardo de Balbuena's 1604 panegyric *La grandeza mexicana*. The Spanish poet's ode features an intriguing, sonorous representation of the busy city waterways that situates these spaces outside of the city's harmonious grid:

> Cruzan sus anchas calles mil hermosas
> acequias que cual sierpes cristalinas
> dan vueltas y revueltas deleitosas,
>
> llenan de estrechos barcos, ricas minas
> de provisión, sustento y materiales
> a sus fábricas y obras peregrinas.
>
> . . . . . . . . . . . . . . . . . . . . . . . . . .
>
> Entra una flota y otra se despide,
> de regalos cargada la que viene,
> la que se va del precio que los mide,
>
> su sordo ruido y tráfago entretiene
> el contratar y aquel bullirse todo
> que nadie un punto de sosiego tiene.[12]
>
> A thousand beautiful canals and dikes
> cross its wide streets
> with delightful, crystalline curves,[13]

straits filled with ships, rich mines
of provisions, [delivering] sustenance and materials
to mills and celebrated works.

. . . . . . . . . . . . . . . . . . . . . . . . . . . .

One fleet enters and another takes its leave,
the arriving one filled with gifts,
the departing one heavy with the price of its wares,

it amuses with deafening noise and maritime traffic,
bustling with commerce and abuzz with noise,
that no one has even a moment's peace.

These verses represent the Mexico City canal as the site of a rich exchange of goods from around the world. They underscore sounds of the mercantile space as lively but also disruptive, especially in contrast with the ordered harmonies of Baker's resounding city. Before the local poet's ear, the cacophonous waterways, filled with foreign sounds and voices, become "sordo ruido," or "deafening noise," a nonsensical din that blends into the background.

Balbuena's muted voicing of the canals embodies haptic and sonic frequencies that can be useful for delving into Black and African presence in the cityscape. As an audio-spatial imagining, echolocation is especially well-suited for aquatic environments like the poem describes, for sound waves travel more freely in liquid. As an analytical lens for considering the sounds of Afro-descent in seventeenth-century Mexico City, these links with water recall the city's prominent—and problematic—waterways and also relate to the wet heterotopia of the Middle Passage.

Although *La grandeza mexicana* offers little specific information about the exact sonorities that one might hear, there is little doubt that the city's multiethnic voices resonated in his aquatic setting. In fact, the Mexico City channels and shipping canals themselves symbolized the disruptive potential of Black, African, and Indigenous people and other lower castes before the ordered cityscape. Indeed, throughout the colonial period, waterways were a source of wealth and trade, but there was also a great deal of anxiety about them as the site by which outside influences could infiltrate the metropolis and disorder urban harmonies. In an overview of sixteenth-century canal renovations, Barbara Mundy argued that the wet spaces of Mexico City reflected anxiety about uprisings among marginalized communities who might take tactical advantage of the city's numerous canals and dikes.[14] Furthermore, it is possible to read the aquatic trade routes that Balbuena envisions as a hallmark of Mexico City as a metonymic representation of the transatlantic exchange of bodies, goods, ideas, and, most pertinently to this study, sound.

Here, echolocation, or listening to sonic mappings of the space that Balbuena's poem describes, enables us to "unhear" the process that takes place in order to script the muted voices of the noisy waterways. In the seventeenth-century, the canals were important recreation spaces. People from all of the city's castes flocked to them to stroll or take a boat ride with family and friends, listen to music, and buy a bite to eat from the street vendors that lined their shores. In fact, the environment does not seem far removed from contemporary Xochimilco, where the canals are filled with *trajinera* tours, vendors selling food and beverages, and, of course, musicians who are happy to serenade you as you float down the waterway. To the unsuspecting ear, these resonances are purely noise. With a bit more historical context, it is possible to hear in them echoes of a vibrant, multicultural depiction of sound from New Spain.

Gemelli Careri compares the canals to the Venice neighborhood of Posillipo, and he details some of the activities that take place there.

> Después de comer fui a divertirme al canal de Jamaica, que es el Posilipo [sic] de México. Se pasea allá en canoas o sean barcas, y si se quiere también por tierra. Va en aquella gran número de músicos y cantores, hombres y mujeres, que compiten entre sí en manifestar la perfección de su canto. En las orillas del canal hay algunas pobres casas de indios, y hosterías para tomar refrigerantes, esto es: chocolate, atole y tamales.[15]

> After eating, I went to enjoy myself at the canal of Jamaica, which is the Posillipo of Mexico. People ride along there in canoes or rowboats, and they also stroll along on land. There are a number of musicians and singers, men and women, who compete among themselves to show off the perfection of their song. On the shores of the canal there are a few poor houses of *indios*, and inns for partaking in refreshments, that is: chocolate, *atole*, and tamales.

While Balbuena's poem represents the Mexico City waterways as symbols of commerce and wealth, Gemelli Careri portrays them as recreational spaces. As a complement to the "deafening noise" that Balbuena decries, the Italian explorer animates the city's watery pathways and fills them with music, dance, food, and boats filled with sightseers who hoped to enjoy an afternoon of repose.

For Gemelli Careri, music stands out as an important part of the Jamaica promenade, and he emphasizes it in other descriptions as well. He relates: "El miércoles, día 19 de mayo, fuí al frecuentado paseo de Jamaica, y ví en el canal muchas canoas en que se bailaba y cantaba al compás de la música, y en la orilla muchas carrozas" (Wednesday, May 19, I went to the much-frequented Jamaica promenade, and I saw many canoes in the canal, in which people danced and sang to the rhythm of music, and on the shore there were many carriages).[16] Here, Gemelli Careri describes lively song and dance that took place on the Mexico City waterways. On another day, he tells readers: "En la tarde fui a Jamaica, donde hubo gran concurso de músicos y de damas coronadas de flores" (In the afternoon, I went to Jamaica, where there was a large competition of musicians and of women crowned with flowers).[17] This reference to a music competition with a popular tone further illustrates the canal's importance for the local music scene of seventeenth-century Mexico. Indeed, by Gemelli Careri's account music was as important in the Jamaica canal during the colonial period as it is today.

Later in his travels, the explorer offers a less favorable account of the canals. His negative tone leaves the reader wondering what might have changed the Italian visitor's perception of these waterways.

> El domingo, día 28, fui en una especie de barca que llaman canoa, hecha de un solo trozo de madera, a pasear al canal de Jamaica. Siendo éste el único pasatiempo que hay en México, acostumbran ir allí mujeres y hombres, viejas y jóvenes, bonitas y feas, con las cabezas adornadas de flores, y pasear después de haber llenado las barrigas de aquellos malos manjares, que como he dicho antes, se venden en las orillas del canal. Si emprendiesen limpiarlo y hacer buscas cómodas, ciertamente sería este paseo muy agradable.[18]
>
> Sunday, the 28th, I went out on a type of boat that they call a canoe, made of a single piece of wood, to ride along the Jamaica canal. Since this is the only pastime there is in Mexico, everyone tends to go there: women and men, old women and young girls, pretty and ugly, with their heads adorned with flowers, and they walk around after having filled their guts with those rotten nectars, which, as I have said before, are sold on the shores of the canal. If they would only clean it, and add a few comfortable details, surely, this promenade would be very agreeable.

Here, unlike in other accounts from Gemelli Careri's narrative, the canals emerge as dingy and disorderly. The negative imagery resonates with other writers' representations of New Spain's non-European inhabitants as simple, unattractive, and unruly. Consequently, one possible interpretation of this passage is that it portrays an area of the canal routes with more Black and Indigenous inhabitants, likely farther removed from the main recreational space and closer to more rural Iztacalco.

While none of Gemelli Careri's descriptions specify the exact sounds that he heard in the Jamaica canal, another written source and its painted complement can amplify the topic. In an essay about New Spanish vicereines, Antonio Rubial cites an episode from Antonio de Robles' *Diario de sucesos notables (1665–1703)*, when Francisco Fernández de la Cueva, Duke of Alburquerque and viceroy from 1702 to 1711 traversed the waterways with his wife, Juana de la Cerda y de Aragón-Moncada. Following Robles' account, Rubial notes that in 1703, the viceregal couple floated through the waterway in a large, lavishly decorated canoe. Ten rowers, a musical ensemble, and a group of smaller canoes accompanied the pair as they made their way down the canal. The scholar draws out differences between Robles's account and Pedro de Villegas's 1706 painting of the scene, *Visita del virrey Francisco Fernández de la Cueva, duque de Alburquerque y su mujer al canal de la Viga*. He perceptively remarks that

> aunque en el cuadro no aparecen ni los diez remeros, ni la banda de música ni las múltiples canoas, la pintura corresponde con bastante exactitud a la descripción de Robles: una dorada embarcación se aproxima a la orilla del canal y en ella van el virrey y su mujer, sentados bajo un toldo. Frente a los virreyes aparecen reclinadas dos damas, tal vez las camareras de la virreina, y una mujer que está a punto de dejar la trajinera. Una comitiva de guardias luciendo uniformes a la moda francesa recibe a los dignatarios y a su séquito a la orilla del canal. Sobre la plaza, frente a la pequeña iglesia de Iztacalco, un forlón de camino tirado por cuatro caballos espera a la pareja para llevarlos de regreso a la capital.[19]

although neither the ten rowers nor the musical band nor the multiple canoes appear in the painting, the piece corresponds with quite a bit of accuracy to Robles' description: a golden vessel nears the shore of the canal and in it travel the viceroy and his wife, seated beneath an awning. Before the viceroys, two ladies appear reclined, perhaps the vicereine's maids, and a woman is about to leave the float. A procession of guards dressed in French-style uniforms receives the dignitaries and their entourage on the shores of the canal. In the plaza, in front of the small Iztacalco church, a carriage pulled by four horses waits for the couple in order to carry them back to the capital.

**7.1**. Detail from Pedro de Villegas, *Visita del virrey Francisco Fernández de la Cueva, duque de Alburquerque y su mujer al canal de la Viga*, 1706. Museo Soumaya, Mexico City. Author's personal collection.

**7.2**. Karl Nebel, "Paseo de la Viga en México." *Viaje pintoresco y arqueolojico sobre la parte mas interesante de la Republica Mejicana, en los años transcurridos desde 1829 hasta 1834.* Beinecke Rare Book and Manuscript Library, Yale University Libraries.

Like Rubial notices, the bands that Robles highlights are strangely (and frustratingly) absent from Villegas' visual representation. Nonetheless, their presence in this watery procession seems likely, especially given the attention that Gemelli Careri gives to the canal's musical atmosphere.

Just as in Gemelli Careri's descriptions, references to Afro-descendant music are far from explicit in accounts of the Duke and Duchess of Alburquerque's outing. Nevertheless, both Villegas's painting and Robles's written account invite speculation about the Black and African sonorities that might have accompanied the journey. One possibility is that the ten costumed rowers who powered the canoe were of African descent. While it is difficult to draw conclusions with any certainty, German illustrator Karl Nebel's lithograph *Paseo de la Viga en México* includes a pair of Black rowers (1829–34, published in 1839). If, indeed, Afro-descendants manned the canal canoes, watery work song with ancestral roots might have accompanied the task. Ochoa Gautier describes a similar phenomenon in eighteenth- and nineteenth-century Colombia, where Black rowers sang *bogas* to lighten their chore.[20]

In addition to the Afro-descendant rowers, Nebel's illustration includes two dark-skinned musicians playing lute-like instruments. The musicians could be *indio* or *mulato*, since their skin tone is barely lighter than their boatman counterparts. While the standing instrumentalist is dressed in Indigenous fashion, his seated companion is shirtless, like the rowers, which I maintain marks him as a member of the same caste. For all this, Nebel's lithograph suggests that Afro-descendant musicians entertained travelers on the Mexico City canal boats. The Villegas painting that Rubial examines offers further evidence of the practice. While the viceregal couple rests beneath a canopy at the back of the boat, a standing figure at the front has his arms outstretched, as if in performance. The individual has his back to the viewer; however, his features are dark, and they sharply contrast with the pale face of a lady-in-waiting sitting next to him. As complements to the lack of details about who made music in written accounts of the Mexico City canals, these two paintings support a hypothesis that Afro-descendants took part in the competitions and performances that graced the waterways.

Just as we have seen with other examples in *Amplifications of Black Sound*, while the written archive inscribes the canal sonorities as "noise" or makes passing references to musical activities, reading multiple sources alongside one another offers a more complete understanding of sounds along the canal. When taking everything into account, it seems likely that Afro-descendant music, voices, and other forms of auditory intervention rang out here, as in other areas of Mexico City. Like Ochoa Gautier and Kevin

Dawson have shown, water was an important space for Afro-descendant communities throughout colonial Latin America and beyond.[21] In light of my readings of Afro-descent in the watery spaces of New Spain's capital, it becomes necessary to draw the Jamaica canal and other Mexico City waterways into this category as well. With such resonances in mind, I ask how might we hear such spaces differently if we were to attend to their Afro-sonic histories and contemporary resonances? How might contemporary understanding of Xochimilco's local symbolism change?

If *Amplifications of Black Sound* has made a case for re-valuing Black and African voices in New Spain's urban spaces, then queries like these are an important next step. While Chapters 3, 4, 6, and 7 point out some present-day echoes of Afro-descendant sound, more research is needed to develop the connections I discuss. As additional readings from this perspective emerge, they will raise significant questions about the twofold construction of most "national" Mexican sounds. Indeed, the two-pronged filter of "European" and "Indigenous" that conditions the ear of most present-day listeners dampens the presence of other sonic practices in Mexican sound cultures. The rich syncretism of African, autochthonous, and European sound traditions that I draw out throughout this book did not simply disappear with Spanish rule. Rather, it persists today in many forms of Mexican music, popular devotional practices, and even the cries of vendors who hawk their wares in the grid-like city streets. The challenges of echolocating such practices do not relate to their scarcity, but rather, to the auditory limits of a listening public whose ears are not attuned to New Spain's rich Afro-descendant sound history. I hope that the "re-tuning" or "unhearing" that takes place in *Amplifications of Black Sound* offers ample fodder for continued research on this and related topics.

# Notes

**A NOTE ON TRANSLATION, NOMENCLATURE, AND TRANSCRIPTIONS**

1. Ndiaye, *Scripts of Blackness*, 141.
2. Cruz, *Selected Works*, 132n5.
3. Ndiaye, 29.
4. Jones, *Staging*, xxiii.
5. Tachtiris, *Translation*, 12.

**INTRODUCTION**

1. New Spain was one of several viceroyalties that the Spanish empire established in the Americas. At its apogee, the territory extended from the southern United States to the Isthmus of Panama and stretched as far as the Philippines.
2. Baker, "The Resounding City," 2.
3. Here, "unheard" refers to sounds that are beyond the listener's physical or psychological capacities. I borrow the term from Tobias Ewé, who maintains that "the unheard lies beyond of the heard—and therefore outside the immediacy of human auditory experience. Unlike the quotidian—almost automatic—activity of hearing, unhearing is not a common activity but a liminal one. This is most conspicuous by the fact that while sound can enter the ear and interface with the cochlea—the spiral-shaped cavity in the inner ear—this does not mean that it is heard. The unheard is a special category given to the sounds just out of earshot: the events that are in excess of the heard. No matter how far we shoot our ears into the surroundings something is always left unheard." Ewé, "The Unheard," 444. As Ewé goes on to explain, through techniques like amplification or repositioning, it is possible to overcome the distance between inaudible sound's physical impact upon the hearing apparatus and its perceptibility. The concept of retuning one's ear in order to attend to previously unheard sounds undergirds all of *Amplifications of Black Sound*. The conclusion will return to it and examine Ewé's work more closely.

4. Bristol, "Blackness and Blurred Boundaries," 78.
5. Bennett, *Colonial Blackness*, 59, table 2.1.
6. Notable publications include Ben Vinson's *Bearing Arms for His Majesty: The Free-Colored Militia in Colonial Mexico*; Herman L. Bennett's *Africans in Colonial Mexico: Absolutism, Christianity, and Afro-Creole Consciousness*; Nicole von Germeten's *Black Blood Brothers: Confraternities and Social Mobility for Afro-Mexicans*; Vinson and Matthew Restall's edited volume *Black Mexico: Race and Society from Colonial to Modern Times*; Bennett's *Colonial Blackness: A History of Afro-Mexico*; Vinson's *Before Mestizaje: The Frontiers of Race and Caste in Colonial Mexico*; Pablo Miguel Sierra Silva's *Urban Slavery in Colonial Mexico: Puebla de los Ángeles, 1531–1706*; Manuel Apodaca Valdez's *Cofradías Afrohispánicas: Celebración, resistencia furtiva y transformación cultural*; Rafael Castañeda García and Juan Carlos Ruiz Guadalajara's two-volume collection *Africanos y afrodescendientes en la América hispánica septentrional: Espacios de convivencia, sociabilidad y conflicto*; and Miguel Valerio's *Sovereign Joy: Afro-Mexican Kings and Queens, 1539–1640*.
7. McKnight and Garofalo, introduction to *Afro-Latino Voices*, xvii.
8. McKnight and Garofalo, xvii–xix.
9. Tomlinson, *The Singing*, 16.
10. Luna, "Sounding the African Atlantic," 585, emphasis in original.
11. Ochoa Gautier, *Aurality*, 3.
12. Ochoa Gautier, 3.
13. de Certeau, "Vocal Utopias," 29–30.
14. de Certeau, 30.
15. Lingold, Mueller, and Trettien, introduction to *Digital Sound Studies*, 1–2.
16. Butler, *The Ancient Phonograph*, 36.
17. Weheliye, *Phonographies*, 25.
18. Weheliye, 25. Since *Amplifications of Black Sound* examines sound writing from the prerecorded era, it is worth noting that neither sonic mechanization nor the rupture of source and sound began in the late nineteenth century. Indeed, although early modern thinkers were less interested in reproducing sonorous interventions than the purveyors of sonic modernity who feature in Weheliye's reading, the period offers numerous examples of vocal manipulation. Bruce R. Smith imagines the Globe Theater as an architectural reproduction of the human vocalizer in his *Acoustic World of Early Modern England* (208), and Jesuit polymath Athanasius Kircher's *Musurgia universalis* (1650) and *Phonurgia nova* (1673) present fantastic devices meant to harness or interrupt acoustical pathways. Among others, these include designs for echoic structures, megaphones, eavesdropping machines, and even a talking statue.
19. Erlmann, *Reason and Resonance*, 31–32.
20. Derrida, *Margins*, xix. Emphasis in original.
21. Spivak, "Can the Subaltern Speak?," 88–89.
22. Du Bois, *The Souls of Black Folk*, 253.

23. Du Bois, 250.
24. Du Bois, 254.
25. Manzella, "The Sites and Sounds," 171.
26. Manzella, 172.
27. Du Bois, *The Souls of Black Folk*, 254.
28. Taylor, *The Archive and the Repertoire*, 2.
29. Gilroy, *The Black Atlantic*, 37.
30. Campt, *Listening to Images*, 6.
31. In this indispensable sorjuanine text, the poet responds to accusations that her intellectual endeavors are impious and overly focused on worldly knowledge. In the epistle's opening, she addresses her anonymous interlocutor, who used the pseudonym Sor Philotea de la Cruz, and begs forgiveness for the long silence that preceded her response. Sor Juana writes: "in this way, of those things that cannot be spoken, it must be said that they cannot be spoken, so that it may be known that silence is kept not for lack of things to say, but because the many things there are to say cannot be contained in mere words." Cruz, *The Answer / La Respuesta*, tr. Powell, lines 88–91, 43.
32. Campt, *Listening to Images*, 45.
33. Judith Lochhead, Eduardo Mendieta, and Stephen Decatur Smith have overviewed the history of sound's relation to affect. As they show, the linkage began with Plato's privileging of harmony in the *Republic*, enjoyed renewed attention during the Renaissance, and then endured well into the Enlightenment, where empirical approaches increasingly mechanized sonic influence. During the nineteenth and early twentieth centuries, scholarship on the topic shifted to a more sentimental plane that reflected philosophical interest in the emotions and personal expression. Modernism ushered in views of auditory affect in constant dialogue with cultural and political structures that (dis)ordered the world. Finally, today, sound's bodily and emotional impact provides ample fodder for sound studies and the so-called affective turn. Lochhead, Mendieta, and Smith, introduction to *Sound and Affect*, 3–17.
34. de Certeau, "Vocal Utopias," 30.

## CHAPTER 1

1. Alemán, *Sucesos de D. Frai Garcia Gera*, 6v.
2. Gage, *A New Survey*, 15.
3. I base this description of García Guerra's entry as viceroy on two sources: Matheo Alemán's *Sucesos* (1613, pp. 5r–6v) and the 1611 directives for clergy and musicians during the ceremony from the Archivo del Cabildo Catedral Metropolitano de México (ACCMM). *Actas de cabildo*, libro 5, f. 236v–237, 14 June 1611, ACCMM; and *Actas de cabildo*, libro 5, f. 238, 17 June 1611, ACCMM.
4. Robert Stevenson lists specific musical advances in the Mexico City cathedral and beyond during García Guerra's years as archbishop and viceroy. Stevenson, "Mexico City Cathedral Music" 112–18.

5. For a description of music in the San Hipólito festivities, see Gemelli Careri, *Viaje*, 186–87.
6. A *coloquio* is a liturgical drama that takes the form of a dialogue. In New Spanish records from this time period, *chanzoneta* often appears as a synonym for villancico. For a sample of musical works from the Mexico City cathedral, see Javier Marín López's description of a rare 1589 inventory of the Mexico City cathedral's choirbooks, "The Musical Inventory of Mexico Cathedral, 1589".
7. *Actas de cabildo*, libro 5, f. 114v, 27 February 1609, ACCMM.
8. *Actas de cabildo*, libro 5, f. 119–119v, 31 March 1609, ACCMM.
9. *Actas de cabildo*, libro 5, f. 166, 7 November 1609, ACCMM. Both Robert Stevenson and Alfredo Nava Sánchez have remarked upon the coincidence of Luis Barreto's heyday in the Mexico City cathedral chapel and García Guerra's tenure as archbishop (1608–11) and viceroy (1611–12). For his part, Stevenson portrays the Dominican priest as one of the singer's key promoters. He notes that as early as February 27, 1609, he [archbishop Francisco García Guerra] insisted that the chapter start paying the 34-year-old male soprano, Luis Barreto, who was a slave, twelve gold pesos monthly. The chapter minutes show that Guerra intervened personally on March 10 and again on March 31 to make sure that this enslaved singer "with such a singularly beautiful voice and such skill in polyphony" received the whole amount in gold, with no discounting. Six years later, Barreto was able to buy his freedom. Stevenson, "Mexico City Cathedral Music" 113–14.

Similarly, Nava Sánchez hypothesizes that "al parecer, la voz del mulato cautivó al dominico y su participación durante las celebraciones fue cada vez más notable" (so it seems, the *mulato*'s voice captivated the Dominican priest and his participation during celebrations was increasingly notable). Nava Sánchez, "El cantor mulato," 113. Indeed, given the extensive privileges that Barreto enjoyed during these years, it seems likely that he benefitted from the archbishop's protection.
10. *Actas de cabildo*, libro 5, f. 236v–237, 14 June 1611, ACCMM.
11. *Actas de cabildo*, libro 5, f. 386v, 28 April 1615, ACCMM.
12. *Actas de cabildo*, libro 5, f. 403v, 7 August 1615, ACCMM.
13. "Diezmos 1604–1627 (Libro de Cuentas de Mayordomía)," "Descargo del mayordomo Gabriel de Rojas," f. 6, 30 September 1604, Archivo del Venerable Cabildo de la Catedral de Puebla (AVCCP), quoted in Morales Abril, "El esclavo negro," 19.
14. Morales Abril, "La música en la catedral," 38n86.
15. Morales Abril, "El esclavo negro," 20.
16. The Franciscan missionary founded San Jose de los Naturales in 1527. For an overview of how Zumárraga received the Indigenous singers that Gante trained, see Spell, "Music in the Cathedral," 294–95.
17. Stevenson, "Mexico City Cathedral Music," 114.
18. Becerra Jiménez, "Enseñanza y ejercicio," 44.
19. *Actas de cabildo*, libro 1, f. 82, 9 January 1652, AHAO; and *Actas de cabildo*, libro 1, f. 112v, 2 February 1653, AHAO.

20. Baker, *Imposing Harmony*.
21. Irving, *Colonial Counterpoint*.
22. Ramos-Kittrell, *Playing in the Cathedral*.
23. *Actas de cabildo*, libro 11, fol. 34, 2 May 1651, ACCMM, quoted in Stevenson, "Mexico City Cathedral Music," 121.
24. According to the *Diccionario de Autoridades*, "indecencia" refers to "immodéstia, falta de urbanidad, decoro y decéncia" (immodesty, lack of manners, decorum, and decency). Published between 1726 and 1739, the *Diccionario de autoridades* is an important resource for scholars of sixteenth- through eighteenth-century literature. A searchable version is available online through the Real Academia Española at https://apps2.rae.es/DA.html. This dictionary is particularly rich in idioms and literary examples. Sebastián de Covarrubias's *Tesoro de la lengva castellana, o española* (1611) is another source for early word usage and meanings. The complete, digitized work is available through the Biblioteca Virtual Miguel de Cervantes at https://www.cervantesvirtual.com/obra-visor/del-origen-y-principio-de-la-lengua-castellana-o-romance-que-oy-se-vsa-en-espana-compuesto-por-el--0/html.
25. Jones, *Staging*, 58.
26. Ramos-Kittrell, *Playing*, 2.
27. See Chapters 3 and 4 for examples of this type of discourse.
28. Aristotle's *De anima* is a key for understanding the construction, for the treatise links voice to animate beings, the soul, and meaning-making. For a discussion of Aristotelian qualities of voice, see Dolar, *A Voice*, 23. These notions influenced philosophers like Jacques Lacan, Derrida, Mladen Dolar, and Adriana Cavarero, all of whom have drawn voice into contemporary discourses on subjectivity. Feldman and Zeitlin overview their contributions. "The Clamor of Voices," 4–7.
29. Moten, *In the Break*, 11.
30. Moten, 12.
31. Gordon, *Voice Machines*, 8–9.
32. Sierra Silva, *Urban Slavery*, 145.
33. Morales Abril, "El esclavo negro," 33–34.
34. Morales Abril, 37–41.
35. *Libro de Actas Capitulares* 0, f. 53v, 10 September 1577, AVCCP, quoted in Morales Abril, "El esclavo negro," 29.
36. Morales Abril, 26.
37. Morales Abril, 30.
38. Testamento del señor canónigo Vera, f. 16v–17v, quoted in Morales Abril, "El esclavo negro," 23.
39. Morales Abril, 27.
40. *Libro de Actas Capitulares* 0, f. 30v–31, 4 May 1576, AVCCP, quoted in Morales Abril, "El esclavo negro," 26.
41. Morales Abril, 28.

42. Nava Sánchez, "El cantor mulato," 106–7.
43. Nava Sánchez, 107.
44. Nava Sánchez, 108.
45. See Nava Sánchez, "La voz descarnada," 37–38, for examples of the debate over falsettists and castrati.
46. Feldman, *The Castrato*, 6.
47. Medina, *Los atributos*, 48.
48. Medina, 51.
49. Hidalgo Lehuedé et al., "De músico a extirpador," 124–26.
50. *Actas de cabildo*, libro 4, f. 36v, 11 December 1590, ACCMM.
51. *Actas de cabildo*, libro 4, f. 102v, 22 April 1594, ACCMM.
52. Morales Abril, "El esclavo negro," 42–43n67.
53. *Actas de cabildo*, libro 4, f. 222, 27 April 1599, ACCMM, quoted in Morales Abril, "El esclavo negro," 43n67, emphasis added.
54. Medina, *Los atributos*, 20.
55. Rosselli, "The Castrati," 150.
56. Baade, "'Hired' Nun Musicians," 298–306.
57. Medina, *Los atributos*, 78.
58. Quoted in Bisaro, "Singing the Community," 108–9.
59. Nassarre, *Escuela Música*, 22.
60. Larson, *The Matter of Song*, 66.
61. Bloom, *Voice in Motion*, 80.
62. Rangan, "The Skin of the Voice," 135, emphasis in original.
63. See Lisa Nielson, "Visibility and Performance," 79–81, for a brief overview of poets and musicians in the early Muslim world.
64. Junne, *The Black Eunuchs*, 7–10.
65. Segal, *Islam's Black Slaves*, 80.
66. Mason Vaughn, *Performing Blackness*, 121–29.
67. Goldberg, *Sonidos negros*, 1–2.
68. In this respect, Olivia Bloechl has remarked that "the 'whiteness' of early modern Europe is a libidinal and political, as well as historical construct, and as such demands critical approaches that are guided, but not bound by historicity. Better historical knowledge, compelling as it is, will not in itself displace the perceived whiteness of early European music, because this perception is not really based on a literal absence of race or racialized people in Europe. It rests instead on a modern correlation of power and prestige with whiteness and a libidinal project of that racial structure on the musical past." "Race, Empire," 79.
69. Wilbourne, "Little Black Giovanni's Dream," 137.
70. Morales Abril, "El esclavo negro," 43n68.
71. Nava Sánchez, "La voz descarnada," 39.
72. Nava Sánchez, 33–34.
73. Lorente, *El porque de la mvsica*, 8.
74. Lorente, 9.
75. Nava Sánchez, "La voz descarnada," 31–32

76. Medina, *Los atributos*, 116.
77. Davies, "Colonialism," 459.
78. Stevenson, "Mexico City Cathedral Music," 113–14.
79. Freitas, "The Eroticism of Emasculation," 206.
80. Nava Sánchez, "El cantor mulato," 108.
81. *Actas de cabildo*, libro 4, f. 202–202v, 11 August 1598, ACCMM.
82. Nava Sánchez, "El cantor mulato," 110.
83. Cerone, *El melopeo*, 328.
84. Nava Sánchez, "La voz descarnada," 36.
85. Lavrín, *Brides of Christ*, 192.
86. As a point of comparison between Barreto and his Afro-descendant peers, Nava Sánchez notes that in 1601, the cathedral paid a mere 20 pesos for clothing for Juan and Antón, the other two enslaved workers. "El cantor mulato," 110.
87. *Actas de cabildo*, libro 5, f. 309v–310, 8 January 1613, ACCMM.
88. In the catalog for a Metropolitan Museum of Art textile exhibit, Amelia Peck singles out fabrics produced for the church as especially precious: "Among the most refined and resplendent artworks produced in New Spain, embroideries created for the Church were made entirely of luxurious silk and gold threads. They demonstrate not only the presence in Mexico of highly skilled artisans— including guild embroiderers originally trained by Spanish masters and who had access to these materials—but also the enormous wealth and resources the Church invested in their commission." Peck, *Interwoven Globe*, 224.
89. Fraser Giffords, *Sanctuaries of Earth*, 210.
90. Here, it is worth noting that while lettered and painted accounts of racial difference in New Spain seek to codify clothing as a sign of subjects' position in the caste system, it appears that actual practices muddied attempts at visual signaling. Ilona Katzew has discussed the topic in her analysis of *casta* painting. *Casta Painting*, 107–9.
91. The reference to Barreto's singing paraphrases Juan Gutiérrez de Padilla's *ensaladilla* "Al establo más dichoso," which I analyze in Chapter 2.
92. Stein, *Music Is My Life*, 134.
93. For an in-depth discussion of race and priesthood, see Pasquier, "Catholicism and Race," 175.
94. Nava Sánchez, "El cantor mulato," 110–11.
95. Sierra Silva, *Urban Slavery*, 2.
96. Sierra Silva, 154.
97. Nava Sánchez, "El esclavo mulato," 32.
98. Nava Sánchez, "El cantor mulato," 111.
99. Here, it is interesting to note that Barreto's case is not the only instance of colonial authorities punishing Africans and Afro-Mexicans with restrictions on their dress. Valerio observes that just a few years after Barreto's attempt to flee, in 1612, the *Audiencia* responded to threats of a massive uprising by forbidding jewelry or rich fabric among Afro-descendant women. Valerio, *Sovereign Joy*, 188.

100. Nava Sánchez, "El cantor mulato," 115.
101. Nava Sánchez, 116–17.
102. Nava Sánchez, 118.
103. Moten, *Stolen Life*, 129.
104. In a musicological response to Moten's theory of fugitivity, Feldman remarks that "Moten's 'music' instead produces a disturbance, a set of contrary desires, a space for new subjectivities (if 'subjectivity' applies at all) and new ways of mapping them, hence a 'paraontological' corrective to the rationalist Europeanist traps that musicology has never really been able to shake off." Feldman, "Fugitive Voice," 13.
105. Moten, *Stolen Life*, 124.
106. Campt, *Listening to Images*, 24.
107. Campt, 26.
108. *Actas de cabildo*, libro 5, f. 402v–403, 73 August 1615, ACCMM.

## CHAPTER 2

1. The seventeenth-century manuscript version of this piece is from Mexico City Cathedral Choirbook II. The Mexico City Cathedral archive houses the original document, and Musicat's "Libros de Coro" digital database makes a small portion of the book available as "P01." In addition, Rodríguez Mata's *Passio secundum Matthaeum* appears in the Carmen Codex, a collection of liturgical music that was found at the Convento de Nuestra Señora de la Encarnación. Brothers, introduction to *Passions*, xivn32. For a transcription of the *Passio secundum Matthaeum* as well as several other works by Rodríguez Mata, see Matthew Grey Brothers's edition, *Passions*.
2. The Spanish style or *more hispano* refers to liturgical music that follows the Mozarabic rite, as opposed to the Roman liturgy. Passions set in this style originated in Andalucía during the fifteenth century, possibly in the Málaga cathedral. Increased use of polyphony distinguishes Hispanic passions from Roman ones and heightens the most moving parts of Gospel texts. New Spanish chapelmasters continued the tradition and transformed it to accommodate New World voices and realities. See Brothers, introduction to *Passions*, vii–viii, for an extensive discussion of the genre.
3. *Actas de cabildo*, libro 5, f. 427v, 29 March 1616, ACCMM.
4. Stevenson, "Mexico City Cathedral Music," 118–19.
5. Brothers, introduction to *Passions*, x.
6. Brothers, xi.
7. Brothers, ix.
8. Marianne Tråvén has studied music written for castrati during the mid- to late seventeenth and eighteenth centuries, and she indicates that their tessitura fell somewhere between a3 to f5, similar to the mezzo-soprano range. "Voicing the Third Gender."

9. For all of its merits, Robert Stevenson's 1968 article "The Afro-American Musical Legacy to 1800" is an example of this approach. While there is little doubt that that Atlantic trade routes put African and European music into contact, it can be difficult to pinpoint "African" melodic or rhythmic elements in the Black villancicos. In this respect, Mario Ortiz observes: "Se cita con frecuencia el empleo de hemiolas, contratiempos y síncopas, pero no debemos olvidar que todos estos recursos rítmicos eran muy comunes en la música vernacular europea de la época, y que por lo tanto al encontrarlos en las negrillas, éstos son solamente las versiones (o imaginaciones) europeas de lo que los africanos hacían con sus ritmos. De la presencia de un elemento melódico sería tarea imposible tratar de igualar los sistemas de escalas africanas con el sistema tonal europeo en el cual todos los villancicos se registran" (Scholars frequently cite the use of hemiolas, off-beats, and syncopations, but we should not forget that all of these rhythmic resources were very common in European vernacular music of the day, and thus, that upon finding them in villancicos, these were only European versions [or imaginings] of what Africans did with their rhythms. With respect to the presence of a melodic element, it would be impossible work to try to equate African scales with the European tonal system in which villancicos were written). Ortiz, "Villancicos de *negrilla*," 127.
10. Ndiaye, *Scripts of Blackness*, 16.
11. Sabat de Rivers, "Blanco, negro," 248.
12. Baker, "The 'Ethnic Villancico,'" 400–401; and Cashner, "Imitating," 175–79.
13. Morales Abril, "El esclavo negro," 36.
14. Morales Abril, 37–38.
15. Jones, "Singing High," 41. Despite historical and geographic distance, Alisha Jones's analysis of African American countertenors in gospel settings, and especially her interviews with singer Patrick Dailey, can be useful for imagining how early performers like Barreto and Vera might have perceived the impact of their high voices on gender or racial identities. Furthermore, Jones raises questions about self-presentation that are equally pertinent, at least to the degree by which the enslaved singers had autonomy over their own personae.
16. Unless otherwise indicated, musical references to Fernández's works are from Aurelio Tello's transcription of the *Cancionero*. Fernández, *Cancionero musical*, 75–80, 158–60, and 284–90. For the lyrics, I use Ireri Chávez Bárcenas's transcriptions, "Singing in the City of Angels," 157–58, 168, and 270. English translations are mine.
17. In his edition of Fernández's *Cancionero*, Tello notes that the soprano's opening "güi-güi-ri-güi" is "texto de puro valor fonético" (a text of pure phonetic value; LXXV). From my perspective, a reading of the text as a negative response to his interlocutor is much more convincing, particularly given numerous representations of Afro-descendant singers as disruptive in other villancicos. I thank Ireri Chávez Bárcenas for this observation.
18. Feldman, "Castrato Acts," 404.

19. Morales Abril, "El esclavo negro," 36n49. The observation supports Morales Abril's conjecture about Fernández's connections to Juan de Vera, who disappears from the archive around 1617, before Gutiérrez de Padilla's arrival in Puebla during the early 1620.
20. Nava Sánchez, "El cantor mulato," 119.
21. See my remarks on the whiteness of Western classical music in Chapter 1.
22. Baker, "The 'Ethnic Villancico,'" 402.
23. Chávez Bárcenas, "Native Song."
24. Egan, "Lyric Intelligibility," 209.
25. Jones, "Sor Juana's Black Atlantic," 269.
26. To date, there are conflicting accounts of Fernández's life and trajectory in New Spain during the early 1600s. While scholars have long accepted the biographical details that Robert Stevenson put forth in his 1984 article on Puebla's chapelmasters, Morales Abril's revision of available records outside of Puebla has given a clearer picture of Fernández's activities in both Guatemala and the City of Angels. Stevenson, "Puebla Chapelmasters"; Morales Abril, "Gaspar Fernández."
27. Chávez Bárcenas, "Native Song," 64.
28. Chávez Bárcenas, "Singing," 80.
29. Chávez Bárcenas, 82.
30. Chávez Bárcenas, 157.
31. Chávez Bárcenas, 158.
32. Chávez Bárcenas, 158.
33. Chávez Bárcenas, 160.
34. Chávez Bárcenas, 79–80.
35. Chávez Bárcenas, 158.
36. Chávez Bárcenas, 270.
37. Chávez Bárcenas, 270.
38. von Germeten, *Black Blood*, 45.
39. Cashner, "Imitating Africans," 144.
40. Gutiérrez de Padilla, "Al establo más dichoso," 45–46. All translations of "Al establo más dichoso" are Cashner's from *Villancicos about Music*, 43-47.
41. Cashner, "Imitating Africans," 161.
42. Bassein, *Women and Death*, 37.
43. Bassein, 38.
44. Eidsheim, *The Race of Sound*, 101.
45. Rowe, *Black Saints*, 197.
46. Fracchia, *"Black but Human,"* 32.
47. Cashner, "Imitating Africans," 161–62.
48. Horswell, *Decolonizing*, 41.
49. Freitas has discussed the castrato in the early modern sexual imaginary in detail. See his "The Eroticism of Emasculation," especially 214–23.
50. Cashner, "Imitating Africans," 163.
51. Gutiérrez de Padilla, "Al establo más dichoso," 46.
52. Lipski, *Latin American Spanish*, 98.

53. While most scholars mention villancicos' invocations of Black and African dance traditions that tantalized audiences throughout the Atlantic, more research is needed to understand how these portrayals might relate to Afro-diasporic rituals.
54. Ngou-Mve, "Los orígenes de las rebeliones," 13.
55. Ghadessi, *Portraits of Human Monsters*, 139.
56. Fol. 64v, quoted in Pérez Marín, *Marvels of Medicine*, 86.
57. See Barquera et al., "Origin and Health Status," for a review of the biological study that identified the remains' origins.
58. Gutiérrez de Padilla, "Al establo más dichoso," 46, brackets mine.
59. Cashner, "Imitating Africans," 169.
60. Cascales, *Cartas philologicas*, 44.
61. Freitas, "The Eroticism of Emasculation," 204.
62. Cascales' angelic rendering of capón singers resonates with approaches to voice in early modern musical and religious thought. Indeed, Nava Sánchez has shown that well-known theorists like Pietro Cerone and Andrés Lorente imagined skilled vocalization as an echo of celestial harmony. Nava Sánchez, "La voz descarnada," 26–30.
63. Brewer-García, *Beyond Babel*, 52.
64. Brewer-García, 54–55.
65. Cashner, "Imitating Africans," 173.
66. Here, I refer to the musical scores' silence before a performer's extra-linguistic interventions, including audible breaths, sighs, footsteps, and more. While one could argue that the Black and Indigenous sounds that villancico lyrics capture are their own form of glossolalia, my reading distinguishes between the "official" performance that writing prescribes and the irreproducible, embodied vocalization of that text.
67. Fiol-Matta, *The Great Woman Singer*, 67.
68. Fiol-Matta, 69.
69. Fiol-Matta, 68.
70. Fiol-Matta, 72–73.
71. Fiol-Matta, 74.
72. de Certeau, "Vocal Utopias," 29.
73. Cashner, "Imitating Africans," 174.
74. See Baker "Latin American Baroque," 441, for a summary of contemporary reimaginings of this ilk.
75. Cashner, "Imitating Africans," 179.

## CHAPTER 3

1. Gemelli Careri, *Viaje*, 28–29. *Viaje a la Nueva España* is the sixth book of Gemelli Careri's travel narrative *Giro del mondo*. I cite from José María de Agreda y Sánchez's 1927 translation to Spanish. English translations are mine.
2. Rama, *The Lettered City*, 5.

3. Gemelli Careri, *Viaje*, 30–31.
4. Bennett, *Africans in Colonial Mexico*, 27.
5. Martínez, "Settler Colonialism," 114.
6. Rama, *The Lettered City*, 6.
7. Dewulf, *Afro-Atlantic Catholics*, 7–8.
8. Taylor, *The Archive and the Repertoire*, 22.
9. Quoted in Gembero Ustarroz "Muy amigo de música," 113–14.
10. I attend to this topic in *Hearing Voices: Aurality and New Spanish Sound Culture in Sor Juana Inés de la Cruz*, particularly in chapter 5. Furthermore, Sara Gonzalez addresses it in *The Musical Iconography of Power in Seventeenth-Century Spain and Her Territories*, and Timothy Foster furthers discussion of intersections of sound, power, and politics in *Music and Power in Early Modern Spain: Harmonic Spheres of Influence*.
11. Konetzke, *Colección de Documentos*, 45.
12. Hernández Reyes, "*Festín*," 340.
13. Gutiérrez de Medina, *Viage*, 27.
14. Gutiérrez de Medina, 27–28.
15. Hernández Reyes, "*Festín*," 344.
16. Valerio, *Sovereign Joy*, 178.
17. Curcio-Nagy, *The Great Festivals*, 43.
18. For general discussions of public ritual and political authority in New Spain, see Curcio-Nagy's *The Great Festivals of Colonial Mexico City*; Alejandro Cañeque's *The King's Living Image: The Culture and Politics of Viceregal Power in Colonial Mexico*, especially chapter 4; and Frances L. Ramos' *Identity, Ritual and Power in Colonial Puebla*.
19. Valerio, *Sovereign Joy*, 170.
20. Valerio, 172.
21. Valerio, 212.
22. Valerio, *Sovereign Joy*, 174.
23. Voigt, "The Archive," 28.
24. Curcio-Nagy, *The Great Festivals*, 58 and 176n54.
25. Hernández Reyes, "*Festín*," 341.
26. Hernández Reyes, 347.
27. Valerio, *Sovereign Joy*, 195.
28. Matluck Brooks, *The Dances*, 156.
29. Matluck Brooks, 168.
30. Matluck Brooks, 169.
31. Torres, *Festín*, emphasis added. This edition does not include page numbers for *Festín*.
32. Valerio, *Sovereign Joy*, 186.
33. Hernández Reyes, "*Festín*," 349.
34. Torres, *Festín*.
35. Torres.

36. Torres.
37. Curcio-Nagy, *The Great Festivals*, 58–59.
38. Campt, *Listening to Images*, 25–26.
39. Valerio, *Sovereign Joy*, 208.
40. Valerio, 201.
41. Torres, *Festín*, emphasis added.
42. Torres.
43. Torres.
44. Valerio, *Sovereign Joy*, 199–202.
45. Gonzalez, *The Musical Iconography*, 161.
46. Hernández Reyes, "*Festín*," 353.
47. Hernández Reyes, 354.
48. Torres, *Festín*.
49. Gemelli Careri, *Viaje*, 172–73.
50. Stein, "The Musicians," 185.
51. Rafael Figueroa Hernández, e-mail message to author, November 5, 2022.
52. D'Amico, "Cumbia," 33.
53. Figueroa Hernández, *Son jarocho*, 77–83, and García de León and Rumazo, *Fandango*, 19–22. I thank Rafael Figueroa Hernández for directing me toward the *son jarocho* resources that inform this section's interpretation.
54. van Orden, *Music, Discipline, and Arms*, 252.
55. See Watanabe-O'Kelly, "The Equestrian Ballet"; van Orden, *Music, Discipline, and Arms*, 235–84; and Jessica Goethls, "The Patronage Politics of Equestrian Ballet."
56. Stein, "The Musicians," 183–84.
57. Bordas Ibáñez, "Coreografía," 249.
58. Gemelli Careri, *Viaje*, 16–17.
59. Guijo, *Diario*, vol. 1, 199–200. All translations of this source are mine.
60. Valerio, *Sovereign Joy*, 66.
61. Motta Sánchez, "Tras la heteroidentificación," 123.
62. Motta Sánchez, 124.
63. Bordas Ibáñez, "Coreografía," 247–48.
64. van Orden, *Music, Discipline, and Arms*, 238.
65. Motta Sánchez, "Tras la heteroidentificación," 126.
66. Motta Sánchez, 128.

## CHAPTER 4

1. Davies, "Making Music," 64.
2. von Germeten, *Black Blood*, 83; and Luna García, "Vista de espacios," 38.
3. "Autos hechos a petición," Cofradías y archicofradías, caja 1586, expediente 32, f. 1, 1673, AGN.
4. "Autos hechos a petición," Cofradías y archicofradías, caja 1586, expediente 32, f. 4, 1673, AGN.

5. "Autos hechos a petición," Cofradías y archicofradías, caja 1586, expediente 32, f.8, 1673, AGN.
6. As a complement to the ways order, harmony, race, and composure intersect in the Preciosa Sangre de Cristo's petition, see Ndiaye's description of a conflict between two Sevillian confraternities at the city's 1604 Holy Week processions. *Scripts of Blackness*, 138.
7. Jaque Hidalgo and Valerio, "Introduction," 9–10.
8. For a more extensive description of these elements, see Curcio-Nagy, "Giants," 24.
9. Curcio-Nagy, "Giants," 23.
10. Curcio-Nagy, 4.
11. Valerio, *Sovereign Joy*, 156.
12. Rojas, "Esclavos de Obraje."
13. Rojas.
14. Tollis de la Rocca, "Como tienen," 185–87. There are several versions of the lyrics for Tollis de la Rocca's villancico, transcribed with varying degrees of accuracy. I cite from Barbara Pérez Ruiz's transcription of the score in Tello, *Humor, pericia y devoción*.
15. Tollis de la Rocca, 179–84.
16. Ndiaye, *Scripts of Blackness*, 195–96. There are examples of dancers wearing ankle rattles in other Afro-Atlantic contexts. For instance, Dewulf has reproduced several travelers' accounts of dancers wearing bells and chimes in nineteenth-century New Orleans. "Ritual Battles," 26–28. He relates the phenomenon to the influence of enslaved people with Kongolese roots, a number of whom arrived in the territory following the 1762 Treaty of Fontainebleau, when Spain took control of French Louisiana.
17. Budasz, "Central-African Pluriarcs," 7–10.
18. Gaddy, *Well of Souls*, 12–14.
19. Tollis de la Rocca, "Como tienen," 191.
20. Goldberg, *Sonidos negros*, 213, n. 162.
21. Fryer, *Rhythms of Resistance*, 107–8.
22. Matluck Brooks, *The Dances*, 216–17.
23. Muir, *Ritual*, 104.
24. Curcio-Nagy, "Giants," 24.
25. Matluck Brooks includes a detail of the Black giants in León Gordillo's drawing in *The Dances*, 215. Interested readers can also consult a digital version that is part of the Identidad e Imagen de Andalucía en la Edad Moderna database (https://www2.ual.es/ideimand/portfolio-items/corpus-sevilla-ii/#).
26. Valerio, *Sovereign Joy*, 156.
27. Curcio-Nagy, "Giants," 24.
28. Original document reproduced in von Germeten, "Juan Roque's Donation," 86.
29. von Germeten, 83.
30. von Germeten, "Black Brotherhoods," 255.

31. Valerio, *Sovereign Joy*, 105–23.
32. Fromont, "Envisioning Brazil's."
33. Fromont, "Envisioning Brazil's," 133.
34. Quoted in Querol y Roso, "Negros y mulatos," 145.
35. Quoted in Querol y Roso, 145.
36. Bristol, "Blackness and Blurred Boundaries," 89–90.
37. Martínez, "Black Blood," 508n66.
38. Guijo, *Diario*, vol. 1, 52.
39. Will de Chaparro, *Death and Dying*, 90.
40. Curcio-Nagy, "Faith and Morals," 157.
41. Guijo, *Diario*, vol. 1, 142.
42. Guijo, 147–48.
43. "Edicto Inquisitorial que prohíbe la costumbre," Edictos de Inquisición, caja 1256, expediente 3, f. 1, 1643, AGN.
44. Marín López, "A Conflicted Relationship," 48.
45. "Edicto Inquisitorial que prohíbe la costumbre," Edictos de Inquisición, caja 1256, expediente 3, f. 1, 1643, AGN.
46. Guijo, *Diario*, vol. 1, 204.
47. Curcio-Nagy, "Rosa de Escalante's," 255–56.
48. Jones, *Staging*, 59.
49. Jones, 58.
50. Jones, 63.
51. Curcio-Nagy, "Rosa de Escalante's," 255.
52. Curcio-Nagy, 256.
53. "Autos hechos por el comisario," Inquisición, vol. 502, exp. 15, f. 571r, 1663, AGN.
54. "Autos hechos por el comisario," Inquisición, vol. 502, exp. 15, f. 571v, 1663, AGN.
55. "Autos hechos por el comisario," Inquisición, vol. 502, exp. 15, f. 573r, 1663, AGN.
56. Apodaca Valdez, *Cofradías Afrohispánicas*, 173.
57. Apodaca Valdez, *Cofradías Afrohispánicas*, 171.
58. "Denuncia de Luis Pérez," R/475/023, f. 266r, 19 May 1649, Biblioteca Palafoxiana. I am grateful to Manuel Apodaca Váldez for sharing personal photographs of this case with me.
59. von Germeten, *Black Blood*, 43.
60. "Denuncia de Luis Pérez," R/475/023, f. 266r, 19 May 1649, Biblioteca Palafoxiana.
61. "Denuncia de Luis Pérez," R/475/023, f. 267r, 19 May 1649, Biblioteca Palafoxiana.
62. "Denuncia de Luis Pérez," R/475/023, f. 266v, 19 May 1649, Biblioteca Palafoxiana.
63. Biblioteca Palafoxiana, R/475/023, f. 266r, 19 May 1649, "Denuncia de Luis Pérez."
64. Villa-Flores, "El arte de hablar," 256–58.
65. Villa-Flores, 254.
66. María Elisa Velázquez Gutiérrez makes a similar argument about general folk medicine and sorcery among Afro-descendant women in *Mujeres de origen africano* (246), and Diego Javier Luis discusses the authority that Afro-descendant diviners assumed in the Acapulco port in his "Galleon Anxiety." The

observations are astute, and they raise significant questions about intersections among magic, gender, and race in New Spain.
67. Villa-Flores, "El arte de hablar," 255.
68. Villa-Flores, 261.
69. Villa-Flores, 262.
70. Villa-Flores, 251.
71. Bourguignon, "Suffering and Healing," 558–59.
72. Bourguignon, 559–60. For examples of possession trance among women in African and Afro-diasporic contexts, see Bourguignon and also Carine Planke's "The Spirit's Wish: Possession Trance and Female Power among the Punu of Congo-Brazzaville."
73. Cavarero, *For More Than One Voice*, 147–48.
74. Luis, "Galleon Anxiety," 407.
75. Hagedorn, "To Have and to Hold," 146–47; and Viarnés, "Cultural Memory," 134.
76. Argyriadis, "Católicos, apostólicos," 195.
77. Malvido, "Crónicas de la Buena Muerte," 21.
78. Argyriadis, "Católicos, apostólicos," 200–201.
79. Argyriadis, 192–93.

## CHAPTER 5

Epigraph. unknown composer, "El negro Maytinero," Archivo Histórico Arquidiocesano de Guatemala, Catalog num. 90, qtd. in Deborah Singer, "Inclusion Politics/Subalternalization Practices."
1. See Jones, *Staging*, 10–11, for an extensive listing of early modern Peninsular works that feature *habla de negros*.
2. Some villancico lyrics notably engage with local themes. For examples, see Cashner's reading of "Al establo más dichoso" (Gutiérrez de Padilla, "Al establo más dichoso"); Deborah Singer's analysis of villancicos with military themes in relation to slave uprisings in Central America ("Inclusion Politics," 45–50); or Baker's discussion of how Sor Juana's lyrics capture "the harsh reality" of daily life for Afro-descendants ("The 'Ethnic Villancico,'" 404).
3. Lipski, *Latin American*, 98.
4. Singer, "Inclusion Politics," 42.
5. Swadley, "The Villancico," 129–32.
6. Swiadon Martínez, "África," 45.
7. Trambaioli includes a partial catalogue of dances associated with the "guineo" in representations of Black characters in Spanish theater, including the *cumbé*, *zarambeque*, and others. While Trambaioli indicates that these terms may be interchangeable, Jones has supplemented her work with descriptions of individual Black dances. Trambaioli, "Apuntes sobre el guineo," 1773; Jones, *Staging*, 56–66.
8. Trambaioli, "Apuntes sobre el guineo," 1775.
9. Jones, *Staging*, 56; and Goldberg, *Sonidos negros*, 50–87.

10. Goldberg, *Sonidos negros*, 64–72.
11. Ndiaye, *Scripts of Blackness*, 191.
12. Trambaioli, "Apuntes sobre el guineo," 1776.
13. Jones, *Staging*, 66.
14. Ortiz, "Villancicos de *negrilla*," 125–26.
15. Baker, "Latin American Baroque," 441.
16. Singer, "Inclusion Politics," 35.
17. Swiadon Martínez, "Los villancicos de negros," ccxvii.
18. While blood purity, social class, and religion strongly defined race in premodern Europe, Ndiaye observes that the transatlantic slave trade prompted a re-orientation of the contact so that it also reflected physical characteristics. *Scripts of Blackness*, 5.
19. Swiadon Martínez, "Los villancicos de negro," cxvii.
20. I base my translation on David A. Pharies's definition of "tuturuto," which links the word to both astonishment and the sound of a trumpet. "As for *tuturuto*, it could be some kind of extract from *turulato*, *a* adj. 'alelado, sobrecogido, estupefacto' (*DRAE* 1308c) or else a stress-shifted form of *tuturutú* 'sonido de la corneta' (*DRAE* 1309c)." Pharies, *Structure and Analogy*, 221.
21. Swiadon Martínez, "Los villancicos de negros," cxvii.
22. Marshall and Rivera, "Visualizing," 215.
23. See Chapter 2.
24. Swiadon Martínez, "Los villancicos de negros," cxvii–cxviii.
25. "Mángulu" could refer to an ethic group from the Kingdom of Kongo.
26. See Fracchia, *"Black but Human,"* 42–43 for a discussion of this tendency in visual art from Hapsburg Spain.
27. Cruz, *Villancicos*, Villancico xvi, 257, vv. 1–5.
28. Cruz, *Lírica*, Romance 8, 30, vv. 5–11.
29. Cruz, *Lírica*, Romance 8, 30, vv. 32–39.
30. See Eidsheim, *The Race of Sound*, 2–3 for an overview of these themes.
31. Cruz, *Villancicos*, Villancico xvi, 258, v. 29.
32. Cruz, *Villancicos*, Villancico xvi, 257, vv. 14–15.
33. Cruz, *Villancicos*, Villancico xvi, 258, vv. 23–24.
34. Cruz, *Villancicos*, Villancico xvi, 258, vv. 25–26.
35. For instance, in the *Political Essay on the Kingdom of New Spain* (published in 1811 as *Essai politique sure le royaume de la Nouvelle-Espagne*), Alexander von Humboldt relates that "in Mexico and Peru, the Indigenous peoples smoked and snuffed tobacco in powder form. At Moctezuma's court, the nobles used tobacco smoke as a narcotic, not only for their siestas after dinner but also in order to sleep in the morning, immediately after the morning meal, as is still the custom in several parts of equinoctial America." Humboldt, *Political Essay*, 29.
36. Sánchez, *Lyra*, 291, vv. 92–97.
37. Sánchez, *Lyra*, 291, vv. 103–7.
38. Sánchez, *Lyra*, 291, v. 115.

39. Cruz, *Villancicos*, Villancico 232, 27, vv. 19–20.
40. Krutitskaya, *Pliegos de villancicos*, 9. Villancico Segundo, Negro, 21, vv. 9–12. With respect to how Santillana's imagery resembles Sor Juana's, it is noteworthy that the two poets were contemporaries. Krutitskaya has drawn out other similarities between their work elsewhere in Santillana's 1688 set for the Nativity of the Blessed Virgin Mary. See *Pliegos de villancicos*, note 4, 12.
41. Lord, *Music*, 147.
42. Eidsheim, *The Race of Sound*, 15.
43. Waisman, *Neglo celeblamo*, vol. 3, 26, vv. 1–10. I thank Omar Morales Abril for drawing my attention to Waisman's anthology of villancicos from Spain and Spanish America.
44. Waisman, *Neglo celeblamo*, vol. 3, 26, vv. 18–23.
45. Baker, "The 'Ethnic Villancico,'" 406.
46. Brewer-García, *Beyond Babel*, 54–55.
47. Bennett, *Africans in Colonial Mexico*, 54–78; and Midlo Hall, *Slavery*, 2–7.
48. See Swadley, "The Villancico," 133; and Cashner, "Imitating Africans," 163, for detailed descriptions
49. van Orden, *Music, Discipline, and Arms*, 83.
50. Swiadon Martínez, "Los villancicos de negro," xxxv–xxxvi.
51. Swiadon Martínez, xxxiv–xxv.
52. Swiadon Martínez, "Fiesta y parodia," 294.
53. Hagedorn, "'Where the Transcendent Breaks,'" 222–23.
54. Cruz, *Villancicos*, Villancico 258, 72, vv. 33–36.
55. Cruz, *Villancicos*, Villancico 258, 72, vv. 37–40.
56. Cruz, *Villancicos*, Villancico 258, 72, vv. 41–49.
57. I will return to this villancico in Chapter 6 to offer additional perspectives on it.
58. Swiadon Martínez, "Villancicos de negro," xxvi.
59. Swiadon Martínez, xxvi.
60. Cruz, *Villancicos*, Villancico ix, 247, vv. 13–16.
61. Aurelio Tello refers to the products of such co-creations as "villancicos de precisión" and remarks upon their frequency among lyrics written for composers auditioning for chapelmaster positions. He describes the process: "La tradición de escribir letras con alusiones musicales se remonta, cuando menos, a comienzos del siglo XVII. Esto fue uno de los signos de la barroquización del género, al dotar a las letras de un [sic] información cuasi críptica derivada de la teoría de la música" (The tradition of writing lyrics with musical allusions dates back to at least beginning of the seventeenth century. This was one of the signs of the genre's Baroquization, in giving the lyrics a quasi-cryptic subtext derived from music theory). Tello, "El villancico," 40.
62. Charters, *A Language*, 27–29.
63. Cruz, *Villancicos*, Villancico ix, 247, vv. 25–36.
64. For a discussion of angelic choruses in Ascension iconography, see Finley, *Hearing Voices*, 106–7.

65. Swiadon Martínez, "Fiesta y parodia," 291.
66. Pérez de Montoro, *Obras posthumas*, 265.
67. For additional examples of the conflation of Afro-descendant and Indigenous dance forms in early modern Hispanic texts, see Trambaioli's readings of Lope de la Vega's *Servir a señor discreto* and his *La dama boba* ("Apuntes sobre el guineo" 1780–83).

## CHAPTER 6

1. Eidsheim, *The Race of Sound*, 16.
2. Georgina Sabat de Rivers has highlighted the need for intersectional frameworks that examine popular representations in villancicos in concert with the poet's own marginality as a cloistered woman living in the Americas

> Sor Juana nos envía signos lingüísticos bien marcados cuando quiere señalar variedades raciales, pero, humanista cristiana, también nos expresa claramente la capacidad de cada uno de estos tipos, sea indio o negro, de hablar de modo perfecta la lengua de sus conquistadores o dueños. Esta mujer valiente que conoció y sufrió las limitaciones de su época nos transmite, por medio de lo que les pone en la boca a estos personajes, sus cualidades sobresalientes e intereses, pero también los puestos de desventaja que ocupan en la sociedad en que viven. El ámbito sonoro de los claustros de las catedrales servía de vehículo a expresiones de protesta apenas veladas en loores a la Virgen o a los santos; estas expresiones cumplían, al mismo tiempo, su cometido de denuncia en una sociedad cristiana que, sin embargo, permitía la esclavitud o exigía la sumisión por el color de la piel. Sabat de Rivers, "Blanco, negro," 25

> Sor Juana sends well indicated linguistic signs when she wants to highlight racial diversity, but as a Christian humanist, she also clearly expresses the capacity of each of these types, whether *indio* or *negro*, to speak the language of their conquerors or owners perfectly. This courageous woman who knew and suffered the limitations of her time transmits to us, by means of what she put in the mouths of these characters, their distinguishing qualities and interests, but also the disadvantaged positions that they occupied in the society in which they lived. The sonorous environment of cathedral cloisters served as a vehicle for expressions of protest that were thinly veiled in praise for the Virgin or the saints; these expressions accomplished, at the same time, their task of denunciation in a Christian society that, nevertheless, permitted slavery or demanded submission because of skin color 3.

3. For this chapter, I owe a debt of gratitude to Nicholas Jones, whose thoughtful comments about my lack of engagement with race in *Hearing Voices: Aurality and New Spanish Sound Culture in Sor Juana Inés de la Cruz* (University of Nebraska Press, 2019) prompted me to rethink my reading of Sor Juana's inscriptions of Black and African voices. Jones, review of *Hearing Voices*, 185.
4. Fra Molinero, "Los villancicos negros," 21.
5. Baker, "The 'Ethnic Villancico,'" 407.

6. Jones, "Sor Juana's," 268.
7. Baker, "The 'Ethnic Villancico,'" 402.
8. Ortiz, "Villancicos de *negrilla*," 125.
9. Eidsheim, *The Race of Sound*, 7.
10. Marín López, "A Conflicted Relationship," 49.
11. Marín López, 57; Pedelty, *Musical Ritual*, 67.
12. Quoted in Ortiz, "Villancicos de *negrilla*," 128.
13. Loreto López, "Campanas," 75–85.
14. Toop, *Sinister Resonance*, 75.
15. Cruz, *Villancicos*, Villancico 230, 24, vv. 1–2.
16. Cruz, *Villancicos*, Villancico 299, 138, vv. 1–4.
17. Toop, *Sinister Resonance*, 76.
18. Castillo, "Horror (Vacui)," 88–89.
19. Tenorio, *Los villancicos*, 161.
20. Kirk, *Sor Juana Inés de la Cruz*, 87.
21. Cruz, *Villancicos*, Villancico 258, 72, vv. 45–47.
22. Trambaioli, "Apuntes sobre el guineo," 1774.
23. Trambaioli, 1774.
24. Méndez Plancarte annotates the *seises*' response in his edition of the *Obras completas*: "'Los *Versículos*' con cuya traducción formó Sor J. este *juguete*, y cuyo texto latino añade tras cada copla, son los que preceden a las 'Lecciones' de cada uno de los 3 Nocturnos, en los Maitines litúrgicos del 15 de agosto. Sólo les añadió, en cuarto lugar, la hermosa Antífona '*Dignare me laudare to*' . . ., de las Vísperas del Común de Nuestra Señora" (The Bible verses with whose translation Sor Juana formed this wordplay, and whose Latin text concludes each *copla*, precede the 'Lessons' of each of the three nocturnes, in the matins liturgy for August 15. She only added, in the fourth verse, the beautiful Antiphon '*Dignare me laudare to*' . . . from the Common of the Blessed Virgin Mary). Cruz, *Villancicos*, 396.
25. Cruz, *Villancicos*, Villancico 258, 73, vv. 78–81.
26. Line 79 features an untranslatable play on words that links the colloquial phrase "meterse en *docena*" (to interrupt) with "una *docena* [de]" (a dozen) choirboys.
27. Cruz, *Villancicos*, Villancico 258, 72, vv. 33–41.
28. See Valerio, *Sovereign Joy*, 65–79, for a discussion of the election of festival kings and queens as an early modern Afro-diasporic practice.
29. By all accounts, Afro-Mexican confraternities thrived in seventeenth-century New Spain. In addition to the nine lay societies that von Germeten lists (see Chapter 5), Miguel Valerio specifically highlights the all-woman sisterhood of St. Efigenia. Valerio, *Sovereign Joy*, 191.
30. von Germeten, *Black Blood*, 44.
31. See Jones, *Staging*, 35–47, for a discussion of this tradition on the Peninsular stage.
32. Fracchia, *"Black but Human,"* 29–32.

33. Cruz, *Villancicos, Villancico* 258, 73, vv. 64–70.
34. Erin Kathleen Rowe traces devotional images of Black saints in the confraternities at least as far back as the late sixteenth century. *Black Saints*, 58.
35. Franco Mata, "Valores artísticos," 527.
36. Cruz, *Villancicos, Villancico* 258, 73, vv. 52–55.
37. Quoted in Vélez de Guevara, *El diablo cojuelo*, 207–8.
38. Cervantes, *The Complete Exemplary Novels*, xxx–xxxi.
39. Boyd, "Cervante's Exemplary Prologue," 52.
40. Katz and Lazos, "The Rediscovery," 23.
41. Fuller, *Between Two Worlds*, 80.
42. Cruz, *Villancicos, Villancico* 258, 73, vv. 57–62.
43. Swiadon Martínez, "Fiesta y parodia," 299.
44. Martínez-San Miguel, "From *American Knowledge*," 275–76.
45. Swiadon Martínez, "Los personajes," 600–601.
46. Valerio, *Sovereign Joy*, 190.
47. Cruz, *Villancicos, Villancico* lviii, 314, vv. 1–8.
48. There is evidence of this practice among pre- and post-Contact Indigenous groups, and it persists in contemporary rituals. For instance, Dorothy Hosler observes the presence of ankle rattles on small clay effigies from pre-Classic Tlatilco, an agricultural community in the Valley of Mexico. *The Sounds*, 233. Among present-day Uto-Aztecan groups, Hosler draws attention to the use of metal ankle rattles in Yaqui and Huichol deer dances (245).
49. Cruz, *Villancicos, Villancico* lviii, 315, vv. 25–28.
50. Cruz, *Villancicos, Villancico* lviii, 315, vv. 29–32.
51. Baker, "The 'Ethnic Villancico,'" 406–7.
52. Cruz, *Villancicos, Villancico* lviii, 315, vv. 34–39.
53. Cruz, *Villancicos, Villancico* lviii, 315, v. 40–44.
54. Cruz, *Villancicos, Villancico* lviii, 315–16, v. 45–60.
55. Revelation 12:1, from the Douay-Rheims translation of the Latin Vulgate Bible.
56. von Germeten, *Black Blood*, 83.
57. Hernández, *Immaculate Conceptions*, 31.
58. Fracchia, Graves, and Rosales, panel discussion.
59. Rowe, *Black Saints*, 7.
60. Recent studies have begun to address this absence by reading national symbols through an Afro-Mexican lens. Key contributions include B. Cristina Arce's *México's Nobodies: The Cultural Legacy of the Soldadera and Afro-Mexico Women* and Ricardo Wilson's *The Nigrescent Beyond: Mexico, the United States and the Psychic Vanishing of Blackness*. Likewise, in reading that attends to the diasporic resonances of *son jarocho*, regional folk music from Veracruz, Elisabeth Le Guin has remarked upon this tendency in musicology. She notes how nationalist imaginings of sound production emphasize the region's "indigenous and European" roots while marginalizing African influence. Le Guin, "One Fine Night," 269.

61. Jones, "Sor Juana's," 271.
62. Beasley, "Performing Zora," 49.
63. Beasley, 56.
64. Derrida, *Specters of Marx*, 18.
65. Derrida, 44–45.
66. Campbell, "DJing Archival," 488.

## CONCLUSION

1. My use of the verb "restitute" is a deliberate echo of Enrico Mario Santí's observation that "as a critical practice, restitution is supplementary in character—in compensating for a previous lack it exceeds rather than simply restores the original" Santí, *Ciphers of History*, 87.
2. Jones, "Debt Collecting," 214–15.
3. Campt, *Listening to Images*, 45.
4. Mark Smith has underscored echo's importance as a means of engaging with the sonic past: "An echo is nothing if not historical. To varying degrees, it is a faded facsimile of an original sound, a reflection of time passed. It invites a habit of listening that not only allows us to locate origin (temporally and spatially) but, more important, to test authenticity: how illustrative the sound was of the historical moment in which it was produced." Smith, "Echo," 55.
5. Eidsheim, *The Race of Sound*, 13.
6. Sterne and Akyama, "The Recording," 553.
7. In an influential study of how sound and music reimagine racial identities, Josh Kun maintains that audiotopias "are both sonic and social spaces where disparate identity-formations, cultures *and* geographies historically kept and mapped separately are allowed to interact with each other as well as enter into relationships whose consequences for cultural identification are never predetermined." *Audiotopia*, 23.
8. Ewé, "The Unheard," 444.
9. Ewé, 444.
10. Hameed, "Black Atlantis," 108.
11. Jones, *Staging*, 50.
12. Balbuena, *Grandeza*, 170–71.
13. The use of "revuelta" is word play that encompasses curve and revolt.
14. Mundy, *The Death*, 194.
15. Gemelli Careri, *Viaje*, 102.
16. Gemelli Careri, 153.
17. Gemelli Careri, 156.
18. Gemelli Careri, 151–52.
19. Rubial Garcia, "Las virreinas," 20–21.
20. Ochoa Gautier, *Aurality*, 31–75.
21. Ochoa Gautier, *Aurality*; and Dawson, *Undercurrents*.

# Bibliography

## MANUSCRIPT SOURCES

Archivo del Cabildo Catedral Metropolitano de México (ACCMM), *Actas de cabildo*, libro 4, f. 036–036v, 4 December 1590, in *Musicat*-Actas de cabildo y otros ramos. Base de datos de las catedrales en México, Puebla, Oaxaca, Guadalajara, Morelia, Mérida y Durango, registro MEX79000463, available at www.musicat.unam.mx.

ACCMM, *Actas de cabildo*, libro 4, f. 36v, 11 December 1590, *Musicat*-Actas de cabildo y otros ramos, registro MEX 79000464, available at www.musicat.unam.mx.

ACCMM, *Actas de cabildo*, libro 4, f. 102v, 22 April 1594, *Musicat*-Actas de cabildo y otros ramos, registro MEX 79000511, available at www.musicat.unam.mx.

ACCMM, *Actas de cabildo*, libro 4, f. 202–202v, 11 August 1598, *Musicat*-Actas de cabildo y otros ramos, registro MEX 79000511, available at www.musicat.unam.mx.

ACCMM, *Actas de cabildo*, libro 5, f. 114v, 27 February 1609, *Musicat*-Actas de cabildo y otros ramos, registro MEX 37000008, available at www.musicat.unam.mx.

ACCMM, *Actas de cabildo*, libro 5, f. 119–119v, 31 March 1609, *Musicat*-Actas de cabildo y otros ramos, registro MEX 37000010, available at www.musicat.unam.mx.

ACCMM, *Actas de cabildo*, libro 5, f. 166, 7 November 1609, *Musicat*-Actas de cabildo y otros ramos, registro MEX 37000016, available at www.musicat.unam.mx.

ACCMM, *Actas de cabildo*, libro 5, f. 236v–237, 14 June 1611, *Musicat*-Actas de cabildo y otros ramos, registro MEX 38000034, available at www.musicat.unam.mx.

ACCMM, *Actas de cabildo*, libro 5, f. 238, 17 June 1611, *Musicat*-Actas de cabildo y otros ramos, registro MEX 37000019, available at www.musicat.unam.mx.

ACCMM, *Actas de cabildo*, libro 5, f. 309v–310, 8 January 1613, *Musicat*-Actas de cabildo y otros ramos, registro MEX 79000511, available at www.musicat.unam.mx.

ACCMM, *Actas de cabildo*, libro 5, f. 386v, 28 April 1615, *Musicat*-Actas de cabildo y otros ramos, registro MEX 37000052, available at www.musicat.unam.mx.

ACCMM, *Actas de cabildo*, libro 5, f. 402v–403, 73 August 1615, *Musicat*-Actas de cabildo y otros ramos, registro MEX 37000066, available at www.musicat.unam.mx.

ACCMM, *Actas de cabildo*, libro 5, f. 403v, 7 August 1615, *Musicat*-Actas de cabildo y otros ramos, registro MEX 37000066, available at www.musicat.unam.mx.

ACCMM, *Actas de cabildo*, libro 5, f. 427v, 29 March 1616, *Musicat*-Actas de cabildo y otros ramos, registro MEX 37000093, available at www.musicat.unam.mx.

AGN, Cofradías y archicofradías, caja 1586, expediente 32, fs. 1–35, 1673, "Autos hechos a petición de la Cofradía de la Preciosa Sangre de Cristo, fundada en la parroquia de la Sta. Virgen y Mártir Santa Catarina, sobre la preferencia de lugar en las procesiones y actos públicos."

AGN, Edictos de Inquisición, caja 1256, expediente 3, fs. 1, 1643, "Edicto Inquisitorial que prohíbe la costumbre de hacer oratorios privados en las casas, tales como: nacimientos, altares a la Virgen María y otros Santos, donde se ponen retratos de personas que ya murieron y se reúnen hombres y mujeres a comer, beber, ca."

AGN, Inquisición, vol. 502, exp. 15, fs. 571–82, 1663, "Autos hechos por el comisario de la Puebla de los Angeles, contra diferentes personas que se hallaron en un oratorio."

Archivo Histórico de la Arquidiócesis de Oaxaca (AHAO), *Actas de cabildo*, libro 1, f. 82, 9 January 1652, in *Musicat*-Actas de cabildo y otros ramos, registro OAX 25000490, available at www. musicat.unam.mx.

AHAO, *Actas de cabildo*, libro 1, f. 112v, 2 February 1653, *Musicat*-Actas de cabildo y otros ramos, registro OAX 25000380, available at www.musicat.unam.mx.

Biblioteca Palafoxiana, R/475/023, f. 266–68, 19 May 1649, "Denuncia de Luis Pérez contra Mariana de la Cruz, mulata libre por hacer bailes música y danzas en un novenario."

### MUSICAL SCORES

Fernández, Gaspar. *Cancionero musical de Gaspar Fernandes*, vol. 1. Transcribed, edited, and with an introduction by Aurelio Tello and in collaboration with Juan Manuel Lara Cárdenas. Mexico City: Instituto Nacional de Bellas Artes / Centro Nacional de Investigación, Documentación e Información Musical Carlos Chávez, 2001.

Gutiérrez de Padilla, Juan. "Al establo más dichoso." Transcribed by Andrew Cashner. In Cashner, *Villancicos about Music*, 193–217.

Rodríguez Mata, Antonio. *Passions*. Transcribed, edited, and with an introduction by Matthew Grey Brothers. Middleton, WI: A-R Editions, 2012.

Salgado, Tomás. "Qué tambén somo gente la nengla." Transcribed by Leonardo Waisman. In *Neglo celeblamo, Pañolo burlamo: La negrilla en España y en América*, vol. 2, edited by Leonardo Waisman, 598–603. Self-published, 2021.

Tollis de la Rocca, Mateo. "Como tienen los morenos." Transcription by Barbara Pérez Ruiz. In *Humor, pericia y devoción: Villancicos en la Nueva España*, edited by Aurelio Tello, 176–92. Mexico City: Centro de Investigaciones y Estudios Superiores en Antropología Social and Instituto Nacional de Bellas Artes, 2013.

## WORKS CITED

Alemán, Matheo. *Sucesos de D. frai Garcia Gera arcobispo de Mejico, a cuyo cargo estuvo el govierno de la Nueva España*. Mexico: En la enprenta de la viuda de Pedro Balli, 1613.

Apodaca Valdez, Manuel. *Cofradías Afrohispánicas: Celebración, resistencia furtiva y transformación cultural*. Leiden, The Netherlands: Brill, 2022.

Arce, B. Cristina. *México's Nobodies: The Cultural Legacy of the Soldadera and Afro-Mexico Women*. Albany: State University of New York Press, 2017.

Argyriadis, Kali. "'Católicos, apostólicos y no-satánicos': Representaciones contemporáneas en México y construcciones locales (Veracruz) del culto a la Santa Muerte." *Revista Cultura y Religión* 8, no. 1 (January-June 2014): 191–218.

Baade, Colleen. "'Hired' Nun Musicians in Early Modern Castile." In *Musical Voices of Early Modern Women: Many-Headed Melodies*, edited by Thomasin LaMay, 287–310. Burlington, VT: Ashgate, 2005.

Baker, Geoffrey. "The 'Ethnic Villancico' and Racial Politics in 17th-Century Mexico. In *Devotional Music in the Iberian World, 1450–1800: The Villancico and Related Genres*, edited by Tess Knighton and Álvaro Torrente, 399–408. Burlington, VT: Ashgate, 2007.

———. *Imposing Harmony: Music and Society in Colonial Cuzco*. Durham, NC: Duke University Press, 2008.

———. "Latin American Baroque: Performance as a Post-Colonial Act?" *Early Music* 36, no. 3 (2008): 441–48.

———. "The Resounding City." In *Music and Urban Society in Colonial Latin America*, edited by Geoffrey Baker and Tess Knighton, 1–20. Cambridge: Cambridge University Press, 2011.

Balbuena, Bernardo de. *Grandeza mexicana*. Edited by Asima F. X. Saad Maura. Madrid: Cátedra, 2011.

Barquera, Rodrigo, Thiseas C. Lamnidis, Aditya Kumar Lankapalli, Arthur Kocher, Diana I. Hernández-Zaragoza, Elizabeth A. Nelson, Adriana C. Zamora-Herrera, et al. "Origin and Health Status of First-Generation Africans from Early Colonial Mexico." *Current Biology* 30, no. 11 (June 2020): 2,078–91.

Bassein, Beth Ann. *Women and Death: Linkages in Western Thought and Literature*. Westport, CT: Greenwood Press, 1984.

Beasley, Myron M. "Performing Zora: Critical Ethnography, Digital Sound, and Not Forgetting." In *Digital Sound Studies*, edited by Mary Caton Lingold, Darren Mueller, and Whitney Trettien, 47–63. Durham, NC: Duke University Press, 2018.

Becerra Jiménez, Celina G. "Enseñanza y ejercicio de la música en la construcción del ritual sonoro en la catedral de Guadalajara." In *Enseñanza y ejercicio de la música en México*, edited by Arturo Camacho Becerra, 21–69. Guadalajara: Centro de Investigaciones y Estudios Superiores en Antropología Social, El Colegio de Jalisco, Universidad de Guadalajara, 2013.

Bennett, Hermann L. *Africans in Colonial Mexico: Absolutism, Christianity, and Afro-Creole Consciousness*. Bloomington: Indiana University Press, 2005.

———. *Colonial Blackness: A History of Afro-Mexico*. Bloomington: Indiana University Press, 2010.

Bisaro, Xavier. "Singing the Community: Plainchant in Early Modern *petites écoles*." In *Listening to Early Modern Catholicism: Perspectives from Musicology*, edited by Daniele Filippi and Michael J. Noone, 94–11. Leiden: Brill, 2017.

Bloechl, Olivia. "Race, Empire, and Early Music." In *Rethinking Difference in Music Scholarship*, edited by Olivia Bloechl, Melanie Lowe, and Jeffrey Kallberg, 77–108. Cambridge: Cambridge University Press, 2015.

Bloom, Gina. *Voice in Motion: Staging Gender and Shaping Sound in Early Modern England*. Philadelphia: University of Pennsylvania Press, 2007.

Bordas-Ibáñez, Cristina. "Coreografía y música en las fiestas ecuestres del siglo XVIII: Los juegos de parejas." *Revista de Musicología* 32, no. 2 (July 2009): 245–67.

Bourguignon, Erika. "Suffering and Healing, Subordination and Power: Women and Possession Trance." *Ethos* 32, no. 4 (Dec. 2004): 557–74.

Boyd, Stephen. "Cervantes's Exemplary Prologue." In *A Companion to Cervantes's Novelas Ejemplares*, edited by Stephen Boyd, 47–68. Woodbridge, UK; Tamesis, 2005.

Brewer-García, Larissa. *Beyond Babel: Translations of Blackness in Colonial Peru and New Granada*. Cambridge: Cambridge University Press, 2020.

Bristol, Joan. "Blackness and Blurred Boundaries in Mexico City." In *A Companion to Viceregal Mexico City, 1519–1821*, edited by John F. López, 76–94. Leiden: Brill, 2021.

Brothers, Matthew Grey. Introduction to *Passions*, vii–xi. Edited by Matthew Grey Brothers. Middleton, WI: A-R Editions, 2012.

Budasz, Rogério. "Central-African Pluricarcs and Their Players in Nineteenth-Century Brazil." *Music in Art* 3, no. 1–2 (Spring-Fall 2014): 5–31.

Butler, Shane. *The Ancient Phonograph*. New York: Zone Books, 2015.

Campbell, Mark V. "DJing Archival Interruptions: Remix Praxis and Reflective Guide." In *The Routledge Handbook of Remix Studies and Digital Humanities*, edited by Eduardo Navas, Owen Gallagher, and xtine burrough, 488–99. New York: Routledge, 2021.

Campt, Tina. *Listening to Images*. Durham, NC: Duke University Press, 2017.
Cañeque, Alejandro. *The King's Living Image: The Culture and Politics of Viceregal Power in Colonial Mexico*. New York: Routledge, 2004.
Cascales, Francisco. *Cartas philologicas, es a saber, de letras hvmanas, Varia erudicion, Expilcaciones de lugares, Lecciones curiosas, Documentos poeticos, Obseruaciones, ritos, i costumbres, i muchas sentencias exquisitas*. Murcia: Luis Verós, 1634.
Cashner, Andrew. "Imitating Africans, Listening for Angels: A Slaveholder's Fantasy of Social Harmony in an 'Ethnic Villancico' from Colonial Puebla (1652)." *Journal of Musicology* 38, no. 2 (2021): 141–82.
———, editor. *Villancicos about Music from Seventeenth-Century Spain and New Spain*. Web Library of Seventeenth-Century Music, no. 32 (Nov. 2017), https://doi.org/10.53610/VCBM8408.
Castañeda García, Rafael. "Piedad y participación femenina en la cofradía de negros y mulatos de San Benito de Palermo en el Bajío novohispano, siglo XVIII." *Cofradías de negros y mulatos en la Nueva España: Devoción, sociabilidad y resistencias*, edited by Rafael Castañeda García, special issue of *Nuevo Mundo Mundos Nuevos*, 2012, https://doi.org/10.4000/nuevomundo.64478.
Castañeda García, Rafael and Juan Carlos Ruiz Guadalajara, editors. *Africanos y afrodescendientes en la América hispánica septentrional: Espacios de convivencia, sociabilidad y conflicto*. 2 vols. San Luis Potosí: El Colegio de San Luis, 2020.
Castillo, David R. "Horror (Vacui): The Baroque Condition." In *Hispanic Baroques: Reading Cultures in Context*, edited by Nicholas Spadaccini and Luis Martín-Estudillo, 87–104. Nashville, TN: Vanderbilt University Press, 2005.
Cavarero, Adriana. *For More Than One Voice*. Translated by Paul Kottman. Redwood City, CA: Stanford University Press, 2005.
Cerone, Pietro. *El melopeo y maestro. Tractado de mvsica Theorica y pratica: En que se pone por extenso, lo que vno para hazerse perfecto Musica ha menester saber: y por mayor facilidad, comodida y claridad del Lector, esta repartido en XXII Libros*. Naples: Por Juan Bautista Gargano y Lucrecio Nucci, 1613.
Cervantes, Miguel de. *The Complete Exemplary Novels*, 2nd ed. Edited by Barry Ife and Jonathan Thacker. Translated by Barry Ife. Oxford, UK: Oxbow Books, 2013.
Charters, Samuel. *A Language of Song: Journeys in the Musical World of the African Diaspora*. Durham, NC: Duke University Press, 2009.
Chávez Bárcenas, Ireri. "Native Song and Dance Affect in Seventeenth-Century Festivals in New Spain." In *Acoustemologies in Contact: Sounding Subjects and Modes of Listening in Early Modernity*, edited by Emily Wilbourne and Suzanne G. Cusick, 37–64. Cambridge, UK: Open Book Publishers, 2021.
———. "Singing in the City of Angels: Race, Identity, and Devotion in Early Modern Puebla de los Ángeles." PhD diss., Princeton University, 2018.

Cruz, Juana Inés de la. *The Answer / La respuesta*, expanded ed. Edited and translated by Electa Arenal and Amanda Powell. New York: Feminist Press of the City University of New York, 2009.

———. *Lírica personal*. Vol. 1 of *Obras completas de sor Juana Inés de la Cruz*, edited by Alfonso Méndez Plancarte. Mexico City: Fondo de Cultura Económica, 1995.

———. *Villancicos y letras sacras*. Vol. 2 of *Obras completas de sor Juana Inés de la Cruz*, edited by Alfonso Méndez Plancarte. Mexico City: Fondo de Cultura Económica, 1995.

———. *Selected Works*. Edited by Anna More. Translated by Edith Grossman. New York: Norton, 2016.

Curcio-Nagy, Linda. *The Great Festivals of Mexico City*. Albuquerque: University of New Mexico Press, 2004.

———. "Rosa de Escalante's Private Party: Popular Female Religiosity in Colonial Mexico City." In *Women in the Inquisition: Spain and the New World*, edited by Mary E. Giles, 254–69. Baltimore, MD: Johns Hopkins University Press, 1999.

———. "Giants and Gypsies: Corpus Christi in Colonial Mexico City." In *Rituals of Rule, Rituals of Resistance: Public Celebrations and Popular Culture in Mexico*, edited by William H. Beezley, Cheryl E. Martin, and William E. French, 1–26. Wilmington, DE: Scholarly Resources, 1994.

———. "Faith and Morals in Colonial Mexico." In *The Oxford History of Mexico*, edited by William H. Beezley and Michael C. Meyer, 151–82. New York: Oxford University Press, 2000.

D'Amico, Leonardo. "Cumbia Music in Colombia: Origins, Transformations, and Evolution of a Coastal Music Genre." In *Cumbia! Scenes of a Migrant Latin American Music Genre*, edited by Héctor Fernández L'Hoeste and Pablo Vila, 29–48. Durham, NC: Duke University Press, 2013.

Davies, Drew Edward. "Colonialism and Music in Habsburg New Spain." In *A Companion to Viceregal Mexico City, 1519–1821*, edited by John F. López, 439–65. Leiden: Brill, 2021.

———. "Making Music, Writing Myth." In *Music and Urban Society in Colonial Latin America*, edited by Geoffrey Baker and Tess Knighton, 64–82. New York: Cambridge University Press, 2011.

Dawson, Kevin. *Undercurrents of Power: Aquatic Culture in the African Diaspora*. Philadelphia: University of Pennsylvania Press, 2018.

de Certeau, Michel. "Vocal Utopias: Glossolalias." *Representations*, no. 56 (Autumn 1996): 29–47.

Derrida, Jacques. *Margins of Philosophy*. Translated by Alan Bass. Chicago: University of Chicago Press, 1982.

———. *Specters of Marx: The State of the Debt, the Work of Mourning, and the New International*. Translated by Peggy Kamuf. New York: Routledge, 1994.

———. "Ritual Battles from the Kongo Kingdom to the Americas." In Fromont, *Afro-Catholic Festivals*, 23–41.

Dillon, Elizabeth Maddock. *New World Drama: The Performative Commons in the Atlantic World, 1649-1849*. Durham, NC: Duke University Press, 2014.

Dolar, Mladen. *A Voice and Nothing More*. Cambridge: MIT Press, 2006.

Du Bois, W. E. B. *The Souls of Black Folk*. Chicago: A. C. McClurg, 1903.

Egan, Caroline. "Lyric Intelligibility in Sor Juana's Nahutal *tocotines*." *Romance Notes* 58, no. 2 (2018): 207–18

Eidsheim, Nina Sun. *The Race of Sound: Listening, Timbre and Vocality in African American Music*. Durham, NC: Duke University Press, 2019.

Erlmann, Veit. *Reason and Resonance: A History of Modern Aurality*. Brooklyn: Zone Books, 2010.

Ewé, Tobias. "The Unheard." In *The Bloomsbury Handbook of the Anthropology of Sound*, edited by Holger Schulze, 443–62. New York: Bloomsbury, 2021.

Feldman, Martha. "Castrato Acts." In *The Oxford Handbook of Opera*, edited by Helen M. Greenwald, 395–418. Oxford: Oxford University Press, 2014.

———. *The Castrato: Reflections on Natures and Kinds*. Oakland: University of California Press, 2015.

———. "Fugitive Voice." *Representations* 154, no. 1 (Spring 2021): 10–22.

Feldman, Martha, and Judith T. Zeitlin. "The Clamor of Voices." In *The Voice as Something More: Essays toward Materiality*, edited by Martha Feldman and Judith T. Zeitlin, 3–33. Chicago: University of Chicago Press, 2019.

Figueroa Hernández, Rafael. *Son jarocho: Guía histórico-musical*. Xalapa, Veracruz: CONACULTA-FONCA, 2007.

Finley, Sarah. *Hearing Voices: Aurality and New Spanish Sound Culture in Sor Juana Inés de la Cruz*. Lincoln: University of Nebraska Press, 2019.

Fiol-Matta, Licia. *The Great Woman Singer: Gender and Voice in Puerto Rican Music*. Durham, NC: Duke University Press, 2017.

Foster, Timothy M. *Music and Power in Early Modern Spain: Harmonic Spheres of Influence*. New York: Routledge, 2022.

Fracchia, Carmen. *"Black but Human": Slavery and the Visual Arts in Hapsburg Spain, 1480–1700*. Oxford: Oxford University Press, 2019.

Fracchia, Carmen, Yinka Esi Graves, and Miguel Ángel Rosales. Panel discussion about *Gurumbé: Canciones de tu memoria negra*. Birbeck Institute of the Moving Image, virtual, May 21, 2021.

Fra Molinero, Baltasar. "Los villancicos negros de sor Juana Inés de la Cruz." *Chiricú Journal: Latina/o Literatures, Arts, and Cultures* 5, no. 2 (1988): 19–34.

Franco Mata, María Ángela. "Valores artísticos y simbólicos del azabache en España y Nuevo Mundo." *Compostellanum: Revista de la Archidiócesis de Santiago de Compostela*, 36, no. 3–4 (1991): 467–531.

Fraser Giffords, Gloria. *Sanctuaries of Earth, Stone, and Light: The Churches of Northern New Spain, 1530–1821*. Tucson: University of Arizona Press, 2007.

Freitas, Roger. "The Eroticism of Emasculation: Confronting the Baroque Body of the Castrato." *Journal of Musicology* 20, no. 2 (Spring 2003): 196–249.

Fromont, Cécile, ed. *Afro-Catholic Festivals in the Americas: Performance, Representation, and the Making of Black Atlantic Tradition*. University Park: Pennsylvania State University Press, 2019.

Fromont, Cécile. "Envisioning Brazil's Afro-Christian *Congados*: The Black King and Queen Festival Lithograph of Johann Moritz Rugendas." In Fromont, *Afro-Catholic Festivals*, 117–39.

Fryer, Peter. *Rhythms of Resistance: African Musical Heritage in Brazil*. London: Pluto Press, 2000.

Fuller, Amy. *Between Two Worlds: The Autos Sacramentales of Sor Juana Inés de la Cruz*. Cambridge, UK: Modern Humanities Research Association, 2015.

Gaddy, Kristina. *Well of Souls: Uncovering the Banjo's Hidden History*. New York: W. W. Norton, 2022.

Gage, Thomas. *A New Survey of the West Indies, Or, The English American His Travail by Sea and Land*, 2nd ed. London: E. Cotes, 1655.

García de León, Antonio, and Liza Rumazo. *Fandango: El ritual del mundo jarocho a través de los siglos*. Veracruz: CONACULTA, Instituto Veracruzano de Cultura and Programa de Desarrollo Cultural del Sotavento, 2006.

Gembero Ustárroz, María. "Muy amigo de música: El obispo Juan de Palafox (1600–1659) y su entorno musical en el Virreinato de Nueva España." In *Juan Gutiérrez de Padilla y la época palafoxiana*, edited by Gustavo Mauleón Rodríguez, 55–130. Puebla: Secretaría de Cultura y Gobierno del Estado de Puebla, 2010.

Gemelli Careri, Juan Francisco. *Viaje a la Nueva España*. Translated by José María de Ágreda y Sánchez. Mexico: Sociedad de Bibliófilos Mexicanos, 1927.

Ghadessi, Touba. *Portraits of Human Monsters in the Renaissance: Dwarves, Hirsutes, and Castrati as Idealized Anatomical Anomalies*. Kalamazoo, MI: Medieval Institute Publications, 2018.

Gilroy, Paul. *The Black Atlantic: Modernity and Double Consciousness*. New York: Verso, 1993.

Goethls, Jessica. "The Patronage Politics of Equestrian Ballet: Allegory, Allusion, and Satire in the Courts of Seventeenth-Century Italy and France." *Renaissance Quarterly* 70, no. 4 (Winter 2017): 1,397–448.

Goldberg, K. Meira. *Sonidos negros: On the Blackness of Flamenco*. New York: Oxford University Press, 2019.

Gonzalez, Sara. *The Musical Iconography of Power in Seventeenth-Century Spain and Her Territories*. New York: Routledge, 2016.

Gordon, Bonnie. *Voice Machines: The Castrato, the Cat Piano, and Other Strange Sounds*. Chicago: University of Chicago Press, 2023.

Guijo, Gregorio Martín de. *Diario de Guijo, 1648–1664*, 2 vols. Edited by Manuel Romero de Terreros. Mexico: Editorial Porrúa, 1952.

Gutiérrez de Medina, Cristóbal. *Viage de tierra, y mar, feliz por mar, y tierra, que hizo El Excellentissimo Señor Marques de Villean mi señor, yendo por virrey, y*

*Capitan General de la Nueva España en la flota que embió su Magestad este año de mil y seiscientos y quarenta, siendo General della Roque Centeno, y Ordoñez: Su Almirante Juan de Campos*. Mexico: Imprenta de Iuan Ruyz, 1640.

Hagedorn, Katherine. "To Have and to Hold: Possession Performance in Afro-Cuban Regla de Ocha." In *Women and New and Africana Religions*, edited by Lillian Ashcraft-Eason, Darnise C. Martin, and Oyeronke Olademo, 145–65. Santa Barbara, CA: Praeger, 2009.

———. "'Where the Transcendent Breaks into Time': Toward a Theology of Sound in Afro-Cuban Regla de Ochá." In *Theorizing Sound Writing*, edited by Deborah Kapchan, 216–32. Middletown, CT: Wesleyan University Press, 2017.

Hameed, Ayesha. "Black Atlantis." In *We Travel the Space Ways: Black Imagination, Fragments, and Diffractions*, edited by Henriette Gunkel and Kara Lynch, 107–28. Bielefeld: transcript Verlag, 2019.

Hernández, Rosilie. *Immaculate Conceptions: The Power of the Religious Imagination in Early Modern Spain*. Toronto: University of Toronto Press, 2019.

Hernández Reyes, Dalia. "*Festín de las morenas criollas*: Danza y emblemática en el recibimiento del virrey marqués de Villena (México, 1640)". In *Dramaturgia y espectáculo teatral en la época de los Austrias, España y América*, edited by Judith Farré Vidal, 339–58. Madrid: Iberoamericana-Vervuert, 2009.

Hidalgo Lehuedé, Jorge, Nelson Casto Flores, Alberto Diaz Araya, and Priscila Cisternas. "De músico a extirpador: Algunas notas sobre Francisco Otal en Lima y La Plata de 1613 a 1618." *Allpanchis* 44, no. 81–82 (2013): 119–54.

Horswell, Michael J. *Decolonizing the Sodomite: Queer Tropes of Sexuality in Colonial Andean Culture*. Austin: University of Texas Press, 2010.

Hosler, Dorothy. *The Sounds and Colors of Power: The Sacred Metallurgical Technology of Ancient West Mexico*. Cambridge, MA: MIT Press, 1994.

Humboldt, Alexander von. *Political Essay on the Kingdom of New Spain: A Critical Edition*, vol. 2. Edited by Vera M. Kutzinski and Ottmar Ette. Translated by J. Ryan Poynter, Kenneth Berri, and Vera M. Kutzinski. Chicago: University of Chicago Press, 2019.

Irving, D. R. M. *Colonial Counterpoint: Music in Early Modern Manila*. New York: Oxford University Press, 2010.

Jaque Hidalgo, Javiera, and Miguel Valerio. "Introduction: Negotiating Status through Confraternal Practices." In *Indigenous and Black Confraternities in Colonial Latin America: Negotiating Status through Religious Practices*, edited by Javiera Jaque Hidalgo and Miguel Valerio, 9–34. Amsterdam: Amsterdam University Press, 2022.

Jones, Alisha Lola. "Singing High: Black Countertenors and Gendered Sound in Gospel Performance." In *The Oxford Handbook of Voice Studies*, edited by Nina Sun Eidsheim and Katherine Meizel, 35–54. New York: Oxford University Press, 2019

Jones, Nicholas R. "Debt Collecting, Disappearance, Necromancy: A Response to John Beusterien." In *Early Modern Black Diaspora Studies: A Critical*

*Anthology*, edited by Cassander L. Smith, Nicholas R. Jones, and Miles P. Grier, 211–22. Cham: Palgrave Macmillan, 2018, pp. 211–22.

———. Review of *Hearing Voices: Aurality and New Spanish Sound Culture in Sor Juana Inés de la Cruz*, by Sarah Finley. *Bulletin for Spanish and Portuguese Historical Studies* 44, no. 1 (2019): 184–86.

———. "Sor Juana's Black Atlantic: Colonial Blackness and the Poetic Subversions of *Habla de negros*." *Hispanic Review* 86, no. 3 (Summer 2018): 265–85.

———. *Staging habla de negros: Radical Performances of the African Diaspora in Early Modern Spain*. University Park: Pennsylvania State University Press, 2019.

Junne, George H. *The Black Eunuchs of the Ottoman Empire: Networks of Power in the Court of the Sultan*. New York: I. B. Tauris, 2016.

Katz, Esther, and Elena Lazos. "The Rediscovery of Native 'Super-Foods' in Mexico." In *Eating Traditional Food: Politics, Identity and Practices*, edited by Brigitte Sébastia, 20–47. New York: Routledge, 2017.

Katzew, Ilona. *Casta Painting: Images of Race in 18th-Century Mexico*. New Haven, CT: Yale University Press, 2005.

Kircher, Athanasius. *Musurgia universalis sive Ars magna consoni et dissoni*. 2 vols. Rome: Haeredum Francisci Corbelletti/Typis Ludovici Grignani, 1650.

———. *Phonurgia nova*. Kempten: Per Rudolphum Dreherr, 1673.

Kirk, Stephanie. *Sor Juana Inés de la Cruz and the Gender Politics of Knowledge in Colonial Mexico*. New York: Routledge, 2019.

Konetzke, Richard. *Colección de Documentos para la Historia de la Formación Social de Hispanoamérica, 1493–1810*, vol 2, tomo 1 (1593–1659). Madrid: Consejo Superior de Investigaciones Científicas, 1958.

Krutitskaya, Anastasia, ed. *Pliegos de villancicos de la catedral de México, siendo maestro de capilla Antonio de Salazar (1688–1714)*. Mexico City: Universidad Nacional Autónoma de México and Escuela Nacional de Estudios Superiores Unidad Morelia, 2022.

Kun, Josh. *Audiotopia: Music, Race and America*. Berkeley: University of California Press, 2005.

Larson, Katherine R. *The Matter of Song in Early Modern England: Texts in and of the Air*. Oxford: Oxford University Press, 2019.

Lavrín, Asunción. *Brides of Christ: Conventual Life in Colonial Mexico*. Stanford, CA: Stanford University Press, 2008.

Le Guin, Elisabeth. "One Fine Night in Veracruz." *The Americas* 39, no. 3 (Fall 2021): 265–300.

Lingold, Mary Caton, Darren Mueller, and Whitney Trettien. Introduction to *Digital Sound Studies*, edited by Mary Caton Lingold, Darren Mueller, and Whitney Trettien, 1–25. Durham, NC: Duke University Press, 2018.

Lipski, John M. *Latin American Spanish*. New York: Longman Group Limited, 1994.

Lochhead, Judith, Eduardo Mendieta, and Stephen Decatur Smith. Introduction to *Sound and Affect: Voice, Music, World*, edited by Judith Lochhead, Eduardo

Mendieta, and Stephen Decatur Smith, 1–33. Chicago: University of Chicago Press, 2021.

Lord, Suzanne. *Music in the Middle Ages: A Reference Guide*. Westport, CT: Greenwood Press, 2008.

Lorente, Andrés. *El porque de la mvsica en qve se contiene los qvatro artes de ella, canto llano, canto de organo, contrapunto, y composición, y en cada vno de ellos nvuvas reglas, razon abreviada env tiles preceptos, aune n las cosas mas dificiles, tocantes a la Harmonia Musica, nvmerosos exemplos, con clara inteligencias, en estilo breve, que al Maestro deleytan, y al Discipulo enseñan, cuya direccion se vera sucintamente anotada antes del Prologo*. Alcalá de Henares: Nicolás de Xamares, 1672.

Loreto López, Rosalva. "Campanas, esquilones, y esquilitas: El espacio y el orden de la sonoridad conventual en la Pueba de los Ángeles del siglo XVIII." In *Espacios en la historia: Invención y transformación de los espacios sonoros*, edited by Pilar Gonzalbo Aizpuru, 75–96. Mexico City: El Colegio de México, Centro de Estudios Históricos, 2014.

Luis, Diego Javier. "Galleon Anxiety: How Afro-Mexican Women Shaped Colonial Spirituality in Acapulco." *The Americas* 78, no. 3 (July 2021): 389–413.

Luna, Kathryn de. "Sounding the African Atlantic." *William and Mary Quarterly* 78, no. 4 (October 2021): 581–616.

Luna García, Sandra Nancy. "Espacios de convivencia y conflicto: Las cofradías de la población de orgen africano en Ciudad de México, siglo XVII." *TRASHUMANTE: Revista Americana de Historia Social*, no. 10 (2017): 32–52.

Malvido, Elsa. "Crónicas de la Buena Muerte a la Santa Muerte en México." *Arqueología Mexicana*, no. 76 (2005): 20–27.

Manzella, Abigail G. H. "The Sites and Sounds of Music in *The Souls of Black Folk*." In *Resounding Pasts: Essays in Literature, Popular Music, and Cultural Memory*, edited by Drago Momcilovic, 159–76. Newcastle upon Tyne, UK: Cambridge Scholars Publishing, 2011.

Marín López, Javier. "A Conflicted Relationship: Music, Power and the Inquisition in Vice-Regal Mexico City." In *Music and Urban Society in Colonial Latin America*, edited by Geoffrey Baker and Tess Knighton, 43–63. Cambridge: Cambridge University Press, 2011.

———. "The Musical Inventory of Mexico Cathedral, 1589: A Lost Document Rediscovered." *Early Music* 36, no. 4 (2008): 575–96.

Martínez, Ignacio. "Settler Colonialism in New Spain and the Early Mexican Republic." In *The Routledge Handbook of the History of Settler Colonialism*, edited by Edward Cavanagh and Lorenzo Veracini, 109–24. New York: Routledge, 2017.

Martínez, María Elena. "Black Blood of New Spain: *Limpieza de sangre*, Racial Violence, and Gendered Power in Early Colonial Mexico." *William and Mary Quarterly* 61, no. 3 (July 2004): 479–520.

Martínez-San Miguel, Yolanda. "From *American Knowledge: The Constitution of a Colonial Subjectivity in the Writings of Sor Juana Inés de la Cruz*." Translated by

Isabel Gómez. In *Selected Works* by Sor Juana Inés de la Cruz, edited by Anna More, 272–80. New York: Norton, 2016.

Marshall, Wayne, and Raquel Z. Rivera. "Visualizing Reggaeton: Editor's Notes." In *Reggaeton*, edited by Raquel Z. Rivera, Wayne Marshall, and Deborah Pacini Hernández, 215–17. Durham, NC: Duke University Press, 200.

Mason Vaughn, Virginia. *Performing Blackness on English Stages, 1500–1800.* Cambridge: Cambridge University Press, 2005.

Matluck Brooks, Lynn. *The Dances of the Processions of Seville in Spain's Golden Age.* Kassel: Edition Reichenberger, 1988.

McKnight, Kathryn Joy, and Leo J. Garofalo. Introduction to *Afro-Latino Voices: Narratives from the Early Modern Ibero-Atlantic World, 1550–1812*, edited by Kathryn Joy McKnight and Leo J. Garofalo, ix–xxiii. Indianapolis, IN: Hackett Publishing Company, 2009.

Medina, Ángel. *Los atributos del capón: Imagen histórica de los cantores castrados en España.* Madrid: Instituto Compultense de Ciencias Musicales, 2003.

Midlo Hall, Gwendolyn. *Slavery and African Ethnicities in the Americas: Restoring the Links.* Chapel Hill: University of North Carolina Press, 2005.

Morales Abril, Omar. "Gaspar Fernández: Su vida y obras como testimonio de la cultura musical novohispana a principios del siglo XVII." In *Enseñanza y ejercicio de la música en México*, edited by Arturo Camacho Becerra, 71–125. Guadalajara: Centro de Investigaciones y Estudios Superiores en Antropología Social, El Colegio de Jalisco, Universidad de Guadalajara, 2013.

———. "El esclavo negro Juan de Vera: Cantor, arpista y compositor de la catedral de Puebla (*florevit 1575–1617*). In *Música y catedral: Nuevos enfoques, viejas temáticas*, edited by Jesús Alfaro Cruz and Raúl Heliodoro Torres Medina, 43–59. Mexico City: Universidad Autónoma de la Ciudad de México, 2010.

———. "La música en la catedral de la Puebla de los Ángeles (1546–1606). Primera Parte: Magisterio de capilla." *Heterofonía: Revista de Investigación Musical*, no. 129 (July-December 2003): 9–47.

———. "Villancicos de remedo en la Nueva España." In *Humor, pericia y devoción: Villancicos en la Nueva España*, edited by Aurelio Tello, 11–39. Mexico City: Centro de Investigaciones y Estudios Superiores en Antropología Social and Instituto Nacional de Bellas Artes, 2013.

Moten, Fred. *In the Break: The Aesthetics of the Black Radical Tradition.* Minneapolis: University of Minnesota Press, 2003.

———. *Stolen Life.* Durham, NC: Duke University Press, 2018.

Motta Sánchez, J. Arturo. "Tras la heteroidentificación: El 'movimiento negro' costachiquense y la selección de marbetes étnicos." *Dimensión Antropológica* 13, no. 38, (Sept/Dec., 2006): 115–50.

Muir, Edward. *Ritual in Early Modern Europe*, 2nd ed. Cambridge: Cambridge University Press, 2005.

Mundy, Barbara. *The Death of Aztec Tenochtitlan, the Life of Mexico City.* Austin: University of Texas Press, 2015.

Nassarre, Pablo. *Escuela Música según la práctica moderna*, dividida en primera, y segvnda parte. Zaragoza: Herederos de Diego de Larumbe, 1724.

Nava Sánchez, Alfredo. "El cantor mulato Luis Barreto: La vida singular de una voz en la catedral de México en el amanecer del siglo XVII." In *Lo sonoro en el ritual catedralicio: Iberoamérica, siglos XVI–XIX*, edited by Patricia Díaz Cayeros, 105–20. Mexico City: Universidad Autónoma de México and Universidad de Guadalajara, 2007.

―――. "El esclavo mulato Luis Barreto clérigo y mejor cantor de las Indias en el tránsito del siglo XVI al XVII." Bachelor's thesis, Universidad Nacional Autónoma de México, 2005.

―――. "La voz descarnada: Un acercamiento al canto y al cuerpo en la Nueva España." In *Presencias y miradas del cuerpo en la Nueva España*, edited by Estela Roselló Soberón, 21–44. Mexico City: Universidad Nacional Autónoma de México and Instituto de Investigaciones Históricas, 2011.

Ndiaye, Noémie. *Scripts of Blackness: Early Modern Performance Culture and the Making of Race*. Philadelphia: University of Pennsylvania Press, 2022.

Ngou-Mve, Nicolás. "Los orígenes de las rebeliones negras en el México colonial." *Dimensión Antropológica* 6, no. 16 (May/August 1999): 7–40.

Nielson, Lisa. "Visibility and Performance." In *Concubines and Courtesans: Women and Slavery in Islamic History*, edited by Matthew S. Gordon and Kathryn A. Hain, 75–99. New York: Oxford University Press, 2017.

Ochoa Gautier, Ana María. *Aurality: Listening and Knowledge in Nineteenth-Century Colombia*. Durham, NC: Duke University Press, 2014.

Ortiz, Mario. "Villancicos de *negrilla*: Imaginando al sujeto afro-colonial." *Calíope: Journal of the Society for Renaissance and Baroque Hispanic Poetry* 11, no. 2 (2005): 125–37.

Pasquier, Michael. "Catholicism and Race." In *The Oxford Handbook of Religion and Race in American History*, edited by Kathryn Gin Lum and Paul Harvey, 172–90. New York: Oxford University Press, 2018.

Peck, Amelia, ed. *Interwoven Globe: The Worldwide Textile Trade, 1500–1800*. New York: Metropolitan Museum of Art, 2013.

Pedelty, Mark. *Musical Ritual in Mexico City: From the Aztec to NAFTA*. Austin: University of Texas Press, 2004.

Pérez Marín, Yarí. *Marvels of Medicine: Literature and Scientific Enquiry in Early Colonial Spanish America*. Liverpool: Liverpool University Press, 2020.

Pérez de Montoro, Joseph. *Obras posthumas y lyricas sagradas de D. Joseph Pérez de Montoro*, vol. 2. Madrid: Oficina de Antonio Marín, 1736.

Pharies, David A. *Structure and Analogy in the Playful Lexicon of Spanish*. Tübingen: Max Niemeyer Philips, 1986.

Planke, Carine. "The Spirit's Wish: Possession Trance and Female Power among the Puno of Congo-Brazzaville." *Journal of Religion in Africa* 41, Fasc. 4 (2011): 366–95.

Querol y Roso, Luis. "Negros y mulatos de Nueva España (Historia de su alzamiento en Méjico en 1612)." *Anales de la Universidad de Valencia*, 12, no. 90 (1931–32): 141–53.

Ramírez Uribe, Claudio. "*Sarabanda tenge que tenge* . . . Evidencias de prácticas religiosas bantú en un villancico en la catedral de Puebla del siglo XVII." *Estudios de Historia Novohispana*, no. 66 (January-June 2022): 47–79.

Rama, Ángel. *The Lettered City*. Translated by John Charles Chasteen. Durham, NC: Duke University Press, 1996.

Ramos, Frances L. *Identity, Ritual, and Power in Colonial Puebla*. Tucson: University of Arizona Press, 2012.

Ramos-Kittrell, Jesús A. *Playing in the Cathedral: Music, Race, and Status in New Spain*. New York: Oxford University Press, 2016.

Rangan, Pooja. "The Skin of the Voice: Acousmatic Illusions, Ventriloquial Listening." In *Sound Objects*, edited by James A Steintrager and Rey Chow, 130–48. Durham, NC: Duke University Press, 2019.

Rak, Ric, Rack! *Tumba La-Lá-La: Los villancicos negros de sor Juana*. FONCA and mott@rte, 2008.

Rojas, Rosa Elena. "Esclavos de Obraje: Consuelo en la Devoción. La cofradía de la Santa Veracruz Nueva fundada por Mulatos, Mestizos y Negros. Coyoacán, siglo XVII." *Cofradías de negros y mulatos en la Nueva España: Devoción, sociabilidad y resistencias*, edited by Rafael Castañeda García. Special edition of *Nuevo Mundo Mundos Nuevos*, 2012. https://doi.org/10.4000/nuevomundo.64339.

Rosselli, John. "The Castrati as a Professional Group and a Social Phenomenon, 1550–1850." *Acta Musicologica* 60, no. 2 (May-August 1988): 143–79.

Rowe, Erin Kathleen. *Black Saints in Early Modern Global Catholicism*. Cambridge: Cambridge University Press, 2020.

Rubial Garcia, Antonio. "Las virreinas novohispanas: Presencias y ausencias." *Estudios de Historia Novohispana*, no. 50 (January-June, 2014): 3–44.

Sabat de Rivers, Georgina. "Blanco, negro, rojo: Semiosis racial en los villancicos de Sor Juana Inés de la Cruz." In *Crítica semiológica de textos literarios hispánicos: Vol. II de las Actas del Congreso Internacional sobre Semiótica e Hispanismo celebrado en Madrid en los días del 20 al 25 de junio de 1983*, edited by Miguel Ángel Garrido-Gallard, 247–55. Madrid: Consejo Superior de Investigaciones Científicas, 1986.

Sánchez, Vicente. *Lyra poética*. Zaragoza: Manuel Roman, Impressor de la Universidad, 1688.

Santí, Enrico Mario. *Ciphers of History: Latin American Readings for a Cultural Age*. New York: Palgrave Macmillan, 2005.

Segal, Ronald. *Islam's Black Slaves: The Other Black Diaspora*. New York: Farrar, Straus and Giroux, 2001.

Sierra Silva, Pablo Miguel. *Urban Slavery in Colonial Mexico: Puebla de los Ángeles, 1531–1706*. New York: Cambridge University Press, 2019.

Singer, Deborah. "Inclusion Politics/Subalternalization Practices: The Construction of Ethnicity in *Villancicos de negros* of the Cathedral of Santiago de Guatemala (16th–18th Centuries)." *Revista de Historia*, no. 80 (July-December 2019): 33–53.

Smith, Bruce R. *The Acoustic World of Early Modern England: Attending to the O-Factor.* Chicago: University of Chicago Press, 1999.
Smith, Mark M. "Echo." In *Keywords in Sound,* edited by David Novak and Matt Sakakeeny, 55–64. Durham, NC: Duke University Press, 2015.
Solórzano Periera, Juan de. *Emblemata regio politica.* Madrid: García Morras, 1653.
Dewulf, Jeroen. *Afro-Atlantic Catholics: America's First Black Christians.* Notre Dame, IN: University of Notre Dame Press, 2022.
Spell, Lota M. "Music in the Cathedral of Mexico in the Sixteenth Century." *Hispanic American Historical Review* 26, no. 3 (1946): 293–319.
Spivak, Gayatri Chakravorty. "Can the Subaltern Speak?" In *Colonial Discourse and Post-Colonial Theory: A Reader,* edited by Patrick Williams and Laura Chrisman, 66–111. New York: Routledge, 2013.
Stein, Daniel. *Music Is My Life: Louis Armstrong, Autobiography, and American Jazz.* Ann Arbor: University of Michigan Press, 2012.
Stein, Louise. "The Musicians of the Spanish Royal Chapel." In *The Royal Chapel in the Time of the Habsburgs: Music and Court Ceremony in Early Modern Europe,* edited by Juan José Carreras and Bernardo García García, 173–94. Woodbridge, UK: Boydell Press, 2005.
Sterne, Jonathan and Mitchell Akiyama. "The Recording that Never Wanted to be Heard and Other Stories of Sonification." In *The Oxford Handbook of Sound Studies,* edited by Trevor Pinch and Karin Bijsterveld, 544–60. New York: Oxford University Press, 2011.
Stevenson, Robert. "The Afro-American Musical Legacy to 1800." *Musical Quarterly* 54, no. 4 (October 1968): 475–502.
———. "Mexico City Cathedral Music: 1600–1750." *The Americas* 21, no. 2 (October 1964): 111–35.
———. "Puebla Chapelmasters and Organists: Sixteenth and Seventeenth Centuries: Part II." *Inter-American Music Review* 6, no. 1 (1984): 29–59.
Swadley, John. "The Villancico in New Spain 1650–1750: Morphology, Significance and Development." PhD diss., Canterbury Christ Church University, 2014. Canterbury Research and Theses Environment.
Swiadon Martínez, Glenn. "África en los villancicos de negro: Seis ejemplos del siglo XVII." In *La otra Nueva España: La palabra marginada en la Colonia,* edited by Mariana Masera, 40–52. Mexico City: Universidad Nacional Autónoma de México and Editorial Azul, 2002.
———. "Fiesta y parodia en los villancicos de negro del siglo XVII." *Anuario de Letras: Lingüística y Filología,* no. 42–43 (2004–05): 285–304.
———. "Los personajes del villancico de negro en su entorno social." In *Actas del XV Congreso de la Asociación Internacional de Hispanistas "Las dos orillas,"* vol. 2, edited by Beatriz Mariscal and María Teresa Miaja de la Peña, 595–604. Mexico City: Fondo de Cultura Económica, 2007.
———. "Los villancicos de negro en el siglo XVII." PhD diss., Universidad Nacional Autónoma de México, 2000.
Tachtiris, Corine. *Translation and Race.* New York: Routledge, 2024.

Taylor, Diana. *The Archive and the Repertoire: Performing Cultural Memory in the Americas*. Durham, NC: Duke University Press, 2003.

Tello, Aurelio. "El villancico de precisión en los exámenes de oposición para maestros de capilla (1708–1750): Cinco casos de catedrales novohispanas." In *Humor, pericia y devoción: Villancicos en la Nueva España*, edited by Aurelio Tello, 39–68. Mexico City: Centro de Investigaciones y Estudios Superiores en Antropología Social and Instituto Nacional de Bellas Artes, 2013.

Tenorio, Marta Lilia. *Los villancicos de Sor Juana*. Mexico City: El Colegio de México, 1999.

Toop, David. *Sinister Resonance: The Mediumship of the Listener*. New York: Continuum, 2010.

Tomlinson, Gary. *The Singing of the New World: Indigenous Voice in the Era of European Contact*. Cambridge: Cambridge University Press, 2007.

Torres, Nicolás de. *Festín hecho por las morenas criollas de la muy noble y muy leal Ciudad de México al recibimiento, y entrada del Excellentísimo Señor Marqués de Villena, Duque de Escalona, Virrey de esta Nueva España*. Mexico: Imprenta de Francisco Robledo, 1640.

Trambaioli, Marcella. "Apuntes sobre el guineo o baile de negros: tipologías y funciones dramáticas." In *Memoria de la palabra: Actas del VI Congreso de la Asociación Internacional Siglo de Oro*, edited by María Luisa Lobato and Francisco Domínguez Matito, 1773–83. Madrid: Iberoamericana, 2004.

Tråvén, Marianne. "Voicing the Third Gender—The Castrato Voice and the Stigma of Emasculation in Eighteenth-Century Society." *Etudes Epistémè: Revue de littérature et de civilisation (XVIe–XVIIIe siècles)*, no. 29 (2016). https://doi.org/10.4000/episteme.1220.

Valerio, Miguel. *Sovereign Joy: Afro-Mexican Kings and Queens, 1539–1640*. New York: Cambridge University Press, 2022.

van Orden, Kate. *Music, Discipline, and Arms in Early Modern France*. Chicago: University of Chicago Press, 2005.

Velázquez Gutiérrez, María Elisa. *Mujeres de origen africano en la capital novohispana, siglos XVII y XVIII*. Mexico City: Instituto Nacional de Antropología e Historia y Universidad Nacional Autónoma de México Programa Universitario de Estudios de Género, 2006.

Vélez de Guevara, Luis. *El diablo cojuelo*. Edited by Adolfo Bonilla y San Martín. Vigo: Librería de Eugenio Krapf. 1902.

Viarnés, Carrie. "Cultural Memory in Afro-Cuban Possession: Problematizing Spiritual Categories, Resurfacing 'Other' Histories." *Western Folklore* 66, no. 1–2 (Winter/Spring 2007): 127–59.

Villa-Flores, Javier. "El arte de hablar por el pecho: Adivinación, vetriloquismo y esclavitud entre mujeres africanas en Nueva España durante el siglo XVII." In Castañedad García and Ruiz Guadalajara, *Africanos y afrodescendientes*, 249–71.

Vinson, Ben. *Bearing Arms for His Majesty: The Free-Colored Militia in Colonial Mexico*. Stanford, CA: Stanford University Press, 2002.

———. *Before Mestizaje: The Frontiers of Race and Caste in Colonial Mexico*. New York: Cambridge University Press, 2017.
Vinson, Ben, and Matthew Restall, eds. *Black Mexico: Race and Society from Colonial to Modern Times*. Albuquerque: University of New Mexico Press, 2009.
Voigt, Lisa. "The Archive and the Festival." *Journal of Festive Studies* 1, no. 1 (Spring 2019): 27–35.
———. *Spectacular Wealth: The Festivals of Colonial South American Mining Towns*. Austin: University of Texas Press, 2016.
von Germeten, Nicole. *Black Blood Brothers: Confraternities and Social Mobility for Afro-Mexicans*. Gainesville: University Press of Florida, 2006.
———. "Black Brotherhoods in Mexico City." In *The Black Urban Atlantic in the Age of the Slave Trade*, edited by Jorge Cañizares-Esguerra, Matt D. Childs, and James Sidbury, 248–68. Philadelphia: University of Pennsylvania Press, 2013.
———. "Juan Roque's Donation of a House to the *Zape* Confraternity, Mexico City, 1623." In *Afro-Latino Voices: Narratives from the Early Modern Ibero-Atlantic World, 1550–1812*, edited by Kathryn Joy McKnight and Leo J. Garofalo, 83–103. Indianapolis, IN: Hackett Publishing Company, 2009.
Waisman, Leonardo. *Negro celeblamo, Pañolo burlamo: La negrilla en España y en América*, vol. 1. Self-published, 2021.
Watanabe-O'Kelly, Helen. "The Equestrian Ballet in Seventeenth-Century Europe—Origin, Description, Development." *German Life and Letters* 36, no. 3 (1983): 198–212.
Weheliye, Alexander. *Phonographies: Grooves in Sonic Afro-Modernity*. Durham, NC: Duke University Press, 2005.
Wilbourne, Emily. "Little Black Giovanni's Dream: Black Authorship and the 'Turks, and Dwarves, the Bad Christians' of the Medici Court." In *Acoustemologies in Contact: Sounding Subjects and Modes of Listening in Early Modernity*, edited by Emily Wilbourne and Suzanne G. Cusick, 135–65. Cambridge, UK: Open Book Publishers, 2021.
Will de Chaparro, Martina. *Death and Dying in New Mexico*. Albuquerque: University of New Mexico Press, 2007.
Wilson, Ricardo. *The Nigrescent Beyond: Mexico, the United States and the Psychic Vanishing of Blackness*. Evanston, IL: Northwestern University Press, 2020.

# Index

Page numbers in *italic* refer to figures.

Acapulco, 113, 149–50
acousmatic blackness, 185–89
Afro-descendant people
  masculinity and, 72–77
  sexuality and hypersexualization of, 42–43, 69–73, 140, 197
  uprisings and, 74–76, 233n99
  whiteness and, 72, 193
  *See also* Black women
Afro-descendant sound
  acousmatic blackness and, 185–89
  *castrati* (eunuch singers) and, 31–39
  *decencia* (decency) and, 24–25, 138–39
  new methodology for, 213–25
  phonographic approach to, 3–15
  politics of representation and, 89–92
  regulation and suppression of, 136–44, 186–87
  *tiples* (sopranos) and, 21–23, 24, 25–29. *See also* Barreto, Luis; Vera, Juan de
  urban planning and, 87–89
  *See also* dance; political ceremonies; religious ceremonies
*afromestizaje*, 208–9

agency
  Afro-descendant people and, 5
  Barreto and, 46
  Black women and, 66–68, 96–109
  in Juana Inés de la Cruz's *villancicos*, 162, 190, 193
  modes of, 98
  voice and, 25
Aguiar y Seijas, Francisco de, 120
Agurto y Loaysa, Joseph de, 190
Akiyama, Mitchell, 215
"Al establo más dichoso" (At the happiest stable) (Gutiérrez de Padilla), 68–74, *75*, 77–80, 82–83
*aleglía*, 197–98
Alfonso, Francisco, 22
amaranth, 197–98
anamorphism, 189, 198
"Andrés do queda el ganado" ("Andrés, where are the cattle") (Fernández), 56, 63–65, *65*
Angola, Juan, 83
Apodaca Valdez, Manuel, 142
archives, 3–15, 88
Archivo del Cabildo Catedral Metropolitano de México, 21, 31
Argaiz, Gregorio de, 89–91, 93

Argyriadis, Kali, 150–52
Aristotle, 34–35, 231n28
Armstrong, Louis, 46
Ascencio, Alonso, 42
Atlantic Ocean, 217–18

Baade, Colleen, 33
Bacon, Francis, 34
Baker, Geoffrey
   on Afro-descendant sound, 213, 216
   on dance, 169
   on harmony, 1–2, 99
   on Juana Inés de la Cruz, 184
   on Mexico City, 87–88
   on race and music in Cuzco, 23
   on *villancicos de negros*, 60–61
Balbuena, Bernardo de, 218–20, 221
banjo, 129
Barreto, Luis
   career of, 22–23, 24, 35–36, 42–46
   as *castrato*, 27, 54, 59
   escape attempt and manumission of, 21, 46–51
   García Guerra and, 230n9
   Rodríguez Mata and, 53, 54
   vocal commodification of, 25–27, 49
   wages and privileges of, 21, 29, 44–46
Bassein, Beth Ann, 70–71
basses (*contrabajos*), 21, 54, 74
*batá* drums, 174–75
Beasley, Myron, 209
Becerra Jiménez, Celina G., 23
Bell, Alexander Graham, 6
bells, 125, 187, 201, 209
Bennett, Herman, 3
Berliner, Emile, 6
Bermúdez, Pedro, 22, 54
*Black Atlantis* (Hameed), 217–18
Black Confraternity of the Monastery of Nuestra Señora de la Merced, 133–34

Black women
   agency of, 66–68, 96–109, 143, 192–93
   confraternities and, 142–44
   dance and, 92–93, 94–111, 140–44, 148–50, 175–77
   in Fernández's *villancicos*, 66–68
   as fortune tellers, 120, 145–50
   political ceremonies and, 92–93, 94–111
   popular religious practices and, 140–44
   in Rodríguez Mata's work, 54
   in *Villancico* 258 (Juana Inés de la Cruz), 175–77, 192–200, 206–8
   in *Villancico* lviii (Juana Inés de la Cruz), 200–208
blackface performance, 56, 80, 161, 195
Bloechl, Olivia, 232n68
Bloom, Gina, 35
Bonilla y San Martín, Adolfo, 196–97
Bordas Ibáñez, Cristina, 112–13, 115
Bourguignon, Erika, 148
Brewer-García, Larissa, 79, 169–70
Brioso, Pablo, 133–34
Bristol, Joan, 3
Broschi, Carlo (Farinelli), 29
Brothers, Matthew Grey, 53–54
Budasz, Rogério, 129
Buonaccorsi, Giovanni, 37–38
Buonanni, Filippo, *165*
Bustamante, Hernando, 30
Butler, Shane, 8

Cádiz, 180–81
Calderón de la Barca, Pedro, 154
*camote*, 199
Campbell, Mark V., 210
Campt, Tina, 13–14, 48, 104–5, 207, 214
*canario*, 179
*Cancionero musical* (Fernández), 61, 62. *See also* "Andrés do queda el ganado" ("Andrés, where

are the cattle") (Fernández); "Fransiquiya donde bamo" ("Francisquiya, where are we going") (Fernández); "Negrinho tiray vos" (Fernández)
*Capital* (Marx), 25–26
capital punishment, 75–76
Carlos IV, 112
Cascales, Francisco, 78–79
Cashner, Andrew, 68–69, 72–73, 74, 77–78, 79, 82–83
caste system, 3
Castillo, David, 189
*castrati* (eunuch singers)
   Black males as, 31–39
   history of, 29–39
   in Italy, 26, 29–30, 59
   in New Spain, 21, 29, 30–39
   qualities of, 59, 65
   Rodríguez Mata and, 54
   in Spain, 36–37
castration
   as financial strategy, 32
   prisoners of war and, 36–37
   as punishment, 75–77
Castro Flores, Nelson, 30–31
Cavarero, Adriana, 148–49, 231n28
*Cecilia Valdés* (Roig), 81
*celoso extremeño, El* (Cervantes), 37
Cerda y de Aragón-Moncada, Juana de la, 222–24
Cerone, Pietro, 44, 237n62
Certeau, Michel de, 6–7, 14, 82
Cervantes, Miguel de, 37, 197
Céspedes, Francisco de, 27, 28
*chanzonetas*
   Mexico City Cathedral and, 20, 21, 171–75
   Rodríguez Mata and, 53
   Vera and, 22
chastity, 33
Chávez Bárcenas, Ireri, 61, 62–63, 64–65

Chimalpahin, 133
Christmas
   giants and, 131
   Gutiérrez de Padilla's *villancico* (1651) and, 157–61
   Juana Inés de la Cruz's *villancico* (1678) and, 162–63
   Pérez de Montoro's lyrics (1688) and, 180–81
   "Que tambén somo gente la nengla" (Salgado) and, 166–69
   role of *villancicos* in, 56
   *villancico* (1657) and, 177–78
Cisternas, Priscilla, 30–31
Colón, Domingo "Mingo," 82
*coloquios*, 21
Comilla, Miguel de, 144
confraternities
   in "Como tienen los morenos" (Tollis de la Rocca), 126–32
   funerals and, 132–35
   religious processions and, 122–26
   role and importance of, 120–22
   uprisings and, 75
   women and, 142–44
Conrado, Gaspar, 135
"Consulta del consejo de las Indias sobre los servicios personales de los indios" (Guidance from the Council of the Indies about the personal services of the indios) (1596), 91
*contrabajos* (basses), 21, 54, 74
*contraltos*, 21. *See also* Fernández, Ruth
Convento de Nuestra Señora de la Encarnación, 54
convents, 187
Coronación de Christo de Señor Nuestro (confraternity), 123
Coronado, Luis, 54
Corpus Christi
   confraternities and, 123–24
   dance and, 99–100, 128

Corpus Christi (*continued*)
  Fernández's *villancicos* and, 66
  giants and, 130, 131
  role of *villancicos* in, 56
  Vera and, 22, 27
Correa, Juan, 204–6, *205*
Covarrubias, Sebastián de, 231n24
cowboy dance (*danza de los vaqueros*), 116–17
Crooke, Helkiah, 34
Cruz, Mariana de la, 142–44
*Cum pro nostro pastorali munere* (Sixtus V), 30
*cumbé*, 110–11
"Cumbées" (Murcia), 156–57
*cumbia*, 110–11
Curcio-Nagy, Linda
  on Afro-descendant dance, 99–100, 104
  on agency, 97
  on confraternities and religious ceremonies, 123–24, 131, 135–36
  on regulation of Afro-descendant sound, 140, 141, 144
Cuzco, 23

Dailey, Patrick, 235n9
D'Amico, Leonardo, 110–11
dance
  Black women and, 92–93, 94–111, 140–44, 148–50, 175–77
  in "Como tienen los morenos" (Tollis de la Rocca), 128–30
  confraternities and, 123, 124, 128–30
  in Gutiérrez de Padilla's *villancicos*, 157–59
  Indigenous people and, 93–94
  in Juana Inés de la Cruz's *villancicos*, 190–91
  politics of representation and, 89–92
  popular religious practices and, 135, 138–42
  role in *villancicos de negros*, 155–57, 169–77, 178–81
  ventriloquism and, 148–50
*danza de los vaqueros* (cowboy dance), 116–17
*danza de uma hacha* (torch dance), 110
Dash, Julie, 36
Davies, Drew Edward, 42, 119–20
Dawson, Kevin, 224–25
*De anima* (Aristotle), 34–35, 231n28
*De instuaranda aethiopum salute* (Sandoval), 72
death, 70–73, *71*
*decencia* (decency), 24–25, 138–39
Derrida, Jacques, 9–10, 210, 231n28
Descartes, René, 9, 170
Dewulf, Jeroen, 88, 240n16
*diablo cojuelo, El* (*The Limping Devil*) (Vélez de Guevara), 196–97
*Diario de sucesos notables (1665–1703)* (Robles), 222–24
Diaz, Sebastian, 121
Díaz Araya, Alberto, 30–31
Díaz del Castillo, Bernal, 114
*divino Narciso, El* (*The Divine Narcissus*) (Juana Inés de la Cruz), 198
"Do bana" (song), 11–13
Dolar, Mladen, 36, 231n28
Douglass, Frederick, 26, 48
Du Bois, W. E. B., 10–14

echoes and echolocation, 209–11, 214, 215–25
Edison, Thomas, 6, 8
Egan, Caroline, 61
Eidsheim, Nina Sun, 71–72, 166, 183, 185–89, 214
*Emblemata regio politica* (Solórzano Pereira), 115
Enríquez de Almanza, Martín, 75–76
*ensalada* and *ensaladilla*
  features of, 68, 160

Gutiérrez de Padilla and, 68–74, 75, 77–80, 82–83
Juana Inés de la Cruz and, 178–80, 188, 189–200
*Entierro de San Ignacio* (Zendejas), 135
*Entretenimientos y ivegos honestos, recreaciones christianas para que en todo género de estados se recreen los sentidos, sin que se estrague el alma* (Diversions and honest games, Christian pastimes to delight the senses in all states, without corrupting the soul) (Remón), 196–97
equestrian displays and ballets, 111–17
Erlmann, Viet, 9
*Escuela Música según la práctica moderna* (Nassarre), 34
Estrada Medinilla, María de, 92–93
eunuch singers. See *castrati* (eunuch singers)
Ewé, Tobias, 216–17, 227n3

"fama de que es Dios hombre, La" (The news that God became man) (Sánchez), 163–64
Farinelli (Carlo Broschi), 29
*Fatal Contract, The* (Hemings), 37
Feldman, Martha, 30, 59, 234n104
Felipe IV, 92
Fernández, Gaspar, 56–60, *58*, 61, 62–68, *65*, 80–81
Fernández, Ruth, 72, 80–82
Fernández de la Cueva, Francisco, 222–24
*Festín hecho por las morenas criollas de la muy noble y muy leal Ciudad de México al recibimiento, y entrada del Excellentísimo Señor Marqués de Villena, Duque de Escalona, Virrey de esta Nueva España* (Torres), 92–93, 94–109
Figueroa Hernández, Rafael, 111
Fiol-Matta, Licia, 72, 80–82

food, 159–60, 196–99
*Forma y Levantado de la Ciudad de México* (Gómez de Trasmonte), 1–2, *2*
fortune tellers, 120, 145–50
Fra Molinero, Baltasar, 184
Fracchia, Carmen, 72, 193–94
Franco, Bartolomé, 29, 43
Franco Mata, María Ángela, 195
"Fransiquiya donde bamo" ("Francisquiya, where are we going") (Fernández), 63, 65–68
Fraser Giffords, Gloria, 45
Freitas, Roger, 43
Fromont, Cécile, 88, 133, 207
Fryer, Peter, 130
Fuller, Amy, 198
funerals, 120, 132–35

Gaddy, Kristina, 129
Gage, Thomas, 20
*gallarda*, 129
Gante, Pedro de, 23
García de León, Antonio, 111
García Guerra, Francisco, 19–21, 134
Garofalo, Leo, 4
Gemelli Careri, Giovanni Francesco, 85–86, 109–11, 113–14, 220–22, 224
Germeten, Nicole von, 66–68, 120, 132, 133, 143, 192
Ghadessi, Touba, 76
giants, 123, 127–28, 130–32
Gilroy, Paul, 10, 13–14
glossolalia, 82
Goldberg, K. Meira, 37, 38, 130, 155
Gómez de Trasmonte, Juan, 1–2, *2*
Góngora, Luis de, 154
Gonzalez, Sara, 107
Gonzalez de Santiago, Cathalina, 149–50
Gordon, Bonnie, 26
*grandeza mexicana, La* (Balbuena), 218–20, 221
Graves, Yinka Esi, 206

Grossman, Edith, xi–xii
Guadalajara, 23
Guijo, Gregorio Martín de, 113–14, 134, 136–37, 139, 140
*Gurumbé: Canciones de tu memoria negra* (*Gurumbé: Afro-Andalusian Memories*) (2016 film), 206
Gutiérrez de Medina, Christóbal, 92–95
Gutiérrez de Padilla, Juan, 59–60, 68–74, 75, 77–80, 82–83, 157–61
Guzmán, Luis Enrique de, 113–14

*habla de negros* (blackspeak)
 dance and, 156
 in Fernández's *villancicos*, 63, 66–68
 in Gutiérrez de Padilla's *villancicos*, 69–71, 74, 157–61
 in Juana Inés de la Cruz's *villancicos*, xi–xii, 61, 154, 162–63, 176–77, 190–92, 199, 202–3
 origins and features of, xi–xii, 25, 36, 60–61, 74, 154–55, 158
 in Sánchez's lyrics, 163–64
 in *Tumba La- Lá-La:* (Rak Ric Rack!), 208–9
"hablar por el pecho" (speaking from the chest), 145–50
Hagedorn, Katherine, 174–75
Hameed, Ayesha, 217–18
harmony
 confraternities and, 121–26, 134–36
 echolocation and, 215–25
 equestrian ballets and, 111–17
 in Fernández's *villancicos*, 62, 64
 in Gutiérrez de Padilla's *villancicos*, 77–79
 in Juana Inés de la Cruz's *villancicos*, 188–89, 191, 197, 202
 Mexico City and, 1–2, 85–89
 neo-Platonic concept of, 85–86, 170, 214–15
 political ceremonies and, 88–89, 93–109
 Puebla and, 88–89, 91
 *villancicos de negros* and, 153–54, 156, 168–69, 170–81
Hemings, William, 37
Hernández, Juan, 21, 48, 53
Hernández, Rosilie, 206
Hernández Reyes, Dalia, 92, 100, 101, 103, 108
Hippodamus, 86
*Historia verdadera de la Conquista de la Nueva España* (Díaz del Castillo), 114
Hollar, Wenceslaus, 71
horsemanship, 111–17
Horswell, Michael, 73
Hosler, Dorothy, 247n48
Humboldt, Alexander von, 243n35
Hurston, Zora Neale, xii, 209

*Illusions* (1982 film), 36
*inconcussum* (unshakeable), 9
Indigenous people, 23, 93–94
*influencia*, 102–3
Inquisition
 blasphemous utterances and, 178
 "ethnic music" and, 186–87
 popular religious practices and, 89, 138, 139, 140–44
 as source, 5, 119
 ventriloquism and, 145–50
Irving, David, 23

James the Moor-slayer, 206
Jaque Hidalgo, Javiera, 122
Jazz Loft Project, 7
Jones, Alisha Lola, 57, 235n9
Jones, Nicholas R.
 on Afro-descendant sound, 38, 213–14
 on agency, 88
 on dance, 24, 140–41, 155, 156, 218, 242n7
 on *habla de negros* (blackspeak), xii

on Juana Inés de la Cruz, 184
on *Tumba La- Lá-La:* (Rak Ric
Rack!), 208–9
on *villancicos de negros*, 61
Juana Inés de la Cruz, Sor
on Black voices, 164
food-based plays on words by,
196–99
*habla de negros* (blackspeak) and,
xi–xii, 61, 154, 162–63, 176–77,
190–92, 199, 202–3
poetic representations of Afro-
descendants by, 184–85, 189–208
resonances in contemporary culture
of, 208–11
on silence, 14
theoretical approach to *villancicos
negros* by, 185–89
voice vs. vocalization and, 183–84
*See also specific villancicos*
Junne, George, 36

Kallman syndrome, 71–72
Katz, Esther, 198
*Kebra Nagast* (Ethiopian epic), 96
Kircher, Athanasius, 170, 228n18
Kirk, Stephanie, 190
Krutitskaya, Anastasia, 244n40
Kun, Josh, 248n7

Lacan, Jacques, 231n28
Larson, Katherine, 35
laughter
in *chanzonetas* for Feast of St. Peter
(1672) and, 172
in Juana Inés de la Cruz's *villancicos*,
154, 176, 197, 203
regulation of Afro-descendant
sound and, 139
in *Tumba La- Lá-La:* (Rak Ric
Rack!), 209
in *villancicos de negros*, 170
Lavrín, Asunción, 44

Lawrence Berkeley National
Laboratory, 6
Lazos, Elena, 198
Le Guin, Elisabeth, 247n60
Lehuedé, Jorge Hidalgo, 30–31
León Gordillo, Nicolás de, 131
Library of Congress, 6
*Libro de todas las cosas* (Quevedo), 154
Lingold, Mary Caton, 7
Lipski, John, 60, 74, 154
*Listening to Images* (Campt), 13
Lochhead, Judith, 229n33
Lopez, Tomás, 31
López de Hinojosos, Alonso, 76–77
López Pacheco Cabrera y Bobadilla,
Diego, 92–109
Lord, Suzanne, 164–66
Lorente, Andrés, 40, 237n62
Loreto López, Rosalva, 187
Luciano, Miguel, 160
*lucumí*, 149–50, 174–75
Luis, Diego Javier, 149
Luna, Kathryn de, 4–5, 213

Manzella, Abigail, 11–12
"Mapa del Orden con que se haze la
Solemne Procesión del Corpus
Christi en la Sta. Metropolitana
y Patriarcal Iglesia de Sevilla en
1747" (Map of the Order of the
Solmen Process of Corpus Christi
in the Holy Metropolitan and
Patriarchal Church of Sevilla in
1747) (León Gordillo), 131
*Margins of Philosophy* (Derrida), 9–10
Marín, Juan, 31–32
Marín, Matheo, 21
Marín López, Javier, 126, 138, 186
Marshall, Wayne, 160
Martín, Pedro, 83
Martínez, Ignacio, 86–87
Martínez, María Elena, 134
Martínez de Castro, Gerónimo, 78–79

Marx, Karl, 25–26
masculinity, 72–77
Matluck Brooks, Lynn, 101–2, 110, 130, 240n25
Maundy Thursday procession, 124–26
McKnight, Kathryn, 4
"Me & te sola Mors separabit" (Hollar), 71
Medina, Ángel, 30, 32, 33–34, 36, 42
*Meditations on First Philosophy* (Descartes), 9
*melopeo y maestro, El* (Cerone), 44
Méndez Plancarte, Alfonso, 246n24
Mendieta, Eduardo, 229n33
Mersenne, Marin, 34, 170
Mexico City
    Afro-descendant uprisings in, 74–76
    canals of, 218–25, *223*
    confraternities in, 120, 123–24, 134
    Corpus Christi in, 123–24
    García Guerra's entry in, 19–21
    Gómez de Trasmonte's map (1628) of, 1–2, *2*
    harmony and, 1–2, 85–89
    political ceremonies in, 19–21, 88–89, 92–93, 94–111, 113–14
    population of, 3
    regulation of Afro-descendant sound in, 136–37, 139–40
    religious ceremonies in, 88–89
Mexico City Cathedral
    Agurto y Loaysa and, 190
    Ascencio and, 42
    *chanzonetas* and, 20, 21, 171–75
    García Guerra's entry in Mexico City and, 20–21
    Indigenous people as musicians in, 23
    Juana Inés de la Cruz's *villancicos* in, 175–77, 190
    Rodríguez Mata and, 53–54
    Santillana and, 164–66
    *tiples* (sopranos) in, 21, 31. See also Barreto, Luis
    *villancico* for Christmas (1657) in, 177–78
Midlo Hall, Gwendolyn, 170
Miguel, Yolanda Martínez-San, 199
Mingo and His Whoopie Kids, 81
Morales Abril, Omar
    on Marín, 31–32
    on Vera, 22–23, 27–29, 38, 56–57, 59, 63, 80–81, 236n26
    on *villancicos de negros*, 62
Moreschi, Alessandro, 29
*Mortalitum nobilitas* (Hollar), 71
Moten, Fred, 25–26, 48
Motta Sánchez, J. Arturo, 114–15, 116–17
Mueller, Darren, 7
*Muerte de San Francisco Javier* (Conrado), 135
Muir, Edward, 130–31
*Mujer del Apocalipsis* (Villalpando), 204–6, *205*
Mundy, Barbara, 219–20
Murcia, Santiago de, 156–57
*musica humana*, 39–40, 91
*musica instrumentalis*, 39–40
*musica mundana*, 39–40
Musicat database, 23
*Musurgia universalis* (Kircher), 228n18

*Narrative of the Life of Frederick Douglass, An American Slave* (Douglass), 26, 48
Nassarre, Pablo, 34
National Museum of American History, 6
Nava Sánchez, Alfredo
    on Barreto, 21, 22–23, 29, 42, 43, 44, 47, 48, 230n9
    on *castrati* (eunuch singers), 38–39, 40–42
    on music theory, 237n62
    on *villancicos de negros*, 60

Ndiaye, Noémie
  on agency, 88
  on dance, 128, 155
  on *habla de negros* (blackspeak), xi, xii
  on racemaking, 55
  on transatlantic slave trade, 243n18
Nebel, Karl, *223*, 224
necromancy, 213–14
"Negrinho tiray vos" (Fernández), 56, 57–60, *58*
"Negros y mulatos de Nueva España (Historia de su alzamiento en Méjico en 1612)" (Negros and mulatos from New Spain [History of their uprising in Mexico in 1612]) (Querol y Roso), 132–33
Ngou-Mve, Nicolás, 75–76
*Novelas ejemplares* (*Exemplary Novels*) (Cervantes), 197

Oaxaca, 61, 166–69
Ochoa Gautier, Ana María, 4, 5, 224–25
Orden, Kate van, 111, 115, 170
Ortiz, Mario, 156–57, 185, 186, 213, 235n9
Otal, Francisco, 30–31

Pacheco y Osorio, Rodrigo, III Marqués de Cerralbo, 20
Pacini Hernandez, Deborah, 160
Palafox y Mendoza, Juan de, 89–91, 93
*paradeta*, 129–30
Partridge, Dan, 7
*Paseo de la Viga en México* (Nebel), *223*, 224
*Passio secundum Matthaeum* (Rodríguez Mata), 53–54
Peck, Amelia, 233n88
Pedelty, Mark, 186
*pepitoria*, 196–97
Peralta, Antonio de, 141–42

Pérez de la Serna, Juan, 48
Pérez de Montoro, José, 180–81
Pérez de Ribera, Lucas, 143
Pérez Marín, Yari, 76–77
*petite mort*, 70–71, *71*
Pharies, David A., 243n20
Philip IV, 112
phonograph, 6
phonography, 3–15, 55
*Phonurgia nova* (Kircher), 228n18
Pisa, Pedro de, 31–32
*Plátano Pride* (Luciano), 160
Plato, 86, 229n33
pluriarc, 128–29
political ceremonies
  Black women and, 92–93, 94–111
  equestrian ballets and, 111–17
  García Guerra's entry in Mexico City and, 19–21
  harmony and, 88–89, 93–109
  Indigenous dance and, 93–94
  politics of representation and, 89–92
*Political Essay on the Kingdom of New Spain* (Humboldt), 243n35
polysemy
  *Festín hecho por las morenas criollas* (Torres) and, 96, 99
  Juana Inés de la Cruz and, 189, 193–200
*El porque de la mvsica* (Lorente), 40
Preciosa Sangre de Cristo (confraternity), 121–22, 124
Puebla
  harmony and, 88–89, 91
  Juana Inés de la Cruz's *villancicos* in, 162–63
  political ceremonies in, 88–89
  regulation of Afro-descendant sound in, 141–44
  religious ceremonies in, 88–89
  representations of Afro-descendant sound in, 89–92

Puebla Cathedral
  Barreto and, 60
  Fernández and, 56–60, *58*, 61, 62–68, *65*, 80–81
  Gutiérrez de Padilla and, 59–60, 68–74, *75*, 77–80, 82–83, 157–61
  *See also* Vera, Juan de

"Que tambén somo gente la nengla" ("We negros are people too") (Salgado), 166–69, *168–69*
Querol y Roso, Luis, 132–33
Quevedo, Francisco de, 154

race
  language and, xi–xiii. *See also habla de negros* (blackspeak)
  timbre and, 60, 161–69
  urban planning and, 86–89
  voice(s) and, 22–25, 35–36
  *See also* Afro-descendant people; Afro-descendant sound; Indigenous people
Rak Ric Rack! 15, 208–11
Rama, Ángel, 86, 87
Ramírez Uribe, Claudio, 60
Ramos-Kittrell, Jesús, 23–24
Rangan, Pooja, 36
Reconquest, 170, 206
Regla de Ochá, 174–75
Reiros, Bernardo de, 121
religious ceremonies
  harmony and, 88–89
  politics of representation and, 89–92
  popular practices and, 135–44
  Santa Muerte and, 150–52
  sources on, 119–20
  ventriloquism and, 145–50
  *See also* confraternities
remixing, 208–11
Remón, Alonso, 196–97
repertoire, 12–13, 88
*Republic* (Plato), 229n33

*Response to Sor Philotea de la Cruz* (Juana Inés de la Cruz), 14
revenant, 210
Reyes, Dalia Hernández, 95
Rivas y Angulo, Felipe de, 109–11
Rivera, Francisco, 23
Rivera, Pedro de, 23
Rivera, Raquel Z., 160
Robles, Antonio de, 222–24
Rodríguez, Francisco, 79–80
Rodríguez de Mesa, Alonso, 44
Rodríguez Mata, Antonio, 53–54
Roig, Gonzalo, 81
Rojas, Rosa Elena, 124–26
*Romance* 8 (Juana Inés de la Cruz), 162
Roque, Juan, 132
Rosales, Miguel Ángel, 206
Rosselli, John, 32–33
Rowe, Erin Kathleen, 72, 207, 247n34
Rubial, Antonio, 222–24
Ruiz de Morales y Molina, Antonio, 28
Rumazo, Liza, 111

Sabat de Rivers, Georgina, 245n2
Salgado, Tomás, 166–69, *168–69*
Salzedo, Pedro de, 31
San Antonio Vocal Arts Ensemble, 83
San Benito de Palermo (confraternity), 123
Sánchez, Vicente, 163–64
Sandoval, Alonso de, 72
Santa Muerte, 150–52
Santa Veracruz Negra (confraternity), 124–26
Santí, Enrico Mario, 248n1
Santillana, Gabriel de, 164–66
*sarambeque*, 130
Scott, Jimmy, 71–72
Segal, Ronald, 37
self-flagellation, 122
Sepúlveda, Martín de, 20
sexuality
  dance and, 138–40

death and, 70–73, *71*
hypersexualization of Afro-descendant people and, 42–43, 69–73, 140, 197
Sierra Silva, Pablo, 27, 47
silence, 14
Singer, Deborah, 154, 157
Sixtus V, Pope, 30
Smith, Bruce R., 228n18
Smith, Mark, 248n4
Smith, Stephen Decatur, 229n33
Smith, W. Eugene, 7
Smithsonian Institute, 6
"Sogno di Giovannino Moro" (poem), 37–38
Solórzano Pereira, Juan de, 115
*son jarocho*, 110–11
sopranos. See *tiples* (sopranos)
*The Souls of Black Folk* (Du Bois), 10–14
Spivak, Gayatri Chakravorty, 10
stars, 203–6, *205*
Stein, Daniel, 46
Sterne, Jonathan, 215
Stevenson, Robert
  on Afro-descendant sound, 24–25, 83, 235n9
  on Barreto, 42, 230n9
  on Indigenous musicians, 23
  on Vera, 236n26
*Summa, y recopilacion de chirvgia, con vn Arte para sangrar muy vtil y prouechosa* (Summary, and compendium of surgery, with a very useful and beneficial guide to blood-letting) (López de Hinojosos), 76–77
Swiadon Martínez, Glenn, 60, 154–55, 173–75, 180, 199–200

Tachtiris, Corine, xii
Taylor, Diana, 12–13, 88
*Te Deum laudamus* (hymn), 20
Tello, Aurelio, 235n17, 244n61

Tenorio, Martha Lilia, 190
*tenors*, 21, 57, 63–64, 77, 167–68
Teresa of Ávila, 105–7
*Tesoro de la lengva castellana, o española* (Covarrubias), 231n24
timbre, 59, 60, 64–65, 154, 161–69
*tiples* (sopranos)
  Black males as, 21–23, 24, 25–29, 31–39. See also Barreto, Luis; Vera, Juan de
  in Fernández's *villancicos*, 62–68
  Rodríguez Mata and, 54
  training of, 39–42
  See also *castrati* (eunuch singers)
tobacco, 163
*tocotín*, 181
Tollis de la Rocca, Mateo, 126–32
Tomlinson, Gary, 4
Toop, David, 187, 188
torch dance (*danza de uma hacha*), 110
Torres, Nicolás de, 92–93, 94–109
Torres y Rueda, Marcos de, 134
Trambaioli, Marcella, 155, 156, 190, 242n7
translation, xi–xii
transubstantiation, 123. See also Corpus Christi
Tråvén, Marianne, 234n8
Trettien, Whitney, 7
tromba marina, 164–66, *165*
"Tromba marina" (Buonanni), *165*
trumpet, 105, 123, 126, 164
*Tumba La- Lá-La: Los villancicos negros de sor Juana* (Rak Ric Rack!), 208–11
Twain, Mark, xii

Urquiola y Elorriaga, Juan Bautista de, 143–44

Valerio, Miguel
  on Afro-descendant sound, 38, 200, 213
  on agency, 88, 96, 97–99, 105, 107

Valerio, Miguel (*continued*)
  on all-woman sisterhoods, 246n29
  on confraternities and religious ceremonies, 122, 124, 131, 133
  on dance, 101, 102
  on knights, 114
  on uprisings, 233n99
Vaughn, Virginia Mason, 37
Vega, Lope de, 154, 190
Vega Sarmiento, Pedro de, 48
Velasco, Luis de, 74–75
Velasco y Castilla, Luis de, 134
Vélez de Guevara, Luis, 196–97
ventriloquism, 145–50
Vera, Antonio de, 27, 28, 32
Vera, Juan de
  career of, 21–23, 24, 35–36
  as *castrato*, 27, 32, 59
  Fernández and, 56–59, 62–68, 80–81
  vocal commodification of, 25–29
  wages and privileges of, 22, 27–29
Veracruz, 74–75, 124, 151–52, 163
*Viage de tierra, y mar* (Gutiérrez de Medina), 92–94
*Viaje a la Nueva España* (Gemelli Careri), 85–86, 109–11
Villa-Flores, Javier, 145–48, 149
Villalpando, Cristóbal de, 204–6, *205*
*Villancico* 230 (Juana Inés de la Cruz), 188
*Villancico* 232 (Juana Inés de la Cruz), 164
*Villancico* 258 (Juana Inés de la Cruz), 175–77, 180, 189–200
*Villancico* 258 (Juana Inés de la Cruz), 35
*Villancico* 299 (Juana Inés de la Cruz), 188
*Villancico* ix (Juana Inés de la Cruz), 178–80
*Villancico* lviii (Juana Inés de la Cruz), 200–208

*Villancico* xvi (Juana Inés de la Cruz), 162–63, 209–10
*villancicos*
  origins and features of, 55–56, 88
  See also *ensalada* and *ensaladilla*
*villancicos de negros* (Black *villancicos*)
  bells in, 125, 187, 201, 209
  Black males sopranos and, 56–57. *See also* Barreto, Luis; Vera, Juan de
  Black voices in, 161–69
  body and dance in, 155–57, 169–77, 178–81
  confraternities in, 126–32
  Gutiérrez de Padilla and, 157–61
  harmonization of Afrodescendant sounds and bodies in, 153–54, 156, 168–69, 170–81
  origins and features of, 56
  research on, 54–55, 60–61
  as sources on Afro-descendant practices and customs, 181–82
  theoretical approach to, 185–89
  as vocal archive, 60–61
  *See also* Fernández, Gaspar; Gutiérrez de Padilla, Juan; *habla de negros* (blackspeak); Juana Inés de la Cruz, Sor
*villancicos de remedo* (ethnic villancicos), 56–57
*villano*, 129–30
Villarubia, Joan de, 31
Villaverdes, Cirilio, 81
Villegas, Pedro de, 222–24, *223*
*Virgen del Apocalipsis* (Correa), 204–6, *205*
Virgin of the Apocalypse, 204–6, *205*
*Visita del virrey Francisco Fernández de la Cueva, duque de Alburquerque y su mujer al canal de la Viga* (Villegas), 222–24, *223*
Vizcarrondo, Fortunato, 82

voice(s)
　commodification of, 25–29, 49
　Juana Inés de la Cruz and, 162
　music theory and religion on, 34–35
　phonographic approach to, 3–15
　politics of racial difference and, 161–69
　race and, 35–36, 48–49
　recovery of, 213–15
　Teresa of Ávila and, 105–7
　timbre and, 60, 64–65, 154, 161–69
　ventriloquism and, 145–50
　vocalization and, 8–10, 183–84
　women and, 21, 30. *See also* Black women
Voigt, Lisa, 88, 99

Weheliye, Alexander, 8
whiteness, 72, 193
Wilbourne, Emily, 37–38
Will de Chaparro, Martina, 134
women's voice(s), 21, 30. *See also* Black women

Ximeno, Fabián, 24–25, 35
Xochimilco, 220, 225

"Y tu abuela onde etá" (song), 82
Yanga, Gaspar, 74–75

Zendejas, Miguel Jerónimo, 135
Zumárraga, Juan de, 23

www.ingramcontent.com/pod-product-compliance
Lightning Source LLC
Chambersburg PA
CBHW030528230426
43665CB00010B/803